F...r's

TAHITI &
FRENCH POLYNESIA

1st Edition

919.62

Where to Stay and Eat
for All Budgets

Must-See Sights
and Local Secrets

Ratings You Can Trust

Fodor's Travel Publications   New York, Toronto, London, Sydney, Auckland
www.fodors.com

FODOR'S TAHITI & FRENCH POLYNESIA
Editor: Alexis C. Kelly

Editorial Contributor: Christina Knight
Writers: Caroline Gladstone, Bob Marriott, Carrie Miller

Production Editors: Evangelos Vasilakis & Astrid deRidder
Maps & Illustrations: David Lindroth, *cartographer*; Bob Blake, Rebecca Baer, *map editors*; William Wu, *information graphics*
Design: Fabrizio LaRocca, *creative director*; Guido Caroti, Siobhan O'Hare, *art directors*; Tina Malaney, Chie Ushio, Ann McBride, Jessica Walsh, *designers*; Melanie Marin, *senior picture editor*; Moon Sun Kim, *cover designer*
Cover Photo: ImageGap/Alamy
Production Manager: Matthew Struble

1st Edition

ISBN 978-1-4000-0683-0

ISSN 1942-6003

SPECIAL SALES
This book is available at special discounts for bulk purchases for sales promotions or premiums. Special editions, including personalized covers, excerpts of existing books, and corporate imprints, can be created in large quantities for special needs. For more information, write to Special Markets/Premium Sales, 1745 Broadway, MD 6-2, New York, New York 10019, or e-mail specialmarkets@randomhouse.com.

AN IMPORTANT TIP & AN INVITATION
Although all prices, opening times, and other details in this book are based on information supplied to us at press time, changes occur all the time in the travel world, and Fodor's cannot accept responsibility for facts that become outdated or for inadvertent errors or omissions. So **always confirm information when it matters,** especially if you're making a detour to visit a specific place. Your experiences—positive and negative—matter to us. If we have missed or misstated something, **please write to us.** We follow up on all suggestions. Contact the Tahiti & French Polynesia editor at editors@fodors.com or c/o Fodor's at 1745 Broadway, New York, NY 10019.

PRINTED IN THE UNITED STATES OF AMERICA

10 9 8 7 6 5 4 3 2 1

Be a Fodor's Correspondent

Your opinion matters. It matters to us. It matters to your fellow Fodor's travelers, too. And we'd like to hear it. In fact, we need to hear it.

When you share your experiences and opinions, you become an active member of the Fodor's community. That means we'll not only use your feedback to make our books better, but we'll publish your names and comments whenever possible. Throughout our guides, look for "Word of Mouth," excerpts of your unvarnished feedback.

Here's how you can help improve Fodor's for all of us.

Tell us when we're right. We rely on local writers to give you an insider's perspective. But our writers and staff editors—who are the best in the business—depend on you. Your positive feedback is a vote to renew our recommendations for the next edition.

Tell us when we're wrong. We're proud that we update most of our guides every year. But we're not perfect. Things change. Hotels cut services. Museums change hours. Charming cafés lose charm. If our writer didn't quite capture the essence of a place, tell us how you'd do it differently. If any of our descriptions are inaccurate or inadequate, we'll incorporate your changes in the next edition and will correct factual errors at fodors.com immediately.

Tell us what to include. You probably have had fantastic travel experiences that aren't yet in Fodor's. Why not share them with a community of like-minded travelers? Maybe you chanced upon a beach or bistro or B&B that you don't want to keep to yourself. Tell us why we should include it. And share your discoveries and experiences with everyone directly at fodors.com. Your input may lead us to add a new listing or highlight a place we cover with a "Highly Recommended" star or with our highest rating, "Fodor's Choice."

Give us your opinion instantly at our feedback center at www.fodors.com/feedback. You may also e-mail editors@fodors.com with the subject line "Tahiti & French Polynesia Editor." Or send your nominations, comments, and complaints by mail to Tahiti & French Polynesia Editor, Fodor's, 1745 Broadway, New York, NY 10019.

You and travelers like you are the heart of the Fodor's community. Make our community richer by sharing your experiences. Be a Fodor's correspondent.

Happy traveling!

Tim Jarrell, Publisher

CONTENTS

MAPS

ABOUT THIS BOOK

Our Ratings

Sometimes you find terrific travel experiences and sometimes they just find you. But usually the burden is on you to select the right combination of experiences. That's where our ratings come in.

As travelers we've all discovered a place so wonderful that its worthiness is obvious. And sometimes that place is so experiential that superlatives don't do it justice: you just have to be there to know. These sights, properties, and experiences get our highest rating, **Fodor's Choice,** indicated by orange stars throughout this book.

Black stars highlight sights and properties we deem **Highly Recommended,** places that our writers, editors, and readers praise again and again for consistency and excellence.

By default, there's another category: any place we include in this book is by definition worth your time, unless we say otherwise. And we will.

Disagree with any of our choices? Care to nominate a place or suggest that we rate one more highly? Visit our feedback center at www.fodors.com/feedback.

Budget Well

Hotel and restaurant price categories from ¢ to $$$$ are defined in the opening pages of each chapter. For attractions, we always give standard adult admission fees; reductions are usually available for children, students, and senior citizens. Want to pay with plastic? **AE, DC, MC, V** after restaurant and hotel listings indicate if American Express, Diners Club, MasterCard, and Visa are accepted.

Restaurants

Unless we state otherwise, restaurants are open for lunch and dinner daily. We mention dress only when there's a specific requirement and reservations only when they're essential or not accepted—it's always best to book ahead.

Hotels

Hotels have private bath, phone, TV, and air-conditioning and operate on the European Plan (aka EP, meaning without meals), unless we specify that they use the Continental Plan (CP, with a Continental breakfast), Breakfast Plan (BP, with a full breakfast), or Modified American Plan (MAP, with breakfast and dinner) or are all-inclusive (including all meals and most activities). We always list facilities but not whether you'll be charged an extra fee to use them, so when pricing accommodations, find out what's included.

Many Listings
- ★ Fodor's Choice
- ★ Highly recommended
- ⊠ Physical address
- ✛ Directions
- ⌂ Mailing address
- ☎ Telephone
- 🖷 Fax
- ⊕ On the Web
- ✉ E-mail
- 🎫 Admission fee
- ⊙ Open/closed times
- Ⓜ Metro stations
- ▭ Credit cards

Hotels & Restaurants
- 🏨 Hotel
- ⤷ Number of rooms
- ⚭ Facilities
- ⅠⓄⅠ Meal plans
- ✕ Restaurant
- ⌕ Reservations
- ⤢ Smoking
- 🍸 BYOB
- ✕🏨 Hotel with restaurant that warrants a visit

Outdoors
- 🏌 Golf
- ⛺ Camping

Other
- ☺ Family-friendly
- ⇨ See also
- ⊠ Branch address
- ☞ Take note

WHEN TO GO

French Polynesia is in the Southern Hemisphere and straddles the Tropic of Capricorn, giving the area two seasons. Summer, also the rainy season, is from November to April when the humidity and rainfall is highest, and winter, although it's never cold, has less humidity and rainfall.

Maximum temperature in the Society Islands is around 85°F (29°C) in the summer and 80°F (27°C) in the winter, with the year-round average being a pleasant 79°F (26°C). The water temperature of the lagoons is a fairly constant 77°F (25°C).

The islands have an average eight hours of sunshine a day; the Tuamotu group gets the most sun. When it rains it certainly pours, and three-quarters of the rain falls between November and April, but the heavy showers are often short-lived, though they can, of course, go on for a day or two. The islands rarely experience severe tropical storms; however, sailors should avoid November to March, as this is when storms do occur. Weather, being the unpredictable entity that it is, will produce perfectly dry days in the wet season and rainy days in the dry season, so be prepared for a mixed bag.

The northern island groups—the Tuamotu and Marquesas—are noticeably warmer and can be wetter than the Society group. The southern islands of the Gambier and Austral groups are slightly cooler, especially at night when a sweater is recommended. In touristy terms the high season runs from June to mid-November and over the Christmas holidays. The monthlong folkloric festival of Heiva takes place throughout July on almost all islands. Its program of cultural performances and dance competitions creates a lot of interest and hotel rooms may be hard to secure on Tahiti and Moorea.

Climate

The following are average daily maximum and minimum temperatures for two major cities in French Polynesia.

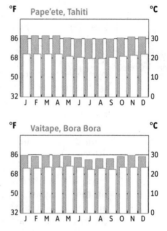

WHAT'S WHERE

TAHITI ISLAND	Tahiti is often used to denote French Polynesia as a whole but officially it's the name of the largest of the 118 islands and atolls that comprise the French protectorate. The island resembles a misshapen "figure 8"—the big loop at the top is Tahiti Nui and the smaller one is Tahiti Iti. The two loops meet at the Taravao isthmus in the southeast. The mountainous interior has many commanding peaks; the highest are Mt. Orohena (7,352 feet) and Mt. Aorai (6,785 feet). The capital, Pape'ete, and the international airport, Faa'a, are in the island's northwestern corner. A 116-km (72-mi) paved road encircles Tahiti Nui.
MOOREA	Moorea, 19 km (12 mi) northwest of Tahiti, can be reached by an eight-minute flight or a 30-minute ferry trip. The island is triangular or heart-shaped with two deep bays, Cook and Opunohu, gouged out of the northern side. Jagged peaks rise sharply over the bays; the highest point is Mt. Tohiea (3,960 feet [1,207 meters]), which sits on a ridge that surrounds a vast valley. Measuring only 51 square mi with one 40-mi coastal road, it's easy to explore Moorea's villages and beaches by car in a day. Many hotels are located near the two bays, with a smattering of accommodation near the airport on the northeast tip, and several clustered near each other at Hauru Point on the northwest corner. The ferry pulls into the township of Vaiare on the east coast, and the administrative center of Afareaitu is a little farther south. The island is ringed by a fringing reef, which encloses a narrow, though very beautiful, lagoon.
BORA BORA WITH MAUPITI	Bora Bora is 260 km (163 mi) northwest of Tahiti. The main island, which sits in a lagoon surrounded by a ring of islets, is dominated by Mt. Otemanu (2,385 feet [727 meters]) and Mt. Pahia (2,168 feet [661 meters]). The airport is on Motu Mute in the northwest and Vaitape, the main town, is on the west coast. Maupiti, a quiet, remote piece of paradise with no international resorts or hotels, lies 25 mi west of Bora Bora. Its airport is on a *motu* (islet) to the north; the port is on the main island.

HUAHINE	Huahine is actually two islands—Huahine Nui and Huahine Iti—connected by a bridge. It's 110 mi northwest of Tahiti and is 75 square km (29 square mi). The main village of Fare sits on the northwest coast; the airport and the historic village of Maeva (which was once the royal seat of power) are on the shores of Lake Fauna Nui in the north. There is low to moderate tourist development on the island—just two resorts (with 32 and 41 bungalows and rooms, respectively) and about nine small lodges and family pensions. Huahine Iti, the more remote and quieter of the two halves, has the best beaches.
TUAMOTU ARCHIPELAGO	Tuamotu is the largest of the five Polynesian archipelagos with 76 islands scattered in a 2,092-km (1307-mi) chain from northwest to southeast across the South Pacific Ocean. The nearest island of the group is 300 km (187 mi) from Tahiti. Only 41 are inhabited, and travelers tend to visit four: Rangiroa, Tikehau, Manihi, and Fakarava—Rangiroa is the largest atoll in the Tuamotu and one of the largest in the world. The Tuamotu are flat circular atolls, only about 20 feet (6 meters) above sea level with large lagoons in the middle. The archipelago is also the center of pearl farming in French Polynesia and there's at least one pearl farm on each of the four main islands that conducts free guided tours and has pearls for sale.
OTHER ISLANDS	The twin islands of Raiatea and Tahaa share the same lagoon, separated only by a 4-km-wide (2.5-mi-wide) channel. Although they lie between Bora Bora and Huahine, they are considered "secret" remote destinations that have managed to escape any large-scale tourism development. The Marquesas Islands, an archipelago of 12 volcanic islands, are about 1,400 km (875 mi) northeast of Tahiti. The most visited islands are Nuku Hiva (the administrative capital), Hiva Oa (where artist Paul Gauguin lived and is buried) and Ua Pou (the most populous). The Gambier Islands are much farther south. Mangareva, the only island in the group with tourist accommodations, is more than 1,600 km (1,000 mi) southeast of Tahiti and is considered the capital of the pearl industry. The Austral Islands lie about 600 km (31 mi) south of Tahiti. The main island of Rurutu is a mecca for humpback whales and has a hotel constructed of coral.

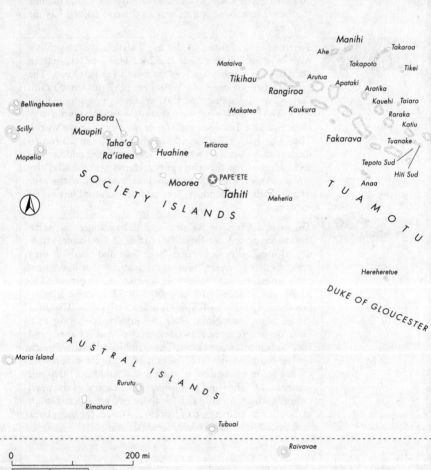

Tahiti & French Polynesia

Motu One
Hatutu
Eiao

MARQUESAS ISLANDS

Nuku Hiva
Ua Huku
Ua Ua Pou   Fatu Huku
Hiva Oa
Tahuata
Motane
Fatu Hiva

Tepoto Nord   Napuka

DISAPPOINTMENT ISLANDS

Pukapuka

Takume   Fangatau
Taenga   Raroia   Fakahina

SOUTH PACIFIC OCEAN

Makemo   Nihiru
Rekareka
Marutea Nord
Tauere   Tatakoto
Haraiki   Hikueru
Reitoru   Amanu
Marokau   Hao
Akiaki
Vahitahi   Pukurua
Reao
Nengonengo
Paraoa   Tavana
Manuhangi   Vairaatea   Pinaki
Ahunui

A R C H I P E L A G O

Anuanuraro
Anuanuranga
Nukutepipi   Vanavana   Tureia

ISLANDS

Tenaroro   Tenerunga
Vahanga   Marutea Sud
Matureivavoa
Tematangi   Moruroa
Maria Est
Fangataufa

GAMBIER ARCHIPELAGO

Mangareva
Morane   Taravai   Rikitea
Akamaru   Temoe

TROPIC OF CAPRICORN

QUINTESSENTIAL
TAHITI & FRENCH POLYNESIA

Delving into the Deep

These waters teem with brilliant hued fish, monstrous manta rays, tranquil turtles, steely sharks, and elegant eels. Rangiroa's huge lagoon, especially the aptly named "shark wall" at Tiputa pass, is legendary and a good place to seek these treasures.

You'll find three types of dives in French Polynesia: lagoon dives in shallow, secure waters; cliff dives along the sides of underwater volcanoes; and diving the "passes"—the turbulent channels where the ocean and lagoon waters meet. But snorkeling in the clear lagoon waters is the most popular activity of all. Novices get instantly hooked as they don a mask, poke their head under the water, and see little Nemo up close or watch a harmless little ray dance by. And if that wasn't enough, delicate coral is right at the doorstep of many bungalows.

Sleeping with the Fishes

Overwater bungalows say "Tahiti" like nothing else and have been known to cast a spell over those who catch a glimpse of the thatched huts floating in aqua-blue lagoons. You'll certainly yearn to stretch out on the balcony, climb down the ladder to splash in the cool blue, or fall asleep to the gently lapping water when you see one for the first time. These four stilted mini-havens have romance stamped all over and some hoteliers are building nothing but them. Reportedly started in Moorea by the Bali Hai Boys—three Californian adventurers who came to the island in the 1950s and became hotel owners—today's best options are undoubtedly those located on the motus in Bora Bora's lagoon; the most expensive look straight out to majestic Mt. Otemanu. Watching the fish through the glass floor panels is mesmerizing and no doubt why the locals call it Tahitian television.

Mention your upcoming trip to French Polynesia and people tend to go dreamy-eyed. Past travelers even turn green with envy. Here are a few reasons why.

Picture Postcard Views

Brochures often lie...but the camera never does. That's why everyone will go weak at the knees when you show them your French Polynesia pics. Tahiti has mountains shrouded in mist and cascading falls; Moorea has razor-jagged peaks towering over fantastic azure blue bays; Bora Bora's lagoon of seven shades of blue, surrounding an island of majestic and foreboding basalt mountains, is magnificent. The tiny low-lying atolls surrounding the main Society Islands are everyone's idea of a deserted island—you can walk around most of them in no time at all, picking up coconut husks and climbing up low-leaning palm trees. Pink sand beaches and miles of narrow coral reefs and tiny islets edge the vast lagoons of the Tuamotu.

Tattooing & Dance

Tattoos are serious business in French Polynesia. They come from the ancient Tahitian word *tatau*, roughly meaning "to mark something." Ancient Polynesians believed a tattoo displayed a person's *mana* or life force, and could ward off evil spirits. Missionaries banned tattooing in 1797 but today the art is thriving.

Being the killjoys they were, the London Missionary Society also banned dancing; the sexually explicit *upa'upa* dance, the forerunner to today's vigorous hip-shaking trademark Tamure dance, was too much for the brethren. The ban forced the art underground and men and women danced in secret for years. Today, you can catch a dance performance at most resorts, Moorea's Tiki Village, and the outdoor stage at Pape'ete's To'ata Square, which hosts dance performances and competitions during the Heiva Festival.

IF YOU LIKE

Romance

The smell of fragrant tiare blossoms isn't the only thing in the air. Love is everywhere in French Polynesia.

Canoe Service. When you're marvelously marooned in an overwater bungalow, breakfast arrives not with a knock on the door, but with a swish of a paddle. A feast of tropical fruits, French pastries, and champagne will be delivered to your door and you can savor on your balcony without leaving your love nest.

Dolphin Duet. Here's a chance to kiss and cuddle a stranger on your honeymoon. The Moorea Dolphin Center's special romance encounter lets couples caress the cute cetaceans, swim by their side, and learn all about the life and loves of the bottlenose dolphin. It's certainly a moment to cherish.

Picnics for two. Stretches of white sand and palm-fringed motu are perfect picnic places. A boatman comes calling, whisks you across the lagoon, sets up a table for two at the water's edge, unwraps the picnic basket, mixes the drinks, and then disappears for several hours leaving you in splendid solitude.

Far Pavilions. Total privacy is guaranteed at the last bungalow on the pier, which is often called the Horizon bungalow. There are no near neighbors, just a private balcony, a couple of sun lounges, the lagoon, and view for two.

Flower power. Ladies bearing floral leis say welcome, frangipanis and hibiscus are strewn over beds, and there are petal baths waiting to be drawn in sumptuous spas. It's a heady bouquet that'll have lovers swooning.

Island Hopping

So many islands, so little time…but not if you plan your island-hopping jaunt with precision.

Passes to Paradise. French Polynesia has 118 islands. Fortunately, Air Tahiti flies to 46 of them from Pape'ete. It's also possible to fly from Bora Bora directly to Rangiroa in the Tuamotus. There are five different Air Tahiti Airpasses that allow you to fly from island to island within one archipelago or, in one case, from Moorea to the islands of the Tuamoto. The Bora Bora Pass, for example, covers Moorea, Huahine, Raiatea, Bora Bora, and Maupiti.

Maupiti Express. A cheap and cheerful option—that includes mixing with the locals—is hopping aboard the Maupiti Express ferry in Bora Bora. Four days a week it travels to Raiatea and Tahaa and back in the one day, and three days a week it goes to Maupiti and back.

Cargo Cult. If burly sailors and long days at sea sound like your thing, there are several freighters that deliver goods to the outlying islands. The most comfortable trip is aboard the *Aranui 3*, a cargo and passenger ship that departs Pape'ete every fortnight on a 13-day voyage to the Tuamotu and the Marquesas islands. While the goods are being unloaded in ports such as Nuka Hiva, Ua Pou, and Fakarava, passengers are taken on excursions. This is an adventure, with cocktails at 6 PM.

Wind in your Sails. Do you want to be the captain of your own boat? There are yachts aplenty for charter in the sailing capital, Raiatea. It's the ultimate freedom.

Living the Robinson Crusoe Life

With 118 islands flung over an area the same size as Europe (1.5 million square mi to be exact), there's definitely an island with your name on it and a dash of civilization to go with it.

Less is Maupiti. Just 25 mi west of Bora Bora, Maupiti is a world away when it comes to swanky sophistication. Home to just 1,200 people on a 5.3-square mi main island with five little motu, it's easy to get a way from it all here. There are no international resorts; just 14 pensions with no more than seven rooms each. Bedding down at Kuriri Village on Motu Tiapaa, a mile from the main island, will be a tonic for the soul.

Wild thing. Rangiroa's most remote resort, the Kia Ora Sauvage, is an hour and 20 minute boat ride across the huge lagoon. The Sauvage (that's savage) has no electricity—there is a generator—or phone connections, and just five bungalows. Hosts Bernard and Mahine will prepare three meals a day for you and take you to excellent snorkeling and dive sites.

Artists' Recluse. Stay at Relais Moehau pension on Hiva Oa and you'll be just a 15-minute walk from Paul Gauguin's grave and a thousand smiles from care. There's even hot water and TV in the rooms.

Coral comfort. Way off in the Austral Islands, 375 mi from Tahiti, is the isle of Rurutu. At the Pension Teautamatea you'll be spoiled with hot showers and bike rides, but be warned the island is made of coral and very hilly.

To Splurge

Luxury awaits those who have a fistful of dollars...and a few dollars more.

St Regis Resort, Bora Bora. If celebrity spotting is high on the agenda, book a week at this posh pad and see who turns up. Chances are superstars (like Nicole Kidman and hubby Keith Urban who honeymooned here) will be canoodling in the three-bedroom royal suite. If that's taken, nestle into a two-room overwater villa with private pool and ask your butler to book a helicopter flight over the island.

Tahaa Island Spa Relais & Chateau. Relais & Chateau scoured the Pacific to find a resort worthy of its imprimatur. The luxury collection of hotels and restaurants found it on a tiny motu just off Tahaa. Choose an overwater villa with views of Bora Bora 30 mi away, or take the plunge into your very private villa pool. This is paradise found—but only by a few.

Bora Bora Cruises. Imagine sitting at tables perched on the beach, set with fine linen and china, as the warm waters lap over your feet. How about watching a movie (*South Pacific,* if you please) on a canvas screen strung between two coconut trees? You get the idea; it's six days of bliss in a sleek white yacht with 37 elegant cabins. You'll drop anchor at Tahaa, Huahine, Raiatea, and Bora Bora and then discover them by canoe, on horseback, or from your oh-so-soft deck chair.

GREAT ITINERARIES

TASTE OF TAHITI

The heat and humidity can make touring and island-hopping a bit of a chore. To ensure it's smooth sailing all the way, you could stay at least three nights on each island and scrap an island or two, or add extra days. You'll also need to brush up on your French, as there's very little English spoken once you get away from the resorts and hotels. You won't find much English spoken at small restaurants either, and most signs are also in French.

Days 1–2: Starting in Pape'ete

If your flight gets in at night, head to one of the resorts near the airport. The Inter-Continental Tahiti Resort has great views of the lagoon and Moorea in the distance. In the morning, take *L'Truck* or a cab to the public market to buy a sunhat and watch the catch of the day arrive. By mid-morning you should be on flight or ferry to Moorea (the ferry allows time to mix with locals and watch the island loom into view).

If your international flight arrives in the early morning, head to the market then get straight on a flight or ferry to Moorea. Check in to your hotel and spend the afternoon in the lagoon swimming and snorkeling, or wander through the tropical gardens. Active folk might want to rent a bike and hit the road.

Days 3–4: Exploring Moorea

On Day 3, take a 4WD safari to see soaring jagged peaks from various angles and a bird's-eye view of Cook and Opunohu Bays. Visit one of the South Pacific's first Christian churches and stop off at the Moorea Fruit Juice Factory for free fruit juice samples—the pineapple is delicious. Have a spa treatment in the afternoon and then head to the Tiki Village for an evening of traditional music, fire dancing, and feasting. Spend Day 4 on the lagoon feeding sharks and rays, or take a hike to the PaoPao Valley.

Days 5–6: Off to Bora Bora

Catch an early flight to Bora Bora for your overwater bungalow experience. ■TIP→ **Pay a bit more to stay on a motu for fantastic views of Mt. Otemanu.** Hit the lagoon straight away either on a two-hour cruise or half-day lagoon excursion with snorkeling or zip around on a Jet Ski. Mix with the happy crowd (and maybe a celeb) at Bloody Mary's that night, or if you love cultural shows book a Polynesian dance and buffet dinner—a good choice is Hotel Bora Bora.

The next day rent a car, scooter, or bike and head off around the island (allow four hours if you're cycling the entire 20-mi route) or join a quad bike tour and zoom over hills or along deserted beaches. You could also check out the old World War II guns and fantastic views on a 4WD jeep tour or visit the Lagoonarium and swim with the fishes. Shop for pearls in Vaitape in the afternoon, then relax with sunset drinks at your resort.

Days 7–8: Wrapping it up in Tahiti

If you're heading back to Tahiti on Day 7, have an early swim and canoe breakfast and take an afternoon flight to Pape'ete and poke around the town stopping at the Notre Dame Cathedral and the colonial style Town Hall (the Mairie). Eat like a local at the *roulettes* (food caravans) at Vaiete Square near the port. Get an early start for one of the beaches, around Puna'auia on the west coast the next morning, or any of the legendary surf breaks, such as the notorious Teahupoo on Tahiti Iti. Dine at Coco's Restaurant

on your last night to the sound of the waves lapping only a few feet away.

If you get to spend another evening on Bora Bora, have breakfast delivered to your bungalow by canoe, then spend the morning kayaking, snorkeling, or swimming at your resort and take another tour—like scuba diving, parasailing, a submarine or helicopter ride, or an aqua safari—in the afternoon. Plan dinner somewhere romantic like a motu or an outdoor restaurant. Take an early flight to Tahiti the next morning and join a half-day circle island tour, or rent a car and hit the 94-mi road that circles both Tahiti Nui and Iti. Heading west from Pape'ete stop at Maraa Grotto, the Marae Arahurahu (the best religious site on Tahiti) and the Museum of Tahiti and Her Islands.

14 DAYS OF BLISS

Days 1–8: Eight Crazy Nights

If you have 14 days, spend the first six nights as above (one in Pape'ete, two in Moorea and three in Bora Bora), then catch the Maupiti Express ferry and head to either Raiatea or Maupiti and stay in a pension for two nights. On Maupiti cycle around the main island or hike to the cliff of Hotu Parata for a fantastic view. On Raiatea get a dose of Polynesian spirituality at the Taputapuatea Marae, the largest of these ancient religious sites, and venture into the jungle on a kayak trip along the Faaroa River.

Days 9–10: Shoot the Pass & Sip Wine

On Day 9 head back to Bora Bora (by ferry or plane) and fly to Rangiroa; depending on schedules you may have to fly via Tahiti, which means you won't arrive in Rangiroa until late afternoon.

If you arrive in the afternoon, relax at your hotel or pension overlooking the vast lagoon or Tiputa Pass. If you don't have a view of the pass (where the lagoon opens to the ocean) cycle or walk down to the public viewing area where people congregate to watch the dolphins.

The next day "shoot the pass," which means taking a diving or snorkeling tour of Tiputa Pass where you'll drift with the current at high tide among the dolphins, rays, sharks, and hundreds of other species of marine life that love the pass, too. If you're not a diver, sign up for an all-day tour of the Blue Lagoon or Ile aux Recifs (an amazing area with abovewater coral fashioned in strange shapes) or one that combines the two places. If you've had enough lagoon trips, take the half-day tour to Vin de Tahiti—French Polynesia's only vineyard—to sample the vintage. Be sure to bring back your favorite bottle to accompany dinner.

Days 11–12: The Marquesas

On Day 11, fly to Nuku Hiva in the Marquesas for two nights. Plan an excursion to the Hatukau Valley to see the magnificent waterfall and ancient places of worship. Visit the artisans at work and pick up a souvenir at one of the sculptors workshops in the village of Taiohae.

Days 13–14: Downtime in Pape'ete

On your 13th day, fly back to Pape'ete and spend a few hours wandering around the town, dining at the roulettes or lying by the pool. Take a circle island trip or play golf at the Olivier Breaud International Golf Course on your last day. That is, if you have any energy left.

Tahiti

Written by
Caroline
Gladstone

THE NAME TAHITI CONJURES UP dreamy images of idyllic islands floating in azure lagoons fringed by palm trees and white sandy beaches. But few people realize that Tahiti is actually the heart of French Polynesian, a vast expanse of 118 islands stretched across the South Pacific Ocean. The island has most of the trappings of the modern world with five-star resorts, boutiques selling top-end labels, and a bustling port city. Pape'ete, the capital of Tahiti (and French Polynesia), has 131,5000 people—around 69% of French Polynesia's total population.

Though Tahiti is usually a stopover for many vacationers heading to the outer islands, it offers many attractions to tempt them beyond a one-night stay. Its assets are its natural attractions—soaring, cloud-swathed mountains, deep valleys, rivers, waterfalls—and ancient temple ruins that dot its valleys. And while the outlying islands have more impressive beaches, Tahiti (1,043 square km [403 square mi]) offers an untamed landscape of both wild black sand beaches and quiet lagoons. Tahiti Iti, just 80 km (50 mi) from the capital, offers the opportunity to chill out completely and find a quiet spot by the beach.

While it's the busiest of the islands, Tahiti still exudes a laid back charm that's incredibly seductive: nobody rushes, races, or worries unduly. People still fish for supper in the lagoon, and amazingly, roosters and chickens can still be seen scratching around not far from the presidential palace.

ORIENTATION & PLANNING

ORIENTATION

TAHITI NUI

Tahiti belongs to the Society Archipelago located in the western half of French Polynesia. Its nearest neighbors are Moorea, 19 km (12 mi) to the northwest, and Tetiaroa 48 km (30 mi) due north. The airport, the capital Pape'ete, and the cruise and ferry ports are all in the northwest. The six resorts are on the northwest coast, all within 9 km (6 mi) of the airport. Most pensions are in the city or on the west coast; the exception is Le Relais de la Maroto in the center of the island.

PAPE'ETE

Pape'ete is in the northwest corner of Tahiti, facing the Sea of the Moon and the island of Moorea. Most attractions—including Place Vaiete, the town's center; the cruise and ferry ports; tourist office; and shops—are located along Boulevard Pomare, the town's main road that runs for about 3 km (2 mi) along the waterfront. Pape'ete Market (Le Marche) is two blocks behind the tourist office.

TAHITI ITI

This peninsula to the southeast of Tahiti Nui is joined to the main island at Taravao by an isthmus. It has a circumference of about 64 km (40 mi); however, there is no car access to the remote east coast. The legendary surf break, Teahupoo, is on the south coast; Mt. Roniu (4,340 feet [1,223 meters]) is in the center. Seven villages, each with at least one pension, dot the island.

PLANNING

GETTING HERE & AROUND

Tahiti is the international arrival point for French Polynesia. Faa'a (pronounced Fa-a-a) International Airport is 5 km (3 mi) west of Pape'ete. Passengers with hotel bookings will be met at the airport by a representative and driven to their hotel in a minivan or bus. If you don't have a booking, you can take the public bus, *L'Truck,* from the main road outside the airport to the city (130 CFP), or an expensive taxi (about 2,000 CFP in the day; 2,500 CFP at night).

L'Truck are colorful jaunty vehicles, with a separate driver's compartment at the front and an open-sided section behind with long benches for passengers. There are three different types of L'Trucks for different routes. The red and white buses go west of Pape'ete to the Centre Moan Nui shopping center at Puna'auia, a distance of about 8 km (5 mi) taking in most of the resorts of the west side but not the Le Méridien. The east side buses are green and white and go as far as Mahina (near Point Vénus), a distance of around 10 km (6 mi). You catch the west coast buses behind the market in Rue du Marechal Foch and the east coast buses on Boulevard Pomare opposite the cruise ship dock. West coast buses run Monday through Friday 6 AM–midnight; east coast buses stop at 5 PM each night. There's limited service on Saturday and none on Sunday. Long distance buses are orange and white and leave from the visitors center on Boulevard Pomare and travel partially around the island. However, the schedules don't allow you to circle the island in one day. Buses depart on the hour between 6 AM and noon and then stop; the next departure from Pape'ete is at 4:30 PM. There are no night or weekend services. Fares around Pape'ete environs are 130 CFP one-way and 200 CFP at night (west side only).

A car's a good option if you're staying a few days. There are seven rental car agencies in Tahiti including Avis, Daniel Rent-a-Car, Europcar, Hertz, and Tahiti Rent-a-Car, which all have outlets at the airport and in downtown Pape'ete. Rates start at around 7,000 CFP a day. Most also rent scooters and bicycles; biking may be tough on the hilly Coastal road. The road around Tahiti Nui is 114 km (71 mi), and is measured in kilometer markers called PKs. It's not possible to drive around Tahiti Iti; paved roads only reach as far as 18 km (11 mi) on both north and south sides of the smaller island.

Two ferry companies—*Aremiti* and *Moorea Ferry*—operate between Pape'ete and Moorea, leaving regularly from the ferry port on Boulevard Pomare.

You can catch taxis at the airport, at stands near Pape'ete's Centre Vaima, or just flag them down along the road. They are a very expensive way to get around though. It will cost around 3,000 CFP (or about US$30) to go only a few miles.

BANKS & There are several banks along Pape'ete's Boulevard Pomare and Rue du
MONEY General de Galle. Most have ATMs that are open 24 hours a day. Banks are generally open Mon. to Fri. from 7:45–11:30 AM and from 1–4 PM.

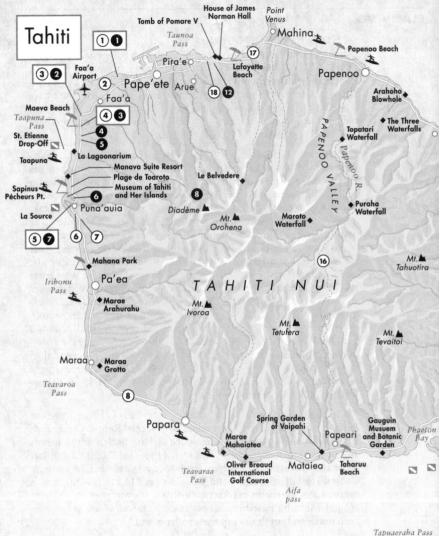

Tahiti

① ①

③ ② Faa'a Airport

② Pape'ete

Maeva Beach
Taapuna Pass
④ ③
④
⑤
St. Etienne Drop-Off
Taapuna

La Lagoonarium
Manava Suite Resort
Plage de Toaroto
Museum of Tahiti and Her Islands

Sapinus Pécheurs Pt.
⑥
La Source
⑤ ⑦ ⑥ ⑦ Puna'auia

Mahana Park
Pa'ea
Irihonu Pass
Marae Arahurahu

Maraa
Maraa Grotto
Teavaroa Pass

⑧

Papara
Teavaraa Pass
Marae Mahaiatea
Oliver Breaud International Golf Course
Aifa pass

Faa'a

Pira'e
Arue
⑰ Lafayette Beach
⑱ ⑫

Tomb of Pomare V
House of James Norman Hall
Point Venus
Mahina
Papenoo Beach
Papenoo
Arahoho Blowhole
The Three Waterfalls
Topatari Waterfall
Puraha Waterfall

PAPENOO VALLEY
Papenoo R.

Le Belvedere
⑧
Diadème
Mt. Orohena
Maroto Waterfall

TAHITI NUI
⑯

Mt. Tahuotira
Mt. Ivoroa
Mt. Tetufera
Mt. Tevaitoi

Spring Garden of Vaipahi
Papeari
Gauguin Musuem and Botanic Garden
Phaeton Bay
Mataiea
Taharuu Beach

Tapuaeraha Pass

The Marado

KEY
① Hotels
● Restaurants
◇ Dive Sites
⚓ Surf Sites

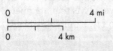

0   4 mi

0   4 km

TOP REASONS TO VISIT TAHITI

Natural splendor. Everything's big on French Polynesia's biggest island—towering mountains, giant waterfalls, and deep valleys.

Surf's up, and up. If you're on a quest for legendary waves you've come to the right place. Experts can tackle Teahupoo in Tahiti Iti, otherwise head to Tahiti Nui's beaches—Papenoo, Point Vénus, or Paea.

Heavenly Voices. Listen to the "singing Mamas," the Tahitian ladies dressed all in white wearing beautifully decorated straw hats, as they sing at the Paofai Protestant Temple on Pape'ete's Boulevard Pomare every Sunday at 10 AM.

Shaken & Stirred. If you miss the amazing Heiva festival in July, make sure you catch a traditional dance show, complete with costume changes and fire twirlers, at one of the resorts.

Some banks stay open through the lunch break, but close earlier. The Banque de Polynesie at Cathedral Square is open Monday to Thursday 7:45 AM to 3:30 PM and Friday from 7:45 AM to 2:30 PM.

There's an ATM and branches of the Banque Socredo and Banque de Polynesie at Faa'a Airport. There are banks in the main shopping centers in Puna'auia, Arue, Taravao, and other towns around Tahiti Nui, as well as ATMs. Take cash to Tahiti Iti to be on the safe side.

ESSENTIALS

Banks Banque de Polynesie (☎ 46–79–79). Banque Socredo (☎ 41–51–23). Banque de Tahiti (☎ 41–70–00).

Car Rentals Avis Pacific Car (☎ 54–10–10 in Pape'ete, 85–02–84 at the airport). Daniel Rent-A-Car (☎ 82–30–04 in Pape'ete, 81–92–32 at the airport). Europcar (☎ 45–24–24 in Pape'ete, 86–61–96 at the airport). Hertz Rent-a-Car (☎ 42–04–71 in Pape'ete, 82–55–86 at the airport ⊕ www.hertz-tahiti.com). Tahiti Rent-a-Car (☎ 81–94–00 in Pape'ete).

Emergencies S.M.U.R. (mobile emergency and CPR unit) (☎ 15). Sea Rescue (☎ 42–12–12). Police (☎ 17 or 46–73–73 Pape'ete, 58–46–56 Puna'auia, 57–11–11 Taravao). Fire Emergencies (☎ 18). Hopital de Pape'ete (☎ 41–01–01). Hopital de Taravao (☎ 57–76–76). Private Medical Clinics (☎ 46–18–90 Clinque Paofai, 46–04–25 Clinque Cardella).

Ferries Aremiti (☎ 50–57–57 or 50–57–91 aremiticruise@mail.pf). Moorea Ferry (☎ 50–11–11 or 56–43–44 ⊕ www.mooreaferry.pf).

Medical Facilities Hopital de Pape'ete (☎ 41–01–01). Hopital de Taravao (☎ 57–76–76). Private Medical Clinics (☎ 46–18–90 Clinque Paofai, 46–04–25 Clinque Cardella).

Visitor Info GIE Tahiti Tourisme (⊠ Fare Manihini, Waterfront, Blvd. Pomare ☎ 50–57–12 ⊙ Mon.–Fri. 7:30–5:30, Sat. 8–4, Sun. 8–1).

WHEN TO GO

Tahiti has two seasons: the wet (November–April) and the dry (May–October). The latter is also slightly cooler and is the high season for travel. The hottest months are February and March with temperatures rising to around 27°C (81°F); July and August are the coolest months with temperatures at around 24°C (76°F).

The Heiva music and dance festival takes place in July along with an arts festival. Other events include the Billabong Pro Surfing competition at Teahupoo in late April and early May, and Tattoonesia, a meeting of Polynesian and foreign tattoo artists, in November.

TAKE IT ALL IN

3 Days: Check into your resort (those with a pool and beach a few miles out of Pape'ete are ideal) and then take L'Truck into town. Wander around the town, checking out the lively city market (Le Marche)—make sure you venture upstairs—Notre Dame Cathedral, the town hall, the Presidential Palace, and the waterfront. At night take a seat at one of the *roulottes* (food trucks) at Place Vaiete for a cheap and cheerful dinner. On day two climb aboard a 4WD for an excursion to the interior that crosses over the old volcanic crater and visits waterfalls and sacred sites. Relax with an evening spa treatment at your resort. On day three, rent a car and drive around the west coast visiting the Maraa Grotto, museums, and botanical gardens and beaches. Or explore the lagoon by Jet Ski, water-ski, or go scuba diving or fishing.

5 Days: With two additional days, you can relax in near solitude on Tahiti Iti on your fourth day. Take L'Truck there or rent a car and check into a groovy pension. On your last day, watch the surfers at Teahupoo, take a half-day boat tour, or hike along either the north or south coast (the mountain views are stunning) before you're get ready to head home.

HEALTH & SAFETY

Stay alert when driving around Tahiti's coastal road. The east coast road, in particular, has several bends and is narrow in parts. Vandals have spray-painted over signs indicating towns (in more than a few places), making it hard to know where you are from your car seat. Play it safe, drive at a reasonable speed, and have patience. And whenever possible, opt for bottled water.

EAT RIGHT, SLEEP WELL

Tahiti has an array of options to accommodate the visitors who tend to breeze in for one or two nights before flying out to the islands. There six resorts, complete with pools, spacious gardens, multiple restaurants, and sports facilities (some with spas) located within a 10- to 15-minute drive of the city. With beach locations and views across to Moorea, they are perfect places to relax for a couple of days and get a glimpse of the traditional dance shows staged several times a week.

Budget travelers can choose from a handful of downtown three-star hotels and a smattering of family-run pensions within a 10- to 15-minute walk of the city. Beyond the capital, accommodation is comprised

TOURING TIPS

Parlez-vous Francais? Brush up on your French before you arrive in Pape'ete, as this is the mother tongue—the majority of people on the street speak only French and all signs are in French. However most shopkeepers, especially the pearl shops, speak English.

Go West Young Man (or Woman). If time is limited and you're renting a car, hit the west coast rather than the east. There's more to see and exploring museums takes time so

you'll need several hours. If you have two days, circle the whole island, including Tahiti Iti.

Take the Bus. If you want to save money, take L'Truck. Check with the tourist office in Pape'ete for schedules, as operation can be erratic and don't operate on Sundays.

of pensions of varying standard, usually quite reasonably priced and often situated by the lagoon.

Tahiti's restaurants offer every possible cuisine. Don't expect too many bargains, but if you shop around you're likely to find affordable Asian dishes. If you want to mix and mingle with the locals, head to the roulottes at Place Vaiete, where you'll find a variety of delicious quick meals such as pizza, chow mein, and fish at reasonable prices.

WHAT IT COSTS IN FRANC COURS PACIFIQUE (CFP)					
	¢	$	$$	$$$	$$$$
RESTAURANTS	under 1,600	1,601–2,200	2,201–3,000	3,001–4,000	over 4,000
HOTELS	under 9,000	9,001–15,000	15,001–25,000	25,001–45,000	over 45,000

Restaurant prices are for a main course at dinner. Hotel prices are for a double room in high season, excluding 10% tax, 10%–15% service charges, and meals plans (except at all-inclusives).

EXPLORING TAHITI

The coastal road that circles the exterior of both Tahiti Nui and Iti is measured in *pointe kilometrique* markers, known as PKs. PK0 begins in Pape'ete and markers go in both clockwise and counterclockwise directions, meeting in Taravao, which is PK60 counterclockwise and PK54 clockwise.

The west coast has the most sights and the most traffic; it's wise to set out early on a driving tour to avoid peak-hour traffic. Grab a map so you know whether a sight is at PK10 clockwise or counterclockwise. While the distances are not far, there is quite a lot to see on the west coast—beaches, surf breaks, museums, gardens and an excellent golf course—and it may take much longer than you think.

Tahiti Nui also has a handful of short interior roads. While a standard car can access the roads to the Belvedere lookout, the Three Waterfalls, and the start of the walking and 4WD trails in the Papenoo Valley, it's not possible to cross the island from north to south, or south to north, without a 4WD.

> **DID YOU KNOW?**
>
> Pape'ete Harbour is a magnet for jet-setters. Microsoft cofounder Paul Allen likes to bring his huge motor yacht, *Octopus,* to town, while the mega yacht *ICE,* owned by a Russian billionaire, is often in port.

The PK marker system also operates in Tahiti Iti, beginning in Taravao, the town at the isthmus. There are two roads: the north road of 18 km (11 mi) from Taravao to Tautira and the south road, also measuring 18 km (11 mi) from Taravao to Teahupoo. The southeast and east coasts of Tahiti Iti can only be accessed by boat, bicycle, or foot. There is one inland road, leading from near Taravao up onto the Taravao Plateau and Taravao's lookout, also called the Belvedere.

PAPE'ETE

SIGHTS

⑤ Centre Vaima. Pape'ete's first shopping center houses 65 stores over three levels. The red-roofed building has stood on Boulevard Pomare, almost directly across from the cruise port, since 1977. Apart from stylish boutiques and jewelery shops, there are restaurants, airline offices, travel agencies, and tour operators. ✉*Bound by Blvd. Pomare, Rue Lagard, Place Notre Dame, and Rue Jeanne d'Arc* ☎*42–44–14 or 42–68–47* ⊕*www.centrevaima.com* ⊙*Mon.–Fri. 9–5:30, Sat. 9–noon.*

❶ Maison de la Culture. The nation's cultural center is housed in a traditional Polynesian design, octagonal building which has a theater, cinema, exhibition space, and a library. Located on the waterfront, almost adjacent to Place To'ata, this is the place to catch dance performances, film festivals, and cultural activities. Some events are free; others cost around 1,000 CFP per show. The center's Tahitian name is Te Fare Tauhiti Nui. ✉*646 Blvd. Pomare* ☎*54–45–44* ⊕*www.maisondela-culture.pf* 📖*Library free* ⊙*Library: Mon.–Fri. 9–5:30.*

❼ Notre Dame Cathedral. This is the center of the Catholic community in Pape'ete, as well as a quiet and cool retreat from the hot and sticky city. Built in 1875 and restored in 1987, this buttercup-yellow church with a red roof and high steeple sits pretty in its own square just a block behind the market. The altar is always decorated with beautiful tropical flower arrangements and the church fills with light from a dozen stained-glass windows. Choirs sing in the upstairs area under a pitched timber ceiling adorned with cast-iron chandeliers. ✉*Place Notre Dame, cnr of Rue Jeanne d'Arc* ⊙*Daily, 8–5; Saturday mass* 6 PM.

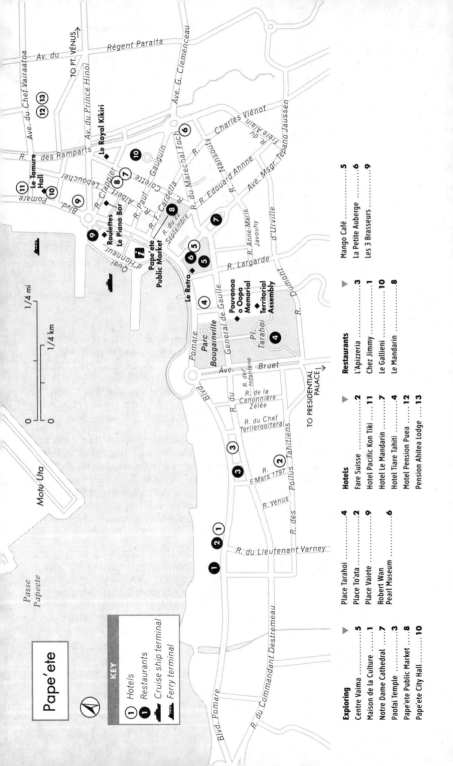

Pape'ete

KEY

▶ Hotels 5
● Restaurants 1
⚓ Cruise ship terminal ... 7
⚓ Ferry terminal ... 3

Exploring

Centre Vaima 5
Maison de la Culture 1
Notre Dame Cathedral 7
Paofai Temple 3
Pape'ete Public Market ... 8
Pape'ete City Hall 10

Place Tarahoi 4
Place To'ata 2
Place Vaiete 9
Robert Wan
Pearl Museum 6

Hotels ▶

Fare Suisse 2
Hotel Pacific Kon Tiki 11
Hotel Le Mandarin 7
Hotel Tiare Tahiti 4
Motel Pension Puea 12
Pension Ahitea Lodge 13

Restaurants ●

L'Apizzeria 3
Chez Jimmy 1
Le Gallieni 10
Le Mandarin 8

Mango Café 5
La Petite Auberge 6
Les 3 Brasseurs 9

CLOSE UP

A Walking Tour of Pape'ete

As most travelers stay in a hotel in or within 10 mi of Pape'ete, they start their explorations in the city. A walking tour should start at ❾Place Vaiete (near the tourist office) and proceed south along Boulevard Pomare where you can stop at the ❺Centre Vaima shops, the ❻Robert Wan Pearl Museum, the ❸Paofai Protestant Temple, and the ❷Place To'ata and cultural center, then turn around and walk back again along the waterfront side looking at the outrigger canoes, the cruise ships in port, the yachts, and the Moorea ferries coming and going. Finding yourself back at the tourist office, wander along either the Rue Francois Cardella or the Rue Du 22 Septembre for a block to come to the Pape'ete ❽Public Market , where you can buy just about anything. Then walk to the ❼Notre Dame Cathedral and any of the other sights, including the Territorial Assembly (French Polynesia's parliament), the Presidential Palace, and ❿Pape'ete City Hall .

❸ **Paofai Temple.** This pale pink church with white timber filigree work and a clock tower topped with green steeple is right on the main road a 100 yards or so from the harbor and the area set aside for dozens of outrigger canoes. Inaugurated in 1873, it is the principal Protestant place of worship on the island and is sometimes listed by its French name *Eglise Evangelique*. The interior is supported by two rows of huge oak handcrafted and painted columns. A Sunday service, with beautiful singing and the chance to see the local ladies dressed in white and wearing decorative straw hats, is not to be missed. ⊠ *Cnr Blvd. Pomare and Rue de Temple* ☉ *Sunday 10* AM.

❿ **Pape'ete City Hall.** Alternatively known in French as *Hotel de Ville* and *Mairie,* this impressive building, opened in 1990, is a replica of Queen Pomare's mansion—who ruled in 1845 when Tahiti became a French Protectorate—which once stood at Place Tarahoi (*see listing below*). The town hall is the office of the mayor of Pape'ete and is open to the public during business hours and when art and historical exhibitions are held on the third floor gallery. The buttercup-yellow building has spacious wraparound terraces on two levels decorated with cream balustrades and columns. ⊠ *Cnr Rue Paul Gauguin and Rue Colette* ☎ 41–57–00 ☒ *Free* ☉ *Mon.–Fri. 9–5:30.*

❽ **Pape'ete Public Market (Marché de Pape'ete).** You could spend hours wandering around this lively market, which sells almost everything from fruit and vegetables to fish and handicrafts to jewelry and Monoi oil. Watch the mamas weave baskets from palm fronds and at around 4 PM watch as the catch of the day is unloaded. There are food outlets downstairs and more shops and a small café and live band playing upstairs. The market opens very early (around 5 AM) and on Sunday it's filled with Tahitian women buying food for their family's Sunday lunch. ⊠ *Between Rue du 22 Septembre and Rue Francois Cardella* ☎ 42–80–39 ☉ *Mon.–Sat. 5–6, Sun. 5:30–9* AM.

❹ **Place Tarahoi.** Once the compound of Tahiti's 19th-century royal family, today it's the center of French Polynesia's territorial government. The square houses the French Polynesian Assembly (⊙ *Mon.–Fri. 9–5*) on one block and the elaborate Presidential Palace (⊙ *by appointment only*), with expansive gardens and fountain, on another. Nearby is a memorial to Tahitian World War I hero and Tahitian independence advocate Pouvanaa o Oopa (1895–1977). Although this area has witnessed many political demonstrations in recent years, it's incredibly peaceful on weekends and even roosters and chickens roam freely just beyond the impressive palace gates. ⊠ *Ave. Bruat* ☎ *47–21–34.*

> ### STAY CONNECTED
>
> Many hotels and resorts have public Internet facilities in their lobbies and business centers, but Pape'ete also has many Internet cafés. **ABC Diffusion** (☎ *45–29–29*). **Cynernesia** (☎ *85–43–67*). **La Maison de la Press** (☎ *50–93–93*). **Maison de la Culture** (☎ *54–45–44*). **Mana Rock Café** (☎ *50–02–40*). **Tiki Soft Café** (☎ *88–93–98*).

② **Place To'ata.** This huge waterfront square, about half a mile south of Place Vaiete, is the venue for the Heiva festival dance performances. International rock concerts are also held at the outdoor stage, which can hold 5,000 people. At quieter times it's the place to sit and watch all the harbor activities including the outrigger canoe teams training for race events. There are a few outdoor take-out snack bars operating in the afternoon and at night. ⊠ *Blvd. Pomare.*

❾ **Place Vaiete.** This open space, in front of the cruise dock and next to the tourist office, is the heart of Pape'ete. The square comes alive when cruise ships are in town with a craft market and traditional bands performing in the lovely iron bandstand decorated with lacework and replica 19th-century French lanterns. Every night about 30 roulottes open their shutters for business, selling great food at reasonable prices. Originally the site of the first territorial parliament (held in 1945), the square was reopened in 2001 after a major upgrade that included new seating, paving, and lovely French-style lampposts. ⊠ *Blvd. Pomare.*

❻ **Robert Wan Pearl Museum.** Pearl pioneer Robert Wan's lovely museum is one of a kind. Here you'll see a pearl-encrusted prayer book that belonged to Charles II of France (AD 840–870) and, among other treasures, a copy of the rosary beads (with 57 pearls) presented to Pope John Paul II in 1987. There's also a retail section selling single pearls, jewelry, and Wan's line of skin products that contain extracts of nacre, the mother-of-pearl shell. Groups of two or more can arrange a free-guided tour with five days' notice. ⊠ *Vaima Centre, Blvd. Pomare, near the Paofai Temple* ☎ *46–15–55* ⊠ *Free* ⊙ *Mon.–Sat. 9–5.*

TAHITI NUI

Tahiti uses PK markers on its circle island road. This measuring system starts in Pape'ete and divides the island into two halves—the north/east coast and the west/south coast. The PK markers use the same numbers in the east (clockwise) as they do in the west (counterclockwise), so drivers must pay attention to what side of the island they are on. Tahiti

Nui does have four coasts, but some maps (including ours) only divide the island into the north/east coast and the west/south coast.

WEST/SOUTH COAST

The west coast is everything west of Pape'ete all the way down to the town to Taravao and its junction with Tahiti Iti. This coast contains the airport, all the resorts (with the exception of the Radisson Plaza Resort), several good restaurants in the town of Puna'anuia, a couple of good beaches, marae, a couple of sizeable towns, the only golf course, and coastal areas with great views to the interior mountain ranges. If driving, allow at least a half-day to explore these sights.

TOWNS **Faa'a.** Pronounced Fa-ah-ah, this town is a commune (municipality area) of greater Pape'ete and houses the international and domestic airport, the Sheraton Hotel, and the InterContinental Tahiti resort, along with a Faa'a town hall built in Polynesian style. The University of Tahiti sits on the side of the mountain above the town. It's more heavily populated that Pape'ete itself, although you won't see much of the place as your airport transfer whisks you along the highway to your resort.

Puna'auia. This, another densely populated commune of Pape'ete, is both a town and the general name of the area that stretches for several miles from around PK11 to PK18. There's a good beach, the Lagoonarium (an aquarium in the lagoon), two resorts—Sofitel Tahiti Resort and Le Méridien Tahiti (separated by about 4 mi)—and the Museum of Tahiti and her Islands, while the township itself has banks, a shopping center with a huge supermarket, and a post office. The road leads to the village of Paea (PK22) which is the spot to stop to explore Marae Arahurahu.

Papara. This sizeable town produces much of Tahiti's vegetables and has Tahiti's only golf course (the Olivier Breaud International) along with a good (black-sand) surf beach. Nearby are the remains of the once massive Marae Mahaiatea. You'll find St. Michel's church in the town itself, and three pensions in the area. ⊠*Near 35.6 counterclockwise, Coastal road.*

Mataiea. Paul Gauguin lived in a bamboo hut (long-since gone) on the banks of the Vaihiria River in Mataiea between 1891 and 1893. A museum in his honor is located in nearby Papeari (PK51.2). Two decades later the English poet Rupert Brooke arrived in the town, fell in love with the local chief's daughter, wrote some of his best work, but returned to England after WWI broke out in 1914, after only a three-month sojourn in Tahiti. Mataiea has a calm, black-sand beach and a pleasant white chapel, *Eglise jean-Baptiste,* built in 1931. ⊠*Near PK 45 counterclockwise, Coastal Road.*

Papeari. Tahiti's oldest village is home to the Paul Gauguin Museum (*see review below*) and the adjacent Botanic Gardens. There are great views from here to the majestic mountains of Tahiti's interior. ⊠*PK 51.2 counterclockwise, Coastal road.*

Taravao. The town's location on the isthmus that connects Tahiti Nui and Tahiti Iti made it the perfect location for a fort, which the French duly built in 1844. Today it's used as an army-training center. The PK markers meet at Taravao and here—to evoke the old Scottish song—you either "take the high road or the low road" to explore Tahiti Iti. The town has a post office, banks, shops, a hospital, and a couple of good restaurants. ✉ *PK 60 counterclockwise, Coastal road.*

BEACHES Tahiti has both white- and black-sand beaches. The black beaches, which sparkle in the sunlight, were formed from eroded lava and are very hot in the heat of the day. Most resorts have a narrow patch of white sand at their doorstep. Away from the resorts, there are very few beaches that fulfill that South Seas Paradise fantasy. However, drive along until you see a patch of sand and then investigate whether it's a public beach or not—if in doubt just ask someone who looks like a local and they should know.

Maeva Beach. This picturesque stretch of white sand lies just west of the Sofitel Tahiti Resort, which is still referred to as the Sofitel Maeva Resort, despite a name change. To get there take L'Truck from Pape'ete and get off at the Outumaoro bus stop, or ask the driver for the Sofitel stop. Wander towards the hotel and then look around for the beach. ✉ *Around PK 10 counterclockwise, Coastal road.*

Plage de Toaroto. This is the official name for the lovely stretch of white sand just west of the Le Méridien Resort in the Puna'auia area. It has good snorkeling and there's a nearby park with public showers and toilets. If you're driving look out for the Tapeara'a Pereo'a Mataeinaa park, which is in front of the beach at PK 15. ✉ *PK 15 counterclockwise, Coastal road.*

Mahana Park. A mile or so west of Toaroto Beach is this family-friendly beachside park complete with a little restaurant. The stretch of white sand is lovely, the snorkeling is good, and folks play soccer and volley ball in the park. ✉ *18.5 PK counterclockwise, Coastal road, Paea.*

Taharuu. This black-sand beach, not far from the Gauguin Museum, is popular with surfers, but it's also a good place for a refreshing dip. **Maoti Surf Shop** (☎ *57–73–45*) has surf clothing, body boards, and secondhand surfboards. ✉ *PK 50, Coastal road, Papeari.*

SIGHTS **Gauguin Museum and Botanic Gardens.** These two sights are side by side. The museum has 25 small original works by the famous artist who lived in Tahiti and the Marquesas Islands for the last 12 years of his life. The other major works are replicas, which can be a disappointment. On the upside, the gardens, which cover 340 acres and were created by American physics professor Harrison Smith in 1922, are beautiful with plenty of walking trails and great views over the lagoon. ✉ *PK 51.2, Coastal road, Papeari* ☎ *56–40–52* ▭ *Museum 400 CFP, gardens 200 CFP* ⊘ *Daily 9–5.*

Le Lagoonarium. You can't miss this open-air aquarium in a fenced -off part of the lagoon as there's a huge model of a shark at the entrance. Here you can swim and snorkel with rays, turtles, eels, and hundreds of colorful reef fish. There's a lagoonarium on many islands, and the safe environment obviously appeals to many people. Guides are on hand to

CLOSE UP

Touring the Interior

1

Even when the peaks are shrouded in clouds, you'll get the best glimpse of Tahiti's spectacular interior—soaring, jagged peaks; rivers; deep valleys; hills covered in virgin rain forest—as you fly into Pape'ete. The island's highest peak, Mt. Orohena, is a mighty 7,352 feet (2,241 meters) and the triple-spired Diadème (4,333 feet [1,321 meters]) is remarkable for its shape rather than height.

Getting to the interior is not easy, though. Only a handful of inland roads—a 4WD is required on most of them—branch off the main coastal road, and there's just one road that crosses Tahiti Nui from north to south. While the 39-km (24-mi) road, which connects the towns of Papenoo (in the north) and Papeari (south), is best experienced with a guide, it can be done on your own by foot or 4WD. Starting in the north, the trail begins at Papenoo (on the coastal road at around PK 18 clockwise) and cuts through the wide Papenoo Valley, alongside the river of the same name. En route you pass three waterfalls at various intervals: Topatari at about 5 km (3 mi) inland, Vaiharuru farther on, and then Puraha. Sixteen km (10 mi) inland you'll reach the Vaituoru Pool, which is perfect for a swim. Almost miraculously you'll come across the only accommodation in the interior, **Le Relais de la Maroto** (☎57–90–29 maroto@mail.pf). The pension, with three bungalows, 26 rooms, and a good restaurant, gets heavily booked, so call ahead if you're planning to stay here. The road south passes by the Anapur marae and travels through a 656-foot (200-meter) tunnel and on past Lake Vaihiria. Farther south you'll encounter Marae Vaihiria, which has extensive remains including an arti-ficial canal. The inland road finishes near Papeari.

If you want to head inland, but only have a car, head to Belvedere lookout (*see the North Coast/East Coast touring section*), which is perched 1,968 feet (600 meters) above sea level. There are great views of the Papenoo Valley to the east and the mighty peaks to the south. If you're keen to hike you can set out from here, following clearly marked trails to Mt. Aorai (6,776 feet [2,206 meters]) in the south, Tahiti's third highest peak. It takes a full day to summit Mt. Aorai and get back to the city, so consider spending the night in one of the two huts, en route. Hiking operator **Polynesian Adventure** (☎42–25–95 ⊕www.polynesianadventure.fr.st) conducts two-day hikes here.

If you have a 4WD vehicle or just want to hike, you can also go inland to the Hitiaa lava tubes, which were formed by lava flows that are big enough to walk through. The turnoff to the trail is at the town of Hitiaa on the east coast (PK 39.9 clockwise). The rocky trail to the tubes is more than 8 km (5 mi) long and once there you'll need a strong flashlight to navigate your way inside. A guide is recommended, and several operators including **Tahiti Rando-Trek** (☎73–04–69) run this excursion.

Travelers with limited time, or no desire to set off on their own, have a choice of several operators who run half-day and full day excursions across the interior. Try **Tahitian Excursion** (☎82–69–96 ⊕www.tahitian-excursion.com) or **Tahiti Safari Expedition** (☎42–14–25 ⊕www.tahiti-safari.com).

dive down and bring up a turtle for view and to feed the sharks at noon every day. ⊠*PK 11.4, Coastal road, Puna'auia* ☎*43–62–90* ✉*900 CFP* ⊙*Daily 9–5:30.*

Maraa Grotto. This park, with meandering pathways leading to ferny grottoes (caves), has lovely gardens and crystal clear pools. You can walk into the caves and adventurous folk can even swim to the Paroa Grotto, an underwater cavern. Like many of Tahiti Nui's attractions, it's not sign-posted well in advance, so slow down around PK 28 and look out for the car park. ⊠*PK 28.7, Coastal road* ✉*Free.*

Marae Arahurahu. Beautifully restored and maintained, this ancient religious site is the most spectacular on the island and is used as a backdrop for historical reenactments during the July Heiva festival. There is a large stone tiki (god-like image) in the grounds and legend says that the spirit of a warrior, who was cremated here, still lingers. ⊠*PK 22.5, Coastal road, Paea* ✉*Free.*

Museum of Tahiti and Her Islands. Located at the Pointe des Pecheurs (fishermen's point), this is one of the best museums in the South Pacific. Situated on the site of an ancient marae, its exhibits tell the story of Polynesian history and culture dating back thousands of years. You'll see replicas of old sailing boats, tools, and artifacts and learn all about tattooing and the traditional skills of weaving and quilt making. ⊠*PK 14.6, not far from Le Méridien Tahiti Resort, Coastal road* ☎*54–84–35* ✉*850 CFP* ⊙*Tues.–Sun. 9:30–5:30.*

Oliver Breaud International Golf Course. The only golf course on the island, and the only 18-hole course in French Polynesia, this 6,944-yard, 72-par course is set on a former cotton and sugar cane plantation. It's the venue for the Tahiti Open International each July. The course sits on the largest piece of flat land on the island. ⊠*PK41, Coastal road* ☎*57–40–52 or 57–40–32 for the Club House* ✉*9 holes with cart 12,000 CFP; 18 holes with cart, 21,000 CFP* ⊙*Daily 8–5; Club House: 8–6.*

Spring Garden of Vaipahi. This lovely haven, on the mountainside of the road at Mataiea, has 75 different species of plants, including the giant elephant ears, as well as a few archaeological relics dotted around the 2.5-acre site. You can wander along paths to ponds and a waterfall and visit the new boutique (constructed in early 2008) to stock up on gardening books and souvenirs. ⊠*PK 49, near the golf course, Coastal road* ☎*47–62–00* ✉*600 CFP* ⊙*Daily 7:30–5.*

NORTH/EAST COASTS

The East Coast extends from Pape'ete around to Taravao, a distance of about 54 km (34 mi). This coast is quieter and less populated than the western side; you can drive for miles without seeing a shop or restaurant. The beaches have black sand and many have perfect conditions for surfers. The most interesting sights are found between Pape'ete and the Three Waterfalls of Fa'arumai, which are just off the coastal road at about PK 23 (clockwise). ■TIP➔ If you like a quiet drive, then this is a perfect half-day's outing.

TOPOGRAPHY

Tahiti (1,043 square km [403 square mi]) is the largest island in French Polynesia. It resembles a misshapen figure eight, with Tahiti Nui in the north and Tahiti Iti (sometimes called the peninsula) in the southeast, joined by an isthmus. Both are extinct volcanoes and have rugged mountains rising almost directly behind the narrow coastal plane. The highest peak is Mt. Orohena (7,352 feet [2,240 meters]) in the center of Tahiti Nui, although the most spectacular is the Diadème—a crown of peaks rising to 4,334 feet (1,321 meters). The Papenoo Valley in the island's north has several waterfalls and rock pools. Tahiti Iti has a mixture of interesting landscapes from the lush cattle-grazing Taravao Plateau, with views of Tahiti Nui, to its highest peak, Mt. Roniu (4340 feet [1,223 meters]). The Te Pari Cliffs, in the southeast, rise dramatically from the sea and are only accessible by boat or foot.

TOWNS **Pira'e and Arue.** Extending from PK2 to PK7, these eastern suburbs of Pape'ete have some very interesting sights. However, signage is seriously inadequate and you may drive right past them. Look for the turnoff to the Belvedere lookout at around PK2.5, and if you like architecture check out the colonial-style *mairie* (town halls), set in tropical gardens, in Pira'e and Arue. The tomb of King Pomare V and the home of American James Norman Hall, who co-wrote the novel *Mutiny on the Bounty*, are in Arue, as is the Radisson Plaza Resort. On a hill above the Radisson is the now-closed Hyatt hotel. ⊠*Between 2.5 and PK 7 clockwise, Coastal road.*

Mahina, Papenoo, and Tiarei. These three towns stretching from around PK10 to PK25 are more of interest for their black-sand beaches and the natural wonders near them: look out for the turnoff into the Papenoo Valley (at around PK 17) and the Arahoho Blowhole and the Three Waterfalls. The most notable man-made attraction is the lighthouse at Pointe Vénus, in Mahina. It overlooks Matavai Bay. ⊠*PK 10 to PK 25 clockwise, Coastal road.*

BEACHES **Lafayette Beach.** There's plenty of room for everyone at this black-sand beach at Arue, stretching for a whopping 2,624 feet (800 meters). It's on the edge of Matavai Bay (where James Cook and other European explorers dropped anchor in the late 1760s), with lovely views to the southwest. The Radisson Plaza Resort is situated on a section of the beach; however, the entire beach is open to the public. There's another black-sand beach a little farther east at Mahina, near the Point Vénus lighthouse. ⊠*PK 7, Coastal road, Arue.*

Papenoo. This black-sand surfing beach stretches for a few hundred yards and is highly rated among the world's surfing fraternity. The waves get a little crowded on the weekend; however, midweek you might have it all to yourself. There are no facilities apart from open space beside the road, where surfers and sightseers park their cars.

BEST BETS FOR CRUISING

Pearl Shop 'Til You Drop. If this is your last port of call, then it's the last chance to get a black pearl. There are many shops along Boulevard Pomare; Pape'ete might close early, but pearls shops never seem to close.

Go Green. Explore Tahiti's huge tracks of jungle on a 4WD full- or half-day trip. You'll climb mountains, ford streams, and swim in water holes.

To Market, To Market. Drink in the colors and flavors of the South Pacific at the Pape'ete public market; buy a hat and pareo and watch the Mamas (official name for mature ladies) weave a straw basket. Sunday mornings open very early for the townsfolk to pick up ready-made Sunday meals.

Dining Roulotte. Colorful caravans festooned with fairy lights set up at 6 PM nightly right in front of Pape'ete's cruise port. Dine like a local on crepes or wok-tossed Chinese meals.

Nearby, at around PK 17, the Papenoo River flows into the sea. ⊠ *PK 16 to PK 17, Coastal road.*

SIGHTS **Arahoho Blowhole.** Look out for the signs denoting the French name *trou du souffleur*. However, you won't miss it because the blowhole is right on—and under—the coastal road and there are always tourist buses around. Water rushes into a cavern and if the swell is just right it shoots out through the hole in the rocks, like a geyser. There's a viewing platform and if the sea's rough, you could get wet. Be careful driving on this section of the road, as there's a narrow, blind corner as you approach the blowhole at PK22. ⊠ *PK 22, Coastal road, Tiarei* 🖼 *Free.*

Le Belvedere. Like most French Polynesian volcanic islands, Tahiti has a *belvedere* or lookout that can be accessed by car (the word means beautiful view). However, the view from this 1,968-foot peak (600 meters) is the loftiest with views of Fautaua Valley, Pape'ete city and port, and Moorea on the horizon. The road to the top is steep and not very wide, so take it easy. There's a restaurant at the top (*see* restaurant review *below*) and the start of a hiking trail to Mt. Aorai. ⊠ *Turn off at PK 2.5, Coastal road, Pira'e.*

The Three Waterfalls. It's an easy walk of about 100 yards from the carpark to the first of these three waterfalls (also known, collectively, as the Fa'arumai Waterfalls)—the 295-foot (90-meter) Vaimahutu cascade. It's 20 minutes farther to Haamarere Iti and Haamarere Rahi falls, which stand side by side and are slightly smaller. You'll need your hiking boots to reach the second set of falls, and bring along a swimsuit and towel as there are places to have a refreshing natural shower. The turnoff is about 200 yards east along the coastal road from the blowhole. ⊠ *Turnoff at PK22.5, Coastal road.*

House of James Norman Hall. The life of this American adventurer, WWI hero, and novelist is displayed at the beautifully restored house where he lived with his wife and children for almost 30 years until his death in 1951. Hall and writer-friend Charles Nordhoff co-wrote the famous *Mutiny on the Bounty* (published in 1932) and *The Hurricane*, among other works. Set in a beautiful garden high on a hill, the house overlooks the bay and beaches. Lunch is available in the tearoom; however, one day's notice is required. ⊠*PK5.5, past Arue town hall, Coastal road, Arue* ☎*50–01–61 museum, 50–01–60 tearoom* ⊕*www.james-normanhallhome.pf* ⊠*600 CFP* ☉*Tues.–Sat. 9–4.*

Tomb of Pomare V. The tomb of Tahiti's last king—Pomare V (1839–1891)—is built of coral stones in the shape of small lighthouse, which has a red door and is topped with a red Grecian urn. The tomb stands on a point at Arue just off the coastal road. Originally built for his mother Queen Pomare IV, Pomare V had her remains exhumed and his were interred instead when he died only a few years later. A nearby cemetery contains the graves of Pomare I, II, III, and IV. ⊠*Turnoff at PK 5.4, Coastal road, Arue.*

Point Vénus and Lighthouse. This point on Matavai Bay has major significance: it is the place where Captain Samuel Wallis landed in 1767 and where James Cook watched the transit of Venus in April 1769. The crew of the infamous *Bounty* also stepped ashore here in 1788 (and did not want to leave), as did the first members of the London Missionary Society, who arrived in 1797. An impressive white lighthouse—Tahiti's only lighthouse—was built in 1867 to commemorate the anniversary of Wallis's arrival; it stands just feet away from the black-sand Vénus Point Beach. There's no sign pointing to the turnoff, but be prepared to swing off the coastal road at PK10. ⊠*Turnoff at PK10, Coastal road.*

TAHITI ITI

Though most people call it Tahiti Iti (little Tahiti), the official name is the Taiarapu Peninsula, which explains why the landmass is sometimes referred to as "the peninsula." Romantics refer to it as *la sauvage* (the wild), as both the landscape and the lifestyle are a reminder of how things used to be in Tahiti many, many decades ago. Compared to its big sister it's a very peaceful place; its rugged eastern side—known as Fenua Aihere—can only be reached on foot or bicycle or by boat.

Two roads, both around 18 km (11 mi) long, branch off from Taravao on Tahiti Nui. The north road runs from Taravao to Tautira; the south road connects Taravao to Teahupoo. People refer to these latter destinations as "the end of the road." Another inland road runs off the north coast road (about one mile east of Taravao) and climbs up to the Taravao plateau. A visit to Tahiti Iti usually involves getting back to nature: trekking along remote coastal roads and mountains, visiting quiet bays and beaches and—in May—taking part in the carnival atmosphere that is the Billabong Pro Surf championships at Teahupoo.

Tahitian History

Tahiti Nui was created by a series of volcanic eruptions about 3 million years ago, and its smaller neighbor was formed 2 million years later. Polynesians, arriving from Raiatea, settled Tahiti between AD 300 and 800. Captain Samuel Wallis, an Englishman, was the first European to land on the island on June 18, 1767, claiming it for Britain. Frenchman Louis-Antoine de Bougainville arrived 10 months later with two ships. Unaware that Wallis had planted the British flag, Bougainville claimed it for France in 1788. Captain James Cook arrived in 1769 to observe the Transit of Venus—the rare sight of planet Venus gliding across the face of the sun—at Matavai Bay. The *Bounty*, with Captain Bligh at the helm, arrived in 1788. Its mission? To collect breadfruit plants that grew profusely on the island. After five months ashore, however, the crew refused to leave. This refusal became one of the leading factors that lead to the infamous mutiny the following year.

The first Protestant missionaries arrived in 1797, an event that is still commemorated with celebrations today. French Catholic priests arrived in the 1830s to the chagrin of the Protestants who had enjoyed their monopoly on saving souls. In the early 1840s Tahitian chiefs, fearing they would come off badly in any hostilities between the British and the French, were tricked into signing documents that made Tahiti a protectorate of France. Tahitian pro-independence fighters waged constant battles with the French to no avail. In 1880 King Pomare V was eventually forced to cede the sovereignty of Tahiti to France. In 1946 Tahiti and all of French Polynesia was deemed a French Overseas Territory.

NORTH COAST

The north coast of Tahiti Iti is steeped in history. Captain Cook moored off it in 1773; a year later Spanish Captain don Domingo de Boenechea arrived and tried to claim the island for Spain, and Scottish writer Robert Louis Stevenson spent time writing a horror story there in 1888. You can travel along the coastal road by L'Truck, but it's best to check schedules with pensions, as they are unreliable and sporadic.

TOWNS **Afaahiti, Pueu, and Tautira.** Pueu has a good surf break, ideal for beginners and body boarders. Taurita is the most remote of the three towns and has fantastic mountain views, two churches, and is the start of the 15-km (9.3 mi) walking track to the Pari Coast and its amazing cliffs. Just off the coast of Afaahiti is Motu Nono, a small islet that can be visited on organized day trips from the town. Pueu and Tautira have at least one pension, while Afaahiti has three or four places to stay.

BEACHES All the pensions along Tahiti Iti's north coast are situated on quiet lagoon beaches, which are perfect places to chill out under a palm tree. However, Motu Nono, the small island off the cost of Afaahiti, is everyone's idea of paradise. To get there, contact **Punatea Village Pension** (☎*57–71–00* ⊕*www.punatea.com*) for a boat transfer to the island. There's also a beach at Tautira, which is dotted with brightly colored outrigger canoes (known as pirogues); the mountain views from this black-sand beach are magnificent.

SIGHTS **Pari Coast Trail.** If you're staying at or visiting the village of Tautira, take the 15-km (9-mi) walking track along the stunningly beautifully—and wild—Pari Coast. Along the way you'll encounter petroglyphs (ancient artworks embedded in rock), marae, and magnificent cliffs. Ask directions from your pension before you head out.

Taravao Plateau. Several hundred meters above the north coastal road is Tahiti Iti's lush agricultural center. Visitors will be shocked to see cattle grazing in the landscape—if not for the tropical trees, one might think they were in Normandy. There's a lookout here (the Taravao Belvedere) where you can see for miles across the isthmus to Tahiti Nui. ✢ *Turn off the North Coastal road about 2 km (1 mi) east of Taravao.*

SOUTH COAST

TOWNS **Toahotu, Vairao, and Teahupoo.** Expect to find a little more action in these three south coast villages than in the north coast towns, as they are visited by surfers making the pilgrimage to the monster wave at Teahupoo. Each village has a handful of pensions, but Teahupoo (the wave itself breaks at Hava'e Pass) is the most developed due to its legendary acclaim and as the venue of the Billabong Pro Surf Championships held in late April to May. It also has several small *snacks* (casual cafés), while its pensions have good restaurants as well. American novelist Zane Grey (who penned dozens of pulp fiction Westerns) ran a deep-sea fishing camp by the lagoon between the villages of Toahotu and Vairao in the 1930s, though nothing remains of it today.

BEACHES **Maui Beach.** This picturesque beach, complete with popular café is located around PK6 along the south coast road. The Maui Cave is a short walk inland.

Teahupoo. Pronounced Cho-Poo, this is the big draw of the region, though people aren't coming for just the beach. Teahupoo is home to the huge left hander wave that surfers the world over come to master. The waves are called Kumbaia tubes and they break out in Hava'e Pass, a gap in the reef. Waves average heights between 6 and 8 feet, though they can get higher. Due to the danger of the reef, it's only recommended for expert surfers. ⊠ *PK16, South Coastal road.*

SIGHTS **Fenua Aihere.** This is the name given to the remote eastern section of Tahiti Iti, which lies between the north coast and the south coast road. A wild and rarely visited area, it's also called Te Pari due to the dramatic Te Pari cliffs. You can walk the 15-km (9.3-mi) Pari Coast trail on your own, but a couple of locals operate overnight, camping excursions. ■TIP➡ **It's best to go with an operator if you want to camp overnight, but you can walk on your own for day trips.** Knowledgeable guides can point out the hidden marae, caves, petroglyphs, and rock formations known as Drums of God Honu Ura and the Queen's Bathtub, which have been created by the pounding surf.

Marae Nuutere. Restored in 1994, this marae is one of several found in Tahiti Iti's interior valleys. There are remnants of altars, meeting areas, and seats where the priest sat during religious ceremonies. ✢ *Turn off South Coastal road around PK9.5 and head inland a short distance.*

WHERE TO STAY

Tahiti's accommodations range from budget city pensions to luxurious resorts in vast tropical gardens. There are two- and three-star hotels in the heart of Pape'ete—which are convenient but not particularly memorable—and a growing number of pensions opening up within a 10- to 15-minute walk of the harbor. The five international resorts are housed in three- to four-story complexes of several wings with huge foyers, two to three restaurants and pools set in gardens on the edge of the lagoon. Only two—the InterContinental and Le Méridien—have overwater bungalows. Prices are cheaper than sister properties on Moorea or Bora Bora. The west and south coasts have a sprinkling of pensions near the bigger towns; the east coast has no accommodations. Le Relais de la Maroto is the only pension in the interior and fills up fast. (*See review in the Touring the Interior box, above.*) Tahiti Iti has about seven pensions with excellent lagoon locations.

PAPE'ETE

RESORTS & HOTELS
$–$$

Hotel Le Mandarin. As the name suggests, there are many Chinese touches in this otherwise contemporary style hotel. Two of the three restaurants have attractive Chinese decor and serve Chinese and western dishes. The six mini-suites have both a double and single bed and a bathtub. It's a well-kept, mid-range hotel conveniently located less than half a mile from the ferry port. **Pros:** Three restaurants, close to the ferry. **Cons:** Not on the waterfront. ⊠ *51 Rue Colette, Pape'ete* ⌂ *B.P. 302, Pape'ete* ☎ *50–3350* ⊕ *www.hotelmandarin.com* ⇌ *31 rooms, 6 suites* ⌂ *In-room: safe (some), refrigerator (some). In-hotel: 3 restaurants, room service, bar, laundry service, concierge, public Internet, airport shuttle, parking (fee)* ⊟ *AE, DC, MC, V.*

$$

Hotel Pacific Kon Tiki. You can party with Pape'ete's nightclub crowd and be steps away from your bed at this budget hotel in the heart of the city's (small) nightlife district. There are two bars on the premises and a nightclub next door, so don't expect to sleep like a baby. Rooms are functional and clean with cane furniture and private bathrooms. ■TIP→ **Ask for one of the 20 seafront rooms so you can watch constant harbor activity.** The friendly staff can arrange car rentals, excursions, and airport transfers. Parking is across the road near the ferry dock. **Pros:** Near harbor, plenty of after hours entertainment at your fingertips. **Cons:** Disco on the premises means it's noisy. ⊠ *271 Blvd. Pomare, Pape'ete* ☎ *54–16–16* ⇌ *36 room* ⌂ *In-room: no a/c (some), safe (some), refrigerator (some), TV (some). In-hotel: restaurant, 2 bars, laundry service, concierge, parking (fee)* ⊟ *AE, MC, V.*

$$

Hotel Tiare Tahiti. This five-story white hotel is in the heart of Pape'ete. The front rooms have great views of the bay, the yachts, and all the comings and goings in the harbor. As it's right on the main road it can get a little noisy, but it's very convenient to all the Pape'ete action. There's an independent restaurant next door and the supermarket's a five-minute walk away. Rooms are clean and unpretentious with bathrooms and TVs. Breakfast is served in a small dining room on the first floor. **Pros:** Excellent harbor-front location. **Cons:** Main road location can be noisy. ✉*417 Blvd. Pomare, Pape'ete* ☎*50–01–00* ⊕*www. hoteltiaretahiti.info* ⌑*38* ☐*In-room: no a/c (some). In-hotel: laundry service, concierge* ☐*AE, MC, V.*

SMALL HOTELS/ GUESTHOUSES
$

🔲**Fare Suisse.** A Swiss-run pension, with the opportunity to taste delicious cheese fondue, is certainly a rare find in Tahiti. Swiss owner Beni runs this modern pension in the Paofai district of Pape'ete, not far from the Paofai Protestant Temple. Two rooms have double beds, the third has two twin beds, and the fourth is ideal for a family with double and single bed. All have private bathrooms with hot water and guests have access to two separate kitchens and a lounge room with TV. A supermarket is nearby. Beni provides free airport transfers and can arrange tours around the island. **Pros:** Clean and affordable; free transfers; fans. **Cons:** Not near harbor or restaurants; no a/c. ✉*Rue des Poilus Tahitiens, Pape'ete* ☎*44–00–30* ⊕*www.fare-suisse.com* ⌑*4 rooms* ☐*In-room: no a/c (some), no phone. In-hotel: kitchen, no elevator, airport shuttle, parking (no fee)* ☐*AE, MC, V.*

$ 🔲**Motel Pension Puea.** This is a sister property to Pension Ahitea Lodge and only a five-minute walk away. It offers comfortable, clean accommodation with private or shared bathrooms all with hot water and fans. Air-conditioning is available at an extra 2,000 CFP a day per room. A kitchenette with microwave and refrigerator are available for guests, as is a TV lounge. Breakfast is included and dinner can be arranged on request. The pension is a half-mile walk from the ferry port. **Pros:** Cheap and cheerful; good location. **Cons:** Some shared bathrooms; basic accommodation. ✉*87 Rue Pasteur Octave Moreau, Pape'ete* ☎*85–43–43* ⌑*8 rooms* ☐*In-room: no a/c (some), no phone, no TV. In-hotel: restaurant, no elevator, laundry facilities, parking (fee)* ☐*AE, MC, V* ⦿*CP.*

$ 🔲**Pension Ahitea Lodge.** This clean and basic pension is located in a large modern two-story house about a half-mile walk from Vaiete Square and most of Pape'ete's attractions. Two rooms have air-conditioning, while the others have fans. Guests have access to a communal kitchen with fridge and microwave; a TV lounge; and a garden pool, which is a welcome sight on a steamy day. The price includes breakfast and taxes and dinner can be arranged and taken in the dining room. **Pros:** Pool; close proximity to Pape'ete; some rooms have a/c. **Cons:** Not all rooms have a/c or private bathrooms ✉*Ave. Vairaatoa (off Ave. du Prince Hinoi), Pape'ete* ☎*55–13–53* ⊕*www.ahitea-lodge.com* ⌑*10 rooms* ☐*In-room: no a/c (some), phone (some), refrigerator (some), TV (some). In-hotel: restaurant, pool, no elevator, laundry facilities, airport shuttle, parking (fee)* ☐*AE, DC, MC, V* ⦿*CP.*

TAHITI NUI

WEST COAST/SOUTH COAST

RESORTS & HOTELS
$$$–$$$$
Fodor'sChoice
★

🔲**InterContinental Resort Tahiti.** It doesn't get any better than this lovely resort, which is surrounded by 30 acres of gardens that includes an enclosed lagoonarium. Watch fish and rays being fed in the morning and the sunset over Moorea in the evening. Hotels rooms have handcrafted wooden beds and spacious bathrooms and are located in two wings; there are also 31 overwater bungalows. There are two "infinity pools" and a man-made white-sand beach. Tahitian women make handcrafts by the pool, which are available for purchase. Acclaimed dance troupe Les Grands Ballets de Tahiti stages a stunning cultural show on Friday and Saturday nights. **Pros:** Great location; has both a lagoon and two pools. **Cons:** No spa or onsite gym. ⊠*PK 7.5, Coastal road, Faa'a* ⌂*B.P. 6014, Faa'a* ☎*86–51–10* ⊕*www.ichotelsgroup.com* ⇗*227 rooms, 2 suites, and 31 overwater bungalows* ⌂*In-room: safe, refrigerator, Internet. In-hotel: 2 restaurants, room service, bar, tennis court, 2 pools, beachfront, diving, water sports, laundry service, concierge, public Internet, airport shuttle, parking (no fee)* ⊟*AE, DC, MC, V.*

$$$–$$$$ ⭐ 🏨 **Le Méridien Tahiti.** All the rooms and suites overlook the lagoon, while the senior suites have expansive terraces. Located at PK15, this is the farthest resort from Pape'ete; guests, however, can take the hotel's free L'Truck bus into town. Like its rival, the Sofitel, Le Méridien claims it occupies the only natural white-sand beach on the island. Whatever the case, the sand is white. The swimming pool, with a sandy bottom, is certainly unique. The resort has a gallery, L'Atelier, where artists display their work and conduct art classes (2,000 CFP an hour for guests). On Friday nights there's a Tahitian dance show. The resort can also organize Tahitian wedding ceremonies in its beautiful grounds. **Pros:** Good beach, wide range of facilities. **Cons:** A bit too far from Pape'ete for a short stay. ⊠*PK 15, Coastal road, Puna'auia* ☎*47–07–07* ⊕*www.lemeridien.com* ⇗*136 rooms, 12 bungalows* ⌂*In-room: safe, refrigerator, Internet. In-hotel: 2 restaurants, room service, 2 bars, tennis court, pool, beachfront, diving, water sports, laundry facilities, laundry service, concierge, public Internet, airport shuttle, parking (no fee)* ⊟*AE, MC, V.*

$$$–$$$$ 🏨 **Sheraton Hotel Tahiti Resort & Spa.** The colonial-style resort, which was refurbished in 2006, has an ideal location between the airport and the city and has a good choice of rooms and activities. The rooms are outfitted with mahogany and cane furniture, marble bathrooms, coconut tree wood floors, and lagoon views. The fitness center operates a full program of classes; there's a dive center on site and entertainment (including a Friday night Polynesian cultural show) most nights of the week. **Pros:** Easy to access the airport and Pape'ete, many facilities. **Cons:** No overwater bungalows. ⊠*PK 2, Coastal road, Faa'a* ☎*86–48–48* ⊕*www.starwood.com/tahiti* ⇗*179 rooms, 10 suites* ⌂*In-room: safe, refrigerator (some), Internet. In-hotel: 2 restaurants, room service, bar, tennis court, pool, gym, spa, beachfront, diving, water sports, bicycles, laundry facilities, laundry service, concierge, executive floor, public Internet, airport shuttle, parking (no fee)* ⊟*AE, DC, MC, V.*

$$$ 🏨 **Sofitel Tahiti Resort.** Shaped like a ship, this resort is situated on Maeva Beach, the only natural white beach on the island. The huge lobby is decorated with Polynesian totem poles and cane furniture with vibrant cushions. Rooms are also brightly decorated in orange, pink, white, green, and yellow fabrics from the Parisian design house Robert Le Heros. A feature of the bedroom is the sheer curtain printed with

CLOSE UP

On the Horizon

1

Scheduled to open in December 2008, **Hotel Tahiti Nui** (⊠ *Ave. Prince Hinoi, Pape'ete* ☎ *42–16–32*), which is managed by the same hotel group that oversees Le Mandarin in Pape'ete, will be the first new hotel to open in or near the city since 2004. About half of the rooms will be suites, but each room will have a balcony, air-conditioning, satellite TV, and a minimalist design featuring ceramic floor tiles, cream walls, and dark-wood features. Other firsts for a city hotel: underground parking, a fitness center, and a pool.

Guests who want to stay in Tahiti for longer than a few days will welcome the opening of **Manava Suite Resort** (⊠ *PK 14, Coastal road, Puna'auia*) as it will offer seven apartments. Scheduled to open in the spring of 2009, the resort will be operated by South Pacific Management, which runs the Pearl Resort chain. The 121 rooms, ranging from standard hotel rooms, to duplexes and three-bedroom apartments, will have a distinctly Polynesian design and be housed in four buildings bordering the lagoon at Puna'auia. The resort will have the largest "infinity pool" on the island and an overwater restaurant.

---

famous sayings of Paul Gauguin; as they are in French, it's best to ask the staff to translate. The grounds are very spacious and there are lovely views of Moorea from the pool. There's a L'Truck stop across the road from the hotel. **Pros:** Great location. **Cons:** Expensive restaurants. ⊠*Puna'auia* ↻*B.P. 60008, Faa'a* ☎*86–66–00* ⊕*www.accorhotels. pf* ⟿*202* ♿*In-room: safe, refrigerator, DVD (some), VCR (some), Internet (some). In-hotel: 2 restaurants, room service, bar, golf, tennis courts, pool, gym, spa, beachfront, diving, water sports, bicycles, laundry service, concierge, executive floor, public Internet, airport shuttle, parking (no fee)* ▭*AE, DC, MC, V.*

SMALL HOTELS/ GUESTHOUSES

$ 🏠**Hiti Moana Villa.** This modern complex of individual bungalows has an enviable position: it's right on the lagoon, is backed by luxuriant rain-forested hills, is close to an excellent surfing beach, and is just 10 minutes from the golf course. The bungalows can accommodate up to four people; four of the bungalows have a kitchen, while all have hot-water private bathrooms, TVs, and refrigerators. The pension has its own bus and motorboat for private tours of the island. Breakfast is available (1,000 CFP per person) onsite and there's a restaurant 300 meters down the road. **Pros:** Excellent position for outdoor activities. **Cons:** No a/c. ⊠*PK 32, Coastal road, Papara* ↻*B.P. 120055, Papara* ☎*57–93–93* ⊕*www.papeete.com/moanavilla* ⟿*8 bungalows* ♿*In-room: no a/c, no phone (some), kitchen (some), refrigerator. In-hotel: restaurant, golf course, pool, beachfront, diving, water sports, no elevator, laundry service, airport shuttle, parking (no fee)* ▭*AE, MC, V.*

¢–$ 🏠**Pension a la Plage.** This charming colonial-style lodge is about a quarter of a mile walk from both Le Méridien resort and a small shopping center, and is just a few minutes walk to the beach. The rooms (some with kitchenettes) have a terrace with a view of the gardens and swimming pool, and are decorated with a Polynesian flair—bright bedspreads and local artwork. Each room has TV, refrigerator, and Wi-Fi (500 CFP per day). All meals can be provided—breakfast is 900 CFP, lunch and dinner 1,500 CFP. The public bus to Pape'ete stops at the front door. **Pros:** Convenient location, reasonably priced, near the beach. **Cons:** No a/c. ⊠*PK 15.4, Coastal road, Puna'auia* 🕾*45–56–12* ⊕*www.pensiondelaplage.com* ⇩*12 rooms* ⌂*In-room: no a/c, kitchen (some), refrigerator, Wi-Fi. In-hotel: restaurant, bar, pool, beachfront, water sports, no elevator, laundry facilities, public Wi-Fi, airport shuttle, parking (no fee)* ⊟*AE, DC, MC, V.*

$-$$ 🏨**Tahiti Airport Motel.** If you have an early or very late flight to catch, or just like looking at planes from the breakfast terrace, then this is the place to stay. It's directly across the road (and up a hill) from the airport—five minutes on foot. The twin, double, and family rooms, which all have private bathrooms, are a little Spartan but the furnishings are pleasant with floral bedspreads and cushions. Rooms are air-conditioned, have Wi-Fi connections, refrigerators, and tea/coffee-making facilities. There is parking for 14 cars. Staff can arrange car rentals and day trips. **Pros:** Convenient location. **Cons:** No leisure facilities. ⊠*PK 2, Coastal road, Faa'a* 🕾*50–40–00* ⊕*www.tahitiairportmotel. com* ⇩*46 rooms* ⌂*In-room: refrigerator, Internet. In-hotel: restaurant, bar, laundry service, concierge, public Internet, airport shuttle, parking (no fee)* ⊟*AE, MC, V.*

¢ 🏨**Te Nahe Toe Toe Puna'auia.** This two-story white house, literally on a white-sand beach, is one of the bargains on the west coast. There are one bungalow and eight rooms in the house; four of the rooms have a/c, but all have private bathrooms with hot water, a living room, and a balcony or terrace. City and airport transfers and excursions can be arranged. There's free use of snorkeling gear and kayaks. Breakfast is served on a terrace overlooking the lagoon and dinner can be arranged (1,500 CFP per person). **Pros:** Good location; good value. **Cons:** Not all rooms have a/c. ⊠*PK 15.5, Coastal road, Puna'auia* 🕾*58–42–43* ⊕*www.pension-tenahetoetoe.net* ⇩*8 rooms, 1 bungalow* ⌂*In-room: no a/c (some), no phone. In-hotel: restaurant, room service, bar, beachfront, diving, water sports, bicycles, no elevator, laundry service, parking (no fee)* ⊟*V* ⍾*CP.*

NORTH COAST/EAST COAST

RESORTS 🏨**Radisson Plaza Resort Tahiti.** Looking to immerse yourself in Polyne-
$$$ sian culture for a few days? Guests at the Radisson can participate in
★ Tahitian dance and cooking classes, though they must leave the wood carving and basket weaving to the Marquesan instructors. The hotel, situated on a long black-sand beach, opened in 2004 making it the newest—to date—in Tahiti. The accommodations here are a mixture of standard rooms, rooms with Jacuzzis on the balcony, two-story duplexes, and suites. All have a modern, western design and are decorated with framed photographs of colonial Pape'ete. A dance show takes place on the beach every Friday night. A free shuttle offers transfers to the city 7 km (4 mi) away. ⊠*PK 7, Coastal road, Arue* 🕾*48– 88–88* ⊕*www.radisson.com/tahiti* ⇩*86 rooms, 26 duplexes, 53 suites* ⌂*In-room: refrigerator, Internet (some). In-hotel: 2 restaurant, room service, 2 bars, pool, gym, spa, beachfront, diving, water sports, bicy-*

cles, laundry service, concierge, executive floor, public Internet, airport shuttle, parking (no fee) ⊟*AE, DC, MC, V.*

SMALL
HOTELS/
GUESTHOUSES
$$
★

⊞**Hotel Royal Tahitien.** Three kilometers (1.8 mi) from the city, this is one of the few options east of the city. It's situated on former royal ground—the Pomare family used to live here. The hotel faces a black-sand beach, has lovely gardens with a Jacuzzi set into black volcanic rocks, and a swimming pool with decorative waterfall. Rooms are well maintained and prices are very reasonable. There's live music (some traditional, some western-style) on the weekends, great views of the lagoon, and good food in the restaurant. **Pros:** Quiet location; lagoon views; lovely gardens. **Cons:** Functional rather than fashionable decor. ⊠*PK 3, Coastal road, Pira'e* ☎*50–40–40* ⊕*www.hotelroyaltahitien. com* ➳*40 rooms* ⌕*In-room: refrigerator, Internet (some). In-hotel: restaurant, bar, pool, beachfront, water sports, no elevator, laundry service, concierge, public Internet, airport shuttle, parking (no fee)* ⊟*AE, DC, MC, V.*

TAHITI ITI

NORTH COAST

SMALL
HOTELS/
GUESTHOUSES
$

⊞**A Pueu Village.** Situated on a quiet bay, this pension has four bungalows each with a double bed and private bathroom with hot water. The decor is rustic Polynesian with rattan walls, bright floral bedspreads, shell artwork, and floral design bed lamps. Each bungalow has a terrace looking across a garden to the lagoon. A variety of excursions including snorkeling trips and boat rides to the Vaipori Grotto can be arranged. Half board is 3,500 CFP per person. **Pros:** Peaceful location, lots of water activities. **Cons:** No a/c, basic facilities. ⊠*PK 9.8, North Coast Road, Pueu* ☎*57–57–87* ⊕*www.pueuvillage.com* ➳*4 bungalows* ⌕*In-room: no a/c, no phone, no TV. In-hotel: restaurant, bar, beachfront, diving, water sports, no elevator, laundry service, parking (no fee)* ⊟*MC, V.*

¢

⊞**Chez Jeannie.** If you like remote locales with fantastic rural and mountain views, you've come to the right place. Chez Jeannine is located on the Taravao plateau, a few miles inland from the both the north and south coast of Tahiti Iti and just a 10-minute drive from Taravao. The views of Tahiti Nui's towering mountains and over the lagoons to either side are fantastic. The pension has rooms and bungalows all with private bathrooms and fans, while some have kitchens. All meals can be provided. The pension has a communal TV lounge and a pool. **Pros:** Great location with mountain views, good value for money. **Cons:** No a/c, basic facilities. ⊠*PK 4, Taravao Plateau Rd., Taravao* ☎*57–07–49* ➳*4 bungalows, 2 rooms* ⌕*In-room: no a/c, kitchen (some), refrigerator (some), no TV. In-hotel: restaurant, bars, pool, gym, spa, bicycles, no elevator, laundry service, airport shuttle, parking (no fee)* ⊟*No credit cards.*

¢

⊞**Pension Punatea Village.** This pension is the perfect place to wile away a few days. There are four beachside bungalows with private bathrooms and capacity for four guests, and four rooms, which share two bathrooms, set in a beautiful garden. The restaurant serves three meals a day, specializing in fish from the nearby village of Pueu. Breakfast and dinner cost 3,000 CFP; lunchtime picnic baskets can be arranged for 900 CFP. Excursions to nearby Motu Nono and picnics at the Vaipori Grotto, a cave at the southeast tip of Tahiti Iti, can be arranged. The pension has intriguing piece of therapeutic equipment, a kind of personal sauna, known as a far-infrared dome sauna which is said to detoxify the body. **Pros:** Ideal location, good value, lots of activities. **Cons:** No a/c, some shared bathrooms. ⊠ *PK 4.7, North Coast Road, Araahiti* ☎ *57–71–00* ⊃*4 bungalows, 5 rooms* ⟟*In-room: no a/c. In-hotel: restaurant, bar, pool, spa, beachfront, water sports, no elevator, laundry service, concierge, airport shuttle, parking (no fee)* ▤*DC, MC, V.*

¢–$ ▦**Te Hi Hi O Te Ra.** This three-room pension in Tautira is one of the only places to stay in this remote section of Tahiti Iti. Tautira has an "edge of the world" feel about it; it's on a black-sand beach and is backed by mountains covered in thick foliage. This is a get-away-from-it-all experience, although the little town has enough parishioners to fill two churches. Rooms are simple and clean, have linen and mosquito nets, and share a hot-water bathroom. There's a lounge with TV and a dining room. **Pros:** Robinson Crusoe experience. **Cons:** Shared bathrooms, no a/c. ⊠ *PK 18, North Coastal road, Tautira* ☎ *57–92–78* ⊃*3 rooms* ⟟*In-room: no a/c, no phone (some). In-hotel: restaurant, bar, beachfront, water sports, no elevator, laundry facilities, parking (no fee)* ▤*No credit cards.*

SOUTH COAST

SMALL
HOTELS/
GUESTHOUSES
$

▦**Pension Chayan.** This tranquil pension, located in a lovely garden with its own waterfall, is just a short walk from the beach and Vairoa lagoon. There are four bungalows, each with one bedroom, private bathroom with hot water, kitchen, and balcony. All meals can be provided and are served in the *fare potee* or main house, which in this case is a lovely white house with a balcony. There are free kayaks and excursions can be arranged to the nearby Vaipori grotto. Teahupoo is only 3 mi to the east. **Pros:** Lovely setting, self-contained bungalows. **Cons:** No a/c. ⊠ *PK 14, South Coastal road, Vairoa* ☎ *57–46–00* ⊕*www.pensionchayantahiti.pf* ⊃*4 bungalows* ⟟*In-room: no a/c, no phone, kitchen, refrigerator. In-hotel: restaurant, bar, beachfront, diving, water sports, no elevator, laundry facilities.* ▤*DC, MC, V.*

$–$$ ▦**La Vague Bleue (also called Tauhanihani Village Lodge).** It means "the blue wave" and the pension pays homage to one of the biggest and most dangerous waves in the world—Teahupoo. The wave itself is accessed via a short boat ride to a place called Hava'e Pass. The pension is literally right on the beach, and each of the six bungalows can accommodate four people (one king bed and two singles) and have kitchen and hot-water bathroom, fan, TV, terrace, and tea- and coffee-making facilities. There are free kayaks, and tours can be organized to the grotto and the "wave" itself. **Pros:** Good value; good location. **Cons:** No a/c. ⊠ *PK 16, South Coastal road, Teahupoo* ☎ *57–23–23* ⊕*6 bungalows* ⊃*6 bungalows* ⟟*In-room: no a/c, safe (some), kitchen, refrigerator. In-hotel: restaurant, bar, beachfront, diving, water sports,* *bicycles, no elevator, laundry facilities, airport shuttle, parking (no fee).* ▭*No credit cards.*

$$ ▦ **Vanira Lodge.** This pension is a must for anyone visiting Teahupoo. ★ The bungalows are very funky, with exposed beams and furniture made from bamboo, varnished tree branches and amazing shaped tree trunks. Two bungalows resemble tree houses with internal stairways and balconies on the top floor, while another has interesting stone walls. All have a kitchenette, hot-water bathroom, and can sleep four people. The pension is on a hill overlooking gardens (where massages take place) and the lagoon. Breakfast is 1,200 CFP per person and other meals are available at "snacks" about a 15-minute walk away. **Pros:** Funky, innovative design. **Cons:** No a/c. ✉*PK 15.6, South Coastal road, Teahupoo* ☎*57–70–18* ⊕*www.vaniralodge.com* ⏎*4 bungalows* ⚐*In-room: no a/c, kitchen, refrigerator, no TV. In-hotel: restaurant, bar, spa (massages only), beachfront, diving, water sports, bicycles, no elevator, laundry service, concierge, airport shuttle, parking (no fee).* ▭*AE, DC, MC, V.*

WHERE TO EAT

There's an enormous array of restaurants in Pape'ete and its nearby suburbs with options ranging from the very top end with sky-high prices to casual cafés in the city's shopping malls. Each of the main resorts has at least two dining areas, one usually a gourmet restaurant under the control of a well-known chef.

French is the main cuisine, although there are many Asian eateries and a sprinkling of other nationalities. It's not hard to find a restaurant with a water view; the restaurants along Pape'ete's main road—Boulevard Pomare—have vistas across the harbor, or you can always grab a great lagoon position at one of the resorts or at the clutch of eateries in the town of Puna'auia, a lively beach and marina district about 15 km (8 mi) west of the city.

Those wanting to save their francs and mix with the locals, should head to the *roulottes,* the mobile food vans selling chow mein, chicken, crepes, steak, and other meals, which open for business at Place Vaiete each day at 6 PM.

RESERVATIONS & TRANSPORTATION
It's always a good idea to book ahead during the high season, especially for the dinner and cultural show performances. Check with a restaurant whether they provide free transfers, as some beyond the city will pick up and deliver you to your hotel.

TIPPING
Tipping is not required, but as Tahiti and Pape'ete get more accustomed to tipping, people will certainly accept tips. Resorts always leave a space on the tab to add a gratuity.

The Brando Island

You could say that art imitated life when Hollywood actor Marlon Brando arrived in Tahiti in 1960 to star in the remake of the 1935 epic *Mutiny on the Bounty*. He played mutineer Fletcher Christian, who met and fell in love with a Tahitian woman in 1788. Brandon met his own Tahitian beauty, Tarita Teripaia, when she was cast as his love interest, Maimiti, in the film. The couple had two children.

Brando bought the island of Tetiaroa in 1966 from the Williams family, Americans who had been given the land by the royal Pomare family of Tahiti, in 1904. The island, which is 48 km (30 mi) north of Tahiti, is actually 13 *motus* (islets) enclosed by a coral reef. One motu, Tahuna Iti, is a natural bird sanctuary.

Brando visited the island frequently until his daughter's death in 1995, after which he was rarely seen in French Polynesia. There was a small hotel on the island but that closed before the actor's death in July 2004. The only inhabitant today is the actor's son, Teihotu. The Brando family apparently sold the island to property developer Richard Bailey for $2 million and there are plans to build an eco-friendly five-star resort to be called The Brando (⊕ *www.brando hotel.com*). This property, to be managed by the InterContinental group, is expected to open in 2010 with 30 villas, though construction work had not begun as recently as mid-2008.

It's not possible to visit the island now, nor will it be while construction takes place. Interestingly, in 2003 Brando allegedly gave his good friend, pop singer Michael Jackson, lifelong use of a quarter of an acre of the land on motu Onetahi, the islet on which the new resort will be built.

PAPE'ETE

HOTEL RESTAURANTS

$–$$$
FRENCH
Fodor'sChoice
★
✕**Le Gallieni.** This is a locals' favorite due to its great food, lively atmosphere, and location on Boulevard Pomare in the same building as the budget style Royal Pape'ete Hotel. Starters include deep-fried crab, and shrimps and scallops with vermouth sauce. Classic international dishes, such as prime rib, also grace the menu. ✉*291 Blvd. Pomare, Pape'ete* ☎*42–05–23* ♨*Reservations essential* ▤*MC, V* ⊙*No dinner Tues.*

$–$$
CHINESE
✕**Le Mandarin.** There's no mistaking you're in a Chinese restaurant at Le Mandarin, situated in the hotel of the same name, just a block from the Pape'ete waterfront. Walls are adorned with frescos of rural scenes including peach blossom trees, pagodas, and fire-breathing dragons, and the ceiling is hung with lanterns. The food's good, too, and fuses Chinese spices with fresh local seafood. Try the spiced lobster if it's on the menu, or the wok-tossed Tahitian shrimp. Duck with Marquesan kumquat and taro-stuffed pork are local twists on classic dishes. A live band plays on Friday and Saturday nights. ✉*51 Rue Colette, Pape'ete* ☎*50–33–50* ▤*AE, DC MC, V.*

1

INDEPENDENT RESTAURANTS

¢–$$ ✕**L'Apizzeria.** This little touch of Italy is a great place to while away a
ITALIAN   few hours in the shady internal courtyard away from the busy water-
★   front road. The tablecloths are red and frescos of Italian scenes adorn
the walls. The pizzas (from 450 to 920 CFP for a mini-pizza) and pas-
tas are excellent, while fish dishes include the mahimahi with garlic,
oregano, and olives. The restaurant is a Pape'ete institution, serving up
wholesome Italian fare since 1968. ⊠*Blvd. Pomare (near Robert Wan
Pearl Museum), Pape'ete* ☎*42–98–30* ▭*MC, V* ⊘*Closed Mon.*

¢–$ ✕**Chez Jimmy.** There's a lovely blend of several Asian cuisines at this
PAN ASIAN   popular eatery not far from Pape'ete Town Hall (le mairie). The Viet-
namese steamed dumplings (known as "raviolis") are said to be legend-
ary, while the Thai Tom Yum soup is also very good. There are also
Chinese dishes using fresh produce from the nearby public market.
⊠*Cnr Rue Collete & Rue des Écoles, Pape'ete* ☎*43–63–32* ▭*AE,
MC, V* ⊘*Closed Sun.*

$$–$$$ ✕**Mango Café.** The decor is bright and breezy with all-white tables and
FRENCH &   chairs and orange, yellow, and green cushions. It's situated next to the
TAHITIAN   busy Vaima Centre, making it an ideal lunch or dinner spot after a
shopping expedition. Dishes that blend Tahitian and French flavors are
the grilled breadfruit topped with foie gras and port wine sauce; and
the tuna with candied ginger. Mains include the hearty red wine beef
stew and rack of lamb. ⊠*Centre Vaima, Rue Jeanne d'Arc, Pape'ete*
☎*43–25–55* ⌂*Reservations essential* ▭*MC, V* ⊘*No dinner Sun. or
Mon., No Lunch Sat.*

$–$$ ✕**La Petite Auberge.** This little restaurant a few blocks back from the
FRENCH &   cruise ship port has a rustic French ambience with vases of fresh flowers
TAHITIAN   everywhere and French and Tahitian ornaments and artwork adorning
the walls. Shrimp in coconut milk and vanilla are a specialty, as are the
desserts, which are homemade. Ask for *le vacherin glace a la vanilla,*
a type of vanilla ice-cream. The friendly staff speaks English, which is
something of a plus in Pape'ete. ⊠*Pont de l'Est, Pape'ete* ☎*42–86–13*
⌂*Reservations essential* ▭*AE, MC, V* ⊘*Closed Sun.*

$–$$ ✕**Les 3 Brasseurs.** This popular café and microbrewery has 20 beers
FRENCH   from around the world on tap. It's right across from the ferry port and
always buzzing with diners and drinkers. Dishes include classic grilled
steaks and fish in variety of styles, including *poisson cru* (raw fish marinated in coconut and lime juice), as well as mussels and duck. Cheaper
choices are the *La Formule due Jour* (special of the day), which includes
a starter or dessert with a main course and glass of beer for 1,950 CFP.
You can taste any four of the beers (in four small glasses) for 800 CFP.
⊠*Blvd. Pomare, Pape'ete* ☎*50–60–25* ▭*MC, V.*

TAHITI NUI

WEST COAST/NORTH COAST

HOTEL RESTAURANTS

$$–$$$ ✕**Le Carre.** Considered one of the best tables in Pape'ete, Le Carre has a
FRENCH   lounge feel due to its subdued lighting, music, and sophisticated ambi-
Fodor'sChoice   ence. Start with lobster ravioli, with peppermint, ginger, and anise; the
★   adventurous might order the breaded pig's foot with roasted scallops

and beets, and a rosemary emulsion. Main dishes include the delicious chef's fish cassolette (stew) flavored with smoked butter, vanilla, and Avatea liqueur. There's a degustation menu, as well as several set menu options that include the two-course option (main and dessert). ⊠ *Le Méridien Tahiti, PK 15, Coastal road, Puna'auia* ☎ 47–07–07 ⌖ *Reservations essential* ⊟ *AE, MC, V.*

$$$–$$$$
FRENCH
★

✕ **Le Lotus.** Bring your credit card to this romantic restaurant perched over the lagoon at the far end of the resort. Several of the dishes were created by the renowned three-star Michelin L'auberge de l'Ill in Alsace, France, with which Le Lotus has an association. You might start with the swordfish mousse on a potato and mussel risotto, move on to duck breast with pan-fried figs and candied onions, and round off with the decadent frozen coconut parfait in a chocolate shell and white mint ice cream. Chef Franck Davi, one of the best in French Polynesia, runs this smart establishment. The four-course degustation menu is pricey. ⊠ *InterContinental Resort Tahiti, PK 7.5, Coastal road, Faa'a* ☎ 86–51–25 ⌖ *Reservations essential* ⊟ *AE, MC, V.*

$$–$$$
FRENCH

✕ **Moevai Restaurant.** Built over the lagoon with floor-to-ceiling windows, this restaurant is a beautiful place to sit and watch the ferries and the planes make their journeys to and from Moorea. At night it's a romantic spot to enjoy succulent local seafood and western dishes with a Tahitian twist. Start with the raw tuna marinated with Tahitian coconut milk with shrimp, mango, and ginger and move on to the thick cut of wahoo (a Pacific Islands fish) with passion fruit sauce. ⊠ *Sheraton Hotel Tahiti Resort & Spa, PK 2, Coastal road, Faa'a* ☎ 86–48–48 ⌖ *Reservations essential* ⊟ *AC, DC, MC, V.*

$$–$$$
JAPANESE

✕ **Sakura.** If you yearn for Japanese cuisine, this teppanyaki restaurant offers the mainstays of the Land of the Rising Sun. Appetizers include mixed tempura and a selection of sushi, while the main course consists of a range of teppanyaki dishes all served with miso soup, mixed salad, and sautéed hibachi vegetables. Choose from salmon, tenderloin, shrimp, pork loin, mahimahi, chicken, lobster, and sea scallop teppanyaki or mix them up in various combinations. Set menus and children's menus and desserts, including flambé vanilla ice cream with rum, are also on offer. ⊠ *Sofitel Tahiti Resort, PK 9, Coastal road, Puna'auia* ☎ 86–66–00 ⌖ *Reservations essential* ⊟ *AC, DC, MC, V.*

INDEPENDENT RESTAURANTS

$–$$
ITALIAN

✕ **Le Casa Bianca.** This is one of a handful of restaurants at Marina Taina, Tahiti's first international marina located about 8 km (5 mi) west of Pape'ete. There are great views of stylish yachts at anchor. The restaurant is decorated with Italian paintings, and pizzas and seafood and fish dishes are the order of the day. The staff speaks English and the menus are in English, too. ⊠ *Marina Taina, PK 9, Coastal road, Puna'auia* ☎ 43–91–35 ⊟ *AE, DC, MC, V.*

$$–$$$$
FRENCH
Fodor's Choice
★

✕ **Coco's.** This romantic restaurant on the edge of the lagoon is perfect for a special night out. The outdoor dining area is a series of small dining nooks within a circular terrace facing a lovely garden. It's especially beautiful at night, dining by candlelight listening to the gentle lap of waves. Dishes such as duck *magret* (lean duck breast) and honey sauce, and beef filet *a la Rossini* (topped with hot foie gras) are served on

1

lovely painted plates. It's an expensive night out, but there are two- and three-course set menus at lunchtime, which go a little easier on the wallet. ⊠ *PK 14.5, Coastal road, Puna'auia* ☎ *58–21–08* ⚑ *Reservations essential* ⊟ *MC, V.*

$-$$
FRENCH
✕ **Le Pink Coconut.** Make sure you arrive before sunset not only to watch the lagoon and Moorea island bathed in a pink glow but to check out the fashionable crowd who frequent this restaurant. Located at Marina Taina, Le Pink Coconut, the trendiest place in town, is a good excuse to put on your best, but still casual, outfit. It serves seafood and Polynesian dishes—the trio of salmon is a favorite. There's live music on Thursday, Friday, and Saturday nights. ⊠ *Marina Taina, PK 9, Coastal road, Puna'auia* ☎ *41–22–23* ⊟ *AE, MC, V* ☺ *Closed Sun. and Mon.*

EAST COAST/NORTH COAST

INDEPENDENT RESTAURANTS

$$$
ECLECTIC
✕ **Le Belvedere Restaurant.** This restaurant is favored by tour groups because of the sensational view from almost 2,000 feet (609 meters) in the hills above Pape'ete. There are sunset and moonlight dining sessions, with sunset being the most popular. You can drive yourself; however, it's a more relaxing experience to take an organized tour, as the road to the top is very steep and narrow in parts. The set menu of salad, french fries, wine or fruit juice, dessert, and a main course (with choices of meat fondue, mahimahi, pepper steak, chicken in red wine, or New Zealand beef shish kebab) includes a round-trip hotel transfer. The restaurant will provide transport to the airport if you have a late flight to catch home. ⊠ *Route de Belvedere, off Coastal road at PK 2.5, Pira'e* ☎ *42–73–44* ⚑ *Reservations essential* ⊟ *AE, MC, V* ☺ *Daily, two sittings: 4:30* PM *and 7* PM.

$-$$
CHINESE
☺
✕ **Le Feng Shui.** If you're heading east of town toward Point Vénus you might want to stop off at this popular Asian restaurant in the town of Arue, not far from the military camp. You can feast on Chinese-style fondue (various meats and vegetables cooked in a pot on your table) or sample the specialty Peking duck or pork with coconut. There's a playground for the kids, too. ⊠ *PK 3.6, Off Coastal road, Arue* ☎ *42–70–50* ⊟ *DC, MC, V* ☺ *Closed Sun.*

TAHITI ITI

Restaurants are few and far between on Tahiti Iti, so your best bet is to eat in your pension, self-cater (after buying groceries at Taravao), eat at one or two of the snacks around the island, or hop in the car and drive to Taravao. There are a few roulottes (restaurant vans on wheels) around Tahiti Iti—often on people's front lawns—so be on the lookout for them as their meals are usually quite reasonable.

INDEPENDENT RESTAURANTS

$-$$$
FRENCH
✕ **Chez Loula and Remy.** This is the big splurge restaurant in the area where you can tuck into delicious plates of fresh seafood laden with lobster, crab, and other delicacies. There's also couscous, paella, various cassoulets (French stews), and wood-fired pizzas on the menu.

⊠*Tautira Rd., Taravao* ☎*57–74–99* ⚑*Reservations essential* ⊟*MC, V* ⊘*Closed Sun.*

¢–$ ✕**La Plage de Maui.** Situated on the south coast road of Tahiti Iti, right
FRENCH on Maui Beach, this restaurant serves fresh seafood such as shrimp,
mahimahi, and tuna. This lovely patch of sand is the only white-sand
beach on the peninsula and is a lovely spot for lunch. Rose Wilkin-
son and Alain Corre, who used to work at the Sofitel Resort Moorea,
decided to really get away from it all and started this restaurant. ⊠*PK
6, South Coastal road, Vairoa* ☎*74–71–74* ⚑*Reservations essential*
⊟*No creit cards* ⊘*Daily 10–6.*

$–$$ ✕**Restaurant Le Manukan.** You can eat in or take away at this stylish
FRENCH little restaurant right at the isthmus. There are classic French/Tahitian
dishes such as beef entrecôte (steak) with coconut or vanilla sauce,
along with a variety of burgers and pizzas. The place heats up on Friday and Saturday nights with dancing to a local live band. ⊠*PK 59.5,
Coastal road, Taravao* ☎*57–77–02* ⚑*Reservations essential* ⊟*MC,
V* ⊘*Closed Sun. and Mon.*

SHOPPING

Pape'ete is the place to shop for everything from the hippest Tahitian
shirt to souvenirs such as pareos, Marquesan carved bowls, ukuleles,
baskets, woven hats, tikis, and monoi oil, which are all available in the
public market. There are plenty of boutiques along Boulevard Pomare
and in Centre Vaima and Fare Tony, and dozens of pearl shops, which
seem to never close. Galleries have exquisite wooden items and paintings. There is little outside the capital, save for a few stores in local
shopping malls and the museum gift shops on the west coast.

PAPE'ETE & TAHITI NUI

BOOKS   **Eurl Vaima Librairie** (⊠*Centre Vaima, Cnr Blvd. Pomare and Rue Jeanne
d'Arc, Pape'ete* ☎*45–57–44* ⊘*Mon.–Fri. 8–5:30, Sat. 8–5*). While the
name suggests otherwise, this is a bookshop not a library. There are
many lovely books, and several in English.

CLOTHING **La Boutique Hinano Tahiti** (⊠*17 Place Notre, Pape'ete* ☎*46–76–76*
BOUTIQUES ⊘*Mon.–Fri. 9–5, Sat. 9–noon*). As well as being a popular brand of
beer, Hinano is a clothing label selling trendy board shorts and surf
gear. This store near the Notre Dame Cathedral also has baseball caps,
girls' and women's wear, swimming costumes, and accessories.

Boutique Le Tiare (⊠*Centre Vaima, 1st level, Cnr Blvd. Pomare &
Rue Jeanne d'Arc, Pape'ete* ☎*42–48–80* ⊘*Mon.–Sat. 9–5:30, Sun.
9–noon*). This bright shop in Pape'ete's best known shopping mall
sells hand-painted shirts and pareos (sarongs) as well as locally made
T-shirts and other items of clothing perfect for lounging.

Te Tare (⊠*Centre Vaima, Blvd. Pomare, Pape'ete* ☎*43–23–30* ⊘*Mon.–
Fri. 9–5, Sat. 9–noon*). The Te Tare label is one of the hippest in the
islands; buy yourself or the man in your life a Te Tare Tahitian shirt, or
a great surf T-shirt or pareo.

GALLERIES **Galerie Antipodes** (✉ *Fare Tony shopping center, Blvd. Pomare, Pape'ete* ☎ *54–05–05 or 54–05–07* ⊕ *www.galerieantipodes.com* ⊙ *Daily 10–5:30*). There's a large selection of local art (including the acclaimed Bora Bora artist Alain Despert), as well as international and aboriginal art.

Galerie des Tropiques (✉ *Place To'ata, Blvd. Pomare, Pape'ete* ☎ *41–05–00* ⊕ *www.galerie-des-tropiques.com* ⊙ *Mon.–Fri. 9–noon, 2–6; Sat. 9–noon*). Situated opposite the Place To'ata (where the huge dance shows take place), this large gallery has several rooms that display the works of French Polynesia's best artists including paintings, carvings, ceramics, and sculptures.

Ganesha Galerie (✉ *Centre Vaima, 2nd floor, Blvd. Pomare, Pape'ete* ☎ *43–04–18* ⊙ *Mon.–Fri. 9–5:30, Sat. 9–noon*). Displays feature the work of craftsmen and -women from across French Polynesia and the Pacific. You'll find stone carved tikis, tapa (bark cloth), wood carvings, and paintings in both traditional and contemporary designs.

GROCERIES **Centre Moana Nui** (✉ *PK 8, Main Coastal road, Puna'auia* ☎ *No phone* & OTHER ⊙ *Mon.–Fri. 9–5:30, Sat. 9–noon*). This is possibly the biggest shop- ESSENTIALS ping mall outside the capital. It's located a few hundred yards south of the Sofitel Resort, near the Marina Taina, which also has many restaurants. You can take the west coast L'Truck bus from Pape'ete to this center, which has a huge supermarket, boutiques, a post office, and an artisans craft shop.

Champion Supermarket (✉ *Rue du General de Gaulle, Pape'ete* ☎ *No phone* ⊙ *Mon.–Sat. 7 AM–7:30 PM, Sun. 6:30–noon*). You can pick up ingredients for dinner, wine and beer, baguettes, and most other essentials at this large supermarket a block behind the Paofai Protestant Temple on Rue du General De Gaulle.

Le Kiosque (✉ *Centre Vaima, ground floor, Blvd. Pomare, Pape'ete* ☎ *64–07–63* ⊙ *Mon.–Fri. 8–6, Sat. 8–noon*). This shop has postcards and stamps, bottled water, candy, and phone cards. There are books and maps, but rarely anything in English.

PEARLS **Robert Wan Pearl Museum (Musee de la Perle)** (✉ *Blvd. Pomare, near Paofai Protestant Temple, Pape'ete* ☎ *46–15–55* ⊙ *Mon.–Sat. 9–5*). This lovely museum also has a retail section where you can purchase single pearls and jewelry (necklaces range from 130,000 to 500,000 CFP) as well as Wan's line of skin-care products that contain nacre, or mother-of-pearl shell. Nacre contains certain proteins that are said to have anti-aging benefits. Wan is the largest pearl producer in the country. There's also a store at InterContinental Tahiti Resort.

Tahia Collins (✉ *Blvd. Pomare & Ave. du Prince Hinoi, Pape'ete* ☎ *54–06–00* ⊕ *www.tahiacollins.com* ⊙ *Daily 9:30–6*). Tahia Collins is another big name in the pearl business. The former beauty queen's boutique is across the road from the cruise dock. Free transfers are provided from hotels.

Tahiti Pearl Market (⊠ *25 Rue Colette, Pape'ete* ☏ *54–30–60* ⊕ *www. tahitipearlmarket.com* ⊗ *Mon.–Sat. 9–5:30, Fri. 9–6, Sun. 10–6*). This huge four-story market claims to have the largest selection of black pearls in French Polynesia with more 150,000 loose pearls on show in Pape'ete and around 70,000 in their Bora Bora store. There's also a range of jewelry and a short movie about pearl production to check out. The company also has a small boutique—the Tahiti Pearl Shop— with a limited range of Italian designed pearl jewelry, located at 349 Blvd. Pomare.

SHOPPING   *See Centre Vaima, in Sights in Pape'ete for information about this out-*
CENTERS   *door shopping center.*

Fare Tony (⊠ *Bounded by Rue du General de Gaulle, Rue Pietonne, and Blvd. Pomare, Pape'ete* ⊗ *Mon.–Fri. 9–5, Sat. 9–noon*). This shopping mall, just a block or two from Centre Vaima, has boutiques, duty free shops, and restaurants.

SOUVENIRS   **Public Market (Le Marche)** (⊠ *Between Rue Francois Cardella and Rue du 22 Septembre, Pape'ete* ☏ *42–48–80* ⊗ *Mon.–Sat. 5 AM–6 PM, Sun. 5–9 AM*). Small gifts such as monoi oil, vanilla, shell necklaces, hats, and baskets are downstairs, while the bigger craft items, as well as pearls and jewelry, are upstairs.

TATTOO   **Mana'o Tattoo Studio** (⊠ *43 Rue Albert Leboucher, Pape'ete* ☏ *42–45– 00* ⊕ *www.manaotattoo.com* ⊗ *Mon.–Sat. 10–6*). The four tattoo art- ists at this studio, which has been operating since 1980, specialize in black and gray tattoos as well as Marquesan and Maori styles.

Simeon & Efaima Huuti (⊠ *Pape'ete market, Pape'ete* ☏ *70–36–34 for Simeon, 42–49–16 for Efaima*). You'll find these tattoo artists at the Pape'ete market place most days of the week—call first to check.

TAHITI ITI

It's best to stock up on essentials at the Hyper Champion (big super- market) in Taravao before you cross over to Tahiti Iti, as there are few shops on Tahiti Iti itself; Taravao also has a post office with pay phones. If you do run out of bottled water, you can always pick some up at the various *snacks* (take-out places) in Teahupoo. There is a craft shop in the center of Vairoa on the southern road where local women sell their wares, which may include printed fabrics, baskets, and *tifaifai* (Tahitian quilts). You may also be lucky to see craftsmen selling carv- ings by the side of the road in Teahupoo.

SPAS

Tahiti has not embraced the spa quite like its western neighbor, Bora Bora. However, most of the resorts do provide massages either in a guest's room or in shady garden spots. Those resorts with dedicated spas offer a menu of treatments that use Tahitian fruits and ingredients such as papaya, monoi oil, and coconut oil. Black volcanic sand is also used in some body scrubs as it's an excellent exfoliant.

PAPE'ETE

INDEPENDENT
SPAS

La Sultane de Saba (⊠*Ave. du Prince Hinoi* ☎*41–34–34* ⊙*Tues.–Fri. 8:30–5, Sat. 8:30–1*). Just off Boulevard Pomare, this exotic eastern themed day spa has a steam bath and offers reflexology, massages, and an array of facials and beauty treatments such as wraps and scrubs.

TAHITI NUI

WEST COAST/SOUTH COAST

SPAS IN
HOTELS &
RESORTS

Le Méridien Tahiti (⊠*PK 15, Coastal road, Puna'auia* ☎*47–07–07* ⊕*www.lemeridien.com* ⊙*Daily 9–6*). There's no full spa at this resort, however there are massages available in guest rooms or in the lovely garden. Prices begin at around 6,500 CFP for an hour.

Sheraton Hotel Tahiti Resort & Spa (⊠*PK 2, Coastal road, Faa'a* ☎*86–48–48* ⊕*www.starwood.com/tahiti* ⊙*Daily 9:30–6*). Indulge in a facial of honey, papaya, coconut milk, and flower essence or treat your feet to reflexology and a pedicure. Massages are available in the spa or your guest room, and there's a hair salon.

Sofitel Tahiti Resort (⊠*PK 9, Coastal road, Puna'auia* ☎*86–66–00* ⊕*www.accorhotels.pf* ⊙*Daily 10–6*). There's no dedicated spa; however, therapists offer an array of massages including sports, relaxation, and "jet-lag revival" in a hotel room set aside on the third level. Also on offer are exfoliating treatments followed by a massage; as well as facials. A 30-minute massage or 30-minute facial costs 6,000 CFP.

NORTH COAST/EAST COAST

SPAS IN
HOTELS &
RESORTS

Radisson Plaza Resort Tahiti (⊠*PK 7, Coastal road, Arue* ☎*48–88–88* ⊕*www.radisson.com/tahiti* ⊙*Daily 9:30–8*). The spa's signature Matavai treatment will leave you totally invigorated. It begins with an exfoliating treatment using black sand and oil followed by a back and scalp massage. The Tihota ute Ute, another exotic scrub, is a subtle blend of brown sugar, Tahitian vanilla, and sweet almond oil.

TAHITI ITI

NORTH COAST

SPAS IN
HOTELS &
RESORTS

Punatea Village Pension (⊠*PK 4.7, North Coastal road, Afaahiti* ☎*57–71–00* ⊕*www.punatea.com* ⊙*By appointment*). It's amazing what you find in Tahiti Iti—this lovely pension has the island's only far-infrared sauna. This technology, also known as sun light saunas, detoxifies your body with heat from sunlight without any sunburn or sun damage. You lie in an igloo-like contraption, with your head poking out one end. If that's a bit too advanced for you, the pension also has a massage chair that will vibrate and massage weary back and leg muscles.

AFTER DARK

Tahiti is really the only island in French Polynesia where you can have a big night out. Pape'ete has several night clubs strung along Boulevard Pomare. Clubs range from those catering to people who want to dance to Tahitian waltzes to those who want to dance to techno. There's also a club running drag shows on the weekends. Night club entry fees are around 1,500 to 2,000 CFP on weekends only, and sometimes only the men get charged. All clubs rage on well into the early hours. You can also catch Polynesian cultural performances—complete with song, dance, and fire twirling—at all the resorts and one or two restaurants. The cultural center (Maison de la Culture) has a full program of drama, dance, and film.

PAPE'ETE & ITS ENVIRONS

COCKTAIL TIME **Le Chaplin's** (⊠ *Blvd. Pomare* ☎ *42–73–05* ⊘ *Daily 6* PM*–1* AM). You'll find more than 50 cocktails on the bar menu at this Centre Vaima bar. There's music and video clips to keep you entertained.

Morrison's Café (⊠ *Centre Vaima, Blvd. Pomare* ☎ *42–78–71* ⊘ *Mon.–Fri. 11* AM*–1* AM*, Sat.–Sun. 4* PM*–1* AM). Have a drink, watch the sunset, and check e-mail at this popular bar just across the road from the cruise dock. There's live music on the terrace on weekends.

Le Retro (⊠ *Blvd. Pomare* ☎ *42–40–01* ⊘ *Daily 10* AM*–11* PM). Decorated like a Parisian café, this bar on the waterfront side of the Centre Vaima is a great place to have a drink at sunset.

Les 3 Brasseurs (⊠ *Blvd. Pomare* ☎ *50–60–25* ⊘ *Daily noon–midnight*). Beer lovers will want to try at least a few of the 20 varieties on tap at this microbrewery-cum-restaurant opposite the ferry port.

LATE-NIGHT **L'Apetahi** (⊠ *Rue du General De Gaulle* ☎ *53–40–80* ⊘ *Mon.–Sat. 6*
BARS & CLUBS PM*–midnight*). If you're a karaoke junkie and fancy dinner as well, then this is the place for you. It's open every night except Sunday, but the karaoke machine cranks up on Thursdays and Saturday nights.

Le Piano Bar (⊠ *Rue des Écoles* ☎ *42–88–24* ⊘ *Drag shows: Fri. and Sat. 1* AM*; bar: daily 10* PM*–3* AM). This is one of the haunts of Pape'ete's *mahu* (*see The Third Sex box below*) community and also the venue for late-night drag shows, to which everyone is welcome.

Le Royal Kikiriri (⊠ *Rue Collette* ☎ *43–58–64* ⊘ *Mon.–Thurs. 9* PM*–1* AM*, Fri.–Sat. 9* PM*–3* AM). If you want to dance the traditional Polynesian two-step, the waltz, the *tamure* (the hip-shaking Tahitian dance), or just shake your booty make this a stop.

Le Tamure Hut (⊠ *291 Blvd. Pomare* ☎ *42–01–29* ⊘ *Daily 9* PM*–1* AM). Situated in the waterfront Royal Pape'ete Hotel, this is one of the city's *in* night spots. You can dance to old and new Tahitian tunes played by a live band from Wednesdays to Saturdays. Another bar with Tahitian music on the same premises is La Cave.

CLOSE UP

The Heiva

1

French Polynesia's most exciting event, which runs from late June to late July, began in 1881, the year after France annexed Tahiti, to mark Bastille Day (July 14). Originally known as Tiuri (the Tahitian word for July), the festival excluded dancing as that had been banned by the missionaries in the 1820s.

Today, though, lavish dance performances dominate the program, and the festival begins with performances by various dance schools, building up to a week of song and dance competitions, each with several categories. It culminates with spectacular shows by the winning troupes, which can number up to 100 dancers. The performances take place at To'ata Square on Pape'ete's waterfront.

Other events include outrigger canoe races around Pape'ete Harbour and across to Moorea and back, and displays of physical prowess including stone lifting, fruit carrying races, coconut cracking, and palm-tree climbing—some events have women's divisions. There's even a contest for Mr. and Miss Heiva, which is based on the contestants' appearance and their ability to perform some of the aforementioned feats.

An arts-and-crafts program runs at the same time involving artists from across French Polynesia, who display their work and demonstrate their weaving, patchwork, painting, and carving skills. Works are displayed at the Aorai Tini Hau Exposition Hall in Pira'e and the Museum of Tahiti and Her Islands west of Pape'ete. Individual song and dance competition tickets range from 1,000 to 2,500 CFP. Heiva celebrations also take place in Bora Bora and Raiatea.

TAHITI NUI

WEST COAST/SOUTH COAST

COCKTAIL TIME **Quinn's Bar** (⊠*PK 2, Faa'a* ☏*86–48–48*). Enjoy a happy hour–priced drink every night between 5 and 6 at the Sheraton Tahiti Resort's popular bar. There's jazz and blues on Wednesdays and live bands on Friday and Saturday.

PERFORMANCES **Captain Bligh Restaurant** (⊠*PK 11.4, Puna'auia* ☏*43–62–90* ⊗*Fri.–Sat. 7 PM*). Another of Tahiti's top dance troupes—O Tahiti E—performs at this restaurant in the same complex as Lagoonarium, complete with seafood buffet (5,100 CFP).

InterContinental Tahiti Resort (⊠*PK7.5 Faa'a* ☏*86–51–10* ⊕*www.ichotelsgroup.com* ⊗*Dinner 7:30 PM, show 8:30 PM*). The acclaimed Les Grands Ballets de Tahiti dance troupe puts on a spectacular show on Friday and Saturday nights complete with a theme buffet—seafood or Polynesian. Prices for dinner and show are 8,400 CFP (Friday) and 7,790 CFP (Saturday).

Le Méridien Tahiti (⊠*PK15, Coastal road, Puna'auia* ☏*47–07–07* ⊕*www.lemeridien.com* ⊗*Fri. 7 PM*). Friday night is the night to catch the lively Polynesian dance show at the Plantation restaurant; price is around 7,500 CFP.

NORTH/EAST COAST

COCKTAIL TIME **Lafayette Bar** (⊠ *Radisson Plaza Resort Tahiti, PK7, Coastal road, Arue* ☎ *48–88–88* ⊕ *www.radisson.com/tahiti* ☽ *Daily noon–10* PM). Pull up a cane chair on the bar's terrace and watch the sun set over Matavai Bay. Sip on a mai tai as Moorea slips into darkness, while you welcome the evening under torchlight.

LATE-NIGHT **Le Royal Tahitien** (⊠ *PK 3, Coastal road, Pira'e* ☎ *50–40–40* ⊕ *www.*
BARS & CLUBS *hotelroyaltahitien.com* ☽ *Fri. 7* PM*–1* AM). This budget hotel, about a mile east of Pape'ete, is a popular place for a good meal and dancing on Friday night. The local Tahitian bands get everyone up on the dance floor before too long.

PERFORMANCES **Radisson Plaza Resort Tahiti** (⊠ *Radisson Plaza Resort Tahiti, PK7, Coastal road, Arue* ☎ *48–88–88* ⊕ *www.radisson.com/tahiti* ☽ *Dinner 7* PM*, show 8* PM). The black sand of Lafayette Beach is the setting for a lively Tahitian dance show every Saturday night. Buffet and performance costs 6,000 CFP and is essential to book.

OUTDOOR ACTIVITIES

Tahiti's rugged landscape draws those keen on exploring the mountainous 4WD trails and ancient marae remains. Guides will also take surfers and body boarders to the legendary surf breaks, while all the usual aquatic activities—diving, snorkeling, fishing, boating, Jet Skiing—are on offer. The island's history is revealed on circle tours that visit temple sights, museums, and the landing sites of Tahiti's first explorers.

BOATING, CANOEING & SAILING

Aroha Pacific (⊠ *Coastal road, Mahina* ☎ *43–67–92*). This all-in-one operator can take you kayaking and snorkeling around Tahiti and the peninsula one day, and trekking through mountain trails the next.

S.A.R.L. Moanareva (⊠ *Pt. Vénus, Coastal road, Mahina* ☎ *42–45–28* ⊕ *www.moanareva.com*). If you want to hit the water on a surfboard, wakeboard, canoe, kayak, long board, paddleboard, or learn to kite surf, then this is the place for lessons and equipment rentals.

Yacht Club de Tahiti (⊠ *PK 4, clockwise, Coastal road, Arue* ☎ *42–78–03*). This operator has introductory and advanced sailing lessons for children and adults and runs competitions at all levels.

CIRCLE ISLAND TOURS

Adventure Eagle Tours (⊠ *Coastal road, Faa'a* ☎ *77–20–03*). Sit back and relax in an air-conditioned minibus as owner William Leeteg takes you on a half-day tour around Tahiti Nui, or a shorter version to the east coast sights. Leetag promises no hiking is involved.

DIVING & SNORKELING

Eleuthera Plongee (⊠ *Marina Tania, PK 9, Coastal road, Puna'auia* ☎ *42–49–29* ⊕ *www.eleuthera.pf*). This French outfit has been operating in Tahiti for 10 years taking experienced divers to 30 sites and

The Third Sex

1

If you spend a few days out and about in French Polynesia, you're likely to come across women who aren't actually women. Known publicly as *mahu* or scientifically as "the third sex," this fraction of the population has been raised female from a very young age. Many behave in an effeminate manner, pluck their eyebrows, and wear makeup, while others are more flamboyant, wearing feminine outfits and jewelry. However, these behaviors don't always mean these men are homosexual.

There are many theories as to why the boys are raised as girls, but none have been scientifically proven. Whatever the explanation, mahus were part of the Polynesian culture long before the Europeans arrived in the late 18th century. Captain Bligh, of *Mutiny on the Bounty* fame, wrote about mahus in his ship's log. Things took a turn for the worse when thousands of French troops arrived in French Polynesia in the 1960s to work in the nuclear testing program and some of the Mahus began prostituting themselves to earn money.

---

training newcomers. They will take you on wreck dives, shark dives, and night dives.

Iti Diving International (⊠*PK6, South Coastal road,Vairao* ☎*57–77–93*). The waters around Tahiti Iti are pristine, and this operator knows all the good cave sights and where the big fish hang out.

Scuba Trek Tahiti (⊠*PK 4,Coastal road Arue* ☎*42–23–55*). This operation is run by the Tahiti Yacht Club. Three dives take place per day to sights around the north coast of the island, with prices starting at 4,800 CFP per dive; there are discounts for multiple dives.

FISHING
Tahitian International Billfish Association (⊠*Marina Taina Club House, Puna'auia* ☎*42–37–14*). This organization can give you the lowdown on the International Billfish Tournament that takes place every March. It also organizes fishing trips.

4WD EXCURSIONS
Patrick Adventure (⊠*Pape'ete* ☎*83–29–29*). Patrick, a local guide, take visitors on an amazing 4WD cross-island adventure past waterfalls and lakes. Stops include Vaihiria Lake to see the blue-eyed eels.

GOLF
Olivier Breaud International Golf Course (⊠*Coastal road, Papara* ☎*57–40–52*). Situated on a beautiful piece of land known as the Atimaono estate, which was once a cotton plantation and then a rum factory, the 18-hole course is extraordinarily beautiful and challenging.

HIKING
Hina Trekking (⊠*Tamanu Center, Puna'auia* ☎*58–22–63*). Treks include the picturesque Orange Tree Plateau in the Punaaru Valley (inland from Puna'auia), the Belvedere, and Mt. Aorai.

HORSEBACK RIDING

L'Amour de la Nature a Cheval (⊠ *PK 2.5, North Coastal road* ☎ *43–50–79*). The wide-open spaces of the Taravao Plateau are the perfect place to let horses run free. There are one-hour rides to lookouts, while day rides include picnics.

Club Equestre de Tahiti (Equestrian Club of Tahiti) (⊠ *PK 2, Coastal road, Pira'e* ☎ *42–70–41*). The club offers trail rides to Pape'ete's rural areas and riding lessons.

LAGOON EXCURSIONS

Tahiti Iti Tours & Surf (⊠ *PK 10, South Coastal road, Vairao* ☎ *57–97–39* ⊕ *www.tahitiititourandsurf.pf*) This Tahiti Iti–based company shows you wild and remote Tahiti by boat. There are hourly, half-day, and full-day excursions, complete with wakeboarding, waterskiing, and fishing if requested.

QUAD BIKES

Tahiti Aventures (⊠ *InterContinental Tahiti Resort, PK 7.5, Coastal road, Faa'a* ☎ *29–01–60 mobile phone* ⊕ *www.tahiti-aventures.com*). Based at the InterContinental Tahiti Resort, this operator has five ATVs (all terrain vehicles) or quad bikes to have you zooming over hills in the Papenoo Valley. They also operate Jet ski tours around the lagoon.

SURFING

Toa Moana Surf School (⊠ *Fare Tony, Blvd. Pomare, Pape'ete* ☎ *81–12–90 pascal-luciani@mail.pf*). Tahiti's surf is mythic among surfers the world over. To learn how to surf the barrels and reef breaks, check out this Pape'ete-based operator, which offers packages of 10 lessons and will take you to various hot spots around the island.

Tura'I Mataare Surf School (⊠ *PK 18.3 counterclockwise, Coastal road, Paea* ☎ *41–91–37* ⊕ *www.tahitisurfschool.info*). With more than 10 years' experience, this operator can teach you the tricks and take you to the great breaks.

WATERSKIING

Water Ski Club of Tahiti (⊠ *PK 7, Coastal road, Puna'auia* ☎ *45–39–36* ⊕ *www.tahitiskiclub.com*). Part of the French Federation of Water Ski-ing, the club provides wakeboarding lessons, as well as all levels of water skiing including mono ski, barefoot ski, and advanced water skiing.

Moorea

WORD OF MOUTH

"I'd pick Moorea over Bora Bora pretty much any-time. Moorea doesn't have that classic "picture in a frame" ringed lagoon, but it has some darn nice beaches, a fine lagoon in places, and a wide range of accommodations and activities. It's also easy to get to, just a short ferry ride from Tahiti. Development isn't as concentrated, so almost the entire shoreline is attractive. The interior is more accessible, and there are some pretty bays that serve as anchorages for passing yachts."

—ALF

Written by
Caroline
Gladstone

MOOREA IS CALLED THE "SISTER island" of Tahiti and its proximity—just 19 km (12 mi) away across the Sea of Moon—has assured a steady stream of both international and local visitors. Many Tahitians have holiday homes on Moorea and hop over in their boats or take the 30-minute ferry. The draw is South Seas island charm and a relatively slow-paced life. Moorea is an eighth of the size of Tahiti but packs all the classic island features into its triangular shape. Cutting into the northern side of the island are the dramatic Opunohu Bay and Cook's Bay, the latter backed by the shark-toothed Mt. Mouaroa and home to many resorts and restaurants. Between the two bays majestic Mt. Rotui rises 2,020 feet (616 meters) and steep, jagged mountain ridges run across the island. From the Belvedere lookout there are awesome views of these bays and mountains, including the tallest peak—the thumb-shaped Mt. Tohiea reaching 3,960 feet (1,207 meters) into the clouds.

Moorea is ringed by a coral reef enclosing a beautiful and quite narrow lagoon. Unlike other islands in the Society group, Moorea has only a couple of *motu* (islets) and they are located off the northwest corner. The island's rugged peaks and deep bays are said to be the inspiration for James A. Michener's mythical isle of Bali Hai, although historians dispute this claim. It's also believed to be the "birthplace" of the legendary overwater bungalow: a trio of Californian guys who came to Moorea in the 1950s and became known as the Bali Hai boys reportedly dreamt up this unique style of hotel room. Today there are seven resorts and about 24 smaller hotels and pensions, acres of pineapple plantations, and one of only two golf courses in French Polynesia.

ORIENTATION & PLANNING

ORIENTATION

MOOREA
Moorea is 19 km (12 mi) northwest of Tahiti, accessible via a 10-minute plane or 30-minute ferry ride. It has a triangular shape with two deep bays cut into the middle of its north side. The airport is at Temae on the northeast corner, which also has the best beach. The port is at Vaiare, 5 km (3 mi) south of the airport. Steep ridges run in a semicircle from the northwestern corner to the southeastern corner of the island; a lush valley sits in the middle. Most tourist infrastructure is on the north coast around the bays and at Hauru Point on the northwest corner.

PLANNING

GETTING HERE AND AROUND
Moorea is the easiest island to get to from Tahiti. Four different vessels make the 19-km (12-mi) crossing, taking 30 to 50 minutes depending on their size and the number of vehicles they carry. All boats depart from the Gallieni Quay in the heart of Pape'ete. Fares range from 900 to 1,060 CFP one-way.

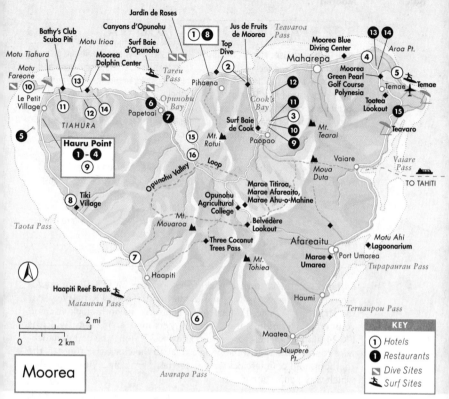

Moorea

TOP REASONS TO VISIT MOOREA

The lush paradise. Moorea retains an authentic island feel, with many traditional villages to be discovered on a circle-island tour. Pineapple plantations dot the hillside, residents tend their luxuriant gardens, and wild rain forest dominates the inland peaks.

Take a hike. This is the place to put on the walking boots and head for the hills. There are ridge and valley walks and treks to high points for awesome views.

Arts and Culture. Moorea is home to more artists than any other island in French Polynesia. There are painters, woodcarvers, and sculptors, and jewelers working with pearls and shells. For cultural entertainment, check out vigorous hip-shaking, the swishing of grass skirts, evocative drumming, and the blaze of fire-dancing at the Tiki Village.

Cheap sleeps. Moorea has the greatest concentration of pensions, guesthouses, and villa rentals in French Polynesia which means there's a wide choice of affordable accommodation.

Distances on the island are marked in kilometers and PK (*pointes kilometer*) markers are on the side of the road. The 0 PK marker is at the airport at Temae. Distances are measured in both clockwise and counterclockwise directions. The markers meet at Haapiti, which is PK 24 along the clockwise route, and PK 37 along the counterclockwise route. Note that some people refer to the clockwise route as the southern, and counterclockwise as the northern route. Just remember which way you're going.

Though you can rent cars, scooters, and bicycles on Moorea, the 137-sqaure-km (53-square-mi) island is extremely rugged, so it's advisable to take an organized 4WD safari tour to see the island's interior. The coastal road, however, is flat and at just 61 km (38 mi) is an easy drive and a good day's cycle trip, but only if you're very fit and can handle the humidity. You can also rent bugsters (they look like small dune buggies) and "fun bikes," which are a cross between a bike and a car and involve both people pedaling. Most resorts can also rent bicycles to their guests. Three rental car companies—Albert Rent-a-Car, Avis Pacificar, and Europcar—have booths at the airport. Rates are competitive and range from 8,500 to 10,000 CFP (depending on car size) for a 24-hour rental period. There's a gas station—Total Tiahura—at Petit Village with a mechanic on duty six days a week.

Air Moorea, a division of Air Tahiti, operates an eight-minute flight between Tahiti and Moorea, about 40 times a day, with one-way fares costing 4,200 CFP (daytime) and 8,400 CFP (night flights). Air Tahiti connects Moorea with Bora Bora about three times a day; with Huahine daily; and with Raiatea about six days a week. A "Bora Bora Airpass" (one of several air passes) will connect Tahiti-Moorea, Huahine, Raiatea, Bora Bora, and Maupiti-Tahiti and cost 36,800 CFP.

If your hotel is not picking you up at Moorea Airport, you can prepay for a transfer when you buy your domestic air ticket at Tahiti-Faa'a airport in Pape'ete and look for the Moorea Transport coach operator on you arrival. You can also take a taxi, but they are pretty expensive. An average fare from the airport to the west coast (near the InterContinental resort) is more than US$35. The night fares can be double the day prices. There's also the famous *L'Truck* public transport that takes passengers from the ferry port at Vaiare to various hotels along the north and northwest coast; all you need do is hail it down.

ESSENTIALS

Airlines Air Moorea (☎86-42-42 ⊕ www.airtahiti.pf).

Banks Banque de Polynesie (☎56-14-59 in Maharepa or 56-12-02 in Le Petit Village, Hauru Point). **Banque Socredo** (☎56-13-06 or 56-18-63). **Banque de Tahiti** (☎56-13-29).

Boats & Ferries Aremiti (☎50-57-57 or 50-57-91 aremiticruise@mail.pf). **Moorea Ferry** (☎50-11-11 or 56-43-44).

Car Rentals Albert Rent-a-Car (☎55-21-10 ⊕ www.albert-transport.net). **Avis Pacificar** (☎56-32-68 ⊕ www.avis-tahiti.com). **Europcar** (☎56-34-00 ⊕ www.europcar.pf). **Rent a Bike/Rent a Scoot** (☎71-11-09). **Teihotu Location** (☎56-52-96).

Emergencies Emergency Telephone Number (☎17). **Cook's Bay Police Station** (☎56-13-44). **Cook's Bay Pharmacy** (☎55-20-75). **Moorea Hospital/Pharmacy in Afareaitu** (☎56-23-23 and 56-24-24). **Varari Pharmacy** (☎56-38-37).

Taxis Mr. Albert Haring (☎56-39-66). **Mr. D'esli Monoihere Grand** (☎73-37-19). **Mr. Edbar Ienfa** (☎56-19-54). **Mrs. Elisabeth Teraiharoa** (☎56-14-93). **Taxi Justin** (☎56-10-13).

Visitor Info Moorea Visitors Bureau (✉ Le Petit, Hauru Point ☎56-29-09 ⊕ www.gomoorea.com ⊙ Mon.–Thurs. 8–4).

TAKE IT ALL IN

3 Days: Settle in at your hotel and cycle around the local area. Moorea's tourist spots are a little spread out along the north side. Have an afternoon swim and a sunset cocktail. On your second day, take a 4WD safari tour into the interior, check out the waterfalls, the Belvedere lookout, and finish at the Moorea Fruit Juice Factory. Spend your last day on the lagoon, letting the experts take you to the best snorkeling and to ray and shark feeding spots. Relax with a BBQ on a motu and laze under a palm tree. At night soak in the culture by watching the vibrant dancers at the Tiki Village. If you prefer some quieter culture there's a Polynesian floor show at the Sofitel Moorea Resort. ■ TIP➡ The Sofitel show is only on twice a week, compared with Tiki Village shows from Tuesday to Saturday.

5 Days: Follow the above itinerary and then on your fourth day, hike along a valley trail: choose from the Vaiare-Paopao Route, the Three Coconut Trees Pass, or the Opunohu Valley Loop. Relax with a spa

TOURING TIPS

Rent a car or scooter: this is the best way to travel the 61-km (37-mi) road around the island. Taxis are notoriously expensive and *L'Truck* is not always available.

Some brochures and flyers (and even one map) refer to the Hauru Point area in the northwest as Haapiti, which is actually a village about 16 km (10 km) farther along the counterclockwise route. It can be confusing, so check with your hotel desk as

to the exact location of a restaurant or activity site.

You'll also see the occasional reference to the location of the former Club Med Resort, which closed down about seven years ago. For the record, it was near the existing Hotel Hibiscus.

treatment afterwards. On day 5, rent a car or scooter and strike out on your own along the 61-km (38-mi) island road.

WHEN TO GO

There are two seasons: the wet summer season from November to April when temperatures peak at 85°F (with night temperatures dropping to around 70°F), and the dry, cooler season from May to October (highs at 82°F, lows at 70°F). Volcanic islands such as Moorea also have their own microclimates and the east coast is a bit wetter than the west.

Moorea's festivals include the Tahiti–Moorea sailing Rendezvous in June; the Heiva Festival (a monthlong celebration of folkloric displays) in July; the Opunohu Valley mountain race in late September; the Rotui 15-km race in October; and the Rotui triathlon on December 30.

EAT RIGHT, SLEEP WELL

Moorea has a much more diverse selection of dining and eating options than other islands in the Society group. Most of the hotels and restaurants are on the northern side, grouped around Hauru Point on the northwest and along the 3-mi strip from Cook's Bay to Maharepa. There are a few small hotels dotted on the west and south coasts as well. Restaurants range from upscale resort restaurants and independent French eateries (both expensive and moderately priced) to cafés, pizza and burger joints, and *Roulottes* around the Cook's Bay-Maharepa area. Roulottes specialize in rotisserie chicken and the classic French Polynesian dish, *poisson cru* (raw tuna marinated in lime and coconut milk). Many restaurants provide patrons free transfers or charge a small fee. ■ TIP➜ Tipping at restaurants is not expected.

There are only three internationally branded hotels on the island (Sheraton, Sofitel, and InterContinental) together with French Polynesia's own resort chain, Pearl. A new self-catering apartment hotel known as Legends Resort & Spa opened in mid-2008 on the hillside on the northwest coast. There is also a good selection of medium and budget priced pensions, lodges, two campsites, and a couple of villas for whole house rentals.

WHAT IT COSTS IN FRANC COURS PACIFIQUE (CFP)					
	¢	$	$$	$$$	$$$$
RESTAURANTS	under 1,000	1,001– 1,500	1.501– 2,500	2,501–3 ,300	over 3,301– 5,000
HOTELS	under 10,000	10,001– 25,000	25,001– 37,000	37,001– 50,000	over 50,001– 84,000

Restaurant prices are for a main course at dinner. Hotel prices are for a double room in high season, excluding 10% tax, 10%–15% service charges, and meal plans (except at all-inclusives).

EXPLORING MOOREA

Moorea is an easy island to explore by car. The one coastal road is just 61 km (37 mi) long, and the best part of a day is needed to travel the road and stop off at the villages, bays, little churches, and cafés along the way and to travel into the interior to the Belvedere lookout and the *marae* (ancient temples).

The lagoon and bays can be discovered on organized excursions that may include a picnic lunch on one of the motu at the island's northwest corner. There are also small motorboats for hire for a half or full day, with no license required. You won't find too many tracks of endless white sands on Moorea; however, the top resorts have lovely man-made beaches and the lagoon-side pensions and lodges always have at least a little patch of sand.

Half-day and full-day 4WD tours take in all the sights and some areas inaccessible to motorists, while hiking is a great way to see the pineapple and fruit plantations and lush valleys.

EAST COAST

Most visitors arrive on the east coast of Moorea by boat or plane. The airport is in Temae, which is where the kilometer marker system begins with PK 0.

TOWNS
Afareaitu. This village a few miles south of the port of Vaiare is the administrative center and contains the island's *mairie* (town hall) and a small, early 20th-century church. The village was headquarters of the South Seas Academy in the early 19th century, whose mission was to spread the Protestant faith. Nearby is Marae Umarea, the oldest on the island, dating back to AD 900. The two Afareaitu waterfalls, often just called waterfall 1 and 2, are inland from the village via different dirt roads. You can drive to car parks and take a 20- to 30-minute walk to each of them. Pack a swimsuit as there are rockpools ideal for swimming. Afareaitu also has the island's only hospital. ⊠*PK 9, clockwise, Coastal road.*

TOPOGRAPHY

Moorea is a mountainous island with dramatic ridges, peaks, and bays that are best seen from the Belvedere lookout or from a boat out in the lagoon. Its towering peaks are often swathed in cloud. The highest is Mt. Tohieu (3,960 feet [1,207 meters]) standing almost directly behind the Belvedere; Mt. Mouaputa (2,723 feet [830 meters]) has a hole pierced through its summit; Mt. Rotui (2,949 feet [899 meters]) rises dramatically between the two bays; Mt. Moua-roa (2,887 feet [880 meters]) is the iconic shark-toothed mountain you see on all the postcards. The island is an extinct volcano; the bays mark the ancient volcano floor and the semicircular ridge of mountains rising above the Opunohu Valley marks the edge of the crater rim. A narrow, shallow lagoon surrounds the island, itself enclosed by a barrier reef broken in several places by passes to the open sea. Black-and-white sand beaches, all about one-half to a mile long, can be found on several points around the island.

Temae. It's the name of a town, a beach, and the location of the airport. The kilometer marker system begins here with PK 0. There are three rental car companies at the airport and a tourism information kiosk with brochures. Nearby are a couple of pensions and the five-star Sofitel Moorea Resort and Spa. ⊠ *PK 0, Coastal road.*

Vaiare. This is likely to be your first view in Moorea and it's a stunning one. Below cloud-swathed, jagged peaks, the ferry port is a hive of activity during the day. It's adjacent to the marina where dozens of catamarans and yachts moor. Europcar and Avis have desks at the port, and *L'Truck* buses meet each ferry, as do the yellow Moorea Transport minibuses and taxis. There is a stall selling pineapples and fruit, so stock up here. ⊠ *PK 4, clockwise, Coastal road.*

SIGHTS

Lagoonarium. This enclosed part of the lagoon near Motu Ahi, off Afareaitu, is home to turtles, rays, and hundreds of fish. A boat takes visitors from Afareaitu at PK 9 (clockwise) on a very short transfer to the island where they can spend all day swimming, snorkeling, learning about marine life, and even nursing baby sharks. There is also an organized tour that includes a dolphin-spotting cruise followed by a few hours on the island. ⊠ *Motu Ahi* ☎ *56–38–75* 💲 *2,800 CFP (island visit), 7,000 CFP (dolphin cruise/island visit)* ⊘ *Daily 8–5.*

Toatea Lookout. This is a high point of the coastal road, just a short drive north of the airport. All the transfer minibuses stop here to show visitors their first view of the lagoon and Tahiti in the distance. There's also a great view of the Sofitel Moorea's overwater bungalows below. It's a wonderful view and everyone gets his or her photo taken here. ⊠ *PK 1, counterclockwise, Coastal road.*

BEACHES

Teavora & Temae Beaches. These beaches are the best on the East Coast; their names tend to be used interchangeably as they're really one long beach that starts just north of the ferry port and stretches all the way to the airport. The best section is the 1-mile stretch between the airport and the Sofitel Moorea Beach Resort. It can be quite busy on weekends, but especially quiet mid-week or during the low season from January to May. To gain access, look for the public access sign near the Sofitel resort. Expert surfers may want to test their skills on the famous Temae surf break—but beware of the dangerous reef.

NORTH COAST

Stretching some 24 km (15 mi) from east to west the north coast of Moorea has the bulk of the island's tourist infrastructure—hotels, pensions, cafés, restaurants, car rentals, a couple of towns, and the two stunning bays: Cook's Bay and Opunohu.

TOWNS

Maharepa. This village is a collection of tourist shops, eateries, pearl stores, a tattoo parlor, and two small shopping centers. The larger Socredo Centre has one of the island's two post offices, a bank, ATMs, and telephones as well as a pastry shop and café. There are several Roulottes selling reputedly the best *poisson cru* on the island. They open for business around 6 PM. ⊠*PK 3, counterclockwise, Coastal road.*

Pihaena. Between Opunohu and Cook's bays, this is more tourist enclave than village, with a collection of pensions (with restaurants) and the Sheraton Moorea resort and hotel restaurants. The Moorea Juice Factory is just a little inland from the coastal road here; bulky Mt. Rotui looms large directly behind. ⊠*PK 13–14, Coastal road.*

Tiahura. While you won't see this name much, it is the official name for the area on Moorea's northwest corner with the biggest concentration of hotels, restaurants, boutiques, and other shops strung along the main road, or just off it toward the lagoon. Moorea residents like to say there isn't really a main town on the island at all, but Tiahura seems the closest thing to it as far as tourists are concerned. It extends into Hauru Point. The focal point is the Le Petit Village shopping center, housing the **Moorea Visitors Center** (Mon.–Thurs. 9–4), a pearl shop, a bank, souvenirs stores, and an Internet café. ⊠*PK 25–30 counterclockwise, Coastal road.*

SIGHTS

Cook's Bay. This lovely bay, also known as Paopao Bay, has the most dramatic setting and is best appreciated by standing at its eastern or western shore, or better still, from a boat out in the lagoon. The much-photographed shark-toothed mountain of Mouaroa rises steeply behind it, and Mt. Rotui stands at its western side. There's no real township, just a smattering of shops, restaurants, and small hotels along the northeast corner. The village of Paopao sits at the base (or head) of the bay at PK 9.5; it has a **daily market** (☉*Mon.–Sat. 6 AM–5 PM, Sun. 4:30 AM—8 AM*) selling food and local crafts, and nearby is the Van der Heyde art gallery. The Catholic church of St. Joseph sits on the western shore and is decorated with an old wall fresco of the Angel Gabriel. For a spiritual experience par excellence, attend the 10 AM mass on

Sunday morning to hear the hymns and see Tahitians in their Sunday best. ⊠ *PK 6–10.5, Coastal road.*

Opunohu Bay. This is the westerly of the two outstanding bays on the north side of the island, and is actually the place where Captain James Cook dropped anchor in 1777. It is much less developed than Cook's Bay in terms of tourism and is said to be the locals' favorite for this very reason. Most of the Polynesian scenes from the 1984 movie *Bounty,* starring Mel Gibson, were filmed in the bay. Big cruise ships moor here, but because there is no port, passengers are taken ashore in tenders. ⊠ *PK 14–21, counterclockwise, Coastal road.*

Papetoai Temple. This temple is the main attraction of little Papetoai and is also known as the Octagonal Church, due to its eight sides. Protestant missionaries constructed it between 1822 and 1827 deliberately on the site of a former marae in an effort to assert the new religion. The buttercup-yellow church with a red roof was rebuilt in the latter part of the 19th century but remains the oldest European building still in use in the South Pacific. Just one spike-shaped stone remains from the days when it was a marae. The church is often locked, so if you want to see inside, turn up for the Sunday church service. Nearby is the small dock where cruise ship passengers come ashore by tender boats. Craft markets stalls are set up when a cruise ship is in town. ⊠ *PK 21.9, Coastal road, Papetoai* ☉ *Sun. 10 AM–11 AM for church service.*

Jus de Fruits de Moorea. Juice was first pressed at this pineapple processing factory and distillery in 1981. In the early days, four juices—pineapple, grapefruit, orange, and apple—flowed, but now there are 18 juices and beverages including the famous Tahiti Punch (with 10% alcohol) and various liquors made from vanilla and coconut. The factory floor is off-limits for safety reasons but you can watch a video (in French and English) of the pineapple juicing process. The degustation (tasting) of juices and liquors is free. The gift shop sells drinks as well as honey, tea, crystallized fruits, chocolates, and souvenirs such as T-shirts, and even pearls. ⊠ *Inland off PK 12 counterclockwise, Coastal road, Pihaena* ☎ *55–20–00* ⊕ *www.manuteatahiti.com* 🖭 *Free* ☉ *Mon.–Sat. 8–4.*

Moorea Dolphin Center. You can literally kiss and cuddle dolphins here. Four dolphins (ex-performers and retired U.S. Navy dolphins) live in an enclosed section of the lagoon at the InterContinental Moorea Resort and Spa. There are special dolphin encounters tailored for couples, groups, and families involving snorkeling in the lagoon with the creatures, swimming with them by holding on to their fins (called the Apnea program), and learning to teach them tricks. Formerly called Dolphin Quest, the center's open to the public but reservations are essential. ⊠ *PK 26, Coastal road* ☎ *55–19–48* ⊕ *www.mooreadolphincenter. com* 🖭 *Apnea program (30 minutes) 24,300 CFP; discovery (1 hour) 19,800 CFP; Trainer for a Day (3 hours) 45,500 CFP* ☉ *Daily 9–5.*

BEACHES

The two motus off the northwest coast of the island have lovely beaches that can be visited on excursion tours or if you take a boat there yourself and dine at the restaurants.

Opunohu Beach. This public beach, about half a mile long, is on the northeast side of Opunohu Bay. It's popular on the weekends with French and Tahitian families, boys playing soccer, and people picnicking under the trees. There are lovely views back to the bay. Dozens of catamarans belonging to the Moorea Sailing School (*Ecole de Voile de Moorea*) line the shore of one section of the beach. Opunohu Beach is about a mile west of the Sheraton Lagoon Resort. ⊠ *PK 14.5 counterclockwise, Coastal road.*

Motu beaches. When you book a shark feeding and motu picnic excursion you'll head to either Motu Fareone or Motu Moea, or to one of several small islands in either of the two bays. A favorite weekend hangout for locals is the La Plage Beach Restaurant on Motu Moea. The owners organize boat transfers for diners, and you can swim and snorkel at the lovely beach before or after lunch. If you have rented a boat, you can cruise over or paddle a canoe. It's rarely visited by tourists, but well worth it. ⊠ *Offshore, approx. PK 27, Coastal road.*

THE INTERIOR

There are several interesting landlocked sights accessed by roads off the Coastal Road at the north end of the island. They include the famous Belvedere and several marae. Each is just a few miles inland.

SIGHTS

Belvedere. This popular lookout, a few miles inland from Paopao, is the island's highest point accessible by car. From the summit (720 feet [219 meters]) there are commanding views of Opunohu and Cook's bays, Mt. Rotui, surrounding peaks, and the valleys below. The Belvedere road can be accessed at turnoffs from the Coastal Road at the base of both bays. The road from Opunohu Bay winds through the valley of the same name past grazing horses and lush grassland. The Paopao road (from Cook's Bay) turns off the Coastal Road near the small Paopao village and passes pineapple plantations of the Paopao Valley. The roads meet not far from a collection of ancient marae, and then the journey winds steeply to the top. ■ TIP→Use your horn at the corners and bends! There's nothing at the top but the view, save a concrete platform to stand on plus a few chickens and a rooster or two wandering around. ⊹ *Turn off the Coastal road towards the mountain at either PK 9 or PK 18* ▱ *Free* ☉ *24 hours.*

Marae. Just off the Belvedere Road are remains of a few ancient marae. You can just park your car, ATV, or bugster (the preferred mode of transport in these parts) and walk to them. Tetiiroa (sometimes spelled Titiroa and often referred to as the Belvedere marae) has excellent interpretative signs. It's on the edge of a forest, and the "jungle" has taken over: big trees roots have burrowed under the moss-covered stone foundations and trees and vines have sprung up everywhere. A walking track leads through the forest to two smaller marae and the Marae Ahu-o-Mahine with a three-tier altar. A hundred yards or so further along the Belvedere Road are two well-preserved archery platforms, belonging to the Afareaito marae. The sport was considered a sacred game, played by the elite males of the day. ⊠ *Belvedere Rd.* ☏ *Free* ☉ *Daily.*

> ### STAY CONNECTED
>
> Need to check your e-mail while you're away? The following places offer Internet access. In Maharepa, there's **Maria Tapas** (☏ *55-01-80*) and in Paopao there's **Moorea Vision** (☏ *55-01-75*). **Pension Motu Iti** (☏ *55-05-20*) on the Coastal Road on the western side of Cook's Bay is another spot, as is **Tiki@Net** (☏ *No phone*) in Petit Village.

Opunohu Agricultural College. Called the *Lycée Argricole* in French, the college comes in view just before you hit the steep part of the road to the Belvedere. Students run free guided tours of the college's vanilla and coffee tree plantations and tropical flower gardens. It's also a pit stop for a refreshing fruit juice or snack and the starting point for three circular hiking trails that can done on your own or with a guide. Ask for a map or guide for the hikes. ⊠ *Belevdere Rd.* ☏ *56–11–34* ⊕ *www.etablissement-opunohu.com* ☏ *Free plantation tours; free hiking* ☉ *Shop and college: Mon.–Thurs. 8–4:30, Fri. 8–3:30, Sat. 8–2:30. Trail hiking: Mon.–Sat. 8:30–3.*

WEST COAST

The west coast extends from Hauru Point at the northwest corner down to Haapiti, the village where the PK 37 (counterclockwise) and PK 24 (clockwise) markets meet. Once you get beyond Hauru, it's fairly quiet. There are also a few good beaches off the west coast, including Painapo, which is also a beach-cum-restaurant.

TOWNS

Haapiti. The largest village on the remote West Coast is located where the PK 37 counterclockwise and the PK 24 markers meet. Apart from this little honor, it's claim to fame is the impressive twin-towered **Catholic Eglise de la Sainte Famille** (Church of the Holy Family), fashioned from coral and lime and dating back to the late 19th century. It is framed by lush coconut groves, and jagged mountains rise steeply behind it. The village also has a Protestant church, built in 1916. This white and gray church is distinguished by an olive green steeple and a big clock face. The churches are open for Sunday morning service only. The popular surf break at the Matauvau Pass is about a half-mile off shore. ⊠ *PK 37, counterclockwise and PK 24, clockwise, Coastal road.*

Hauru Point. Not really a town per se, but still one of the busiest tourist strips, this 5-km (3.1-mi) strip from PK 25 to PK 30 has shops, excursions operators, small hotels, pensions, and restaurants. ⊠ *PK 25–PK 30, Coastal road.*

SIGHTS

Painapo Beach Paradise. This lovely area, with great lagoon views, is not a public beach: it costs 2,000 CFP for a day pass, which allows you to snorkel along an underwater marked trail, meet friendly rays, and watch a breadfruit cooking and coconut gathering show. Thursday is Polynesian day with dances and a traditional sports and craft exhibition and a Tahitian earth oven feast. You can't miss this place as a huge wooden statue of a Tahitian warrior marks the entrance. Meals are available at the restaurant. ⊠ *PK 34 counterclockwise, Coastal road* ☎ *55-07-90* ⊕ *www.painapobeach.com* 💳 *2,000 CFP* ⊗ *Daily.*

Tiki Village. This replica of a traditional Polynesian village, a few miles south of Hauru Point, has been drawing visitors for 14 years. By day there are fishing and pearl-collecting demonstrations, and artisans are at work weaving, carving stone, painting, and tattooing. At night 60 performers put on a spectacular show complete with grass skirts and fire dancing. The audience gets a lesson in pareo (sarong) tying and hip swinging. ■ TIP ➔ **If you don't want to be dragged up on stage, don't sit in the front.** If you buy a ticket to the nightly show, you receive a free day pass to the village. The village is also well known for its Polynesian wedding ceremonies, which must be booked well in advance. ⊠ *PK 30 counterclockwise, Coastal road* ☎ *55-02-50* ⊕ *www.tikivillage. pf* 💳 *Daytime village tour 2,500 CFP; night performance and dinner 8,700 CFP; show only 4,400 CFP* ⊗ *Tues.–Sat. 11 AM–3 PM; Tues.– Wed. and Fri.–Sat. dinner 7 PM, show 8:45 PM.*

BEACHES

Hauru Point. The point has one long beach that winds in and out of bays and skirts several pensions and hotels for about 5 km (3.1 mi). It's narrow but is wider—and sandier—in some places than others. Unless you're staying at one of the hotels or pensions, you'll have to walk down narrow laneways between hotel complexes to access it. One such laneway is near the Fare Vai Moana Hotel at around PK 28, counterclockwise. ⊠ *PK 25–PK 3, Coastal road* 💳 *Free* ⊗ *24 hours.*

WHERE TO EAT

When it comes to dining in Moorea you'll be spoiled with choices, but you won't have to break the bank. There are some expensive French restaurants, but there are also quite a few mobile *roulottes* (caravans selling hot food and traditional *poisson cru*) and pizza and hamburger joints, Chinese restaurants, and restaurants with live music several times a week. Resort hotels have lovely lagoon front restaurants and usually stage one Polynesian buffet a week followed by a traditional dance show. In an attempt to appease various palates, some resort meals can be quite bland. If you like variety in your dining life, eat at independent restaurants and don't buy the resort meal packages. Most restaurants will pick you up for free, a few may ask for a small transport charge. You'll find most restaurants around the Cook's Bay–Maharepa and Hauru Point districts.

RESERVATIONS & TRANSPORTATION

It is advisable to book for dinner as restaurants around the popular Hauru Point and Maharepa areas get very busy. Check the restaurant's transfer policy at the time of booking. Most restaurants will pick up diners if they are in the same vicinity.

HOTEL RESTAURANTS

$-$$$ ✕**Hotel Les Tipaniers.** This hotel has
ITALIAN two restaurants. Breakfast and lunch are served on the lagoon (where the bar is open until 7 PM daily), and the main restaurant is in a cute thatched bungalow at the hotel's entrance. Lunch choices include pizzas, burgers, salads, and

fish, while evening diners can choose from the set menu (three courses for 3,450 CFP) or from the á la carte menu, where Italian and French dishes dominate and include the classic entrecôte (steak) with béarnaise sauce. ⊠*PK 27, Coastal road, Hauru Point* ☎*56–12–67* ⚑*Reservations essential* ▭*MC, V.*

$-$$ ✕**L'Ananas Bleu.** Breakfast and lunch at "the Blue Pineapple," within
PACIFIC RIM the three-star time-share Bali Hai Club, is popular with guests and visitors. The views over Cook's Bay are superb and breakfast treats such as Tahitian donuts (on weekends) and crêpes are legendary. Lunchtime offerings include steak with fries, salads, hamburgers, and *poisson cru*. On Wednesday nights the restaurant puts on a lavish seafood barbecue (dishes from 1,800 to 3,890 CFP) and a dance performance beginning at 6 PM. ⊠*Cook's Bay* ☎*56–12–06* ⚑*Reservations essential* ▭*MC, V* ☻*No dinner, except Wed.*

$$$$ ✕**Le Matiehani Gourmet.** This lovely restaurant at the Moorea Pearl
FRENCH Resort is considered one of the best on the island and it's also the most expensive. The menu is a three-course degustation, at 8,500 CFP, with five choices of appetizer, seven of main course, and four of dessert. Three of the dishes, including the lobster tournedos, attract an extra supplement (from 600 to 1,000 CFP). You can start with crab tartar on hibiscus and honey jelly, move on to the roasted mahimahi stuffed with lobster with a side of pasta with cuttlefish ink, and finish with Morello cherries soufflé. The resort offers "reduced taxi fares," which you should inquire about when booking. ⊠*PK 3 counterclockwise, Coastal road, Maharepa* ☎*55–17–66* ⚑*Reservations essential* ▭*AE, MC, V* ☻*No lunch. Closed Wed. and Sun.*

$$$-$$$$ ✕**K.** Named after the Kahaia tree from which the restaurant's roof
FRENCH and beams are made, this lovely venue is part of the Sofitel Moorea Resort. Just 28 diners sit at chunky tree trunk tables on groovy chairs and wiggle their toes in the sand. Bohemian candelabras grace every table. The fare is a modern take on French cuisine; there are no heavy

2

sauces and the emphasis is on fresh ingredients prepared in a simple way. The prawns are marinated with tandoori spices and the blue fin tuna steak is marinated with soy sauce, honey, and sesame and cooked to taste. Desserts are light with the exception of chocolate *dacquoise* (a nut meringue) cookie with coconut cream. ⊠*PK 1 counterclockwise, Coastal road, Temae* ☎*55–11–11* ⚖*Reservations essential* ⊟*AE, DC, MC, V* ☉*No lunch.*

$$$–$$$$ ✗**Restaurant Arii Vahine.** The main restaurant at the Sheraton Moorea
FRENCH Lagoon Resort & Spa has a soaring thatched roof, held up by sturdy varnished tree branches, and an array of dangling lights made from hundreds of shells, but it's wise to grab a table on the terrace to take in the superb lagoon view. Interesting seafood dishes to choose from include pan-seared mahimahi crusted with sweet potatoes, caramelized fei bananas (indigenous bananas that can only be eaten cooked), and mango reduction. A dish that combines French and Polynesian flavors is the goat cheese *quenelle* (breaded and lightly fried) served with tomatoes, cucumbers, and sweet Moorea pineapple. A trio of singers and guitarists entertain several nights a week. ⊠*PK 13, Coastal road, Pihaena* ☎*56–11–11* ⚖*Reservations essential* ⊟*AE, DC, MC, V* ☉*No lunch.*

$–$$$ ✗**Sunset Restaurant.** Location and reasonably priced meals are the
ITALIAN attraction at this casual restaurant right on the beach at Hauru Point. Lunch dishes include fish burgers, omelets, and toasted sandwiches while pizzas and pastas (all around 1,550 CFP) are served at dinner. There's a menu for kids, too. Try the mahimahi with coconut sauce or the beef tenderloin with green pepper sauce and finish off with flambé bananas or baked coconut tart. ⊠*Hotel Hibiscus, PK 27 counterclockwise, Coastal road, Hauru Point* ☎*56–12–20* ⊟*MC, V.*

INDEPENDENT RESTAURANTS

$$–$$$$ ✗**Alfredo's.** Established in 1994, Alfredo's is an institution on Moorea
ITALIAN and its free-transfer minibus can be spotted across the island. It's open for lunch and dinner and there's live entertainment (and sometimes a spot of impromptu karaoke) on Thursday and Sunday nights. Start with a cocktail while perusing the menu of soup, pizza, pasta, fresh lobster, and whatever the fishermen have caught that day. ⊠*PK 3 counterclockwise, Coastal road, Maharepa* ☎*56–17–71* ⚖*Reservations essential* ⊟*MC, V* ☉*Closed Mon.*

$ ✗**Allo Pizza.** If you like thin-crusted, wood-fired pizzas then this is defi-
PIZZA nitely the place to come for lunch or dinner. You can eat in or take away. The only concession to the Tahitian palate is the pizza topped with fresh tuna, garlic, and cheese, while there's French influence behind the "five cheese" pizza with Parmesan, mozzarella, goat cheese, Roquefort, and cheddar. There is also a range of salads and a limited dessert menu. Wonderful baguettes straight out of the oven cost 200 CFP each. ⊠*PK 7.8 counterclockwise, Coastal road, Paopao* ☎*56–18–22* ⊟*No credit cards* ☉*Closed Mon.*

$–$$ ✗**Bus Stop.** You'll find this cheerful indoor-outdoor restaurant on the
FRENCH mountain side of the main road, just opposite the Hotel Hibiscus. Lunch in the courtyard is a pleasant way to pass the day, feasting on stuffed crab with salad or shrimp with vanilla sauce. Apple and duck

liver tart is the specialty dish, while the rib-eye steak with blue cheese and fries is reasonable priced at 1,500 CFP. You can eat in or take away any of the meals. ⊠*PK 27 counterclockwise, Coastal road, Hauru Point* ☏*56–41–10* ⊟*No credit cards* ⊘*Closed Wed.*

$$$–$$$$ ✕**La Licorne d'Or.** "The Golden Unicorn" is a charming little spot that
FRENCH   wouldn't be out of place in a French village. The tables are immaculately set for dinner with fine glassware and apricot colored tablecloths, while lunch is more casual. The specialty dish is an intriguing mixture of tempura tuna, shrimps, rice, and ginger sauce, while lighter fare includes smoked salmon and crème fraiche and *poisson cru* "a la Chinois" (Chinese style). ⊠*PK 22 counterclockwise, Coastal road, Papetoai* ☏*56–16–65* ⊟*MC, V* ⊘*Closed Tues.*

$$–$$$ ✕**Le Mayflower.** Lobster ravioli is the specialty dish at this restaurant,
FRENCH   considered one the best on the island, right next to the Hotel Hibiscus. Other seafood dishes with a twist are raw tuna sashimi with ginger and garlic sauce and scallops with Calvados, an apple brandy. Traditional French fare such as beef fillet with foie gras is a hearty choice and might best be followed with a light dessert such as lemon sorbet with vodka, or the local innovation—a half-frozen coconut! ⊠*PK 27 counterclockwise, Coastal road, Hauru Point* ☏*56–53–59* ⌁*Reservations essential* ⊟*MC, V* ⊘*No lunch Sat. and Mon.*

¢–$ ✕**La Plage Motu Moea.** If you want to dine where the locals go, catch
FRENCH   the boat from Hauru Point over to Motu Moea, just off the northwest coast. If you have rented a boat then motor over, or paddle if you have a canoe! It's a casual open-sided fare (bamboo hut) right on the beach serving ultra fresh seafood (try the fish spiced with mint and ginger and served with red cabbage) and the excellent *poisson cru.* There are a few salads on the menu and you may be lucky to be there when the rustle up fondant au chocolate (chocolate pudding with a warm runny center). Ask about boat transfers when you call to make a reservation. ⊠*Approx. PK 27 counterclockwise, Coastal road, Motu Moea, off Hauru Point* ☏*74–96–96* ⌁*Reservations essential* ⊟*No credit cards* ⊘*No dinner. Closed Mon.*

$$$$ ✕**La Plantation.** Dine on French and Cajun food while listening to a jazz
FRENCH   or soul band at this restaurant near Le Petit Village. A favorite dish is slipper lobster (a small relative of the crayfish) served with a vanilla sauce. Crab cakes and Cajun gazpacho spice things up. The decor of all white is plantation style with white cane chairs and tables. It's so popular that those with a bit of money to spare fly in by helicopter from Pape'ete. The best deals are the two set menus—the discovery (4,500 CFP) and the Cajun (5,100 CFP). There are regular party nights with a DJ and dancing into the late hours. ⊠*PK 2 counterclockwise, Coastal road, Hauru Point, Le Petit Village* ☏*56–45–10* ⌁*Reservations essential* ⊟*MC, V* ⊘*No lunch Tues. and Wed.*

$$$–$$$$ ✕**Rudy's Fine Steaks and Seafood.** Try the catch of the day, a succulent fil-
STEAK   let of fish stuffed with crab or the rock lobster medallion. Steak lovers have plenty of choices too or they might prefer the stuffed boneless duck with port wine sauce. It's a happy place with music three times a week. You can't miss it—it's an all-white adobe style building on the mountainside of the main road, not far from the Pearl Resort. It offers free

hotel transfers. ⊠*PK 3 counterclockwise, Coastal road, Maharepa* ☎*56–58–00* ⊕*www.rudysmoorea. com* ▤*MC, V* ⊘*No lunch.*

$$$–$$$$
FRENCH
✕**Te Honu Iti.** "The Little Turtle" is one of the best restaurants on the island. Some people call it Chez Roger as that's the chef's name. There are great views of Cook's Bay and the shark-toothed mountain. The menu is classic French with dishes such as frogs' legs sautéed in garlic and beef tenderloin with brandy sauce. The chef will flambé your lobster or crêpes suzette at your table. This is an expensive night out (the lobster

is 4,700 CFP) but it will be a night to remember, and there's a free shuttle to and from your hotel. ⊠*PK 9 counterclockwise, Coastal road, Cook's Bay* ☎*79–29–98 or 56–19–84* ⌂*Reservations essential* ▤*MC, V* ⊘*Closed Wed.*

WHERE TO STAY

Moorea is said to have one-third of French Polynesia's total hotel capacity with more than 900 hotel rooms, bungalows, family-run lodges, and pensions. However, it still manages to be laid-back and peaceful. There are just three international resorts—Sofitel, InterContinental, and Sheraton—and French Polynesia's own Pearl resort, which are the only accommodations with overwater bungalows. The rest run the gamut from mid-range hotels (some with pools) with between 15 and 37 rooms and bungalows, and family-run pensions, lodges, and self-catering bungalows. Most are located on the lagoon, with one or two in the interior. The new Legends Resort Moorea, which opened in July 2008, is on the hillside overlooking Hauru Point and is a 10-minute drive from the beach. There are a handful of villas and houses available for weekly and longer rentals, plus a couple of camping grounds.

VILLAS & CONDOMINIUMS

$$
▦ **Fare Hamara.** Shaped like a yurt, Fare Hamara is nestled into the hillside overlooking Opunohu Bay, in the shadow of the shark-toothed Mt. Mouaroa. It has two bedrooms and trundle beds in the living room, making it ideal for six people. It's family friendly with a crib and high chair, washer/dryer, and TV. The villa is owned by an American couple, Bob and Mary Hammar, and bookings are made through their U.S. phone number or by e-mailing them. The minimum stay is one week and 10% discounts are given to three-week and monthly rentals. **Pros:** Total seclusion; modern conveniences. **Cons:** Maybe too isolated; no housekeeping. ⊠*PK 17.5 counterclockwise, Coastal road, Opunohu Bay* ☎*253/564–0180 in the U.S.* ⊕*www.farehamara.com hamara@*

harbornet.com 🏠*1 villa* 🛏*In-room: phone, kitchen, refrigerator, DVD, Internet. In-hotel: beachfront, water sports, laundry facilities, airport shuttle, parking (no fee)* ▤*AE, DC, MC, V* ▥*EP.*

$$$ ▦**Robinson's Cove.** You'll feel marooned in paradise when you take up residence at this very stylish villa and look across gorgeous Opunohu Bay from your gently swaying hammock. It's on a white sandy beach—Robinson's Cove—which reputedly was named after a sailor (not Robinson Crusoe) who was aboard one of James Cook's ships when it moored in the bay. The experience will be totally Crusoe as you paddle your canoe to the front door and shower in the outdoor stonewalled bathroom with views across the lagoon. A lovely deck surrounds the whole villa, which has two bedrooms, a living room, kitchen, and an array of funky furnishings and mod cons: dishwasher, microwave, solar hot water system, and Wi-Fi. A guide who greets you will explain the villa and the island's attractions, while a caretaker lives nearby. The villa can sleep a maximum of six adults and two children and is priced according to the number of occupants and includes tax. There's a four-night minimum stay. **Pros:** Luxury hideaway. **Cons:** You'll need a car to get anywhere. ✉*PK 15 counterclockwise, Coastal road, Opunohu Bay* ☎*56–57–08* 🌐*www.robinsonscove.com* 🏠*1 villa* 🛏*In-room: phone, kitchen, refrigerator, no TV, Internet. In-hotel: beachfront, diving, water sports, laundry facilities, concierge, airport shuttle, parking (no fee)* ▤*AE, MC, V* ▥*EP.*

$$$ ▦**Villa Corallina.** This villa should satisfy those who want to "get away from it all." It's on Motu Fareone, a little island minutes off the northwest coast. If you require a bit of action (supermarket, bars, restaurants), take the daily shuttle back to the main island. Four or five people could easily inhabit the spacious 3,000 square feet that include lounge, kitchen, bathroom, bedroom, and a spacious master bedroom suite (750 square feet) serviced daily by housekeeping staff. The villa's decor is unmistakably "South Seas," with bamboo and rattan walls and furniture and tropical print fabrics. Varnished bamboo poles support the kitchen and bathroom. A one-bedroom cottage is located a few hundred feet away in the garden, and this can be rented if the villa is not occupied. Minimum stay is four nights, and three nights at the cottage. **Pros:** Great location. **Cons:** Need to boat to get to town. ✉*Off PK 26, Coastal road, Motu Fareone* ☎*56–36–65* 🌐*www.villacorallina. com* 🏠*2 villas* 🛏*In-room: no a/c, kitchen, refrigerator, DVD. In-hotel: beachfront, water sports, laundry facilities, public Internet, airport shuttle* ▤*No credit cards* ▥*EP.*

RESORTS

$–$$ ▦**Club Bali Hai.** This is the last remaining hotel of a handful that were started by the "Bali Hai Boys," three Californians who came to Moorea in the early 1960s to start a vanilla farm. Instead, they ended up running hotels and invented the legendary overwater bungalow concept. The Club is part time-share, part hotel, and it would be hard to find a more spectacular position in Moorea. It sits on the eastern shore of Cook's Bay with a perfect view of the iconic shark-toothed mountain—Mt. Mouaroa—from almost every angle. There are mountain- and beach-view rooms and beach and overwater bungalows, although the

2

latter are only partially overwater. The five garden rooms have kitch-enettes and several are large enough for families. A grocery store across the road is stocked with a good range of fresh produce. The resort is comfortable without being luxurious and has a very friendly atmo-sphere. It's virtually a one-stop-shop with a free dance performance on Wednesday night (preceded by a seafood barbecue), its own boat for lagoon excursions and sunset cruises, car rental desk, boutique, weekly crab races, and a sunset talk every day (except Wednesday) given by Muk, one of the two surviving "boys." Gather round over a few drinks as he shares stories of the "good old days" of Moorea and his interest-ing exploits. The hotel's best rates are available over the Internet. **Pros:** Spectacular views. **Cons:** Rooms and bungalows need a face-lift. ⊠*PK 8 counterclockwise, Coastal road, Cook's Bay* ☏*56–13–68* ⊕*www. clubbalihai.com* ⋑*33 bungalows, 11 rooms* ⅋*In-room: phone (some), safe (some), kitchen (some), refrigerator (some). In-hotel: restaurant, room service, bar, pool, beachfront, diving, water sports, bicycles, no elevator, laundry facilities, laundry service, concierge, public Internet, airport shuttle, parking (no fee)* ⊟*AE, MC, V* ⦿*EP.*

$-$$ 🏠**Hotel Hibiscus.** This medium-size, budget establishment on the popu-lar Hauru Point strip has neat little beach and garden bungalows and a wing of 12 hotel rooms in the garden. Each room is air-conditioned and has a bathroom with hot water and a small corner kitchenette with fridge. Bungalows are fan-cooled, have a fridge, a wide terrace, and can sleep up to four people. The hotel's beachfront Sunset restaurant is one of the most popular eateries on the Hauru Point strip and serves French, Italian, and local dishes, plus children's menus. Half- and full-board meal plans are available (5,250 and 8,250 CFP, respectively), but if you wish to eat out you can every day of the week as the Hibis-cus is near a handful of cafés and restaurants. Le Petit Village is about a half a mile away. **Pros:** Well located. **Cons:** Not all rooms are air-conditioned. ⊠*PK 27 counterclockwise, Coastal road, Hauru Point* ☏*56–12–20* ⊕*www.hotel-hibiscus.pf* ⋑*29 bungalows, 12 rooms* ⅋*In-room: no a/c (some), phone (some), safe (some), kitchen (some), refrigerator (some), no TV. In-hotel: restaurant, bar, pool, beachfront, diving, water sports, bicycles, laundry service, airport shuttle, parking (fee)* ⊟*AE, MC, V* ⦿*MAP, EP.*

$-$$ 🏠**Hotel Les Tipaniers.** Location is the draw for this popular budget hotel at Hauru Point. It doesn't have a pool but it has a lovely position on the lagoon and a daytime beach restaurant with fantastic views. There's also an Italian restaurant, near the coastal road, which opens in the evening. Bungalows with fridges are near the beach or in the garden and each can accommodate up to four people, while the superior category have telephones, and 13 bungalows have full kitchens. The upscale "vanilla bungalow" has a kitchen and a living room. Interiors are bright and airy with tropical style fabrics and cane bed heads and bed bases. Free activities include outrigger canoes and bicycles. Loca Boat, a company that rents out small boats with no license required, is right next door. A smaller sister property—Tipaniers Iti—is 4 km (2.5 mi) to the east and has three bungalows, each with a kitchen. **Pros:** Good location; good restaurant. **Cons:** No a/c(there are fans). ⊠*PK 27, Coastal road,*

Hauru Point ☎ *56–12–67* ⊕ *www. lestipaniers.com* ⌦ *24 bungalows* ⚬ *In-room: no a/c, phone (some), kitchen (some), refrigerator (some). In-hotel: 2 restaurants, room service, bars, beachfront, diving, water sports, bicycles, laundry service, airport shuttle, parking (no fee)* ⊟ *AE, DC, MC, V* ⦿ *EP.*

$$$-$$$$ ⊡ **InterContinental Moorea Resort & Spa.** The largest resort on the island appears to have it all—choice of garden, beach, or overwater bungalows, spa, Polynesian dancing during the week, a turtle protection center operated in partnership with the government environmental department, a special coral snorkeling park, and four resident dolphins that can be "booked" for personal encounters. The setting is ideal on the northwest corner of the island near Le Petit Village shopping complex and several Hauru Point restaurants. The overwater bungalows, however, are not completely overwater (the balconies are but the rest is over land) and the pool is a little small. Meals can vary in quality, so don't lock yourself into a meal plan but take advantage of the free pickup services from the many nearby restaurants. **Pros:** Dolphins, turtles, and an ideal location. **Cons:** No children's program; small pool; inconsistent meal quality. ⊠ *PK 28.5 counterclockwise, Coastal road, Papetoai* ☎ *55–19–00* ⊕ *www.ichotelsgroup.com* ⌦ *144 rooms* ⚬ *In-room: safe, refrigerator, Internet. In-hotel: 2 restaurants, room service, bars, tennis courts, pool, gym, spa, beachfront, diving, water sports, bicycles, no elevator, laundry service, concierge, public Internet, airport shuttle, parking (no fee)* ⊟ *AE, DC, MC, V* ⦿ *EP.*

$$-$$$ ⊡ **Legends Resort Moorea.** This 50-apartment complex, high on the hill overlooking the InterContinental Resort and the lagoon, opened in July 2008. It's a new concept for Moorea and will be interesting to see if hillside self-catering apartments, with no beach access, take off in an island resort where the lagoon reigns supreme. A regular shuttle takes guests to a private island for swimming and snorkeling. The two- and three-bedroom apartments have terraces with hot tubs and views over the lagoon or to the lofty cloud-swathed mountain ranges. There's a choice of daily or weekly housekeeping (which keeps rates down) and a delicatessen sells groceries and other items for self-catering. There's also an onsite restaurant for those who don't want to cook too often, and in-room massages can be booked. **Pros:** Lofty views; brand-new designer apartments. **Cons:** Need a shuttle service to the beach. ⊠ *Approx. PK 26, Coastal road, Hauru Point* ☎ *83–19–09* ⊕ *www.legendsresort.fr* ⌦ *50 apartments* ⚬ *In-room: safe, kitchen, refrigerator, DVD. In-hotel: restaurant, bar, pool, tennis courts, gym, bicycles, laundry facilities, public Internet, airport shuttle, parking (no fee)* ⊟ *AE, DC, MC, V* ⦿ *EP.*

$$$-$$$$ ⊡ **Moorea Pearl Resort & Spa.** Pearl Resorts encompass the best of French Polynesia with regular dance performances and onsite dive centers to get guests into the lagoon as quickly as possible. This little gem of a resort is a short distance from the Maharepa commercial cen-

ter, near the new golf course, and a 10-minute drive from the airport. There are plenty of activities to enjoy, a gorgeous spa, and even a resident tattoo artist (Herenui Teriitehau) for those guests who want an indelible reminder of their stay. Accommodations range from rooms (located in a wing) to individual bungalows in the garden,

beachfront, and overwater. Eighteen of the garden bungalows have plunge pools. Kids receive a set of beach toys, snorkel gear, life jackets, and a basket of candy. The Matiehani gourmet restaurant is considered one of the best on the island. **Pros:** Everything at your fingertips. **Cons:** Expensive restaurants. ⊠*PK 3, counterclockwise, Coastal road, Maharepa* ☎*55–17–50* ⊕*www.pearlresorts.com* ⬩*95 rooms and bungalows* ⬩*In-room: refrigerator, DVD. In-hotel: 2 restaurants, room service, 2 bars, pool, gym, spa, beachfront, diving, water sports, bicycles, no elevator, laundry service, concierge, public Internet, airport shuttle, parking (no fee)* ⊟*AE, DC, MC, V* ⊺◎*EP.*

$$$–$$$$ ⛺**Sheraton Moorea Lagoon Resort & Spa.** Opened in 2000, this resort is right in front of Mt. Rotui between Cook's and Opunohu bays. There's a 10-acre lagoon at the doorstep, and free activities include pedal boats, kayaks, and outrigger canoes. Fifty-four overwater bungalows are placed in various distances from the beach on three pontoons and are priced accordingly. Bungalows have hardwood floors and timber shutters and sliding glass doors leading out to terraces; the overwater bungalows have stunning views of jagged mountain ridges. Bathrooms have deep claw-foot baths and double vanities. Grounds are spacious and the walkway from the lobby to the main restaurant and boutique leads over a lovely pond and waterfall stocked with huge goldfish. There are three restaurants all with water views; in fact the Toata Bar is on a pontoon. It's only opened in the evening and you can dine here on crêpes and keep an eye out for stingrays and reef tip sharks below. **Pros:** Lovely grounds; three restaurants. **Cons:** No outside restaurants nearby; need a car. ⊠*PK 13, Coastal road, Pihaena* ☎*55–11–11* ⊕*www.starwood.com/tahiti* ⬩*106 bungalows* ⬩*In-room: safe, refrigerator, DVD, Internet (some). In-hotel: 3 restaurants, room service, 2 bars, 2 tennis courts, pool, gym, spa, beachfront, diving, water sports, bicycles, no elevator, laundry service, concierge, public Internet, airport shuttle, parking (no fee)* ⊟*AE, DC, MC, V* ⊺◎*EP.*

$$$–$$$$ ⛺**Sofitel Moorea Resort.** This hotel, on the best beach on the island, reopened in January 2007 after a US$40 million total renovation. Existing bungalows were refurbished and 52 new garden, 15 new beachside, and 19 new overwater bungalows were added. Any room termed "deluxe" is brand-new. The lobby has a minimalist look with an array of furniture from funky chaise longues to '60s-style cane chairs. All bungalows are spacious and uncluttered with king beds draped with romantic nets, positioned to get the best view first thing in the morning. Bed heads are covered with fabric depicting scenes from

two of Paul Gaugin's paintings, while bed lamps have golden shades to bathe the rooms in a warm glow. The resort has a lovely "infinity pool" and a gourmet restaurant, K, which seats just 28 diners in eclectic chairs, none of which are the same. **Pros:** Brand-new accommodations; great gourmet restaurant. **Cons:** No outside restaurants nearby. ⊠*PK 1, counterclockwise, Coastal road, Temae* ☎*55–12–12* ⊕*www.accorhotels.pf* ⇗*114 bungalows* ⌂*In-room: safe, refrigerator. DVD (some). In-hotel: 2 restaurants, room service, 2 bars, pool, gym, spa, tennis courts, beachfront, diving, water sports, bicycles, no elevator, laundry service, concierge, airport shuttle, parking (no fee)* ▤*AE, DC, MC, V* ⍩*EP.*

SMALL HOTELS/GUESTHOUSES

$ ⌂ **Fare Edith.** This family-run accommodation has four bungalows that can sleep three to six people. Two bungalows have two bedrooms each and extra beds in the living room; the other two each have one bedroom and a mezzanine (upper floor) with extra beds. They are equipped with full kitchen, washing machine, living room with TV, and bathroom with hot water. The lagoon setting is perfect and kayaks are provided for exploring this quiet corner of Moorea. **Pros:** Good for families; quiet location. **Cons:** Need a car; not all bungalows have a/c. ⊠*PK 32.5 counterclockwise, Coastal road, Haapiti* ☎*56–35–34* ⊕*www.fareedith.com* ⇗*4 bungalows* ⌂*In-room: a/c (some), no phone, kitchen, refrigerator. In-hotel: beachfront, water sports, bicycles, laundry facilities, parking (no fee)* ▤*No credit cards* ⍩*EP.*

$$$–$$$$ ⌂ **Fenua-Mata'i'oa.** If you want something very different and have money to spare, this luxury four-suite residence is a bit like Louis XIV meets Polynesia and it all works wonderfully. Touches run from bohemian to European with chandeliers, four-poster beds, chaise longues, Oriental carpets, upholstered tub chairs, and gilt mirrors, plus typical island decor of rattan and bamboo. There are two junior suites, a royal suite with two bedrooms and two bathrooms and a collection of exotic—and slightly erotic—art, while the presidential suite is split-level and includes two bedrooms, two bathrooms (one with Jacuzzi) and a small "office" with Wi-Fi–ready computer and printer. The gardens are beautiful and the French owner, Eileen, who has furnished the rooms with pieces she collected in her European travels, provides a very warm welcome. Meals and half-board options are available, together with a weekly Polynesian dance show. **Pros:** Unique accommodation; lovely garden. **Cons:** Everything is pricey. ⊠*PK 25, counterclockwise, Coastal road, Tiahura* ☎*55–00–25* ⊕*www.fenua-mataioa.com* ⇗*4 suites* ⌂*In-room: safe, refrigerator, DVD, Internet. In-hotel: restaurant, room service, bar, beachfront, diving, water sports, bicycles, laundry service, concierge, public Internet, airport shuttle, parking (free)* ▤*MC, V* ⍩*MAP, EP.*

$ ⌂ **La Maison de la Nature.** This budget accommodation deep in the Vaianae Valley is designed for folks who love camping and don't mind roughing it. It's a cross between a backpackers' hostel and a guesthouse with half and full-board options. As the name suggests, the house is tucked away in a natural setting, a few miles inland from the PK 21 clockwise marker (near Haapiti). The owners are avid hikers and conduct mountain hikes and photo safaris and run camps for school children during school holidays. There are four rooms with four single beds, one room with six single beds, and one dorm with 24 beds. The four bathrooms (with warm water) are all shared. The "maison" is solar-powered, has a shared kitchen, living room, library, and restaurant. **Pros:** Eco-friendly; affordable. **Cons:** Warm water can peter out. ☒ *Off PK 21, clockwise, Haapiti* ☎*56–58–62* ⊕*www. lamaisondelanature.com* ⤶*46 beds* ☖*In-room: no a/c, no phone (some), no TV. In-hotel: restaurant, shuttle, parking (no fee)* ▤*AE, DC, MC, V* †◎*|MAP.*

$ 📺**Pension Motu Iti.** The family owners of this five-bungalow pension will mix you a cocktail to sip while you read your e-mails (you can toast the lagoon view from the deck). The pension is on the western shore of Cook's Bay and has great mountain views. Each bungalow has a bathroom with hot water, fan, and TV. There's also a 20-bed dormitory, above the hotel lobby area, which shares bathrooms with hot water. It's a cozy little place with a 60-seat restaurant, open from 6 AM until 8:30 PM daily, serving all-day snacks such as hamburgers, pizzas, and fresh fish. On Sunday at around noon everyone is welcome to take part in the Ma'a Tahiti (traditional Polynesian meal) cooked in an underground oven over hot coals, known as an *ahima'a*. **Pros:** Friendly vibe; traditional Polynesian meals. **Cons:** No a/c. ☒*Cook's Bay* ☎*55–05–20* ⊕*www.pensionmotuiti.com* ⤶*5 bungalows, 1 dorm* ☖*In-room: no a/c. In-hotel: restaurant, room service, bar, beachfront, diving, water sports, bicycles, no elevator, laundry facilities, public Internet, airport shuttle, parking (no fee)* ▤*AE, MC, V* †◎*|EP.*

$–$$ 📺**Residence Linareva.** Swiss owner Florian Pilloud has run this friendly little self-catering pension for 20 years. The residence has a pleasant location on a small beach on the western side of the island, near Haapiti. This is the sleepy side of Moorea with few tourist facilities apart from a take-away pizza parlor (Daniel's Pizza) half a mile down the road and a grocery store a short drive away. The eight bungalows are scattered along the beach and the two largest ones can accommodate four and seven people. Each bungalow has rattan walls decorated with island artwork or pareos; a kitchen equipped with stove, fridge, microwave, and coffeemaker; and a bathroom with hot water. All have ceiling fans while a few also have air-conditioning. All bungalows are Wi-Fi ready (free); otherwise, there's access to dial-up Internet (fee) in the lobby. Each bungalow has a small terrace with a floor fashioned from river flagstones. This is the perfect place to have breakfast, which can be delivered by room service (1,500 CFP per person) if you don't want to make your own. **Pros:** Quiet location; friendly owner; free Wi-Fi. **Cons:** Isolated; car is needed for restaurants and shopping. ☒*PK 24, clockwise, Coastal road, Haapiti* ☎*55–05–65* ⊕*www.linareva.com* ⤶*8 bungalows* ☖*In-room: a/c (some), no phone, safe, Internet. In-hotel: room service (breakfast only), beachfront, diving, laundry service, public Internet, airport shuttle, parking (no fee)* ▤*AE, MC, V* †◎*|EP.*

BEST BETS FOR CRUISING

Climb every mountain. Moorea has lofty peaks, some resembling shark's teeth. To get a good look at the rugged interior, hop aboard a 4WD jungle safari.

Free wheelin'. Get footloose and fancy free on your independent island tour. Hire a car, scooter, or bugster and hit the 61-km (38-mi) road that circles the island.

Make a splash. Nothing beats a few hours on the lagoon, complete with snorkeling and a motu picnic. You can join several tour outfitters to the two motu off the northwest corner of the island.

Flip Out. There are two ways to get close to flipper and friends on Moorea: take one of the dolphin and whale-watching ecotours run by Michael Poole, a marine biologist (originally from California), or have an intimate encounter at the Moorea Dolphin Center at the InterContinental Resort.

OUTDOOR ACTIVITIES

There are ample boat excursion companies to take you to great snorkeling spots on the lagoon and for a barbecue on a motu. There's also Jet Skiing, waterskiing, diving, and other underwater adventures, along with parasailing and helicopter rides. The island's green and rugged interior is visited by several safari tours that will include the Belvedere lookout and the nearby marae and a venture to the waterfalls. Most hotels will be able to book excursions and activities and many operators will pick you up at your front door.

BIKING

Most of the Coastal Road is flat; the best biking is around the two bays—Cook's Bay and Opunohu Bay. Allow a whole day to do the entire 59-km (37-mi) Coastal Road.

Rent a Bike/Rent A Scoot (☎71–11–09). There are lots of two-wheel options for rent, including 18-speed mountain bikes. The operators will deliver to your hotel.

Sun Bike (⊠PK 37 counterclockwise, and PK 24, clockwise, Coastal road, Haapiti ☎56–40–74). Call to see if they can also deliver your bike to you.

DIVING EXCURSIONS

Aquablue (⊠InterContinental Moorea Resort & Spa, PK 28.5, counterclockwise, Coastal road, Hauru Point ☎56–53–53). Nonswimmers and non-divers alike can enjoy this walk along the seabed, fitted with a diver's helmet. Children from six years old can participate. It's based at the InterContinental Moorea Resort at Hauru Point.

DOLPHIN WATCHING TOURS

Dolphin & Whale-Watching Excursions with Dr. Michael Poole (⊠PK 3, Coastal road, Maharepa ☎56–23–22). An adventure, with marine biologist Dr. Poole, is sure to pay off with sightings of spinner dolphins year-round and humpback whales from July to October.

FISHING & BOATING

Moorea Fishing Charters (☎ *56–15–87* ⊕ *www.moorea-fishing.com*). The 29-foot *Riviera* (with flybridge) is ready to go out every day except in rough weather. It can be hired, with crew, by the hour. A maximum of six people is required.

Moorea LocaBoat (⊠ *PK 26, Coastal road* ☎ *78–13–39*). You can hire out a small motorboat (no license required) for two, four, or eight hours. Eight hours costs 13,000 CFP with gas included. To find LocaBoat, wander through Hotel Les Tipaniers to the lagoon and it's just at the right of the hotel beach.

4WD SAFARI

Albert Safari Tours (⊠ *PK 3, Coastal road, Maharepa* ☎ *55–21–11* ⊕ *www.albert-transport.net*). Albert is the island expert and he knows every fascinating place on the hills and the coast.

Inner Island Safari Tour (⊠ *PK 3, counterclockwise Coastal road, Maharepa* ☎ *56–20–09*). You'll be climbing mountains and discovering ancient marae and waterfalls on these trips in eight-seater Land Rovers.

GOLF

Moorea Green Pearl Golf Course Polynesia (⊠ *PK 1.5 Coastal road, Temae* ☎ *56–27–32* ⊕ *www.mooreagolf-resort.com* 🏌 *9 holes with cart, 12,000 CFP; 18 holes with cart, 21,000 CFP* ⊙ *Daily 7:30 AM–5*). The first 9 holes of this Jack Nicklaus–designed golf course opened in late 2007 and work is underway on the next 9, which should be completed in late 2009. It is only the second golf course to be built in French Polynesia (the other is in Tahiti, and was built 35 years ago). The course has holes on the hillside, around the lakes, on the edge of the beach and in the middle of a coconut grove. Clubs and golf carts can be hired.

HIKING

Moorea is a great island for hiking, but the trails are often hard to find so it's advisable to take an organized hiking tour. However, if you wish to set out on your own, there are several routes including the Three Coconut Trees Pass and the Opunohau Vallep Loop. You can start both of these routes at the Agricultural College (also known as the Lycee Argricole); ask the staff for directions.

Mer et Montagne Excursions (☎ *56–16–48 mreetmontagne@mail.pf*). As the French name says, these full-day hikes go to places with fantastic views of the "sea and the mountain." There are hikes in the Opunohu Valley and to the peaks of Rotui and Tohiea.

Tahiti Evasion (⊠ *PK 20 counterclockwise, Coastal road, Papetoai* ☎ *56–48–77* ⊕ *www.tahitievasion.com*). This company runs half- and full-day hikes to the Three Coconut Trees Pass, the "balconies" of Mount Rotui, and several archeological sites.

HORSEBACK RIDING

Ranch Opunohu Valley (⊠*Belvedere Rd.* ☎*56–28–55*). You can saddle up every day (except Monday) for two-hour trails in the morning and afternoon. There's a maximum of six people required for rides to take place; the trails wind past pineapple plantations in the lovely Oponohu Valley and provide fantastic mountain vistas. The owner will pick up from hotels.

JET SKIING

Mahana Wave Runner (⊠*PK 28.5, Coastal road, Hauru Point* ☎*56–20–44*). You can rent out the Jet Skis and go it alone, or go on a guided half-hour or hour-long tour.

KITESURFING

Lakana Fly (⊠*Near the Moorea LocaBoat at PK 26, Coastal road [next door to Hotel Les Tipaniers]* ☎*56–51–58* ⊕*www.lakanafly.com*) Kids from nine years old can have fun with their parents at this adrenaline-filled sport. There are beginner and advanced courses and kite rental.

LAGOON EXCURSIONS

Half- or full-day lagoon trips visit Cook's and Opunohu bays, shark and ray feeding spots, and—on day tours only—a stop at a motu for swimming, snorkeling, and a picnic.

Moorea Mahana Tours (⊠*PK 28.5 counterclockwise, Coastal road,* ☎*56–20–44*), at the InterContinental Moorea Resort & Spa, is a one-stop-shop for lagoon excursions, sunset cruises, Jet Ski rides, and fishing trips.

Shark Tours (⊠*Moorea Camping, PK 27 counterclockwise, Coastal road* ☎*56–14–47*). The name tells you the focus of this group and you'll be friends with the black-tipped denizens of the lagoon by the end of the day.

PARASAILING

Mahana parasail (⊠*PK 28.5, Coastal road, Hauru Point* ☎*56–20–44*). During 10 minutes of pure exhilaration, you'll fly over the two bays and the lagoon, single or tandem. It's owned by the Mahana Wave Runner Jet Ski outfitter.

QUAD BIKING

Rando Quad/ATV Moorea Tours (☎56–16–60 ⊕www.atvmoorea.com).
These guided two- to three-hour tours on quad bikes (aka, all-terrain
vehicles) travel along hidden paths in the interior, to the Belvedere, and
other amazing viewing points. Price is 14,000 CFP for one person on
board and 2,000 CFP for the second passenger.

SCUBA DIVING

Bathy's Diving (⊠PK 28.5 counterclockwise, Coastal road ☎56–31–44
⊕www.bathys.net). Its location at the InterContinental Moorea Resort
& Spa is a short boat ride from Taotoi Pass, which is a favorite haunt of
marine life. There are dives for beginners and experienced divers.

Moorea Blue Diving Center (⊠Moorea Pearl Resort & Spa, PK 3, Coastal
road ☎55–17–04 ⊕www.mooreabluediving.com) This center calls
itself the "shark dive experts." They have 16 different dive sites to
choose from. Divers plunge off a deep drop-off and venture out past
the reef to the open sea.

Scuba Piti (⊠Les Tipaniers Hotel, PK 27, Coastal road ☎56–20–38
⊕www.scubapiti.com). This small operator offers 11 different dive
sites choices; a single dive costs from 6,100 CFP.

Top Dive Moorea (⊠Sheraton Moorea Lagoon Resort, PK 13 counterclockwise, Coastal road, Pinaena ☎56–17–32 ⊕www.topdive.com).
This is one of the most experienced dive operations in French Polynesia, with outlets on five islands.

SNORKELING

Most lagoon excursion operators will include snorkeling as part of the
half- or full-day trip.

Moana Lagoon Excursions (⊠Cook's Bay ☎55–21–10 ⊕www.albert-
transport.net). Operated by the ubiquitous Albert (who runs many
tours on Moorea), these six-hour tours on catamaran or outrigger
canoes involve shark and ray feeding as well as snorkeling.

What to do on Moorea Tours (⊠Club Bali Hai, Cook's Bay ☎56–57–64).
This company is run by Hiro Kelley, son of the late Hugh Kelley, one
of the Bali Hai Boys. Having grown up here, he knows all the good
places around the island.

SUBMARINE

Aquadisco (⊠PK 3, Coastal road, Maharepa ☎56–40–90 ⊕www.
aquadisco.com). This little semisubmersible takes 12 people to out-of-
the-way sites in air-conditioned comfort. There's a free pickup service.

Mer et Montagne Excursions (☎56–16–48). This hiking company also
runs underwater tours in an aquascope (a semisubmersible craft) and
surface trips on glass bottom boats.

SHOPPING

Many creative people have made Moorea their home, choosing its peaceful environment over bustling Pape'ete. They include painters, sculptors, wood carvers, and tattoo artists, many of whom have studios and galleries. Boutiques sell the famous black pearls and others sell pareos (Tahitian sarongs) and original-design clothing and jewelry.

ART GALLERIES

Art Marquisien (⊠ *Cook's Bay Center, near Hotel Aveka* ☎ *56–23–37* ⊕ *www.hotelaveka.com* ⊙ *8–5:30; closed Sun.*). You'll see artworks and Marquesan artisans at work in this workshop and gallery. The best-known carved item is the "tiki" (a representation of a god); delicate pieces made from mother-of-pearl and bone may be on display at various times.

Dany Creations (⊠ *PK 27.5, Coastal road, Hauru Point* ☎ *56–45–96* ⊙ *9–5:30; closed Sun.*). Apart from black Tahitian pearl jewelry, there are many local crafts including wood carvings, basketware, and hand-painted pareos.

Galerie Van der Heyde (⊠ *PK 7, counterclockwise, Coastal road, Paopao* ☎ *56–14–22*). This gallery displays the work of Dutch painter Aad Van der Heyde, who has lived in Moorea for around 30 years. Other displays include Marquesan wood carvings, shell jewelry, tapa cloth, and other South Seas souvenirs.

Green Lagoon Art Gallery (⊠ *PK 3.8, Coastal road, Maharepa* ☎ *56–18–39* ⊕ *www.artoftheworld.info* ⊙ *9–5:30; closed Sun.*). The gallery displays paintings of local artists—island and islander scenes—sculpture, and photographs. Gallery pieces are also exhibited at the InterContinental Moorea Resort & Spa.

CLOTHES & SOUVENIRS

Boutique Polynesia (⊠ *PK 2.7, counterclockwise, Coastal road* ☎ *65–43–48* ⊙ *8:30–5; closed Sun.*). There's an array of colorful Tahitian style shirts for men, women's dresses, and children's and baby clothes, together with pareos. Souvenirs include pearl and leather necklaces and bracelets, and small stone and wood carvings.

Exotica Surf (⊠ *PK 3, Coastal road, Maharepa* ☎ *56–26–34* ⊙ *Mon.–Sat. 8–5:30*). Don't be fooled by its name. If you want a new swimsuit or some beach and resort wear, this is a good place to look. It's in the Commercial Center at Maharepa.

GROCERIES & OTHER ESSENTIALS

Le Petit Village (⊠ *PK 27, Coastal road, Hauru Point* ☎ *No phone*). **Le Socredo Shopping Center** (⊠ *PK 3, Coastal road* ☎ *No phone*).

PEARLS

Eva Perles (⊠ *PK 3 counterclockwise, Coastal road, Maharepa* ☎ *56–10–10* ⊕ *www.evaperles.com* ⊙ *Daily 8–6*). Goldsmith and jeweler Eva Frachon has been working with Tahitian cultured pearls for 18 years. The gallery-store has single pearls and jewelry pieces. Free transfers are available.

Ron Hall's Island Fashion (⊠*PK 9, Coastal road, Paopao* ☎*56–11–06*). This black pearl and clothing boutique has been run by American Ron Hall and his Tahitian son for the past 20 years.

Tahia Collins (⊠*Near Le Petit Village, PK 27, Coastal road* ☎*56–53–59* ⊕*www.tahiacollins.com*). Former beauty queen Tahia Collins (she was Miss Moorea in 1994) has boutiques near Le Petit Village and at the Moorea Pearl Resort and aboard the Paul Gaugin cruise ship. Free pickup from hotels and cruise ships.

TATTOO

James Samuela's Moorea Tattoo (⊠*PK 32 counterclockwise [between Tiki Village and Painepo Beach] Coastal road* ☎*56–25–33* ⊕*www. mooreatattoo.com* ⊗*weekdays 10–4; evenings by appointment*). Traditional tattoo artist James Samuela, who has been practicing for 10 years, is one of only seven artists in French Polynesia who still practices the ancient techniques first used by the ancient warriors of the Marquesas Islands. The ban on traditional tattooing (using sterilized wooden and bone implements) was lifted in 2001.

Cougar Body Art (⊠*Coastal road, PK 11, clockwise* ☎*26–34–96* ⊕*www. cougarbodyart.com*). Artist Jim White, using conventional tattoo methods, will design a personal Tahitian or "western" design for you. The studio is on the east coast, just south of the village of Afareaitu.

Herenui Teriitehau, Moorea Pearl Resort & Spa (⊠*PK 3, counterclockwise, Coastal road, Maharepa* ☎*55–17–50* ⊕*www.pearlresorts. com*). Resident tattoo artist Herenui (Here) Teriitehau has a poolside studio. Using state-of-the-art machinery, he creates traditional-style black ink tattoos.

SPECIALTY ITEMS

Taimana Creations (⊠*Moorea Pearl Resort & Spa, PK 3, Maharepa* ☎*72–52–79* ⊗*Mon.–Sat. 8–5*). If you've always yearned to own a Polynesian ukulele then this is where you'll get one. The boutique also has jewelry.

SPAS

"Taurumi," the Tahitian name for massage, has a long tradition in the islands. The benefits to body and soul have been known for centuries and many therapists on Moorea have been trained in the traditional methods. Oils infused with vanilla or tiare flower may be used and body scrubs will use nature's bounty such as papaya and coconut. You may also find yourself wrapped up in a banana leaf. Bathing is an exotic ritual; there are petal baths with floating with hibiscus and tiare, river baths of fresh water, and rain showers resembling natural waterfalls.

A BRIEF HISTORY

Moorea was born from the forces of volcanic eruptions 3 million years ago. Its name means "yellow lizard," which one legend attributes to the name of a powerful island family. Of the island's ancient temples, the oldest is Umarea on the east coast, dating back to AD 900. A handful of others, discovered in the Opunohu Valley, are believed to be 600 years old.

The valley's farmers worked the rich volcanic soils several centuries before the Europeans arrived in the late 18th century. British explorer Samuel Wallis arrived in 1767, followed by Louis-Antoine de Bougainville in 1768, and James Cook in 1769. Cook actually anchored in Opunohu Bay and not the bay that bears his name. Moorea was the birthplace of the Protestant church in French Polynesia. Representatives of the London Missionary Society fled the tribal warfare of Tahiti and arrived in Moorea with King Pomare II in 1803. The missionaries built their first church at Papetoai in 1822. Europeans planted copra and vanilla plantations, but today it is the pineapple that dominates the agricultural scene. Tourism is, of course, a substantial industry. French Polynesia's iconic overwater bungalows began in Moorea, dreamed up by a trio of Californian entrepreneurs known as the Bali Hai Boys.

Helene Spa (⊠ *InterContinental Moorea Resort & Spa, PK 28.5, counterclockwise, Coastal road, Tiahura* ☎ *55–19–00* ⊕ *www.ichotelsgroup.com* ⊙ *Daily*). This is the home of Helene Spa, the only spa concession on the island. Relax in a river bath, be revitalized with a pineapple, papaya, or grapefruit wrap and scrub, and be cleansed under a waterfall shower.

Mandara Spa (⊠ *Sheraton Moorea Lagoon Resort & Spa, Pihaena* ☎ *55–11–11* ⊕ *www.starwood.com/tahiti* ⊙ *Daily*). Massage rooms have open air balconies overlooking the gardens. Scrubs, masks and wraps use the earth's bounty including coconut milk, tiare flowers, ginger, and the vanilla bean.

Manea Spa (⊠ *Pearl Moorea Resort, Maharepa* ☎ *55–17–50* ⊕ *www.pearlresorts.com* ⊙ *Daily*). Five expertly trained therapists will deliver a long menu of taurumi treatments in the garden spa, or right by the lagoon.

Sofitel Moorea Beach Resort (⊠ *Temae* ☎ *55–12–12* ⊕ *www.accorhotels.pf* ⊙ *Daily*). Here you can escape the world in a papaya cocoon or be revitalized by a hot and cool shell massage, where shells are placed on the body at various pressure points. The refurbished hotel has seven new treatment rooms.

AFTER DARK

While Moorea doesn't really rock well into the wee hours, there's more entertainment here than any other island, with the exception of Tahiti itself. Some restaurants have live music—singers and bands—while the resorts (and some smaller hotels) stage Polynesian dance shows. The Pearl Resort has traditional performances on Wednesday and Friday, and Bali Hai stages its cultural shows on Wednesday as well. It's best to check with individual resorts. The Tiki Village turns on a cultural extravaganza, complete with fire dancing, four nights a week.

COCKTAIL TIME

It's easy to get into the "sundowners" habit (having a drink at sunset) on Moorea. Just pull up a bar stool or ease into a lovely cane chair, order a Mai Tai (a cocktail and the Tahitian word meaning "good") or a cold Hinano (the local beer) and watch the sun go down.

Eimeo Bar (✉*Sheraton Resort Moorea, PK 14, Coastal road, Pihaena* ☎*55–11–11* ⊕*www.sheratonmoorea.com* ⊙*Daily*). You'll be saying "Set 'em up Joe," as soon as you settle onto (rather than into) a huge tree trunk bar stool at this great bar with a panoramic view. A trio entertains from 6 PM.

Motu Iti Bar (✉*Moorea InterContinental Resort & Spa, PK 28.5, counterclockwise, Coastal road, Hauru Point* ☎*55–19–19* ⊕*www.ichotelsgroup.com* ⊙*Daily*). Savoring a breathtaking sunset sinking into the lagoon at this lovely little spot on the island's northwest corner is a great end to the day.

LIVE MUSIC

Hotel Kaveka (✉*PK 9, Coastal road, Cook's Bay* ☎*56–50–50* ⊕*www.hotelkaveka.com*). This lively three-star hotel right on Cook's Bay has a traditional island band playing three nights a week: Tuesday, Friday, and Saturday.

La Plantation de Moorea (✉*PK 26.8, counterclockwise, Coastal road, Hauru Point* ☎*56–45–10* ⊕*www.laplantationmoorea.com* ⊙*Daily*). The entertainment at this all-white restaurant in Le Petit Village runs from three-piece jazz combos and soul bands to Elvis impersonators and funky DJs at the parties held several times a month.

Maria Tapas (✉*Kikipa Centre, PK 6, Coastal road Maharepa* ☎*55–01–70*). This Tex-Mex restaurant and bar is open until 1 AM from Thursday to Saturday and holds salsa dance classes on Wednesday. Live music nights vary, so call ahead. Happy hour is in swing at 6 pm on Thursday and Friday with half-price drinks.

Rudy's Fine Steaks & Seafood (✉*PK 6, Coastal road, Maharepa* ☎*56–58–00* ⊕*www.rudysmoorea.com* ⊙*Daily*). The owner, Syd Pollock, has been running restaurants and bars in French Polynesia for 40 years. Now his elder son, Rudy, is turning on the fun with live music Tuesday, Friday, and Saturday nights to accompany the good food.

PERFORMANCES

Tiki Village (✉ *PK 30, counterclockwise, Coastal road, Hauru Point-Haapiti district* ☎ *55–02–50* ⊕ *www.tikivillage.com* ☉ *Tues., Thur., Fri., Sat. nights, 8:45* PM). At night this replica Tahitian village comes alive with the excitement of hip-shaking and fire twirling as 60 dancers put on a spectacular cultural show.

Bora Bora with Maupiti

WORD OF MOUTH

"When you fly into Bora Bora over its gorgeous lagoon, you can't believe how there can be such a beautiful island. However, its beauty is attracting hotel construction and cruise ships. While the scenery remains unforgettable, the island life is getting touristy. There seemed to be more cruise ships in port during the early part of the week. If you do stay on the island (and are not cruising), you might want to check the cruise schedules to avoid being there when the cruise ship passengers overwhelm Vaitape and anything near it."

—nickn

Written by
Caroline
Gladstone

CHANCES ARE THAT IF YOU were asked to draw your idea of a Pacific island, you might come up with a picture that looks pretty much like Bora Bora—soaring rain-forest covered peaks, a classic lagoon of blues and greens, and a ring of coral reef and tiny islets with lovely beaches and coconut trees. The island itself can be explored in a few hours; there are sweeping beaches in the south and ancient Polynesian temples hidden in the jungle. It's populated by 8,880 Polynesians who love to show visitors their treasured lagoon and its marine inhabitants. They also love to entertain visitors with music and dance.

American writer James A. Michener, who visited more than 40 Pacific Islands during his naval service in World War II, famously called Bora Bora the most beautiful island in the world. Some say it was the inspiration for the enchanted island Bali Hai, which features in his book *Tales of the South Pacific,* and was sung about in the long-running hit musical *South Pacific.* Other sources, however, claim Bali Hai was based on an island in the New Hebrides (now Vanuatu) that Michener could see from his base in Espiritu Santo, Vanuatu's largest island.

Whatever the real story, the island's name means "firstborn" in the Tahitian language and, as people will not tire of telling you, should be spelled *Pora Pora* since there is no *B* in Tahitian. These days few would dream of changing the popular name of a place that is already recognized globally as the ultimate South Seas paradise.

ORIENTATION & PLANNING

ORIENTATION

BORA BORA

Bora Bora is a mountainous island surrounded by a huge lagoon, which at 80 square km (31 square mi) is three times the size of the island. About 30 islets, called *motu,* form a ring around the main island. Vaitape, the principal town, is on the western side of the main island, as is the inter-island ferry port. The airport is 3 mi north on Motu Mute. The Teav-anui Pass, on the western side, is the only navigable passage into the lagoon. Many of the 25 resorts and smaller hotels are grouped around the southern tip near Matira Point. The top end resorts are located on the motu to the east.

MAUPITI

Maupiti also consists of a main island, surrounded by a large lagoon and several long motu. It's 40 km (25 mi) west of Bora Bora but its slow pace and lack of sophistication put it in another world. The town of Vai'ea and the port are in the south; the airport is on a motu to the northeast. There are just 14 small hotels and pensions, most of which are located on the motu near the best beaches.

TOP REASONS TO VISIT BORA BORA

Round-the-clock romance. Bora Bora is a honeymooner's paradise. Its amazing beauty will get every marriage off to a great start, and those in long-term relationships will fall in love all over again.

Fade to blue. The sensationally beautiful lagoon, said to have seven shades of blue, has to be seen to be believed. When you fly in, you'll understand what we mean.

Overwater magic. The iconic overwater bungalow was invented in French Polynesia and this island is home to the swankiest ones—perched atop four stilts with private plunge pools on the terrace. Celebrities love them, too, and you might have a brush with fame.

Underwater magic. Don a mask, snorkel, and flippers to see what lies beneath the watery blue. Advanced divers have both the lagoon and ocean to explore and many creatures to meet, though beginners will be able to mingle with manta rays as well.

PLANNING

WHEN TO GO

Anytime is a good time to visit Bora Bora due to the pleasant average temperature of 80°F (27°C). There are two basic seasons: the dry season from May to October (the Polynesian winter and busiest season) and the wet season from November to April (Polynesian summer), which can be very humid and cloudy. However, the heavy rains are often only short-lived.

The Tahiti Pearl Regatta, a yacht race around the Leeward Islands, takes place in the second week of May, the month-long Heiva Festival is in July, and the Hawaiki Nui Canoe Race is in early November.

GETTING HERE AND AROUND

The quickest way to get to Bora Bora is by plane. Air Tahiti flies several times a day to Bora Bora from Tahiti, with up to 11 flights a day in the high season (June to October). There are also charter and helicopter flights. There are a minimum of three flights a day from Moorea to Bora Bora. Air Tahiti passes for the Society Archipelago are a good option if you're visiting a few islands. *See Air Passes and Flights, in Getting here & Around in Travel Smart French Polynesia for air pass and airline contact information.*

Two passenger cargo ships travel from Pape'ete to Bora Bora on journeys from 14 to 19 hours. The 90-passenger *Vaeanu* and the 12-passenger *Hawaiki Nui* make the slow journey from Pape'ete about three times a week calling at other Society Islands en route. They offer a few cabins, but aren't suitable for tourists, unless "roughing" it's high on the agenda.

L'Truck (the local form of bus) circles the island and can be hailed almost anywhere on the coastal road; it also meets the interisland ferries. There are rental cars, scooters, bugsters (open vehicles similar to

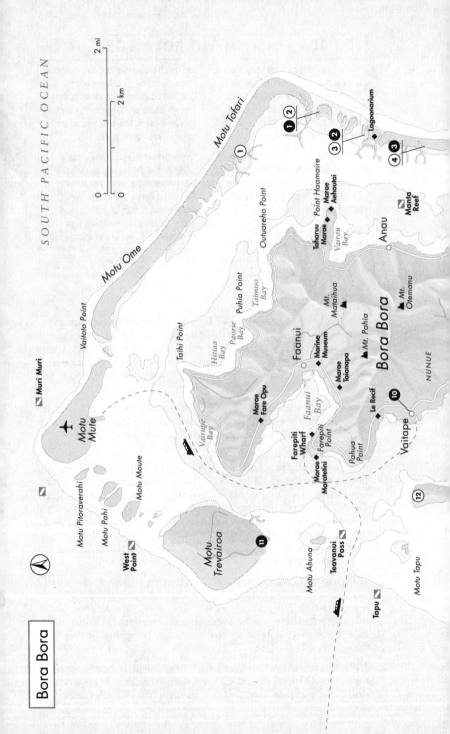

KEY

① *Hotels*
❶ *Restaurants*
▨ *Dive Sites*

Restaurants

▶

Bloody Mary's **7**
La Bounty **4**
Café Aloe **10**
Kaina Hut **8**
Lagoon Restaurant by
Jean-Georges **1**
Le Manu Tuki **5**
MikiMiki Restaurant **11**
Reef Restaurant **3**

Restaurant Matira **6**
Le Tipanie **2**
Villa Mahana **9**

Hotels

▶

Bora Bora Eden
Beach Hotel **5**
Bora Bora Lagoon
Resort & Spa **12**
Bora Bora Nui
Resort & Spa **11**
Chez Rosina **9**
Club Mediterranée
Bora Bora **8**
Four Seasons Bora Bora .. **1**

InterContinental Bora Bora
Resort & Thalasso Spa **4**
Le Maitai Polynesia
Bora Bora **7**
Le Meridien Bora Bora **3**
Rohutu Fare Lodge **10**
St. Regis, Bora Bora **2**
Village Temanuata **6**

dune buggies), and bicycles to rent. It takes about four hours to cycle around the island.

There are four rental car companies: Bora Bora Tours, Europcar, Avis, and Fare Piti Rent-a-Car. Bora Bora Tours and Fare Piti Rent-a-Car also rent scooters. Europcar also has desks at several resorts on the island including Hotel InterContinental Le Moana and Club Med. The majority of resorts and a few pensions such as the Pension Anau-Chez Teipo and Village Temanuata provide bicycles either for free or to rent.

There are several taxi companies on the island that usually operate as a one-man-one-car show. They are quite expensive. If you want to head to the water, water taxis, also expensive (around 8,500 CFP for two people), will pick you up from anywhere in Bora Bora and zip you across the lagoon.

ESSENTIALS

Banks Bank of Polynesia (☎ 60–57–57). **Bank Socredo** (☎ 60–50–10). **Bank of Tahiti** (☎ 60–59–90).

Car Rentals Avis (☎ 67–70–15). **Bora Bora Tours** (☎ 67–70–31 ⊕ www.bora boratours.com). **Europcar** (☎ 67–70–08 in Vaitape, 60–59–52 in Matira ⊕ www. europcar.pf). **Fare Piti Rent-a-Car** (☎ 67–65–28).

Emergencies Police (☎ 60–59–05). **Medical Center** (☎ 67–70–77). **Pharmacy** (☎ 67–70–30).

Ferries Vaeanu (☎ 41–25–35). **Hawaiki Nui** (☎ 45–23–24).

Taxis Heiman Tours (☎ 67–69–32). **JL Transport** (☎ 67–61–27). **Mrs. Dolly Dora Martin** (☎ 67–69–31). **Mrs. Tania Terorohauepa** (☎ 74–49–56). **Simple Tours** (☎ 79–19–31). **VIP Services Bora Bora** (☎ 67–78–77).

Visitor Info Office du Tourism (✉ Vaitape Quay ☎ 67–76–36 ⊙ Mon.–Fri. 9–4).

Water Taxi Bora Bora Taxi Motu (☎ 67–60–61). **Charlie Taxi** (☎ 67–64–37). **Island Taxi Service** (☎ 67–72–25).

TAKE IT ALL IN

3 Days: Take a half- or full-day lagoon excursion with stops for snorkeling, ray feeding, and a barbecue picnic on a motu. On Day 2 rent a car, scooter, or bicycle to explore the coastal road (there are only occasional hills) or take a 4WD excursion to the interior to see the WWII guns and admire sensational views. Shop at Vaitape in the afternoon, or call in at the Pearl Farm. On your third day, zip over the lagoon on a Jet Ski, go scuba diving or game fishing, or try any of the many nautical activities on offer such as swimming with marine life at the Lagoonarium.

5 Days: Follow the above itinerary and then on your fourth day, relax at the resort (think spa treatment), followed by dinner at Bloody Mary's. Or, take in a Tahitian dance show and buffet at a resort. On Day 5 take a helicopter ride, a hike into the interior, or an ATV (All Terrain Vehicle) along a deserted beach.

TOURING TIPS

Hotels, restaurants, and tourist outlets don't have street addresses and are usually listed as being in such-and-such a town. Often the address is given as so many kilometers (km) from the nearest town, such as PK 10, which means 10 km from Vaitape (which is located at PK0). Sounds simple, but it can be complicated because some distances are given for the north section of the 32-km coastal road and some are given for the south section. It's best to ask for directions at the tourism office or your hotel desk.

Most transfers in Bora Bora are by boat and you'll spend a lot of time on water going from hotel to restaurant, hotel to town, and hotel to tourist attraction or activity. Most restaurants, and at least one car hire company, provide free boat and boat/land transfers for people using their services. If you get seasick, make sure you've got Dramamine.

Whatever you desire to do on Bora Bora, the tourist office in Vaitape or your hotel tour desk can arrange it for you. Just ask.

7 Days: With seven days you can do all of the above, plus catch the Maupiti Express over to Raiatea, Tahaa, or Maupiti for the day.

HEALTH & SAFETY

Bora Bora is a very safe destination; even the lagoon waters are calm.

EAT RIGHT, SLEEP WELL

There are 15 hotels and resorts—the greatest number of any island in French Polynesia—and about a dozen family hotels (sometimes called pensions, lodges, or the name of the owner, i.e., "Chez Rosina") spread over the main island and motu. Some hoteliers believe there are too many, but this oversupply has its benefits as attractive deals, such as "stay five nights, pay for four" abound in the off-season (wet season).

International hotels have a selection of restaurants (and offer half- and full-board meal plans at extra cost), a choice of garden, beachside and overwater bungalows, and spas. Honeymooners are feted with private dinners in romantic settings, and breakfasts can be delivered by canoe. Overwater bungalows feature glass floor panels that allow you to see into the lagoon and feed the fish—the locals call them "Tahitian television." Hotels provide boat transfers from airport to resort. The major resorts usually have one Polynesian-themed buffet and dance show per week. Children are welcome at all resorts, most of which offer babysitting services at an extra charge.

The family-run establishments, most often near the lagoon, have no more than 15 bungalows or rooms and offer a traditional Polynesian experience with limited facilities, which sometimes include self-catering amenities. Many don't have restaurants and may not have in-room TVs or a/c, and the most basic don't have hot water. A few have dining rooms where a three-course-meal will be served at night (which will be a set meal and change nightly), while most are located near a restaurant district.

You'll probably encounter the term *fare* (pronounced far-ay) throughout French Polynesia. It means "house", however, in the accommodation business it means a little thatched bungalow. "Bungalow" is an introduced word (and adopted by most of the big resorts) whereas "fare" is a Tahitian word.

There are lots of dining options in Bora Bora. You can wiggle your toes in the sand as you sip French wines and tuck into fresh seafood or dine inches away from the lagoon under Polynesian designed "huts" with soaring cathedral ceilings. You can have light meals at small eateries known as "snacks" in Vaitape and around Matira Point or take a boat over to one of the motu resorts to feast not only on the fine food but sunset views of Mt. Otemanu. The daily catch is always on the menu along with chargrilled meats and a selection of French and international dishes that often includes duck, lobster, shrimp curry, and various fish and meat dishes graced with vanilla sauce—expect to find it on almost all menus (it has a subtle rather than a sweet taste). The signature Tahitian dish is *poisson cru* (raw tuna marinated in lime and coconut milk), and it's generally excellent. You may also be served delicious coconut bread (homemade bread with shredded coconut cooked on a barbecue) at a motu beach picnic. Almost all restaurants provide free transport for diners, with most motu boat transfers operating until around 11:30 or midnight every night. ■TIP→ **Tipping is not expected.**

WHAT IT COSTS IN FRANC COURS PACIFIQUE (CFP)					
	¢	$	$$	$$$	$$$$
RESTAURANTS	under 1,500	1,501–2,500	2,501–3,500	3,500–4,500	over 4,500
HOTELS	under 15,000	15,001–30,000	30,001–65,000	65,001–95,000	over 95,000

Restaurant prices are for a main course at dinner. Hotel prices are for a double room in high season, excluding 10% tax, 10%–15% service charges, and meals plans (except at all-inclusives).

EXPLORING BORA BORA

There are three popular ways to explore Bora Bora: by boat on the lagoon, by 4WD into the interior exploring the hills, and by driving around the 32-km (20-mi) main island road.

While it's very popular to drive around on one's own, if you have limited time it might be better to book an organized Circle Island tour. There are several *marae* (ancient Polynesian temples) and seven remaining WWII guns tucked away in the jungle interior, which are best pointed out by the experts.

If you want to cycle, it takes a good four hours to circle the island.

TOWNS

Vaitape. On the west coast, this is Bora Bora's main town and will be the first port of call for those staying on the main island. It has a marina and public wharf (where transfer boats come and go), a tourist office, police station, three banks, two gas stations, a post office with public phones, phar-

STAY CONNECTED

Aloe (☎*67-78-88*), a popular Internet café in Vaitape, has four PCs and printers, scanners, a web-cam, and choice of French or English keyboards. Half-hour Internet use costs around 1,000 CFP.

macy, and a medical center. Boutiques and eateries are strung along the one main road, which doesn't have a name. Near the police station (the Gendarmerie) is the grave of French yachtsman Alain Gerbault, who single-handedly sailed his yacht around the world in 1923–29, and lived here in the 1930s. There are also a bus stop, taxis, a cyber café, and two charming churches (Catholic and Protestant) painted in pastels with red roofs and steeples. ⊠*PK 0.*

Anau. Anau is almost directly opposite Vaitape on the east coast, although you have to go around the island to get there. Here you'll get a glimpse of authentic Polynesian life. There's one small church with a steeple and a few shops. The lagoon is very narrow at this section, as Motu Piti Anau is only a mile away. There's a great view of Mt. Otemanu from the town. ⊠*PK 18.5 via north road (clockwise).*

Faanui. This village, perched on Faanui Bay, is about 5 km (3 mi) north of Vaitape. It has a lovely pastel pink church in the shadow of a mountain. This area was once the stronghold of the former ruling family, the Pomare, which explains the presence of several marae not too far away. There are a few shops and stalls with brightly colored pareos (sarongs) fluttering in the breeze. Nearby are the remains of the former U.S. naval base, built in 1942. ⊠*PK 5.2 north.*

BEACHES

While Bora Bora has a stunning lagoon it doesn't have stunning beaches on the main island. There are, of course, lovely man-made sandy stretches attached to the international resorts, and nonguests may be able to use them if they eat in the restaurant or have a drink in the bar (but ask permission first). Otherwise, if you are driving or cycling around the main island, it's safe to say you can swim at most beaches as long as you don't have to cross private land to get there. The best beaches are located at Matira at the southern end of the main island and on the motu.

Matira Beach. This lovely beach at the southern most tip of the island graces both sides of Matira Point and is about 1.5 km (1 mi) long. Technically there are two beaches—west and east—with Matira Point in the middle. It's one of the few public access beaches on the island. Several luxurious resorts, shops, eateries, and activity centers are located on or near the beach making it a tourist hub. The beach is located about 6 km

(4 mi) from Vaitape; take a taxi, ride your scooter or bike, or wait for the local, but somewhat unreliable, L'Truck. ⊠*PK 6 south.*

SIGHTS

Marae. These ancient stone temples were religious and social gathering places, as well as the scene of human and animal sacrifices. One or two have been restored and some are adorned with turtle petroglyphs (images cut in stone); the turtle was considered sacred as it was a major source of food. Look for Taharuu Marae at Point Haamaire on the east coast, Aehautai near the Club

Med resort on the southeast coast, and the beautifully restored 164-foot-long(50-meter) Marotetini Marae near the wharf at Faanui Bay on the west coast. The Fare Opu Marae is a little north of Faanui and partially buried under the road. As some are tucked away in the jungle, it is advisable to take a 4WD or Circle Island tour, or ask the tourist office for exact locations. ⊠*Main island.*

WWII Guns. There are seven giant cannons on Bora Bora, perched on the hills above the four points of the island. U.S. servicemen stationed on the island during WWII installed them. Like the marae they can be difficult to find. Their general locations are the hills above Matira Point (about 6.5 km [4 mi] south of Vaitape); Fitiiu Point (on the east coast about 15 km [9 mi] from Vaitape via the southern route); and at Farepiti and Tereia Point (which are 2 km [1 mi] and 8 km [5 mi] north of Vaitape). The best way to see them, or some of them, is on an exciting but very bumpy 4WD tour. ⊠*Main island.*

Bora Bora Lagoonarium. This natural aquarium and water park is located on a private island near the Motu Piti Anau, not far from Le Meridien Resort. The family owners run half-day and full-day visits that include swimming with marine animals, ray and shark feeding demonstrations, circle-island tours in an outrigger canoe, and snorkel visits to the famed coral gardens at the southeast end of the main island. Alternatively, visitors can spend half a day just swimming, exploring, and learning about marine life. The owners also run a small guesthouse, called Pension Lagoonarium, on the main island's east coast. ⊠*Private motu, off Anau* 🕾*67–71–34* ⊕*www.boraboraisland.com/lagoonarium* 🖃*6,200–9,500 CFP* ☉*Daily 8:45–3:45.*

Marine Museum. This small museum at the very northern end of the island is only open upon request (and never on the weekends), so if you want to see 40 models of ancient and modern canoes, tuna fishing boats, and models of legendary ships such as the *Bounty* and the *Kon Tiki*, call before you visit. ⊠*PK 11 north of Vaitape, near Faanui* 🕾*67–75–24* 🖃*Free* ☉*Mon.–Fri. upon request.*

WHERE TO STAY

RESORTS

$$–$$$$ **Bora Bora Eden Beach Hotel.** If you're seeking a Robinson Crusoe experience, this quirky owner-run resort may be the place for you. You'll revel in the solitude and mix and mingle with just a handful of other guests, happy in the knowledge that the resort is completely solar-powered and has fully embraced other eco practices such as recycling and composting. Walk along the quiet beachfront or check out the roaring surf on the ocean side of the motu. There are limited activities (windsurfing and kayaking are free); however, the friendly owner, Vlada Zydek, can organize the usual excursions and motorized sports. Complimentary boat transfers ferry passengers to the village of Anau. All bungalows are by the beach or in a garden setting. **Pros:** An eco-minded resort. **Cons:** Limited activities; no overwater bungalows; no Internet. ⊠ *Motu Piti Aau* ⌂ *B.P. 191, Vaitape* ☎ *60–57–60* ⊕ *www. boraborahotel.com* ⇆ *15 bungalows* ⌂ *In-room: no a/c, safe, refrigerator. In-hotel: restaurant, bar, pool, beachfront, diving, water sports, no elevator, laundry service, concierge* ▤ *AE, MC, V* ⊙ *EP.*

$$$$ **Bora Bora Lagoon Resort & Spa.** This resort is a winner in the location sense. Situated on the northern tip of Motu Toopua, it has wonderful view of Mt. Otemanu on one side and a deserted islet on the other. On the island's southern end is Hiro's Bells—a group of 300-foot-high (91-meter) basalt rocks that resonate like a bell when struck. Accommodation is a mixture of overwater, beachside, and garden bungalows, and a handful have private plunge pools. The most secluded and sought-after accommodations are the six "end of pontoon overwater bungalows" with magnificent mountain views from the bedroom. One- and two-bedroom villas have indoor-outdoor garden showers and the bathroom walls are a mosaic fashioned from shells and volcanic stones. The resort's Maru Spa is the only treetop spa in Polynesia, with treatment rooms hidden between two banyan trees. **Pros:** Great views; huge "infinity pool"; ideal location. **Cons:** Signs of wear and tear in spa. ⊠ *Motu Toopua* ⌂ *B.P. 175, Vaitape* ☎ *60–40–00* ⊕ *www. boraboralagoon.com* ⇆ *76 bungalows* ⌂ *In-room: safe, refrigerator, DVD, Internet (some). In-hotel: 2 restaurants, room service, bars, tennis courts, pool, gym, spa, beachfront, diving, water sports, bicycles, no elevator, laundry service, concierge, public Internet, airport shuttle* ▤ *AE, DC, MC, V* ⊙ *EP.*

$$$$ **Bora Bora Nui Resort & Spa.** At the southern tip of Motu Toopua, this resort is considered to have one of the best beaches in Bora Bora and amazing snorkeling right off the bungalows. It's a large resort with expansive gardens; electric carts are available for those who don't want long walks by the shore or through the coconut groves. Bungalows are elegantly furnished with Indonesian mahogany canopy beds swathed in net and Italian marble baths. A regular shuttle ferries guests to and from Vaitape throughout the day and well into the night for those who want to dine on the mainland. **Pros:** Great beach; regular shuttles to Vaitape; electric carts to tool around in. **Cons:** There's a charge for

A BRIEF HISTORY

Bora Bora, along with Maupiti, is the oldest of the Society Islands at about 7 million years and was formed by volcanic eruptions. No one really knows how long humans have lived on the island, though the first Polynesians are thought to have arrived around AD 400. The island was first known as Vava'u and later Pora Pora, which relates to the myth that it was the first island "drawn out of the sea after the creation of Raiatea" by the gods.

Europeans including Dutch explorer Jacob Roggeveen and Captain James Cook sighted the island in the 18th century; Cook landed in 1777. The London Missionary Society set up a Protestant Church in 1822. Bora Bora became a protectorate of France in 1842. Some 5,000 American soldiers arrived in December 1942 to man the island, which was intended to be a military supply base. They built the runway on Motu Mute and installed eight artillery guns and fuel storage tanks. International tourists began to arrive the 1960s. Hotel Bora Bora, the first international hotel, opened the island's first overwater bungalows in 1961. The hotel closed its doors for renovations October 2008 with plans to reopen in 2010.

airport transfers. ⊠*Motu Toopua* ⬩*B.P. 502, Vaitape* ☎*60–33–00* ⊕*www.boraboranui.com* ⬩*120 bungalows* ♿*In-room: safe, kitchen, refrigerator, DVD, VCR, Internet. In-hotel: 2 restaurants, room service, bars, pool, gym, spa, beachfront, diving, water sports, bicycles, no elevator, laundry service, concierge, public Internet, airport shuttle* ▭*AE, DC, MC, V* ⦿*EP.*

$$$ ▦ **Club Méditerranée Bora Bora.** You can't miss this cluster of huts painted in various colors—pink, orange, and yellow—as you zoom past on a Jet Ski or launch. Like many Club Meds around the world it has a great location but not too many frills. The bungalows are a little Spartan but spacious enough, and are either nestled in a luxuriant coconut grove or on a narrow strip of beachfront. There are no overwater bungalows and no swimming pool; however, guests have access to a private motu where they can swim and sunbathe all day long. This is a good choice for travelers on a budget as all meals, including snacks at any time, and all drinks are included. Free activities include cooking and Polynesian dance classes, and there are group sailing, windsurfing, and snorkeling lessons. **Pros:** All meals included; access to private motu; lots of free activities. **Cons:** Nontraditional style bungalows. ⊠*PK8, Aponapu Bay* ⬩*B.P. 575, Pape'ete, Tahiti* ☎*60–46–04* ⊕*www.clubmed.com* ⬩*150 rooms* ♿*In-room: safe, refrigerator. In-hotel: restaurant, bar, tennis courts, gym, spa, beachfront, diving, water sports, bicycles, no elevator, laundry facilities, laundry service, concierge, public Internet, airport shuttle, parking (no fee)* ▭*AE, MC, V* ⦿*MAP.*

$$$$ ▦ **Four Seasons Bora Bora.** The island's newest resort opened its doors in mid-2008. Like other luxurious resorts on Bora Bora, it's location on an eastern motu provides guests with stunning views of Mt. Otemanu. This is also the island's first resort with a club for teenagers, Teen Island, which has its own beach. There's also a club for younger children. All 100 overwater bungalows, a handful of which have private

plunge pools, can accommodate two adults and two children, or three adults, with children under 18 free. There are also six two-bedroom villas and the ultimate holiday pad, the three-bedroom, four-bathroom villas, situated on the beach in private gardens. **Pros:** Kids club; villas have private pools; great views. **Cons:** Pricey; charge for airport transfers. ⊠*Motu Tofari* ⌂*B.P. 371, Pape'ete, Tahiti* ☎*60–31–30* ⊕*www.fourseasons. com* ⬅*100 suites, 21 villas* ⌂*In-room: safe, refrigerator, DVD, Internet. In-hotel: 2 restaurants, room service, bars, 2 pools, gym, spa, beachfront, diving, water sports, no elevator, children's programs (ages 3–17), laundry service, concierge, public Internet, airport shuttle* ▤*AE, DC, MC, V.* ⦿*EP.*

$$$$ ⬚**InterContinental Bora Bora Resort and Thalasso Spa.** This beautiful and innovative resort features virtually all overwater bungalows, except three two-bedroom family villas on the beachfront. It's the first in the Southern Hemisphere with a Thalasso spa, which uses deep seawater and seaweed in a long menu of therapeutic treatments. Another unique feature is the charming wedding chapel (the only resort chapel in French Polynesia) complete with a glass aisle—you can see coral and fish below—that the happy couple walks on from the door to the altar. The resort has adopted several energy-saving practices including using seawater pumped from 2,500 feet (762 meters) below to cool the air-conditioning system. The beds in each bungalow are situated right in front of floor-to-ceiling windows so you wake up with a view. Decor includes Paul Gauguin prints and Polynesian artworks. A free shuttle runs between the motu and the sister property, the InterContinental Moana Resort, at Matira Point. **Pros:** Lovely swimming lagoon; great views; beautiful bungalows. **Cons:** Pricey. ⊠*Motu Piti Aau* ⌂*B.P. 156, Vaitape* ☎*60–76–00* ⊕*www. ichotelsgroup.com* ⬅*85 bungalows* ⌂*In-room: safe, refrigerator, DVD, Internet. In-hotel: 3 restaurants, room service, 2 bars, tennis court, pool, gym, spa, beachfront, diving, water sports, no elevator, laundry service, concierge, airport shuttle* ▤*AE, DC, MC, V* ⦿*EP.*

$$–$$$$ ⬚**Le Maitai Polynesia Bora Bora.** This mid-range resort is about a 10-minute walk from Matira Beach, and 6 km (4 mi) from Vaitape. Accommodations are a mixture of air-conditioned hotel rooms in two-story wings and beachside and overwater bungalows. Hotel rooms have balconies and views either of the mountain or the lagoon. A recent upgrade widened the beach and added 20 new air-conditioned rooms, nine overwater bungalows, and a second restaurant—Tama'a Maitai, serving Polynesian and seafood dishes—right on the beach. **Pros:** Baby-sitting services are available; rooms and bungalows have great views. **Cons:** No pool; bungalows are fan-cooled only. ⊠*PK6, Matira* ⌂*B.P. 505, Vaitape* ☎*603–000* *48 rooms, 26 bungalows* ⌂*In-room: no a/c (some), safe, refrigerator. In-hotel: 2 restaurants, 2 bars, beachfront, diving, water sports, bicycles, no elevator, laundry service, concierge* ☰*AE, DC, MC, V* ⍅*EP.*

$$$$ **Le Meridien Bora Bora.** One of the original hotels on Bora Bora, this is the place for those who love water activities and marine life. The hotel has its own private lagoon that has developed as a turtle sanctuary since the first injured turtle was brought there for rehabilitation in 1999. Today Le Meridien plays host to the Marine Turtle Protection Centre; guests can swim with the turtles and watch babies being cared for. The resort has a brilliant position—on Motu Piti Aau—with Mt. Otemanu looming directly in front of it. One of its biggest draws is the Miki Miki Bar, designed as a prow of a ship, and an ideal place for sunset cocktails. The majority of accommodations are overwater bungalow, graced with romantic four-poster beds. **Pros:** Private lagoon; onsite spa; wedding ceremonies performed. **Cons:** There's a charge for airport transfers. ⊠*Motu Piti Aau* ⌂*B.P. 190, Vaitape* ☎*47–07–29* ⊕*www.lemeridien.com* *99 bungalows* ⌂*In-room: safe, refrigerator, DVD, Internet. In-hotel: 3 restaurants, room service, 2 bars, pool, gym, spa, beachfront, diving, water sports, bicycles, no elevator, laundry service, concierge, executive floor, public Internet, airport shuttle* ☰*AE, DC, MC, V* ⍅*EP.*

$$$$ **St Regis Resort, Bora Bora.** If you're looking for the ultimate getaway, and are not concerned about breaking the bank, then this is the place to come. The villas, most of which are overwater, have spacious living rooms, a sundeck and terrace, and a personal butler. Some of the overwater bungalows have Jacuzzis, others have private plunge pools. The Royal Estate Villa, where Nicole Kidman and Keith Urban honeymooned in 2006, is set away from the others and has three bedrooms, two bathrooms, a chef's kitchen, a private spa area, and a private beach. The resort has drop-dead beautiful views of Mt. Otemanu. It was also the first resort on the island to have a kids' club. **Pros:** Kids' club; ultimate in luxury; has signature Miri Miri Spa. **Cons:** Very pricey. ⊠*Motu Ome* ⌂*B.P. 506, Vaitape* ☎*60–78–88* ⊕*www.stregis.com/ borabora* *90 bungalows, 1 villa* ⌂*In-room: safe, refrigerator, DVD, Internet. In-hotel: 4 restaurants, room service, 2 bars, tennis court, 3 pools, gym, spa, beachfront, diving, water sports, bicycles, no elevator, children's programs (ages 5–12), laundry service, concierge* ☰*AE, DC, MC, V* ⍅*EP.*

SMALL HOTELS

$$$$ **Chez Rosina.** This pleasant little pension has a mountainside location at Paofai Bay, 4.5 km (2.8 mi) south of Vaitape. There is a dining room onsite, and a TV and VCR in the common living room, along with a communal kitchen and washing machine. This is place to save big bucks on accommodation if you don't mind the simple life. **Pros:**

Linen and mosquito nets provided; the half-board option is available. **Cons:** No a/c; no activities or water sports; only some of the rooms have private bathrooms with hot water. ✉ *PK 4.5, Paofai Bay* 🏠*B.P. 51, Vaitape* ☎*67–70–91* 🌐*www.tahitiguide.com* 🛏*1 bungalow, 5 rooms* ⏃*In-room: no a/c, no phone, no TV. In-hotel: dining room, no elevator, laundry facilities, airport shuttle, parking (no fee)* ⊟*No credit cards* ⦿*EP.*

$$ 🏠**Rohotu Fare Lodge.** This three-bungalow lodge at Paofai Bay is unique in that guests can stay in one bungalow or make an advance booking and rent out the entire property for eight family members or friends. It is situated on the hillside, a few hundred yards from the lagoon; however, the owners provide free shuttles to the beach and free transport to nearby restaurants and grocery stores. Each bungalow has a balcony with view of the lagoon or mountainside, a queen-size canopy bed, and a large bathroom with outdoor garden shower flowing from a statue of a Tahitian woman! Each has a kitchenette with refrigerator, microwave, and coffee machine, perfect for preparing your own breakfast each day. The lodge provides free bicycles and free airport transfers and will rent out kayaks and arrange paid activities such as lagoon excursions. There's a communal lounge and library bungalow with hammock and free Internet in the lobby. Local artwork adorns the bungalows and stone tikis are dotted around the grounds. **Pros:** Lofty views; free bikes and transfers. **Cons:** No restaurant. ✉ *PK 4, Paofai Bay* 🏠*B.P. 544, Vaitape* ☎*70–77–99* 🌐*www.rohotufarelodge.com* 🛏*3 bungalows* ⏃*In-room: no a/c, no phone (some), safe (some), kitchen, refrigerator, no TV. In-hotel: diving, water sports, bicycles, no elevator, laundry service, public Internet, airport shuttle, parking (no fee)* ⊟*MC, V* ⦿*EP.*

$-$$ 🏠**Village Temanuata.** The resort's bungalows—four are at the Iti location—are serviced daily and have double beds, private bathroom with hot water, a ceiling fan, fridge, kettle, and terrace. Two are located on the beach and all the others in the garden. Seven have fully equipped kitchens, while the four newest also have TVs. A breakfast basket of croissants, jam, tea, and coffee is available each morning for a small charge. The property has recently opened a sister location, Village Temanuata Iti, approximately half a mile (800 meters) to the east on what's called the "mountainside" of the main island road. **Pros:** Private bathrooms have hot water; Matira Beach is a short walk away; there are numerous eateries close by. **Cons:** No a/c in the bungalows; there's a fee to rent snorkeling equipment and canoes; no restaurant in the hotel. ✉ *PK 8, Matira Point* 🏠*B.P. 544, Vaitape* ☎*67–75–61* 🌐*www.temanuata.com* 🛏*16 bungalows* ⏃*In-room: no a/c, no phone (some), kitchen (some), refrigerator, TV (some). In-hotel: beachfront, water sports, bicycles (some), no elevator, laundry facilities, airport shuttle (charge), parking (no fee)* ⊟*MC, V* ⦿*EP.*

TOPOGRAPHY

Bora Bora's main island is a caldera, or collapsed volcano. It's about 5 mi (8 km) long and 3 mi (5 km) at its widest, with a circumference of a little more than 20 mi (32 km). It's surrounded by a huge lagoon, which is encircled by about 30 motu (islets) of various shapes and sizes and a fringing coral reef. The motu are flat with the exception of Motu Toopua's one peak of 485 feet (148 meters) and edged with pristine beaches. The island's interior is dominated by the majestic Mt. Otemanu, which at 2,385 feet (727 meters) pierces the clouds. Nearby is Mt. Pahia (2,168 feet [661 meters]), while Mt. Hue (2,054 feet [616 meters]), Mt. Matalhua (1,030 feet [314 meters]), and Mt. Popoti (817 feet [249 meters]) are in the north. The only high point in the south is Mt. Pahonu (456 feet [139 meters]).

WHERE TO EAT

It's advisable to make reservations, often well in advance. Villa Mahana and Bloody Mary's are legendary and people clamor to get into these two on the main island. Most provide free transport for diners. If you want to dine at a resort, especially one on a motu, plan on getting there early as the kitchen will most likely close around 9 PM.

HOTEL RESTAURANTS

$$$$
FRENCH
✕ **Lagoon Restaurant by Jean-Georges.** This is the 16th of the 17 restaurants run by star chef, and New York resident, Jean-Georges Vongerichten. The stunning restaurant at the St. Regis resort, with fantastic Mt. Otemanu views, is suspended over the lagoon. The dishes reflect Vongerichten's Thai French style. Start with bacon wrapped shrimp with passion fruit mustard atop slices of fresh avocado. Follow that up with the exotic spiced chicken with coconut caramel sauce and a citrus salad. Vongerrichten flies in every few months to introduce the new menus. When he's not around, executive chef Romuald Feger, who once worked at Le Cirque in New York, is at the helm. ⊠*St. Regis Resort, Motu Ome* ☎*60–78–88* ⌂*Reservations essential (in the high season)* ▭*AE, DC, MC, V.*

$$$
FRENCH
✕ **Le Manu Tuki.** With 180-degree views of the main island and a wide veranda, alfresco dining doesn't get any better. The resort is perched on a private island just off the far south-eastern coast, and free transfers operate from the Sofitel Bora Bora Beach resort a few hundred yards away. You may find the tandoori-style tuna with "virgin sauce"—so named because none of its ingredients (tomato, basil, lemon juice, garlic, olive oil, and shallots) are cooked—on the menu or the addictive crème brûleè with Tahitian vanilla. You'll feel a million miles from home on this little island and have a view of the "bright lights" of Matria Beach. ⊠*Sofitel Motu Bora Bora, Motu Piti Uu'Uta (off Matira)* ☎*60–56–00* ⌂*Reservations essential* ▭*AE, DC, MC, V.*

$$
CAFÉ ✕ **MikiMiki Restaurant.** If you are not staying at the Bora Bora Pearl Resort, dinner reservations are difficult to get, so make a point to come here for lunch. The resort's boat dock is right at the northwestern tip of Motu Tevairo, and the crossing from the main island only takes 10 minutes or so. The indoor-outdoor restaurant overlooks the pool and serves everything from club sandwiches and paninis to pork ribs and sautéed shrimp with chili sauce. ⊠ *Bora Bora Pearl Resort, Motu Tevairoa* ☎ *60–52–00* ⚬ *Reservations essential* ⊟ *AE, DC, MC, V* ⊙ *Lunch daily 11:30–4.*

$$$–$$$$
FRENCH ✕ **Reef Restaurant.** There are tranquil views of the lagoon from this indoor-outdoor restaurant, which has one of the most innovative menus on the island. Start with a drink at the very funky Bubbles Bar and then perhaps try the medium-rare red tuna, celery puree, pine nuts, and fine slices of foie gras; or splurge on the lobster fricassee with Tahitian Rum, pumpkin chutney, and spicy rice. Finish your meal with pan-fried strawberries topped with Marquesas Island honey and fromage frais ice cream. It's open for breakfast and dinner. ⊠ *InterContinental Bora Bora & Thalasso Spa, Motu Piti Aau* ☎ *60–76–43* ⊟ *AE, DC, MC, V.*

$–$$
AMERICAN ✕ **Restaurant Matira.** The comfortable furniture at this restaurant gives it the feel of a local hangout, while the floor-to-ceiling windows bring the gorgeous lagoon right indoors. Meals range from Chinese specialties to thin-crust pizzas and inexpensive burgers and fries. ⊠ *Hotel Matira, Matira* ☎ *67–70–51* ⚬ *Reservations essential* ⊟ *AE, DC, MC, V.*

$$$
FRENCH ✕ **Le Tipanie.** This lovely restaurant at Le Meridien is built around the resort's private lagoon, which allows you to watch the antics of turtles big and small while you dine. Tasty main courses include roasted Muscovy duck breast with cinnamon and honey, topped with lavender and orange sauce. Finish off with caramelized banana tatin tart and Tahitian tiare flower ice cream. ⊠ *Le Meridien Resort, Motu Piti Aau* ☎ *60–51–51* ⚬ *Reservations essential* ⊟ *AE, DC, MC, V* ⊙ *Daily 6:30 AM–9:30 PM.*

INDEPENDENT RESTAURANTS

$$$
CAFÉ ✕ **Bloody Mary's.** This is Bora Bora's iconic restaurant where you may spot celebrities. If not you can read the long list of movie stars and VIPs who've dined here—from Prince Rainier of Monaco to Jane Fonda and Harrison Ford. The menu items run the gamut from the fresh catch of the day (displayed on ice for you to take your pick) to char grills. The roof is thatched, the floor is sand, and the bar is very popular—and you can buy a T-shirt, too. Be warned, as with all iconic institutions the food may not match the hype, but it's lively most nights of the week

---

WORD OF MOUTH

"If you're staying on one of many hotels on motus, your option for eating outside your hotel is very limited. If your hotel is on a motu, inquire the boat schedule to the main island. Once you get to the island, it's also very difficult to travel on island, especially on days when you have to compete for a few taxis with cruise ship passengers. Upper scale restaurant such as Blood Mary's offers transportation for dinners, but even so, understand very well how you get back to your hotel." —nickn

3

and that's a bonus for night owls. Call for a reservation when you get to the island. ⊠*PK 4 Paofai Bay, Amanahune* ☎*67–72–86* ⊕*www. boraboraisland.com/bloodymarys/index.html* ⚑*Reservations essential* ▤*MC, V* ⊙*Mon.–Sat. 11–3, 6:30–9.*

$$
FRENCH

✕**La Bounty.** Like Café Aloe, this popular hangout on the main island is suited for those watching their francs. Menu items include thin pizzas and a whole array of Italian pastas, along with the local fish (such as mahimahi) given the French treatment, as well as crepes. ⊠*PK 6, Matira* ☎*67–70–43* ▤*MC, V* ⊙*Closed Mondays.*

$–$$
CAFÉ

✕**Café Aloe.** Formerly L'Appetisserie, this café and bakery in Vaitape serves delicious strong French coffee and yummy pastries and tarts, as well as the plate du jour (dish of the day), which maybe be grilled fish and salad. Other snacks include pizza slices and sandwiches. When you're done eating, you can check your e-mails or browse the Web. ⊠*Centre Commercial La Pahia, Vaitape* ☎*67–78–88* ⚑*Reservations not accepted* ▤*No credit cards* ⊙*Open Mon.–Sat., 6 AM–7 PM.*

$$$
FRENCH

✕**Kaina Hut.** Pull up a tree trunk stool and have a drink at the bar (feet in the sand, of course) while waiting for your table. You may find Provencal Bouillabaisse or grilled tuna and shrimp skewers on the menu, or decide to try the local *moana* (a delicate white fish) soup with vegetables and croutons. The catch of the day is always popular, while char-grilled meats are always on the menu. ⊠*PK 3.5, Paofai Bay* ☎*71–10–73* ⚑*Reservations essential* ▤*MC, V* ⊙*Closed Tuesdays.*

$$$$
FRENCH
Fodor'sChoice
★

✕**Villa Mahana.** Set in a Tuscan-style house on one of the main island's quiet lanes, the villa is virtually next door to Bloody Mary's; make sure you book three months ahead of time to snag one of its six tables. Chef Damien Rinaldi-Dovio is said to preside over the very best restaurant in Bora Bora and combines classic French cuisine with French Polynesian flavors in dishes like filet mignon with vanilla cream gnocchi and mahimahi with banana curry. Though this will be a meal to remember, it is an expensive night out, so if you're looking for an inexpensive option, try one of the set menus that range from 90 euros (10,740 CFP) to 125 euros (14,320 CFP) per person. There is a free shuttle bus for diners. ⊠*PK 4, Amanahune* ☎*67–50–63* ⊕*villamahana.com* ⚑*Reservations essential* ▤*AE, DC, MC, V.*

OUTDOOR ACTIVITIES

Bora Bora packs in a wealth of activities for a small place and naturally most occur on or in the lagoon. You can scuba dive, snorkel, feed the sharks and rays, swim with rays and turtles, sail, Jet Ski, jetboat, water ski, fish, ride an underwater aquabike, or cruise around in submarine. On land there's biking, quad biking, hiking, parasailing, and even helicopter rides.

Horseback riding is not available on Bora Bora and tennis is not very popular game due to the heat. The only public court near Vaitape is not in good condition, but some of the resorts have courts. If tennis is important to you, make sure you ask when booking if there's a court.

BIKING

It takes an hour to drive around the island (without stopping too much) and about four hours to cycle. If you don't want to rent a bike, most resorts offer free bikes for their guests to use.

> **DID YOU KNOW?**
>
> Seabow is the cute name for the array of colors in the Bora Bora lagoon: sapphire, turquoise, emerald, aqua, marine, curaçao, and transparent blue.

Bora Bora Tours (✉ *PK 2, Vaitape* ☎ *67–70–31*) will rent you bikes, scooters, and cars. **Fare Piti Rent-A-Car** (✉ *PK 3 north, Fare Piti* ☎ *67–65–28*) also rents out bicycles, scooters, and cars.

BOATING & SAILING

Bora Bora Voile (✉ *Anau* ☎ *67–64–30 boraboravoile@mail.pf*) offers circle island, two-hour, sunset, and full-day cruises on the catamaran *Taaroa III*. It carries 10 to 16 passengers depending on the type of cruise and is also available for charter excursions. **Manu Taxi Boat** (✉ *Vaitape* ☎ *67–61–93 fantantaxiboat@mail.pf*) operates hourly, half-day, and full-day boating trips on the lagoon. It also rents out its four boats for personal use. Licenses may be required for vessels larger than 27 feet.

Moana Adventure Tours (✉ *Paofai Bay* ☎ *67–61–41* ⊕ *www.moana tours.com*) offers glass-bottom boat tours, snorkel safaris on a 68-passenger catamaran, shark and ray safaris for 12 people, and champagne Blue Lagoon Cruises for just six passengers. **Moana Jet Boat** (✉ *Vaitape* ☎ *67–68–10* ⊕ *www.moanajetboat.com*) offers a 2½-hour trip aboard a speedboat that includes snorkeling and feeding the stingrays; maximum of 12 passengers allowed. **Shark Boy** (✉ *Vaitape* ☎ *67–60–93* ✍ *sharkboy@mail.pf*) offers lagoon excursions to feed rays and sharks and snorkel on a choice of four motorboats, a canoe for 12 people, a long boat, or a catamaran.

Sunsail Tahiti (✉ *Uturoa, Raiatea* ☎ *60–04–85* ⊕ *www.sunsail.com. au*), an Australian charter company, is based in Raiatea but cruises the areas around Bora Bora, Huaine, and Tahaa. Sailors must have skippered a charter yacht before to qualify. There are 10 luxury yachts and four catamarans in the fleet. **Taravana** (✉ *Vaitape* ☎ *60–59–31* ⊕ *www. boraboraisland.com/taravana/index.html*), a catamaran, is available for lagoon sunset cruises, full-day excursions to the island of Tupai, and fishing excursions.

FISHING

Moana Adventure Tour (✉ *Paofai Bay* ☎ *67–61–41* ⊕ *www.moanatours. com*) offers two options for keen anglers: lagoon trolling (light tackle fishing in the lagoon) and surface casting for poppers, an excursion that travels to Tupai (10 mi north of Bora Bora); this is a six-hour trip for fishermen with their own equipment.

4WD SAFARIS

Head for the hills with **Tupuna Mountain Safari** (✉ *Vaitape* ☎ *67–75–06* ✍ *tupuna.bora@mail.pf*) to check out the WWII guns. The views across the lagoon and to the islands beyond are spectacular.

GUIDED ISLAND TOURS

Bora Bora Safari Land (✉ *Vaitape* ☎ *67–71–32*) offers island tours in air-conditioned buses, window-down cooled trucks, or an eight-seater Volkswagen van. **Bora Bora Tours** (✉ *Vaitape* ☎ *67–70–31* ⊕ *www. boraboratours.com*) offers a two-hour island tour that stops regularly for sightseeing and shopping. **Charley Transports** (✉ *Vaitape* ☎ *73–73– 31*) has a Land Rover or minivan to take you on an air-conditioned tour of Bora Bora's great sights.

HELICOPTER TOURS

Polynesia Helicopters (✉ *Vaitape* ☎ *67–62–59* ⊕ *www.polynesia-helicopter.com*). Soar over the lagoon for 15 minutes or take a 30-minute return flight to Tupai in a five-seat helicopter.

HIKING

Pahia Heights Adventure (✉ *Vaitape* ☎ *67–77–73*) offers a day trip to the interior that includes a few very steep hills and is for experienced hikers only. There's a picnic at a scenic spot where you can rest and enjoy the sensational views.

JET SKIING

Matira Jet Tours (✉ *Matira Point* ☎ *67–62–73* ⊕ *www.boraborawave runner.com*). Spend two hours circling the island on a two-seater Jet Ski visiting a private island for a lagoon swim and watching the Jet Ski guides climb up a coconut tree to knock down a few for an impromptu snack.

PARASAILING

Bora Bora Para Sail (✉ *Novotel Bora Bora, Matira* ☎ *67–70–34 or 78–27–10* ⊕ *www.boraboraisland.com/parasail/index.html*) will take you to great heights. Customers choose the height they want to fly and can even do side-by-side couple's parasailing. Flights range from 12 to 30 minutes.

QUAD BIKING

Matira Jet Tours also runs Quad Bike trips into the interior of the main island. You can do Jet Ski/quad and quad/snorkeling combinations. Quad bikes or ATVs (all-terrain vehicles) go over hills and through streams, carry two people, and are lots of fun.

UNDERWATER ADVENTURES

Aquabike Aventure (✉ *Tipoto* ☎ *675–091* ⊕ *www.aquabikadventure. com*). You'll feel like one of the Jetsons (albeit in the water), as you motor about in your little scooter built for two. This is certainly a unique way to check out the fish.

Aqua Safari (✉ *Amanahune, near Kaina Hut* ☎ *67–74–83* ⊕ *www. aquasafaribora.com*). This is an underwater walk wearing a diving helmet and wet suit. Participants walk on the seabed a few meters below the surface for 30 to 45 minutes. Passengers awaiting their turn at the underwater walk get to snorkel.

Bora Bora Submarine (✉ *Nunue, south of Vaitape* ☎ *67–74–84* ⊕ *www. boraborasubmarine.com*). You'll be singing the Beatles' classic pop

BEST BETS FOR CRUISING

Little rays of sunshine. Take a snorkeling trip to swim with and feed the rays and watch the experts feed friendly reef sharks. It's a thrill you won't soon forget.

Take a ride. Rent a bicycle, scooter, car, or bugster and head off around the 32-km (20-mi) coastal road, stopping at shops and little villages along the way. If time is limited, head south from Vaitape to Matira where you'll find most of the action anyway.

Lovely lagoon. Kayak, catamaran, submarine, aquabike, jet boat, or Jet Ski—explore the lagoon however you can, it's too beautiful to miss.

Bush exploring. Take a bumpy 4WD trip up the mountainside for a sensational view of the lagoon and far-flung islands. Check out the old WWII guns along the way.

song as you plunge to depths of 100 feet (30 meters) in a yellow submarine with panoramic windows. Passengers watch the sea creatures swim by in air-conditioned comfort.

Bora Diving Centre & Nemo World (⊠*Matira* ☎*67–71–84 or 67–77– 85* ⊕*www.boradiving.com*) are located in Matira and have the same owner. Morning dives are for certified divers (two 45-minute dives); beginners are taught in the afternoon. There are five boats, and hotel and motu resort pickups are arranged.

Moana Adventure Tours (⊠*Paofai Bay* ☎*67–61–41* ⊕*www.moana tours.com*) has been running snorkeling tours for 30 years and offers public and private tours to all the best places in Bora Bora.

SHOPPING

The big-ticket item is always the pearl—black and a few other lustrous colors. There are several art galleries, and boutiques selling pareos, curios, gifts, and souvenirs. Many shops open early, close for an hour and a half for lunch and then open again around 1:30 PM and stay open until 7 PM. Many are closed on Sunday.

GALLERIES

Alain Despert Studio (⊠*Matira* ☎*60–48–15* ⊕*www.despert.com* ☉*By appointment only*). This French artist moved to Bora Bora in 1986, and from his hillside studio above Matira Beach, paints Bora Bora scenes and depictions of tikis, with a slightly naive style, using acrylic and enamel on canvas. He achieved international fame for his painting of a bottle of vodka floating in the Bora Bora lagoon to promote Absolut vodka.

Alain & Linda (⊠*Paofai Bay* ⊕*www.borabora-art.com* ☉*Mon.–Sat. 8:30–6*). The gallery's French owners came to Bora Bora 35 years ago on their honeymoon, loved it, and returned a few years later to live there. The lovely thatched building displays both their works—she paints on canvas and he specializes in hand-painted pareos—and the work of local artists (painters and sculptors) who they nurture and promote. The gallery also sells etchings, tapas (Polynesian painted cloth), and books.

Boutique Paiki (⊠ *Matira Point* ☎ *67–50–84* ⊕ *www.boraboraisland. com/paiki/index.html* ⊘ *Call for an appointment*). This boutique and art gallery is owned by Isa Motuehitu and specializes in Polynesia art and gifts. Her husband Fati, owns Fati Tattoo next door. *See Tattoos below.*

Chez Garrick Yrondi (⊠ *PK4, Amanahune* ☎ *60–57–15* ⊕ *www.yrondi.pf* ⊘ *Call for an appointment*). Garrick Yrondi is a Frenchman who has lived on various islands of French Polynesia since he was two years old. He paints oils and watercolors and sculpts in a Mediterranean style villa studio 4 km (2 mi) south of Vaitape. His 2-meter rose marble statue of a woman, known as *Vahine E ia* is displayed on a tiny island in the lagoon just near Bora Bora airport. You can't miss it.

GROCERIES & OTHER ESSENTIALS

Magasin Chin Lee (⊠ *Vaitape* ☎ *67–73–86* ⊘ *Closed Sunday*). From post cards and toothpaste to Vini cards for your mobile phone, you'll find most things you need at this popular supermarket. There are also upscale items as well, including foie gras and French champagne.

Tiare Market (⊠ *East Matira* ☎ *67–71–38* ⊘ *Closed Daily 1:30–3* PM *for lunch*). You'll find this supermarket near the Novotel and the Sofitel resorts at the southeast end of the island about 8 km (5 mi) from Vaitape. It carries all the essentials—from sunblock to toothpaste—and ingredients for self-catering meals.

PEARLS

The Farm (⊠ *Matira* ☎ *70–06–75* ⊕ *www.borapearl.com* ⊘ *Daily 9–6*). Owned by the 30-year-old Bora Pearl Company, this is one of those one-stop-look-and-shop places that a tour operator might take you to. You can walk along pontoons to see oyster leases in the water and take a free guided tour of the pearl harvesting, jewelry making, and retail sections. It's educational…and tempting.

Matira Pearls & Fashions (⊠ *PK 6.8, Matira Point* ☎ *67–79–14* ⊕ *www. matirapearls.com* ⊘ *Mon.–Sat. 9–5:30*), not far from the InterContinental Hotel Moana, is run by two American guys who have been in business since 1993. The company has its own pearl farm on Raiatea and each pearl comes with a certificate of authenticity and origin.

Robert Wan (⊠ *Main Road, next to the post office, Vaitape* ☎ *67–50–27* ⊕ *www.robertwan.com* ⊘ *Daily 8:30–6*). You'll hear the name Robert Wan all over French Polynesia, as he is the doyen of pearl production and design. There are four of his beautiful boutiques on Bora Bora: in Vaitape, the St Regis Resort, Bora Bora Nui Resort & Spa, and Inter-Continental Le Moana Resort. A free shuttle boat is available to pick up customers from other resorts and transport them to Vaitape.

TATTOOS

Fati Tattoo (✉ *PK 6.6, Matira Point* ☎ *67–50–84* ⊕ *www.boraborais-land.com/fati/index.html* ◷ *Call for an appointment*). Fati Motue-hitu, a Marquesan tattoo artist, runs this tattoo studio that specializes in original Polynesian designs.

3

SPAS

Bora Bora is the spa capital of French Polynesia with eight spas, all located in resorts, offering massage, scrubs, body wraps, facials, and petal baths.

Deep Ocean Spa by Algotherm (✉ *InterContinental Bora Bora Resort and Thalasso Spa, Motu Piti Aau* ☎ *60–76–00* ⊕ *www.deepoceanspa.com* ◷ *Daily 9:30–7*) has the only Thalassotherapy spa in the South Pacific, which means it uses seawater pumped from 2,500 feet (762 meters) below the ocean's surface in therapies to replenish body minerals and restore equilibrium. Before your treatment, take a soak in a private Jacuzzi with views out to Mt. Otemanu.

Manea Spa (✉ *Bora Bora Pearl Beach Resort, Motu Tevairoa* ☎ *60–53–85* ⊕ *www.maneaspa.com*) uses locally made products such as monoi oil and tamanu balm (from the sacred Te Ati tree) in all its treatments; the ingredients are used in Pearl Resort spas across French Polynesia. The all-Tahitian staff are trained in an endless range of massages, four-hand massage technique, and barefoot bodywork.

Maru Spa (✉ *Bora Bora Lagoon Resort & Spa, Motu Toopua* ☎ *60–40–00* ⊕ *www.boraboralagoon.com* ◷ *Daily 8–6*) has the only beachfront/tree-house spa in French Polynesia. Two elevated treatment rooms are hidden among the banyan tees, while the ground floor has a couple's massage room and sunken bath that offers coconut and flower petal soaking treatments with views over the lagoon.

Miri Miri Spa (✉ *St Regis Resort, Motu Ome* ☎ *60–78–40* ⊕ *www.stregis.com/borabora* ◷ *Daily 9:30–6, Jan. to May; 8:30–7, June to Dec.*) is located on its own little island, which is connected to the main resort island by a walkway. It has a little waterfall and pool and the entire spa occupies 13,000 square feet (1,207 square meters). Seven suites provide the ultimate in pampering including the intriguing signature treatment, the Heremoana Facial. It begins with a pressure point massage using warmed black pearls followed by the application of a mother-of-pearl salve, which is part of the Robert Wan cosmetic range; it leaves the face refreshed and hydrated.

AFTER DARK

Bora Bora is a honeymoon resort and its inhabitants tend to stay indoors. However, there are a few bars that stay open late and one late-night club. There are also cultural dance performances you can check out.

The best place for quiet, sunset cocktails are the motu resort bars to the east of the main island or any bar on the main island with a view to Mt. Otemanu and Mt. Pahia.

BARS & CLUBS

Bloody Mary's (⊠*PK 4.8, Paofai Bay* ☎*67–72–86* ⊕*www.borabora island.com/bloodymarys* ⊗*Closed Sun.*). This island institution, named after the famous character in James A. Michener's *Tales of the South Pacific* and the musical *South Pacific*, has been buzzing for almost 30 years. The bar's open late every night of the week except Sunday and there's occasional music.

Club Med (⊠*PK 8, Aponapu Bay* ⊕*www.clubmed.com/borabora* ⊗*Sun.–Fri. until midnight, Sat. until 1* AM). Nonguests pay a cover of 1,000–1,500 CFP, which includes a free drink, to join this party. There's dancing on Saturday nights.

Le Recif (⊠*near Bora Bora Yacht Club, PK 2.5 north, Vaitape* ☎*67– 73–87* ⊗*Fri. and Sat. 11* PM*–3* AM). If you want to drink and dance late into the night, this is the only nightclub on the island. The party goes well past 3 AM and attracts a young, often boisterous crowd of mostly locals who groove to hip-hop, reggae, and funk.

PERFORMANCES

Almost all the big hotels and resorts have a Tahitian dance show once a week where girls wearing grass skirts and coconut bras vigorously sway their hips and sing. The more exciting performances will feature fire dancing, performed by men, as well.

ISLAND-HOPPING

It's possible to do Maupiti in a day trip from Bora Bora; the Maupiti Express leaves Bora Bora Tuesday, Thursday, and Saturday mornings, returning in the late afternoon. It's a quick look but it will be fun mingling with locals and other adventurers.

MAUPITI

You could say Maupiti is a smaller version of Bora Bora—there's a main island sitting in a large lagoon surrounded by several motu that have long, creamy white beaches. Apart from Maupiti's high peaks (Mt. Teurufaaitu is 1,130 feet [344 meters]) being half the size of its neighbor's and its motu being considerably longer, the real difference is the peace, quiet, and unspoiled nature. It's a haven for those wanting to escape the international resorts and Jet Skis and boats zipping across the lagoon. In fact, the locals are doing their best to keep ritzy resorts away. Its 18 square km (7 square mi) are home to only 1,200 people who are involved in agriculture and tourism—melons and copra are the main crops—and there are a handful of pensions and tours available. In name there are two towns—Farauru and Vai'ea—but there's really only one as the two run together with a church, a few offices, and one snack bar. The road is 10 km (6 mi) long and it virtually clings to the coast the whole way; it takes two to three hours to walk it and over an hour to cycle it.

Maupiti is said to be the oldest of the Society Islands, having being formed 4 millions years ago. Excavated graves on the northern motu of Pae'ao date to AD 850, as do some of the marae. There are also ancient turtle petroglyphs (stone carvings) on the main island. Dutch explorer Jakob Roggeveen sighted and recorded the island in 1722 but it remained forgotten for many years. Today, life goes on as it has for hundreds of years and turtles still nest on the isolated beaches. You'll share this untouched landscape with hundreds of seabirds that nest around Vai'ea and the manta rays and fish that inhabit the shallow lagoon. The best snorkeling is at Onoiau, the fast-flowing pass between Pitiahe and Tiapaa motus; it's also the only entrance into the lagoon.

GETTING HERE & AROUND

Maupiti is 315 km (196 mi) west of Tahiti and 40 km (25 mi) from Bora Bora. There are around seven flights a week from Pape'ete in the high season; some days there are no flights, others there are two. Flight time is about an hour direct and two hours with a stopover in Bora Bora or Raiatea. The Maupiti Express ferry operates between Bora Bora and Maupiti, leaving Bora Bora at 8:30 AM Tuesday, Thursday, and Saturday. It returns the same day at 4 PM.

You can't rent cars on the island, but you can walk around the 10-km (6-mi) road in two to three hours, rent a bicycle from a pension, or take an organized island tour or lagoon excursion. You can even walk across the shallow lagoon from the main island to Motu Auira in the west. ⚠ **The island does not have a tourist office.**

ESSENTIALS

Ferry Maupiti Express (✉ *Vaitape Wharf Bora Bora* ☎ *67–66–69* 💷 *2,000 CFP one-way; 3,000 CFP return*).

WHAT TO SEE

Maupiti's pretty low-key and you can really explore it on your own, by bike, or by foot. Pensions will organize a half-day or full-day excursion on the lagoon, which can cost from 2,500 to 5,000 CFP depending on whether a picnic is included.

Tereia Beach is the main island's only beach and it's on the western side of the island. It's often completely deserted and there are no shops. You can even walk across the lagoon at low tide to Motu Auira. The best beaches are on Motu Auira, to the west of Maupiti, and Motu Tuanai, to the east. They are long and white, with crushed coral in the sand. Beaches line the azure blue lagoon and make for classic island paradise vistas with palm trees bending towards the water, while it's only

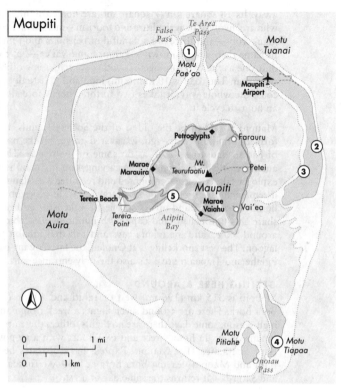

a short walk from the lagoon to the ocean on most motus so there's really two beaches—the calm one and the ocean beach with waves. In the low season (February to May) you may have long stretches of sand to yourself.

Some of the island's marae date to the 9th century. The Marauira marae is on the west coast and Vaiahu marae is on the south. Ancient graves are located on Motu Pae'ao in the north, and turtle petroglyphs are on the north side of the main island. The petroglyphs are often hard to find; ask the pension owner or someone in main village for help.

Hina's Tiare, the little flower known as the *moon goddess* in Tahitian, grows only on Maupiti and Motu Pitiahe in the south.

WHERE TO STAY

There are no big hotels with swimming pools or fancy facilities on Maupiti, nor are there any restaurants (beyond one small snack bar) on the island. The best (and most economical) option is to go with a Modified American plan (aka half board or "demi-pension") or all-inclusive (aka full-board package) at a pension.

Pensions are small, with no more than seven bungalows apiece; some only have one or two fares (another name for bungalow). The best of these are located on the motu as these long islands also have the best beaches. If you're staying on the main island, it's quite easy to get a boat transfer over to a motu and vice versa. Only a handful of pensions have bathrooms with hot water; even fewer have TVs in the room or air-conditioning.

> **TINY TUPAI**
>
> The small island of Tupai is 13 km (8 mi) north of Bora Bora. There are no resorts or hotels on the island, and the only residents are plantation workers.

3

$$ **Fare Pae'ao.** You'll have handy access to historical sites when staying at this pension on the motu of the same name. There are six cute bungalows with private bathrooms (some have hot water) and little terraces from which you can watch incredible sunsets. There are also fully equipped kitchens if you feel like cooking, although a communal dining room does provide all meals. **Pros:** Sea access; linens and mosquito nets provided. **Cons:** No a/c; only some bathrooms have hot water. ⊠*Motu Pae'ao* ⌖*B.P. 33, Vai'ea* ☎*67–81–01* ⊕*www.haere-mai.pf* ⟿*6 bungalows* ⌂*In-room: no a/c, no phone, kitchen (some), refrigerator (some). In-hotel: restaurant, beachfront, water sports, bicycles, no elevator, laundry facilities, airport shuttle* ▤*MC, V* ⍨*MAP.*

$$$$ **Kuriri Village.** This pension is about as remote as you can get on Maupiti. It's on Motu Tiapaa, has five bungalows and miles of beach to explore by snorkel or canoe, which are provided. All bathrooms are shared, but do have hot water. **Pros:** Ceiling fans in the rooms; sea access; mosquito nets and linens provided. **Cons:** No Internet or phone access; no a/c; no private bathrooms. ⊠*Motu Tiapaa* ⌖*B.P. 23, Maupiti* ☎*67–82–23* ⊕*www.Maupiti-kuriri.com* ⟿*5 bungalows* ⌂*In-room: no a/c. In-hotel: restaurant, beachfront, water sports, bicycles, no elevator, airport shuttle* ▤*MC, V* ⍨*MAP.*

¢ **Pension Marau.** This ocean-side pension is a hit with surfers and those who like their holidays to come with an adrenaline rush. The owner of this small place will teach you how to kite surf—a fast-moving sport similar to snowboarding where you're attached to a harness and hang onto what looks like a parasail. Each bungalow can accommodate five people and the bathrooms are spacious but there's no hot water. Meals are available on a half-board and full-board basis. **Pros:** Ceiling fans in the rooms; sea access; mosquito nets and linens provided. **Cons:** No Internet or phone access; no a/c; no private bathrooms. ⊠*Motu Tuanai* ⌖*B.P. 11, Maupiti* ☎*67–81–19* ⊕*www.pension-marau.com* ⟿*7 bungalows* ⌂*In-room: no a/c, no phone (some), no TV. In-hotel: restaurant, beachfront, diving, water sports, bicycles, no elevator, airport shuttle* ▤*No credit cards* ⍨*EP.*

$ **Pension Poe Iti.** Each bungalow, which can sleep up to three people, has hot-water bathrooms, air-conditioning, and a room TV, which is about as glamorous as it gets on Maupiti. It's located on the same motu as the airport (to the east of the main island), and transfers are free. You can be a modern day castaway and when you yearn to see the handful of buildings on the main island village, hop in a canoe and paddle the half-mile channel across. **Pros:** Airports transfers are free; sea access; linens provided. **Cons:** No Internet or phone access; no mosquito nets.

⊠*Motu Tuanai* ☜*B.P. 39, Vai'ea* ☏*74–58–76 maupitiexpress@mail. pf* ⬐*4 bungalows* ♻*In-room: no phone, refrigerator (some). In-hotel: restaurant, beachfront, water sports, bicycles, no elevator, laundry facilities, airport shuttle* ⊟*No credit cards* ⍟*MAP.*

$ ⊡**Pension Tautiare Village.** This guesthouse is quite a departure from most island accommodations. It is a large, newish house on the south coast of the main island about 2 mi from the main village. It has four bedrooms each with private bathroom with hot water and terrace, and one room with a shared hot-water bathroom. All meals are offered and the owners will provide take-away picnics at 1,500 CFP for those who wish to go exploring all day. **Pros:** Ceiling fans in the rooms; sea access; linens provided. **Cons:** No Internet or phone access; no mosquito nets. ⊠*Vai'ea* ⊠*B.P. 16, Vai'ea* ☏*60–15–90* ⬐*5 rooms* ♻*In-room: no a/c, no phone. In-hotel: restaurant, beachfront, water sports, bicycles, no elevator, laundry facilities, airport shuttle* ⊟*No credit cards* ⍟*MAP.*

Huahine

WORD OF MOUTH

"Huahine was an interesting island. We took an inland tour. We were shown where they had/have ancestor worship and we fed the sacred eels. Chicken and roosters run free."

—cd

Written by
Caroline
Gladstone

ALTHOUGH IT LIES BETWEEN MOOREA and Bora Bora, Huahine (pronounced Hu-a-hee-nee or Wha-hee-nee) isn't on the tourist circuit just yet, but it should be. Its near-deserted roads and villages and wooded hills entwined with jungle vines beckon those looking for a little R&R.

Huahine is two islands (Huahine Nui and Huahine Iti) joined by a bridge. What passes for action takes place in the main town of Fare (pronounced far-ay) on Huahine Nui, the northern and bigger island. Away from this little port, life is slow-paced and you'll be lucky to find anyone stirring on a lazy afternoon in any of the villages of Huahine Iti. Most locals ride bicycles and agriculture's still the main industry—plantations grow vanilla and melons.

There are various legends surrounding the island's name. Some say that *hua* means "sex" and *hine* means "woman," while others say the name means "pregnant woman" due to a rock outline on Huahine Nui's Fitii Peninsula. Then there's the legend of Hiro, Polynesia's most famous god. It's said that Hiro rammed his canoe into the island, splitting it down the middle. Not far from the town of Maroe is a rock spire called *Te Moa o Hiro* or "penis of Hiro"—you can't miss it.

ORIENTATION & PLANNING

ORIENTATION

HUAHINE NUI

Huahine Nui contains the airport in the north and Fare, the port and main town, in the northwest; Maeva village, with numerous marae, is in the northeast. A 20-km road (15 mi) road circles the island and crosses over the bridge to Huahine Iti about a mile or so south of the town of Fitii. The views of the two bays—the smaller Bourayne Bay and the sweeping Maroe Bay—are fantastic here.

HUAHINE ITI

Huahine Iti is quieter than its northern neighbor and has four small blink-and-you'll-miss-it villages: Maroe (north), Tefarerii (east), Parea (south), and Haapu (west). Maroe Bay is to the left of the bridge when crossing over from Huahine Nui. There are great views of the bay and the rock protrusion known as Hiro's phallus from Maroe. The island's best accommodation and beaches are found in Parea.

PLANNING

GETTING HERE AND AROUND

Huahine lies 170 km (112 mi) northwest of Tahiti. Air Tahiti operates three to six flights a day from Pape'ete, depending on the season, with flight time of 30 minutes. There's also one flight a day between Moorea and Huahine, and twice daily flights between Bora Bora and Huahine on Tuesdays, Thursdays, and Fridays and daily on the other days. A daily flight (except on Sunday) operates between Raiatea and Huahine.

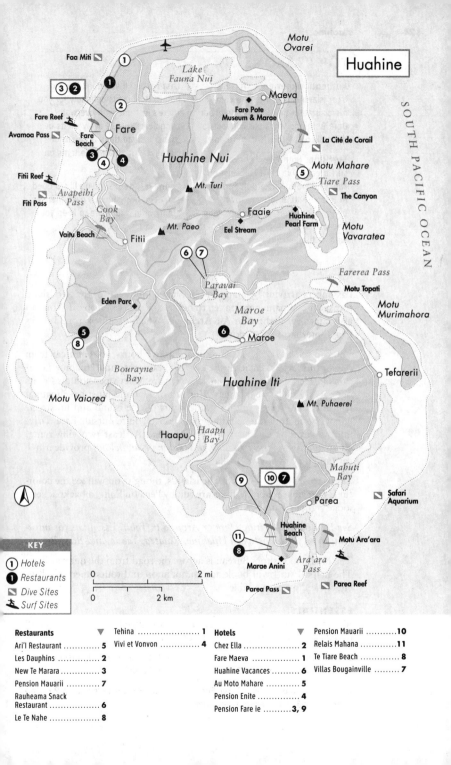

Huahine

SOUTH PACIFIC OCEAN

Motu Ovarei
Lake Fauna Nui
Maeva
Fare Pote
Museum & Marae
Faa Miti
Fare Reef
Avamoa Pass
Fare
Fare Beach
Fitii Reef
Fiti Pass
Avapeihi Pass
Cook Bay
Vaitu Beach
Fitii
La Cité de Corail
Motu Mahare
Tiare Pass
The Canyon
Huahine Nui
Mt. Turi
Faaie
Eel Stream
Huahine Pearl Farm
Motu Vavaratea
Mt. Paeo
Paravai Bay
Farerea Pass
Motu Topati
Eden Parc
Maroe Bay
Maroe
Motu Murimahora
Bourayne Bay
Tefarerii
Motu Vaiorea
Huahine Iti
Mt. Puhaerei
Haapu
Haapu Bay
Mahuti Bay
Parea
Safari Aquarium
Huahine Beach
Motu Ara'ara
Marae Anini
Ara'ara Pass
Parea Pass
Parea Reef

KEY
① Hotels
● Restaurants
◪ Dive Sites
⚓ Surf Sites

0 — 2 mi
0 — 2 km

Restaurants ▼
Ari'l Restaurant **5**
Les Dauphins **2**
New Te Marara **3**
Pension Mauarii **7**
Rauheama Snack Restaurant **6**
Le Te Nahe **8**

Tehina **1**
Vivi et Vonvon **4**

Hotels ▼
Chez Ella **2**
Fare Maeva **1**
Huahine Vacances **6**
Au Moto Mahare **5**
Pension Enite **4**
Pension Fare ie **3, 9**

Pension Mauarii **10**
Relais Mahana **11**
Te Tiare Beach **8**
Villas Bougainville **7**

TOP REASONS TO VISIT HUAHINE

Authentic experience. This laid-back island is free from the commercialization that ravages neighbor Bora Bora and you'll easily adapt to the chilled environment in no time.

Surf's up. Both islands have great surf breaks: Ava Mo'a Pass just off Fare and Motu Aara'ara in Parea in Huahine Iti. Bring your own board, reef shoes, and a good vibe because locals don't like interlopers with "attitude."

Last resort. If you don't like big hotels, Huahine is definitely for you. There's just one with overwater bungalows, tucked away on its own island. Instead there are pensions, cottages, and safari-style tents on the beach.

Myths & legends. If you like a good story and a mysterious past, there's plenty of intrigue here to keep you guessing for days.

Passengers arriving by plane will be picked up by one of the two island transport companies and taken to hotels in a general drop off. You can also charter a flight with Air Archipels, which operates from Tahiti's Faa'a International Airport.

You can see most of the island in about five hours, so rent a car from one of the three agencies in Fare—Avis, Europcar and Huahine Locations (a Hertz agent)—at your leisure; Fare Maeva pension also rents out cars. You'll probably get a Renault or Fiat and most have manual transmissions. There are no traffic lights on the island and no streetlights illuminating the winding roads, once you're outside Fare. Driving, however, is easy as traffic is minimal. At least two villa rental companies (*See Where to Stay, in Huahine Nui, below*) provide a free car (and boat) with each villa.

There are no public buses on the islands, though you will see the colorful *L'Truck* buses about. Taxis are run by Pension Enite, a backpackers' lodge right at Fare wharf.

See By Boat, in Getting Here & Around in Tahiti Essentials for information on ferries between Huahine, Raiatea, Tahaa, and Bora Bora.

The Huahine Visitors Bureau is across the road from the quay at Fare. The helpful staff will book accommodation and tours; there are brochures and maps available.

ESSENTIALS

Airlines Air Archipels (☎ 81–30–30 ⊕ www.airarchipels.com). **Air Tahiti** (☎ 68–77–02 or 60–62–60 ⊕ www.airtahiti.com).

Banks Banque Socredo (✉ Fare ☎ 60–63–60). **Banque de Polynesie** (✉ Fare ☎ 60–61–41). **Banque de Tahiti** (✉ Fare ☎ 68–82–46).

Car Rentals Avis (☎ 68–73–34). **Europcar** (☎ 68–88–03). **Fare Maeva Pension** (☎ 68–75–53 ⊕ www.fare-maeva.com).

Emergencies **Police** (☎*60-63-10 or 68-73-28*). **Medical Center** (☎*68-82-48*). **Pharmacy** (☎*60-61-41*). **Doctors** (☎*68-82-20*).

Taxis **Pension Enite** (☎*68-82-37*).

Visitor Info **Huahine Visitors Bureau** (☎*68-78-81* ⊙ *Mon.-Thurs. 8-4, Fri. 8-3*).

WHEN TO GO

Huahine has a similar climate to the other islands of the Society Archipelago. The warmer wet season (November to April) sees temperatures ranging from 27 to 30° C (80 to 86° F). The cooler, dry season—and peak tourist season—is May through October and temperatures range from 24 to 28° C (75 to 82° F). The lagoon temperature is 26° C (79° F) year-round.

The annual Hawaiki Nui Va'a, the greatest canoe race in the South Pacific, departs from Huahine in late October. One hundred canoes are launched from the west coast, race across the lagoon to Raiatea and finish in Bora Bora three days later.

TAKE IT ALL IN

The combination of Huahine's slow pace and its interesting sights, good hiking opportunities, and extensive bays and blue lagoon mean you'll want to take it easy and explore while you're here. An itinerary of at least three nights is recommended, though five nights is ideal.

3 Days: On Day 1 settle into your accommodation and get your bearings. If you're staying on Huahine Nui, head to Fare for the island action. Spend the day poking around the little port—you'll see Tahaa, Bora Bora, and Raiatea in the distance. Stop by the New Te Marara for a cocktail just in time to watch the spectacular sunset. Sign yourself up for a 4WD circle island tour on Day 2—make sure it also goes into the interior; you might combine this with a half-day outrigger canoe trip and *motu* (islet) picnic lunch. On Day 3 grab one of your pension's free canoes or kayaks and do your own exploring. If you want to see Huahine's "wild side" you might want to pack up and move down to Huahine Iti and stay in a groovy tent at the Fare ie Pension on the beach. You can rent a car and get groceries in Fare. Budget in enough time to be able to stop along the way at cute little churches and the very occasional roadside snack or shop.

5 Days: If you have two more days, you can take the car up to Maeva for your own *marae* (ancient temples) hillside tour. If you saw enough temples on your 4WD tour, opt for one of the many outdoor activities on offer—horseback riding on the beach, a visit to the pearl farm, renting a speedboat, scuba diving, or a hike into the hills. On Day 5 you'll need a rest, so have a swim, a paddle, or surf (at Parea) in the morning and then take it easy in the afternoon.

HEALTH & SAFETY

Huahine is a very safe place to spend a few days. But, as there are no streetlights beyond the main street of Fare, be careful walking or cycling along the roads at night. Carry a flashlight or lantern.

TOURING TIPS

Early nights. There are no street-lights to illuminate the palm tree-lined coastal road that winds around Huahine Nui and Iti, making driving a little bit tricky. If you do drive after dark use high beam as there are usually cyclists and people walking along the road.

Slow down. The island isn't big but there are many marae to discover at Maeva. Give yourself plenty of time to walk around these fascinating sites, right by the Lake Fauna Nui.

Simple life. You won't find sophisti-cated restaurants or any nightlife on the island. It's a step back in time; chill out and enjoy it.

Wise planning. Car rental is pricey, so plan what you want to do so you won't waste money on a car you don't use. If you're staying three days, chill out and get your bearings on arrival, take a lagoon or mountain excursion another day, and hire a car on Day 3.

Conversely, watch out for cyclists and pedestrians on the road after dark and use your high beams when driving.

EAT RIGHT, SLEEP WELL

Don't expect a variety of luxurious accommodations on Huahine. There are only two hotels and only one—the newly renamed Te Tiare Beach Pearl Resort—has overwater bungalows. There are, however, some funky accommodations in Huahine Iti, such as comfortable "tents" with fabulous furnishings and a couple of very good value for money self-catering villas on Huahine Nui where a car and boat come with the daily rate.

Hotels and most pensions have restaurants and can offer half-board (MAP) options, while some small establishments include breakfast and airport transfers. Most of the island's independent restaurants are in Fare. You'll find similar menus at most restaurants and these usually include *poisson cru*, shrimp, and grilled fish, meat, and lobster—most accompanied with vanilla sauce—as well as desserts like coconut tart with vanilla ice cream. Independent restaurants tend to be cheaper and serve bigger portions. There are a couple of roulottes at the wharf in Fare, which sell chow mein, lemon chicken, stir-fries, rice, and pizza. Prices are around 1,100 CFP a dish and portions are big. Tipping is not expected, but will of course be accepted.

WHAT IT COSTS IN FRANC COURS PACIFIQUE (CFP)				
	¢	$	$$	$$$	$$$$
RESTAURANTS	under 1,000	1,001–1,500	1,501–2,500	2,501–3,300	over 3,300
HOTELS	under 8,000	8,001–16,000	16,001–27,000	27,001–40,000	over 40,000

Restaurant prices are for a main course at dinner. Hotel prices are for a double room in high season, excluding 10% tax, 10%–15% service charges, and meals plans (except at all-inclusives).

EXPLORING HUAHINE

It's easy to explore Huahine (75 square km [47 square mi]) by rental car, as there is really only one road, albeit with a few forks in it. When you cross the bridge into Huahine Iti you can go either left to Maroe or right to Parea. The road to Haapu leads off to a dead end.

When crossing from Huahine Iti to Nui the same rule applies. Take the left fork to the "busy" town of Fare and the right fork to the "sacred eel" village of Faaie, via the Belvedere lookout.

Hiring your own boat allows you to circle the island and anchor at the motu; a couple of self-catering villas provide both a car and a boat. There are only one or two restaurants on Huahine Iti; you either eat at your pension, choose a pension with cooking facilities, or drive up to Fare for a wider, though still rather limited, choice.

HUAHINE NUI

TOWNS

Fare. This little town fits the stereotype of a sleepy South Seas port with market stalls lining the road, men fishing from the wharf at sunset, and a few shops and restaurants here and there. However, expect a bit of a traffic jam outside the Fare Super Nui, the island's only supermarket, and a big one at that. There are two parts to Fare: the busy quay or port (mentioned above), which is reached by turning off the main island road, and other businesses, such as the post office, bank, Europcar, pharmacy, restaurant, and Catholic church, which are strung out along the main road for half a mile or so. The quay is the place to watch brilliant sunsets over the distant isles of Tahaa and Bora Bora and pull up a stool to dine at the *roulottes* (food trucks) that open around 6 PM.

Maeva. The historic and cultural heart of Huahine is on the southeast shore of Lake Fauna Nui. Here you can stroll through an open museum of ancient marae or walk a mile-long trail on the hillside that's strewn with archeological sites (see below for more details). The town's other significant attraction is several old fish traps located in the eastern corner of the lake. Fish swim into these triangular structures at high tide and are trapped when the tide runs out. There's also a pleasant little church, a school and playgrounds; at 3 PM you may get caught behind the colorful school bus as it drops kids off at their homes along the main road.

Faaie. If Fare is sleepy, then Faaie—on the east coast about 2 mi south of Maeva—is in a coma. It only wakes when a tour group or individuals stop to the see the blue-eye eels that live in the river. The eels' favorite dish is tinned mackerel and the constant feeding over the years has turned them into little pets—most tour operators include this on a round-island tour. Beyond the eels, there's a small church and corner store and once you go over the Belvedere hill towards the bridge, there's a town hall and primary school (both painted apricot).

BEACHES

Fare Beach. Just a few hundred yards north of Fare quay is a popular beach for locals and the few tourists who discover it. When driving along the main road (from the airport to Fare) turn off to the right near the Europcar rental agency and drive along an unpaved road for 100 yards. There's a stall selling drinks during the day, lots of yachts in the bay, kids playing, people snorkeling, and a distant view of Bora Bora.

STAY CONNECTED

There are two Internet cafés in Fare, both near the quay. **AO Api New World** (☎ 68–70–99) is located above the Tourism Bureau. It costs 15 CFP for one minute—which is cheap for French Polynesia—and the connection is quite fast, although the keyboard is French. **Video Shop Huahine** (☎ 60–67–40) in Fare also has Internet.

Vaitu Beach. This is truly a lovely beach and the inlet is dotted with a few boats at their moorings. It's a bit hard to find this beach, so ask directions at your hotel or the visitors' bureau in Fare. ⚓ *Off the coastal road, west of Fitii.*

SIGHTS

Eden Parc. This large organic garden and orchard was established in 1986 by horticulturalist and committed environmentalist Gilles Te Hau Parzy. It's a self-sufficient park, with a huge collection of tropical fruit trees and medicinal plants, that adopts renewable energy and other ecological practices. Visitors can walk around the gardens, take a two-hour tour, have lunch and sample fruit juices. There's a shop selling jams, sun-dried bananas, herbs, and spices. Lunch costs 1,000 CFP and includes a salad of 10 tropical vegetables followed by flambé bananas with vanilla rum. ⚓ *A mi southwest of Fitii. Follow the sign from Hotel Bellevue.* ☎ 68–86–58 ⊕ *www.edenparc.org* ⬛ *300 CFP* ⊙ *Mon.–Sat. 9–4. Closed mid-Dec.–mid-Jan. End of Feb.–mid-Mar, Oct. 6–26.*

Huahine Pearl Farm. If you've had your fill of pearl farms, this—the only one in Huahine—may change your mind. Both the farm and a separate pottery studio (owned by ex-Californian Peter Owen and his Tahitian-born wife Ghislaine) are located on an island in the middle of the lagoon and a boat will whisk you to one, then the other, from the town of Faaie. You'll learn about the long processes involved before a cultivated pearl is hatched, watch technicians at work, and browse the small boutique where you can check out the couple's pottery: Peter makes the vases and urns and his wife and son paint them with Polynesian designs. ⚓ *Main Road, mile north of Faaie* ☎ 68–73–27 ⊕ *www. huahinepearlfarm.com* ⬛ *Free* ⊙ *10–3, boat transfers every 15 mins.*

Marae & Fare Pote Museum. Maeva is rich in archeological sites; there are the remains of a handful on the shore of Lake Fauna Nui along with

TOPOGRAPHY

Huahine is two mountainous massifs separated by two bays—Bourayne Bay in the west and Maroe Bay in the east—with a short, narrow bridge connecting them. The series of high peaks on both islands are the remains of collapsed volcanoes. The highest is Mt. Turi (2,200 feet [670 meters]) on Huahine Nui, while Mt. Puhaerei on Huahine Iti reaches 1,460 feet (445 meters). The two islands are surrounded by a pristine narrow lagoon with several long motu off the east coast. The lagoon is quite narrow at the northeast corner and contains several ancient fish traps, which look like little thatched houses floating on the water. At the top of the island is Lake Fauna Nui, an almost landlocked body of salt water save for a narrow channel leading into the lagoon. The highest point accessible by car is the Belvedere, a lookout on Huahine Nui that has wonderful views of Maroe Bay and Huahine Iti.

4

a replica of a 19th-century *fare pote* (meeting house). Today the meeting house is used as a museum and cultural center, displaying ancient tools, woven cloth, and historical pictures. It's only open when cruise ships are in port. The 2.5-km (1.5-mi) Matairea-rahi trail is virtually littered with the remnants of ancient temples and islanders' home; some 20 or so can be seen on the trail. The Matairea-rahi Marae was the most important temple in the Society Islands before the building of Taputapuatea on the island of Raiatea, and was used for solemn ceremonies including human sacrifices. Signs, in English and French, can be found near the lakeside marae and the Fare Pote. They explain the meaning of temple design and the purpose of the replica wooden totem poles (some decorated with animals) that are wedged into the stone platforms on the lakeshore. The path leading to the hillside trail, however, is a little tricky to find. You will find the start of the trail a little farther along the road from the public bathroom. ⊠ *Main Rd., Maeva* 🕮 *200 CFP* ☉ *10–4, when cruise ships are in port.*

HUAHINE ITI

A 20-km (14-mi) road circles Huahine Iti but you're unlikely to see much traffic on it, especially in the low season (January to April). The road around the island is dotted with small *magasins* (grocery stores), a few pensions, and one midsize hotel with pool. The villages are so small you only know you've arrived when you see a church or school. The island's interior is densely wooded and jungle-like in parts, the view from the town of Maroe across the bay of the same name is spectacular and the best beach at Parea also has its own marae.

TOWNS

Maroe. Situated on the Maroe Bay, this village has a rotunda on the water's edge, a big billboard style map of the island, a buttercup-colored Protestant church with adjoining church hall, a little restaurant serving fish, and a few baguette sandwiches, and that's about it. It does, however, have a spectacular view over the wide bay where the cruise ships dock. Passengers are brought ashore at Maroe at the rotunda site where they then board *L'Truck* buses for circle tours or meet their 4WD tour operators or rental car agents. If you look to the east you can't miss Te Moa o Hiro, the looming phallus-shaped rock. The restaurant, Rauheama, is a popular watering hole for ship passengers. *See Where to Eat, in Huhine Iti, below, for a full review of the restaurant.*

Parea. With its two sizeable lodgings *(see Where to Stay, in Huhine Iti, below, for a full review)*, a white church, small tidy little houses in secluded lanes off the main road, a restaurant, a roadside snack bar, and the occasional small grocery store, this village—that stretches for a couple of mi with big gaps between most of the infrastructure—could be considered the epicenter of Huahine Iti. The island's best beach is here (at the southern tip) and the Anini Marae (also called the Parea Marae) is virtually standing on the shore. Across the lagoon is Motu Aara'ara. ✛ *At the southwest and southern tip of the island.*

Tefarerii. This tiny village midway down the east coast has a butter-cup-yellow church on one side of the road and a small graveyard on the other, which is backed by rain-forest covered hills. Across the lagoon is Motu Murimahora, a lush island where melon growing is the main activity.

BEACHES
Ara'ara. This is both the name of the motu and a great surfing beach at the southern tip of Huahine Iti. It's about 2 km (1 mi) south of the hotel Relais Mahana. Slow down when you see a sign for the archeological site of Marae Anini. Follow the road to the marae and there's the beach. It's a fantastic place for photos—the black basalt of the marae against the azure blue lagoon. The sand is coral and rocky. The surf is good here and you may see a few surfers out towards the reef. It's a quiet spot, which you just may have to yourself.

SIGHTS
Marae Anini. This marae is located at one of the best locations on the island—virtually on the tip of Parea. It functioned as the island's temple long before Europeans arrived. Sacrifices, including human ones (to Oro the god of war), were said to have taken place here.

WHERE TO STAY

You won't find a dozen big resorts extending their pontoons of overwa-ter bungalows into the lagoon. In fact, the Te Tiare Beach Resort is the island's only luxury hotel with those iconic accommodations and it's hidden away on a private island. Apart from the resort there's only one other hotel with a swimming pool. Keen observers will notice an aban-doned resort just across the lagoon from Maeva. It's what's left of the

Sofitel Maeva, which closed in 2004. Locals say someone has bought it and a new hotel will be built there. In the meantime, Huahine is blessed with a good range of pensions, a few self-catering villas, smart safari-style tents, backpacker hostels, and a camping site. Be warned there are a lot of roosters on Huahine (especially Huahine Iti), and if you're next door to a few you'll be woken up at all hours.

HUAHINE NUI

SELF-CATERING HOUSES

¢–$

Chez Ella. This small complex is five minutes from the airport and five minutes from Fare by car. There are two pleasant little semidetached houses (each with its own entrance) in a nice garden, each with two bedrooms, a bathroom, terrace, and garage. Each house can sleep six people. There's also a separate two-story cottage (or mezzanine as they are called in French Polynesia) that can sleep up to 10 people. The accommodations are neat and clean with bright tropical curtains and bedcovers. There are half-board meal plans at approx 3,200 CFP per person. **Pros:** Well priced; rate includes airport transfers; each accommodation has a fully equipped kitchen and TV. **Cons:** Not near the lagoon or beach. ⊠ *Main Road, near airport road turn-off Fare* ☎ *B.P. 421, Fare 98731* ☎ *68–73–07* ⊕ *www.iaorana-huahine.com* ⇆ *3 houses* ⌂ *In-room: no a/c (some), no phone (some), kitchen, refrigerator, VCR (some). In-hotel: laundry facilities, airport shuttle, parking (no fee)* ⊟ *MC, V* ⌊○⌉ *EP.*

$

Huahine Vacances. These two- and three-bedroom houses, just a stone's throw from the Bay of Maroe, represent the ultimate in freedom. The daily rate includes a small, five-person car and a small motor boat, which can fit six people. The three all-white houses are 100 or so yards away from each other and there's a fourth located high on the hill above the others. They have all the modern conveniences such as a microwave, stove, fridge, TV, iron, washing machine, and hair dryer and are furnished with comfortable sofa and chairs and have double and single beds. Prices are charged according to the number of guests. Fishing gear is also provided, the owner's wife will babysit for a fee, and free airport/port transfers are provided. **Pros:** A large supermarket is only a short drive away; daily rate includes your own car and a small speedboat; stay six nights and get the seventh night free. **Cons:** Not on a beach. ⊠ *PK 10, Huahine Nui's main road* ⊹ *Take a right at the bridge and head towards Faaie* ☎ *BP 10, Fare* ☎ *68–73–63* ⊕ *www.huahinevacances.com* ⇆ *4 houses* ⌂ *In-room: kitchen, refrigerator. In-hotel: spa, beachfront, water sports, bikes, no elevator, laundry facilities, parking (no fee)* ⊟ *MC, V* ⌊○⌉ *EP.*

$$–$$$

Villas Bougainville. This is an identical operation to Huahine Vacances and these villas, only a little distance from each other, compete head to head. There's a boat and car for guests to use, and a choice of fan-cooled or air-conditioned villa. Villas have TVs with satellite reception, DVD players, fully equipped kitchens, washing machines, and choice of two or three bedrooms. Minimum stay is three nights and there are discounts for longer stays. Airport/quay transfers are free, while babysitting can be arranged for a fee. **Pros:** Daily rate includes your own car

A BRIEF HISTORY

Rich archeological sites discovered in Maeva on the island's northeast coast reveal a civilization dating back to AD 850; this area has the greatest concentration of marae (ancient temples) in French Polynesia. The marae are what's left of a royal compound where the island's eight chiefs lived side by side and was totally out of bounds to commoners.

Captain Cook set eyes on the island in 1769 and the first English missionaries arrived in 1809. The island has a history of fierce independence and national spirit; warriors fended off French invaders in 1844 and were engaged in a series of bitter skirmishes until 1897 when the French finally annexed the island. Today there's a strong sense of identity and pride, evident in the number of red and white Maohi flags that can be seen around the island—Maohi are Polynesian ancestors.

and a small boat. **Cons:** Not on a beach. ⚓ *Huahine Nui's main road, take right at bridge and head towards Faaie ⌂BP 258, Fare 98731 ☎60–60–30 ⊕www.villas-bougainville.com ⛱4 villas ⌕In-room: a/c (some), kitchen (some), refrigerator, DVD. In-hotel: beachfront, water sports, laundry facilities, laundry service, airport shuttle, parking (no fee) ⊟MC, V ⏉EP.*

RESORTS
$$$–$$$$

▦ **Te Tiare Beach.** Located on an island just off the southwest tip of Huahine Nui, this is the most luxurious resort in Huahine and the only one with overwater bungalows. Regular complimentary boat transfers run between the resort and Fare quay. Accommodation includes garden, beachside, and overwater bungalows with the latter being either "shallow-water" or "deep-water." All bungalows are spacious and furnished with large rattan sofa, oversize armchairs, marble-top coffee table, and desk; bathrooms have granite double vanities, while overwater bungalow bathrooms have Jacuzzis. Tahitian company Pearl Resorts took over the resort, which opened in 1999, in March 2008. **Pros:** Isolated position with lovely sunset views to Raiatea & Tahaa. **Cons:** Pricey. ⚓ *Motu, off southwest trip of Huahine Iti. ⌂BP 36, Fare 98731 ☎60–60–60, 888/600–8455 ⊕www.tetiarebeachresort.com ⛱41 bungalows ⌕In-room: refrigerator. In-hotel: restaurant, room service, bar, pool, beachfront, diving, water sports, bicycles, laundry service, concierge, public Internet, airport shuttle, parking (no fee) ⊟AE, MC, V ⏉EP.*

SMALL
HOTELS/
GUESTHOUSES
¢–$

▦ **Fare Maeva.** The friendly Tahitian owner, Brian Tissot, is a world traveler and speaks perfect English, which is a bonus. The 10 bungalows are clean and basic, with air-conditioning and a safe. There are also 10 rooms, which are very small, but have the benefit of private bathrooms with hot water. Each bungalow has a stove and small refrigerator. The pension has a very pleasant garden around a small pool and restaurant. Á la carte meals are available or you can opt for half-board (3,000 CFP) with a set dinner menu. Although it has a lagoon-side position, a better beach is located about half a mile away at Fare. You can also rent brand-new Fiat cars here (9,200 CFP per day and cheaper for longer rentals; includes air-conditioner). **Pros:** Friendly owner; restaurant and bar on premise. **Cons:** Basic accommodation. ✉*PK 3, Fare* ⌂*BP 675, Fare 98731* ☎*68–70–68* ⊕*www.fare-maeva.com* ⇨*10 bungalows, 10 rooms* ⌂*In-room: no phone, safe (some), kitchen (some), refrigerator (some). In-hotel: restaurant, bar, pool, beachfront, diving, water sports, bicycles, no elevator, laundry service, concierge, airport shuttle, parking (no fee)* ▭*MC, V* ¶*EP.*

¢ ▦**Au Motu Mahare.** If you yearn to stay on a tiny island and have it (almost) all to yourself—but don't mind character-building cold showers—head to Au Motu Mahare. This new two-bungalow pension opened in late 2007. Each bungalow can sleep up to three people, has a private bathroom and shared kitchens, a barbecue area, and a Fare Pote (a thatched-roof communal area). Each bungalow has a double and single bed and...a sand floor. Owners Kim and Walter also live on the island, which is just off the east coast. They will happily take you by the supermarket, on your way to the motu, to stock up on essentials. **Pros:** The daily rate includes airport transfers and the use of bikes and kayaks; beautiful, isolated location. **Cons:** Basic amenities. ✉*Motu Mahara* ⌂*BP 772, Fare 98731* ☎*77–76–97* ⇨*2 bungalows* ⌂*In-room: no a/c. In-hotel: beachfront, water sports, bicycles, no elevator, airport shuttle* ▭*No credit cards* ¶*EP.*

¢ ▦**Pension Enite.** This basic backpackers' hostels has an ideal position about a minute's walk from Fare quay. Although each of its eight bedrooms has only minimal amenities (double and/or single beds and hanging space), there's a very pleasant living area for mixing and mingling. The restaurant, with a coral floor and decorated with seafaring artifacts, is a great place to be at sunset. It's just a few feet away from the bay. Half-board is included and dinner will almost always feature fish or seafood. There's a two-night minimum stay. The owners also operate guided island tours. **Pros:** Great location near the town of Fare, the port, and restaurants. **Cons:** Minimal amenities. ✉*Fare quay road, Fare* ⌂*BP 37, Fare 98731* ☎*68–82–37* ⇨*8 rooms* ⌂*In-room: no a/c. In-hotel: restaurant, bar, beachfront, diving, water sports, no elevator, airport shuttle, parking (no fee)* ▭*No credit cards* ¶*EP.*

$$ ▦**Pension Fare ie.** These tents will redefine camping for the most outdoor-challenged soul. Two permanent safari-style tents, complete with hardwood floors, timber furniture, funky bedcovers, and indoor bathrooms, sit right on the beach just north of Fare. They can sleep two to four people and the price includes use of bikes, kayaks, snorkeling gear, and free transfers. There's a shared kitchen for whipping up meals, although breakfast can be delivered to your tent for an extra charge. The company, Tahiti Safari, recently opened a bigger all-tent complex on Huahine Iti. **Pros:** Unique accommodation; great beach location. **Cons:** Two double beds in each tent, meaning not much privacy if two couples. ✉*Just off main road, just north of Fare* ⌂*BP 746, Fare 98731* ☎*60–63–77* ⊕*www.tahitisafari.com* ⇨*2 tents* ⌂*In-room: no a/c. In-hotel: room service (breakfast only), spa, beachfront, water sports, bicycles, no elevator, airport shuttle, parking (no fee)* ▭*AE, DC, MC* ¶*EP.*

HUAHINE ITI

RESORTS
$$–$$$

⛫Relais Mahana. This is the island's second-swankiest accommodation, and its brand-new beachfront bungalows, which opened in late 2007, are lovely. They have king beds and daybeds and lots of huge cushions for lounging around on. They have high-pitched ceilings, rattan walls, and cool ceramic tiled floors; furniture includes a stylish long desk with a flat-screen TV at one end. There's a cane table and chairs on the small terrace, just steps away from the lagoon. There are also lagoon-view bungalows (you have to walk down a slight incline to get to the beach) and garden rooms that interconnect and are ideal for families. The large beachfront restaurant, Le Te Nahe, is popular with nonguests. While there's no spa, you only need to walk out the front door and across the road to Kahuna Massage (*see review below*) if you want to a Thai or Shiatsu massage (*see Spas, below, for a full review*). Each Saturday night there's a Polynesian buffet and dance show (5,804 CFP per person). The hotel has free kayaks and snorkel gear, and Jet Skis for hire. **Pros:** Lovely new accommodation on the beach; friendly staff. **Cons:** The older beachfront bungalows are perched on a rocky rise, which you need to walk down. ⌂*Parea* ⌖*BP 30, Fare 98731* ☎*60–60–40* ⊕*www.relaismahana.com* ⇆*22 bungalows, 10 rooms* ⌂*In-room: a/c (some), safe, refrigerator, Internet. In-hotel: restaurant, room service, bar, pool, gym, beachfront, diving, water sports, bicycles, no elevator, laundry service, concierge, executive floor, public Internet, airport shuttle, parking (no fee)* ⊟*AE, MC, V* ⏹*EP.*

SMALL
HOTELS/
GUESTHOUSES
$$
Fodor'sChoice
★

⛫Pension Fare ie. This is a new sister property to the Fare ie on Huahine Nui. The four split-level tents (two garden and two sea view) are similar to those you'd find in African safari camps. Each has two double beds; the beach tents are larger with sofas and a downstairs bathroom. Furnishings are bright and funky, i.e., varnished timber sofas with bright red cushions, ceilings of billowing material, bright patterned bedspreads, and each tent has hardwood floors, fan, chest of drawers, and chairs. The two beachfront tents each have their own outdoor kitchen; the garden tents share a kitchen. The rate includes breakfast, canoe, and bikes. There's even a little marae right on the beach. **Pros:** Unique accommodation; great beachfront position; good kitchens. **Cons:** Two double beds in each tent means two couples don't have much privacy. ⌂*Main road, Parea* ⌖*BP 746, Fare 98731* ☎*60–3–77* ⊕*www.tahitisafari.com* ⇆*4 tents* ⌂*In-room: no a/c (some), no phone, kitchen (some), refrigerator (some), no TV. In-hotel: room service (breakfast only), beachfront, water sports, bicycles, no elevator, airport shuttle, parking (no fee)* ⊟*MC, V* ⏹*BP.*

$–$$$

⛫Pension Mauarii. This pension has an imaginative array of accommodations, including garden bungalows with coral floor bathrooms and big stepping stones; a three-bedroom bungalow for families; and a large bungalow divided into three separate rooms, each with their own toilet but sharing a shower and sink. Garden bungalows have lovely little covered terraces, big tables hewn from enormous tree trunks, and four-poster beds held up with varnished tree branches. The Mauarii company also owns a boutique in Fare, car rental and tour excursions companies, and the airport snack bar. The elevated spa, Divine & Sens, has a Jacuzzi on the terrace with great views, but only offers massages. Several activities such as pareo (sarong) tying and Polynesian handicraft demonstrations are held in the early evening and are complimentary. **Pros:** Friendly staff; good restaurant; great pancakes for breakfast. **Cons:** Nearby roosters are quite loud; bungalows may get uninvited visitors, i.e., baby geckos. ⊠ *Avea Bay, Parea* 🗊 *BP 4121, Fare 98731* ☎ *68–86–49* ⊕ *www.mauarii.com* 🛏 *6 bungalows, 5 rooms* 🚪 *In-room: no a/c, no phone (some), no safe, refrigerator (some), no TV. In-hotel: restaurant, bar, spa, beachfront, diving, water sports, service, concierge, airport shuttle, parking (no fee)* ⊟ *MC, V* ⧦ *EP.*

WHERE TO EAT

4

Dining is mainly confined to Huahine's hotels and pensions, which have a wide selection of dishes from lobster, crab, and fish to meat, duck, and *poisson cru.* If you're looking for a big night out, head to the main town of Fare on Huahine Nui; there's only one independent restaurant on Huahine Iti. As there aren't many restaurants on Huahine, it's best to make reservations, especially in the high season (May to August). ⚠ **Unlike other islands there are a few places that provide restaurant transfers (check with each individual restaurant), and there are no free transfers for people staying on Huahine Iti.**

For something really casual and inexpensive, check out the *roulottes* (food trucks with specialties) at Fare quay, operating near the huge supermarket, Fare Super Nui. Starting around 6 PM, each truck serves up something different. One truck specializes in pizza, while another dishes up huge servings of chicken chow mien, steak and frites (fries), beef and vegetable stir-fries, and lemon chicken. You can eat here or take away, just remember to bring cash as the trucks don't take credit cards.

HUAHINE NUI

HOTEL RESTAURANTS

$$$-$$$$ ✕ **Ari'I Restaurant.** Executive chef Jean Frederic Markacz has a simple
PACIFIC RIM philosophy when creating dishes: use only the freshest local fruit and vegetables combined with fish straight out of the ocean. He incorporates the much-loved vanilla bean with mahimahi and also uses it to create a sauce to accompany a chicken breast stuffed with papaya. Swordfish, red tuna, and lobster are always on the menu. The restaurant has a wonderful position over the water with both lagoon and ocean views. ⊠ *Te Tiare Pearl Resort, Private island, west coast* ☎ *60–60–50* 🍽 *Reservations essential* ⏱ *Daily 7* AM*–9* PM.

$-$$ ✕ **Tehina.** This small poolside garden restaurant, popular with locals,
POLYNESIAN is in the Fare Maeva. Pension guests can either buy a half-board meal plan and receive a set dinner menu (which can change daily) of entrée, main course, and dessert, or choose from the á la carte menu. Dishes include curries (chicken or prawns), prawns cru (a new twist on poisson cru), and char-grilled lobster (at 3,200 CFP). A popular dessert choice is the pineapple tart with coconut milk. Snacks including

sandwiches and burgers are available during the day. ⊠ *Just west of the airport, off the main road, Maeva* ☎ *68–75–53* ▤ *MC, V.*

INDEPENDENT RESTAURANTS

$$–$$$ ✕ **Les Dauphins.** You can't miss Les Dauphins (The Dolphins), as it's right
FRENCH   next to the post office in Fare—the only post office on the island. There are seven tables beautifully set for dinner each night under thatched cover and casual lunch dining in the garden under bright umbrellas. The menu is quite imaginative for Huahine and includes stuffed mussels with garlic butter, sautéed jumbo prawns with cognac, and fillet of duck with honey sauce. There's also confit of duck with potatoes and garlic and, for those with plain tastes, grilled lamp chops. Finish off with the classic French dessert of crème brûlée, or a warm coconut tart with vanilla ice cream. You can order half or full bottles of wine. ⊠ *Fare* ☎ *68–78–54* ⚑ *Reservations essential* ▤ *MC, V* ۞ *Closed Mon.*

$$ ✕ **New Te Marara.** The great location right on the water at Fare quay
SEAFOOD   and a happy vibe are the draws for this restaurant, which despite the name has been operating a few years now. Locals drink their Hinanos (a local beer) as the sun goes down and cocktails are around 500 CFP during happy hour from 5:30–6:30 every night. Menus items include grilled salmon, tuna with vanilla sauce, steamed mahimahi with ginger, or lobster with spicy coconut sauce (3,200 CFP); meat lovers have several options including steak with Roquefort sauce. ⊠ *Fare Quay* ☎ *68–70–81* ⚑ *Reservations essential* ▤ *No credit cards.*

$$ ✕ **Vivi et Vonvon.** This cute balcony restaurant, right in the heart of Fare
FRENCH AND   quay, is also a bookstore. It's open for breakfast, lunch, and dinner
TAHITIAN   serving great food prepared by charming French owner Vivi. Dinner is either á la carte or a set menu of main course and dessert (1800 CFP), possibly grilled fish and vegetables and a tart. Á la carte choices include tuna tartare with papaya salad, and a salad of lentils and hot duck sausage with pistachio and balsamic dressing. It's located up a spiral staircase, a few doors away from the visitors' bureau and Internet café. ⊠ *Fare quay road, Fare* ☎ *60–63–71* ▤ *No credit cards.*

HUAHINE ITI

HOTEL RESTAURANTS

$$ ✕ **Pension Mauarii.** The restaurant at this popular pension prides itself
SEAFOOD   on using local products in 95% of its dishes. You'll find Tahitian dishes such as *Fa Fa* chicken (chicken with taro leaves and coconut milk) and *Punu Pualoro* (smoked beef with coconut cream) on the menu. Lobster and crab, and a medley of both, are house specialties and are huge dishes. If you're brave you can also try mako shark but that might be too much of an ironic twist after a day on the lagoon feeding sharks and rays. Desserts include baked papaya with coconut cream and coconut tart. ⊠ *Parea* ☎ *68–86–49* ⚑ *Reservations essentials* ▤ *MC, V* ۞ *Daily 7:30* AM*–8:30* PM.

$$$ ✕ **Le Te Nahe.** There aren't too many restaurants on Huahine Iti, so
SEAFOOD   this hotel restaurant attracts a crowd of guests and nonguests in the high season. Large windows open onto the lagoon, bringing in cool

breezes. By day it's a casual place and at night white tablecloths are laid and sparkling glassware graces the tables. Lobster takes pride of place on the menu—there's grilled lobster with local vegetables and rice; a degustation plate of lobster, shrimp, and fish; and lobster ravioli, a dish that seems a bit odd for French Polynesia. Rum flambéed Huahine bananas is a lovely dessert and beautifully combines two Tahitian local ingredients. Every Saturday night there's a Polynesian buffet and traditional dance performance (5,804 CFP per person). ⊠*Relais Mahana, Parea* ☎*60–60–40* ⚖*Reservations essential* ▭*MC, V.*

INDEPENDENT RESTAURANTS

¢–$ ✕**Rauheama Snack Restaurant.** This pleasant little thatched hut, with
SEAFOOD a coral floor and pareos hanging from the ceiling, does a brisk trade when cruise ships are in port. It's directly opposite the dock where passengers are ferried ashore, right on beautiful Maroe Bay. It has a very limited menu with the friendly French-speaking Tahitian owner offering baguettes with various fillings such as chicken and salad for those who want a snack and the heartier plat du jour (dish of the day)—which is whatever she's just cooked. It may be a platter of fish and vegetables featuring poisson cru, grilled fish, beans, and salad—with a sizeable portion of fries. The food's good and you can also buy a pareo. ⊠*Main road, Maroe Bay, Maroe* ☎*68–78–41* ▭*No credit cards* ☉*Lunch and dinner only.*

SHOPPING

If you're after jewelry, a pareo, or some surf gear—in Tahitian designs—you'll find them in Fare's port area; there's one long street of shops. You'll have to venture across the lagoon for pearls.

HUAHINE NUI

BOOKS **Vivi et Vonvon** (⊠*Fare Quay, Fare* ☎*60–63–70* ☉*Daily 7:30 AM–8:30 PM*) is a restaurant with a small bookshop attached that specializes in children's books and books on French Polynesia—most are in French.

CLOTHING & **Exotica Shop** (⊠*Fare Quay, Fare* ☎*68–78–21* ☉*Mon.–Sat. 9–5:30*)
FASHION has an eclectic mixture of clothes, jewelry, and gifts, but the range is not really Polynesian. It's on the second level of a small retail complex near the tourism bureau.

Local Style (⊠*Fare Quay, Fare* ☎*68–76–85* ⊕*www.mauarii.com* ☉*Mon.–Sat. 9–5:30*) has a colorful range of surf gear including the Tahitian label, Hinano. There also are shorts, shirts, and bikinis. It shares space with the Hertz rental kiosk.

GROCERIES **Fare Super Nui** (⊠*Quay Road, Fare* ☎*68–84–68* ☉*Daily 8–6*) is a
& OTHER huge supermarket that carries everything from wine and beer to milk,
ESSENTIALS snorkeling gear, and clothes. It even has pigs ready for roasting. This is the hub of life in Huahine.

Magasin Vaimoe (⊠*Near the church, Faaie* ☎*68–81–08* ☉*Daily 7 AM–5 PM*) is just one of several small "corner stores" that dot the island's

BEST BETS FOR CRUISING

Marae mystery tour. Huahine has the best-preserved archaeological remains in French Polynesia, most located in Maeva. In the same open-air complex is a replica Fare Pote (meeting house), which is a cultural museum that's only opened when cruise ships are in port.

Free wheel it. It's possible to see much of Huahine's wild beauty during a four- or six-hour drive, so rent a car. The map's easy to follow and traffic is minimal.

Go off-road. Take a 4WD tour and let the experts show you the island—lookouts, funny blue-eyed eels, and temples—from the back of a truck.

Zoom zoom. Hot tail it around the lagoon and bays on a Jet Ski. Get in line, follow the leader, and discover a laid-back paradise.

Beach picnic. If you have a full day, take a lagoon excursion with motu picnic and shark and ray feeding, and a stopover for snorkeling.

main road. Usually called Magasins, they sell water, beer, snacks, and a limited (and often quite expensive) range of groceries.

PEARLS AND POTTERY   **Huahine Pearl Farm** (⊠ *Motu, off Faaie* ☎ *68–73–27* ⊕ *www.huahine pearlfarm.com* 🚤 *free* ◷ *10* AM–*3* PM) has loose pearls and pearl jewelry, as well as pottery crafted by ex-Californian Peter Owen and his Tahitian-born wife Ghislaine. Take the free boat transfer over to the motu off the village of Faaie, which leaves every 15 minutes.

HUAHINE ITI

There are few shopping opportunities on Huhine Iti apart from corner stores selling ice cream, water, and groceries.

CLOTHING & FASHION   **Mauariki Creations.** (⊠ *Parea* ☎ *73–58–72*) French artist Bertho Franck hand paints pareos in a little studio tucked away in a garden on the main road, a few miles away from Pension Mauarii. They are priced from 2,080 to 2,500 CFP. Just ring to see if it's open, or drive down—it's only 20 to 30 minutes from Fare by car and very scenic.

GROCERIES & OTHER ESSENTIALS   **Magasin Chez Hine.** (⊠ *Parea* ☎ *76–81–27* ◷ *Daily 7–5*) A short drive from Pension Mauarii, this small "corner store" sells beer, water, soft drinks, ice cream, packaged snacks, and a small range of groceries such as tinned food and eggs.

SPAS

Exotic spa treatments have yet to find their way to Huahine. Massage and petal-filled Jacuzzi baths are the only treatments available on the island to date. Massages styles include Thai, shiatsu, and Hawaiian.

HUAHINE NUI

SPAS IN HOTELS & RESORTS   **Te Tiare Pearl Resort** (⊠ *Motu, off southwest tip of Huahine Iti, Fitii* ☎ *60–60—60* ⊕ *www.tetiarebeachresort.com* ◷ *By appointment only*) doesn't have a spa, but in-room massages and yoga sessions can be arranged.

HUAHINE ITI

INDEPENDENT
SPAS

Kahuna Massage (✉ *Main Road, Parea* ☎ *68–89–78* ⊘ *By appointment only*). Hanin Elias runs this massage school and parlor directly across the road from Relais Mahana. He offers Thai, shiatsu, and Lomi Lomi (a Hawaiian technique) massages, as well as a variety of after-sun and after-travel massages. Prices start at 5,000 CFP for 30 minutes.

SPAS IN
HOTELS &
RESORTS

Divine & Sens (✉ *Pension Mauarii, Parea* ☎ *22–43–97* ⊕ *www.mauarii.com* ⊘ *Daily 9–6*) one-room "spa" offers 30-, 50-, and 90-minute relaxation massages. It's 19,000 CFP for a 15-minute Jacuzzi soak and a 45-minute massage. There's a Jacuzzi on the terrace that guests can partake in before or after their services.

AFTER DARK

If you're looking for nightlife you've definitely come to the wrong place. Nightlife consists of dinner and a few drinks at your hotel or pension—most restaurants, both resort and independent, start closing their doors around 9 PM.

HUAHINE NUI

COCKTAIL TIME

New Te Marara (✉ *Fare Quay, Fare* ☎ *68–70–81* ⊘ *Daily noon–9:30 PM*), also a seafood restaurant, has the island's best view of the lagoon and the port activities, as well as the killer sunsets. Happy hour (5:30–6:30 PM) brings the price of cocktails down to 500 CFP.

PERFORMANCES

Te Tiare Pearl Resort (✉ *Private island, off west coast* ☎ *60–60–60* ⊕ *www.tetiarebeachresort.com* ⊘ *Twice a week at 8 PM; days change depending on the number of guests staying*) holds Polynesian dance performances and buffet twice a week. Performances last for 45 minutes.

HUAHINE ITI

PERFORMANCES

Relais Mahana (✉ *Main Road, Parea* ☎ *69–60–40* ⊕ *www.relais mahana.com* ⊘ *Sat. 7:30 PM*) stages a Polynesian dance show by a local group along with a buffet dinner (5,804 CFP per person).

OUTDOOR ACTIVITIES

There's a wide variety of activities on Huahine from the classic lagoon excursion—complete with snorkeling, shark feeding, and motu picnics—to hilltop trekking along marae trails. You can swim with your horse in Lake Fake Fauna Nui, dive in eight different sites, relax on a sunset cruise, Jet Ski over the lagoon, or hire a boat and go fishing. You can find the operators on Fare Quay, unless otherwise noted.

BIKING

Huahine Lagoon (☎ *68–70–00*). You can rent bikes for a few hours or the whole day (eight hours); a half day (four hours) is 600 CFP.

BOATING &
SAILING

Huahine Lagoon (☎ *68–70–00*). Canoes and speedboats (no license is needed to rent) are available for two-, four-, and eight-hour periods. Speedboat costs start at 5,000 CFP for two hours; gas is extra. Canoes are 300 CFP for two hours.

Sailing Huahine Voile (✉ *Along the Fitii road, Fare* ☎ *68–72–49* ⊕ *www.sailing-huahine.com*). This company's 49-foot yacht the "Eden Martin" can be chartered for a whole day with a crew, or you can join a four- or seven-day cruise around the Society Islands with five passengers plus the skipper.

DIVING & **Mahana Dive** (☎ *73–07–17* ⊕ *www.mahanadive.com*). You can choose
SNORKELING from eight sites around both Huahine Nui and Iti including Avapeihi Pass (which connects the ocean with the lagoon and is teeming with marine life), and various drop-offs and coral gardens. Dives start from 5,900 CFP; dive packages can also be bought.

Pacific Blue Adventures (☎ *68–87–21* ⊕ *www.divehuahine.com*). Since its establishment in 1993, Pacific Blue has been working with all levels of divers. Newcomers dive in shallow water off the coast of Fitii, while experienced divers go out beyond the lagoon to Avapeihi Pass, which is famous for its sharks and rays.

4WD TOURS **Huahine Explorer** (☎ *68–87–33* ⊕ *www.iaorana-huahine.com*). A fleet of three eight-seat Land Rovers take folks on half-day tours of both islands visiting marae, vanilla plantations, and local villages. An all-day tour adds a motorized canoe trip with a motu picnic.

Island Eco-Tours (✉ *Motu Maeva* ☎ *68–79–67* ✐ *islandecotours@mail.pf*). These tours are run by American Paul Atallah, an specialist in Polynesian archeology and anthropology. Half-day land tours are on offer, and there's an option to add a half-day lagoon excursion by outrigger canoe complete with a motu picnic.

HIKING **Huahine Randonnees** (☎ *68–81–06*). A great way to learn about the archeological sites of Maeva is to take a half-day hike along the coast and up into the hills. There are also half-day hikes to Huahine Iti's Mt. Puhaerei for groups of two to eight people.

HORSEBACK **La Petite Ferme** (✉ *Main road, one mile north of Fare* ☎ *68–82–98*
RIDING ⊕ *www.huahine-lapetiteferme.com*). Four Marquesan horses, known for their strong but gentle nature, are used for these two-hour trail rides along the beach near Fare; 5,500 CFP per person. For those who want a truly unique experience, tack on "sea-bathing" to the two-hour ride—the horses go into Lake Fauna Nui with you; 7,000 CFP.

LAGOON **Huahine Nautique** (☎ *68–83–15* ⊕ *www.huahine-nautique.com*) seems
EXCURSIONS to have the lagoon covered. There's a full-day circle island tour by boat with ray and shark feeding and a picnic on a motu or outrigger tours and Jet Skiing with a private lobster lunch with the tables and chairs actually set up in a shallow part of the lagoon. If you're on a cruise, they have excursions scheduled to fit in with cruise ship visits.

Moana Turquoise (☎ *77–59–58* ⊕ *www.mauarii.com*). This one-stop-shop runs whale and dolphin cruises, snorkeling trips, circle island boat tours, wakeboarding, and sunset cruises. They also offer VIP tours for two people, and transfers are provided.

Tuamotu
Archipelago

WORD OF MOUTH

"I only took a day trip diving in Rangiroa, but from what I gathered the island is one of the most popular diving destinations. Diving there was unforgettable. I still daydream about it. If you're a confirmed non-diver then Rangiroa is not the best choice for you. But if you are at least thinking about trying it, it's one of the best places for beginners: the water is warm, safe, clear, and shallow."

—KittyKate1993

Written by
Caroline
Gladstone

TUAMOTU MEANS "ISLANDS ON THE ocean's back," and some romantic observers liken them to the backs of surfacing whales. Each is comprised of hundreds of little *motu* (islets), which are clumps of coral, sand, and limestone strung together to form circular or rectangular shapes of white enclosing blue lagoons. Fringed by white beaches and sprouting lush green coconut groves, the motu are the reality of most people's South Seas paradise dreams.

Only 41 of the atolls are inhabited and have a total population of 12,500. Tourists tend to visit only Rangiroa, Fakarava, Tikehau, and Manihi, which have the bulk of accommodations, though services like banks are few and far between. There are only five sizeable hotels in the entire archipelago; most lodgings are family-run pensions. There is no nightlife beyond the resorts, and the few independent restaurants close their doors around 9:30 PM. Surprisingly, there is a vineyard—Rangiroa grows the only grapes in the South Pacific.

Pearl farms thrive in the region due to the warm waters favored by the black pearl oyster, *Pinctada margaritifera*. The islands are well known in diving circles for their spectacular marine life, but are off the radar of the average tourist.

ORIENTATION & PLANNING

ORIENTATION

Tuamotu is the largest of French Polynesia's five archipelagos with 77 atolls and one high island—Makatea—scattered in a vast 2,092-km (1,307-mi) chain. The closest is 350 km (219 mi) from Tahiti; about an hour's flight.

RANGIROA

Rangiroa is the largest of the group and the largest atoll in the South Pacific. It's 354 km (220 mi) northeast of Tahiti, in the northwest corner of the archipelago. It has a circumference of 281 km (175 mi) and a huge lagoon that's roughly 72 km (45 mi) long and 25 km (16 mi) wide. The main village of Avatoru, the airport, ferry port, and most of the accommodations are on a 6-mi piece of land on the northern edge that lies between the two passes—Avatoru and Tiputa. The village of Tiputa, on the east side of Tiputa Pass, is reached by a regular boat service from Ohotu wharf.

FAKARAVA

The oblong Fakarava, the second-largest atoll in Tuamotu, is 120 km (75 mi) southeast of Rangiroa. Garuae Pass, measuring more than a mile across, is located on the northern edge; the narrower Tamakohua Pass is 59 km (37 mi) away to the south. The airport, the main town of Rotoava, and most accommodations are strung along the atoll's only semi-paved road in the northeast corner. The tiny village of Tetamanu (population: about 11) sits beside the Tamakohua Pass.

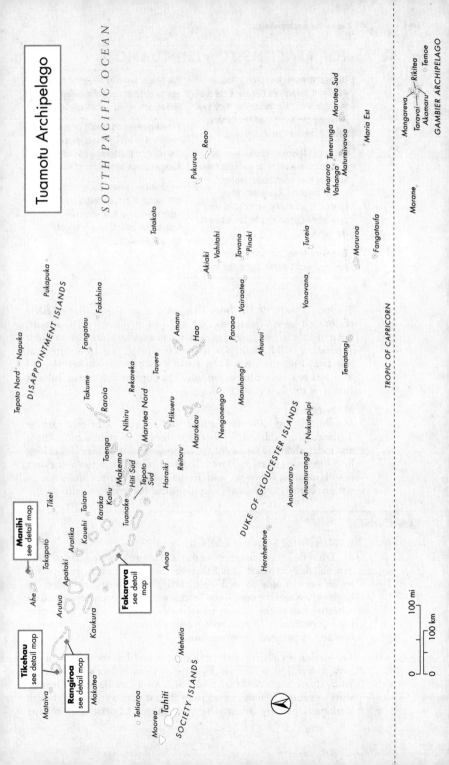

TOP REASONS TO VISIT TUAMOTU

Divers' dream. Rangiroa's Tiputa Pass and Fakarava's Garuae Pass are teeming with "big fauna" as they say in diving circles. Would the "shark cave" appeal to you?

Endless lagoons. You'll never be short of somewhere to swim in these lagoons that even boast lagoons within lagoons. Rangiroa's Blue Lagoon is an idyllic picnic spot with cute black-tipped sharks keen to eat the leftovers.

The slow lane. No one rushes here and you won't either. Cycle the long flat roads, swim at deserted beaches, and snooze under palm trees. Go ahead, you're on vacation.

Finding religion. You'll discover churches in very remote places—like the abandoned village of Otepipi on Rangiroa and Tetamanu in Fakarava.

Stylish castaway. Escape from the world in private villas and retreats—just a few convivial folk, an oil lamps, and miles of beautiful beaches.

TIKEHAU

Tikehau, 14 km (9 mi) from Rangiroa, is an almost perfect circle enclosing a lagoon measuring 26 km (16 mi) in diameter. The airport, town of Tuherahera, several pensions, and a diving center are on Motu Tuherahera in the south. The island's one resort is a 10-minute boat ride away from the town. There are miles of calm lagoon beaches and wild surf beaches on the ocean side. The popular dive site of Tuheiva Pass is on the west coast.

MANIHI

Manihi, 161 km (100 mi) northeast of Rangiroa, is the cradle of the Tuamotu pearl industry. Its first pearl farm was established in 1968, and today about 60 farms dot the lagoon, which measures 30 km long by 6 km wide (18 mi by 4 mi). The airport, the main town of Paeua (also known as Turipaoa), and Turipaoa Pass lie in the atoll's southwestern corner; lodgings are spread around the southern half.

PLANNING

GETTING HERE AND AROUND

Air Tahiti flies about four times a day to Rangiroa, twice a day to Tikehau, and daily to Manihi and Fakarava. Two Air Tahiti passes cover the region but can only be used when staying for a month or longer: the Lagoon Pass and the Bora Bora/Tuamotu Pass. Air Archipels, a charter operator, flies to the Tuamotu. *See Air Passes and Flights, in Getting Here & Around in Travel Smart French Polynesia for air pass information and airline contact information.*

The *Aranui 3* calls regularly at Rangiroa and Fakarava, making 16 voyages a year from Pape'ete. Five ships—*Cobia 3, Dory, Mareva Nui, Saint-Xavier Maris-Stella III,* and *T.M.I. Kura Ora III*—make regular visits to various islands in the group at least once a month. Although working ships, they do carry between six and 12 passengers in basic accommodations (sometimes only on the deck) and are suited to those travelers who don't mind roughing it.

There's little need for a car but if you want motorized transport, there are car and scooter rentals on Rangiroa, and you can rent scooters and motorboats on Fakarava. All four islands have bicycle rentals.

There's is no public transport on the islands apart from the Taxi Boat on Rangiroa that takes people from Ohotu wharf to Tiputa. There is, however, one taxi in Rangiroa.

There are three banks in Rangiroa; there are no banks on Manihi, Tikehau, or Fakarava. The Banque Socredo branch in Avatoru has an ATM. The major resorts take credit cards as do some pensions, but it's wise to bring plenty of cash.

ESSENTIALS

Boats & Ferries *Arani 3* (☎ *42-62-42* ⊕ *www.aranui.com*). *Cobia 3* (☎ *43-36-43*). *Dory* (☎ *42-30-55*). *Mareva Nui* (☎ *42-25-53*). *Saint-Xavier Maris-Stella III* (☎ *42-23-58*). *T.M.I. Kura Ora III* (☎ *45-60-00*).

WHEN TO GO

Tuamotu has two seasons—the wet (November to April) and the dry (May to October). As the archipelago is farther north than the Society group, it tends to be a little hotter than the average 85°F (29°C) in the summer and the average 80°F (27°C) in winter that other islands experience. The wet season can be wetter, too. The upside is more sunny days and a constant lagoon temperature of around 78°F (25°C).

The big event is the Arii Mata Tini Va'a Canoe race, in Rangiroa in late May.

TAKE IT ALL IN

A vacation in the Tuamotus is all about diving and snorkeling, close encounters with wonderful marine life, lazing on pink sand beaches on the edge of translucent lagoons, wandering through small towns that seem frozen in yesteryear, and relaxing under palm trees. However, don't expect to see more than two islands if you only have seven days—the heat will kill you.

3 Days: Just choose one island and experience what's on offer. Go on a lagoon and motu picnic excursions complete with shark feeding and visits to bird islands one day. On another, go drift diving or snorkeling the passes or hop abroad a bike, scooter, or dune buggy to zoom along the one island road.

5 Days: You could see two islands in five days, but that would be pushing it—remember that half a day will be lost just by getting to airports and hotels. It's possible of course, so if you're game, follow the above itinerary on Rangiroa and then head to Manihi for some R & R.

7 Days: Take a three- or four-day cruise around Rangiroa lagoon with Haumana Cruises and then fly to Fakarava for some great diving or snorkeling in the Garuae (also called Ngarue) Pass.

HEALTH & SAFETY

There are no health issues, but remember to pack your reef shoes as walking on coral sea beds is tough on the sole.

The general emergency number for police in French Polynesia is 17.

EAT RIGHT, SLEEP WELL

The Tuamotu Islands have escaped large-scale hotel development and are likely to stay that way, because of their location well off the major tourist track. However, there are adequate rooms to accommodate the divers and castaways who visit these parts.

Rangiroa has the bulk of accommodations with two medium-size hotels—Hotel Kia Ora (63 bungalows) and Novotel Rangiroa Lagoon Resort (38 rooms and bungalows.) There is one upscale resort on each of the other three islands, comprising no more than about 35 bungalows apiece. Other lodgings are a mix of stylish pensions, a couple of "wild" retreats perfect for solitude-seekers, and homely pensions with no more than six bungalows each.

Dining is mostly confined to the resorts and pensions, as there are few independent restaurants beyond Rangiroa. Pension meals—generally cooked by the lady of the house—are usually very tasty and served in large portions. Menus are limited, but change nightly and may include lobster. The resort restaurants offer a big variety of dishes with an emphasis on seafood—tuna, parrotfish, mahimahi (with a variety of sauces) mussels, shrimp, and occasionally escargot. Dessert menus often feature papaya or coconut pie or decadent profiteroles.

All the usual taxes apply; however, sojourn tax is not (yet) added to bills in Manihi or Fakarava. *See Taxes, in Essentials in Travel Smart French Polynesia for more information.*

WHAT IT COSTS IN FRANC COURS PACIFIQUE (CFP)				
	¢	$	$$	$$$	$$$$
RESTAURANTS	under 1,500	1,501–2,000	2,001–2,400	2,401–2,800	over 2,800
HOTELS	under 10,000	10,001–17,000	17,001–32,000	32,001–50,000	over 50,000

Restaurant prices are for a main course at dinner. Hotel prices are for a double room in high season, excluding 10% tax, 10%–15% service charges, and meals plans (except at all-inclusives).

RANGIROA

Rangiroa, or "Endless Sky" in Tahitian, is French Polynesia's largest atoll. A long, narrow grouping of 415 small motu strung together in a misshapen circle, it harbors a lagoon so large the entire island of Tahiti could fit in it. It's also impossible to see from one side of the lagoon to the other.

Rangiroa's tourism industry has been built around the lagoon and the two passes (Avatoru and Tiputa) that connect it to the ocean. Divers

TOURING TIPS

■ The Tuamotus are sleepy, laid-back places, with no nightlife. If it's nightlife you want, look somewhere else.

■ For a diversified experience, book a variety of excursions—drift snorkeling, pearl farm visits, bird island tours, and motu picnics complete with visits to remote villages.

■ If you're torn between which Rangiroa excursions to take, opt for the stunning Ile aux Recifs trip. The coral formations (known as feo) rise meters out of the water.

■ Book a pension with a good view of a pass that connects the lagoon to the ocean. You'll see frolicking dolphins from your terrace.

■ There are no streetlights, so bring a flashlight.

descend on Rangi, as it's nicknamed, to "shoot the pass." The atoll's main town, Avatoru, and the village of Tiputa lie in the northern section of the atoll.

GETTING HERE & AROUND
Avatoru is the name of a town and the general name for the 9.6-km-long (6-mi) piece of land that stretches between the two passes: Avatoru pass is in the west and Tiputa pass is in the east. Ohotu sits on the west side of Tiputa pass and is just a wharf and one or two pensions. Tiputa village is across Tiputa pass on the eastern side.

ESSENTIALS
Banks **Bank de Tahiti** (⊠ *Avatoru* ☎ *96–85–52*). **Banque Socredo** (⊠ *Avatoru* ☎ *96–85–63*). **Banque Socredo** (⊠ *Tiputa* ☎ *93–12–50*).

Car Rentals **Europcar** (☎ *96–03–45* ⊕ *www.europcar.pf*).

Emergencies **Police (gendarmerie)** (☎ *93–03–61*). **Cabinet Medical** (☎ *96–86–00*). **Pharmacie de Rangiroa** (⊠ *Avatoru* ☎ *93–12–35*).

Taxis **Mr. Ignace Tupahiroa** (☎ *77–28–02*).

Visitor Info **Taeo'o No Rairoa Association** (⊠ *Rangiroa* ☎ *68–82–67* ✐ *rangi@mail.pf*).

WHAT TO SEE

TOWNS
Avatoru. Rangiroa's capital is a small village on Avatoru Pass with two churches (Catholic and Mormon) fashioned from coral, a town hall, post office, banks, and a couple of general stores. It has an ideal location with access to the lagoon, the ocean's surf beach, and the pass's good diving spot. To experience a true slice of island life, turn up at 10 AM on Sunday for one of the church services. ⊠ *Main road.*

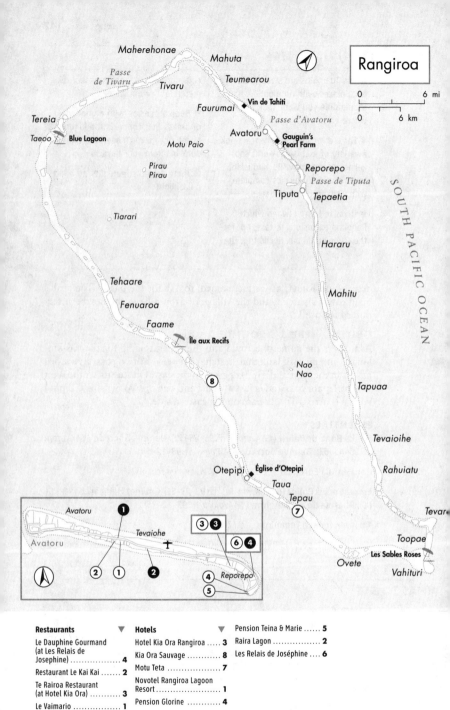

Rangiroa

0 — 6 mi
0 — 6 km

Maherehonae
Mahuta
Passe de Tivaru
Tivaru
Teumearou
Faurumai
◆ Vin de Tahiti
Passe d'Avatoru
Tereia
Avatoru
◆ Gauguin's Pearl Farm
Taeoo ◆ Blue Lagoon
Motu Paio
Reporepo
Pirau Pirau
Passe de Tiputa
Tiputa
Tepaetia
Tiarari
Hararu
Mahitu
Tehaare
Fenuaroa
Faame
Île aux Recifs
⑧
Nao Nao
Tapuaa
Tevaioihe
Rahuiatu
Otepipi ◆ Église d'Otepipi
Taua
Tepau
⑦
Tevar
Toopae
◆ Les Sables Roses
Ovete
Vahituri

SOUTH PACIFIC OCEAN

Avatoru
❶
Tevaioihe
③ ③
⑥ ④
Avatoru
② ① ❷
④
⑤
Reporepo

Restaurants

Le Dauphine Gourmand
(at Les Relais de
Josephine) 4

Restaurant Le Kai Kai 2

Te Rairoa Restaurant
(at Hotel Kia Ora) 3

Le Vaimario 1

Hotels

Hotel Kia Ora Rangiroa 3

Kia Ora Sauvage 8

Motu Teta 7

Novotel Rangiroa Lagoon
Resort 1

Pension Glorine 4

Pension Teina & Marie 5

Raira Lagon 2

Les Relais de Joséphine 6

Tiputa. Rangiroa's other little settlement can be reached by a regular ferry service (called a taxi boat) from Ohotu wharf. Tiputa's well kept, with a few houses enclosed by coral fences, St. Michael's Catholic church, and a little school. A great way to explore the village is by bike, which you can take on the ferry for a small fee (400 CFP return; 200 CFP bicycles, 500 CFP scooters). ✉ *Main road, across the Tiputa Pass.*

Otepipi. This deserted village, complete with church, is on the opposite side of the lagoon to Avatoru, midway between Ile aux Recifs and Les Sables Roses. At least one operator runs a tour there, which is combined with island-hopping and lunch. For tour information, contact Pension Chez Martine (☎ 96–82–67).

BEACHES

Rangiroa has three different styles of beach—the calm, lagoon beaches that are just a patch of sand, the wild surf beaches on the ocean side, and the beaches on the small motus that are located within the lagoon itself. You'll need to rent a boat to reach a motu beach, or take an organized excursion to the Blue Lagoon, the Sables Roses, or Ile aux Recifs for that real castaway experience complete with picnic.

Blue Lagoon. This "lagoon with a lagoon" is a popular excursion. The water is sensationally blue and fringed by white sandy beaches and coconut trees. After an hour's boat ride from Avatoru, the captain anchors off a small island and guests walk across a seabed strewn with coral (reef shoes required), past a few harmless black-tipped reef sharks, and over the island itself to reach the blue lagoon. The seabed is soft and sandy and the views are magical, but the snorkeling, unfortunately, is nothing special.

Ile aux Recifs. The "isle of reefs" is considered the best lagoon excursion of all. Located about an hour due south of Avatoru, it's an area dotted with raised *feo* (coral outcrops), some 16 to 19 feet (5 to 6 meters) above the lagoon. These amazing formations are on the ocean side so you'll have to put on your reef shoes to explore them. They stretch about 300 feet (9 meters) and between them are pools perfect for swimming and excellent snorkeling. Picnics are usually held on one of the larger motus.

Les Sables Roses. This pink sand beach is in the southeast corner of Rangiroa, reached by a two-hour boat trip. The sands contain eroded coral and foraminiferal deposits (the pulverized red shells of tiny sea creatures) which sparkle in the sunlight. Getting here is one of the most expensive lagoon excursions (10,500 to 11,500 CFP for a day trip with picnic), but what you'll get is complete isolation, deserted beaches, and crystal clear water. You could rent a boat and come here on your own, but why would you want to pass up the BBQ and picnic most operators provide?

SIGHTS

Gauguin's Pearl Farm. The farm is an easy walk from the airport on the edge of the lagoon. A guide, who explains the long and laborious process of cultivating Tahitian black pearls, shows around small groups. Tours take 30 minutes and are fascinating; you'll learn about the *Pinctada margaritifera* or black-lipped oyster, and watch technicians insert a nucleus (a small shell bead) into the oyster and attach it with a graft of oyster muscle tissue to begin the pearling process. There's a jewelry boutique but it's not a hard-sell experience: a single top-grade pearl can cost 41,000 CFP (about US$530). ✉ *Near airport, Main road* ☎ *93–11–30* 💲 *Free* ⊙ *Mon.–Fri. 8:30–2, Shop: Mon.–Fri. 8:30–5:30, Sat.–Sun. 9–noon, 3–5.*

> **DID YOU KNOW?**
>
> **Vin de Tahiti** (✉ *Wine cave about 1.6 km (1 mi) east of Avatoru village, Main road* ☎ *96–04–70 in Rangiroa* ⊕ *www.vindetahiti.pf*) is the only vineyard in the South Pacific—the grapes are grown on a motu in Rangiroa's lagoon. Owner Dominique Auroy's estate produces red, white, and rose varieties. Day trips can be arranged to see the vineyard on Motu Ovavan, near the Avatoru Pass, and include a tour of the vines and a tasting at the wine cellar back on Rangiroa. Full-day tours also include a motu picnic. If time is short, you can visit the cellar by yourself for a free tasting.

The Passes. Avatoru and Tiputa passes offer some of the best drift diving in the world. Divers, accompanied by a guide, are dropped off on the ocean side of the atoll into the fast-moving current and are sucked through the pass by the tide. Feeling an amazing adrenaline rush, divers come (literally) face to face with hundreds of fish, along with giant napoleon wrasses, hawksbill turtles, manta and eagle rays, dolphins, and sharks—gray reefs, lemons, hammerheads, and dozens of blacktips. Snorkeling and glass bottom boat trips explore the calmer waters of the Tiputa Pass, and seek out the dolphins that are cavorting in the waves. 🖼 *Snorkeling 4,750 CFP for two hours; dives 5,580–6,800 CFP; glass-bottom boat trips 3,000 CFP for one hour; dolphin watch cruises and snorkeling in quieter waters 4,750 CFP for two hours.*

WHERE TO STAY

Rangiroa has the lion's share of accommodation in the Tuamotu with 200 rooms, most of which are at the four-star Hotel Kia Ora and the three-star Novotel Rangiroa Beach Resort. The other rooms are spread over 24 family pensions.

Every pension has managed to secure a site on or very close to the lagoon. Hotel Kia Ora has the only pool and tennis court on the island and stages Polynesian dance shows twice a week. Those seeking ultimate castaway experiences can either rent a villa on a remote motu or bed down at the five-bungalow Kia Ora Sauvage, located an hour's boat ride across the lagoon.

VILLAS & CONDOMINIUMS

$$$$ ⊞**Motu Teta.** Complete with personal chef and open bar, this villa is straight out of the pages of *Lifestyles of the Rich and Famous*. Located on Motu Tetaraire, a two-hour boat ride from Avatoru, it has two separate residences, the largest of which has three bedrooms and two bathrooms. The other house (just a short distance away) has two bedrooms and one bathroom. Both villas have extensive living and dining areas and a chef prepares all the meals. **Pros:** Ultimate luxury; complete isolation. **Cons:** Ultimate luxury comes with a heavy price tag; complete isolation might not be what you're looking for. ⊠*Motu Tetaraire* ☎*559/447–2525 in U.S.* ⊕*www.yourdreamisland.com* ⇆*2 villas* ⌂*In-room: safe (some), kitchen, refrigerator, DVD, Internet. In-hotel: beachfront, diving, water sports, no elevator, laundry facilities, laundry service, concierge, airport shuttle* ▤*AE, DC, MC, V* ⦿*AP.*

RESORTS

$$$–$$$$ ⊞**Hotel Kia Ora Rangiroa.** The largest hotel in Tuamotu, it's set in expansive grounds, surrounded by a lovely coconut grove with all the facilities expected of a four-star resort. There's a wide range of bungalows including two-story, two-bedroom beach bungalows, bungalows with plunge pools and Jacuzzis, and 10 overwater bungalows. Decor includes ceiling beams carved with ancient Polynesian designs and bathroom mirrors with mother-of-pearl frames. **Pros:** Lovely setting; lots of creature comforts. **Cons:** Very pricey overwater bungalows. ⊠*Main road, Avatoru* ⌂*B.P. 198, Avatoru 98775* ☎*93–11–17* ⊕*www.hotelkiaora.com* ⇆*63 bungalows* ⌂*In-room: safe (some), refrigerator, Internet. In-hotel: restaurant, bar, pool, tennis court, spa, beachfront, diving, water sports, bicycles, no elevator, laundry service, concierge, public Internet, airport shuttle, parking (no fee)* ▤*AE, DC, MC, V* ⦿*EP.*

$$$ ⊞**Kia Ora Sauvage.** In French, *Sauvage* means savage, but the experience on this private island will be gloriously serene. The five-bungalow resort, little sister to Hotel Kia Ora, is 35 km (22 mi) away across the lagoon. There's a two-night minimum stay, but the peaceful experience uninterrupted by phones and TV may have you lingering longer. Rooms are rustic with double beds swathed in mosquito netting, tree branch pillars, and tables fashioned from tree trucks. Oil lamps illuminate the restaurant and bungalows at night, but the generator keeps the water hot in the bathrooms. **Pros:** Castaway experience; pristine beach setting. **Cons:** No a/c, TV, or fans; basic amenities. ⊠*Motu Avea Rahi* ⌂*B.P. 198, Avatoru 98775* ☎*93–11–17* ⊕*www.hotelkiaora. com* ⇆*5 bungalows* ⌂*In-room: no TV. In-hotel: restaurant, bar, beachfront, diving, water sports,*

> ### WORD OF MOUTH
>
> "I just returned from a stay at Kia Ora and highly recommend that you spend a couple of days at Sauvage. It was simply the most amazing travel experience I have ever had. We had the good fortune of being alone, as in the only guests, our first two days on the island. Since we were alone, Bernard, the caretaker, and his family invited us to join them for Christmas dinner. Sublime! I cannot recommend it enough." –mitchrc

no elevator, concierge, airport shuttle, no children under 18 ▭*AE, D, DC, MC, V* ⊠*EP.*

$$$–$$$$　▦**Novotel Rangiroa Lagoon Resort.** Located halfway between the airport and Tiputa Pass, this three-star hotel has a restaurant and bar popular with divers relaxing at day's end. The garden is lovely, has a gold-fish pond, and is dotted with bungalows. Ocean-view bungalows have access to a small sunbathing patch of crushed coral rather than a beach. All have queen and single beds and a separate bathroom that can be sectioned off with a sliding door. **Pros:** Lovely gardens; great views from restaurant; friendly staff. **Cons:** Very rocky beach; little space to sunbathe. ⊠*Avatoru* ⊕*B.P. 17, Avatoru 98775* ☎*93–13–50* ⊕*novotel-rangiroa-lagoon-resort.com* ⇆*16 bungalows, 22 garden rooms* ⚅*In-room: safe, refrigerator. In-hotel: restaurant, bar, beachfront, diving, water sports, bicycles, no elevator, laundry service, concierge, airport shuttle, parking (no fee)* ▭*AE, DC, MC, V* ⊠*EP.*

SMALL HOTELS/GUESTHOUSES

$　▦**Pension Glorine.** This budget pension has an ideal position near Ohutu wharf and its restaurant and terrace have great views over the lagoon. Hostess Glorine has a reputation for wonderful home-cooked meals; her specialties include tuna carpaccio and baked lagoon fish au gratin, which could make up for the lack of hot water in the bathrooms and the basic nature of the six rooms. There are bicycles for hire and excursions can be booked. **Pros:** Great location; good food; friendly atmosphere. **Cons:** Cold water; basic amenities. ⊠*Main road, Ohutu about 6 km (3.7 mi) from airport* ⊕*B.P. 17, Avatoru 98775* ☎*96–04–05* ⊘*pensionglorine@mail.pf* ⇆*6 bungalows* ⚅*In-room: no a/c (some), no TV. In-hotel: restaurant, bar, beachfront, diving, water sports, bicycles, no elevator, laundry service, concierge, airport shuttle, parking (no fee)* ▭*MC, V* ⊠*MAP.*

$　▦**Pension Teina & Marie.** Situated on the water near the Ohutu ferry wharf, this is a good choice for budget travelers who don't mind cold showers. There are four two-bedroom bungalows with share bathrooms and three beach bungalows and a family bungalow, all with private bathrooms. Prices include taxes, half board, and airport transfers. Meals, including lobster twice a week, are served in a large communal dining room with adjoining living room with TV. There's also a terrace for alfresco dining. **Pros:** Good location; good value. **Cons:** Some shared bathrooms; cold water in bathrooms. ⊠*Main roadroad, Ohutu 6 km from airport* ⊕*B.P. 51, Avatoru 98775* ☎*96–03–94* ⊘*pensionteinasimone@caramail.com* ⇆*10 bungalows* ⚅*In-room: no safe, no TV no a/c. In-hotel: restaurant, bar, beachfront, diving, water sports, bicycles, no elevator, airport shuttle, parking (no fee)* ▭*MC, V* ⊠*MAP.*

$$　▦**Raira Lagon.** This pension, less than a mile from the airport, also runs its own excursions to the Blue Lagoon. There are 10 small bungalows, each with private bathroom with hot water. Meals, which often feature local lobster prepared with various sauces, are served in an open-sided thatched restaurant. At night it can get a bit lively—for Rangi—when local traditional entertainers sometimes perform and often invite guests up to dance as well. **Pros:** Friendly atmosphere; good location. **Cons:** No a/c; basic accommodations. ⊠*Avatoru* ⊕*B.P. 87, Avatoru 98775*

☎93–12–30 ⊕*www.raira-lagon.pf* ⟿*10 bungalows* ⌂*In-room: no a/c, no TV. In-hotel: restaurant, bar, beachfront, diving, water sports, bicycles, no elevator, laundry service, airport shuttle, parking (no fee)* ⊟*AE, MC, V* ⓘⓄⓘ*MAP.*

$$ ⓣⓣ **Les Relais de Joséphine.** This lovely pension on Tiputa Pass, is the place to watch acrobatic dolphins swimming against the current. French owner Denise Josephine Caroggio tells you the best time to keep a look out for them from her terrace. There are six bungalows decorated with Balinese furniture including a lovely four-poster bed, a daybed, and padded sun lounges on private decks. Each has a ceiling fan and a small portable air-conditioning unit. Meals are served on the terrace overlooking the pass. **Pros:** Stylish rooms; great location on pass. **Cons:** No beach access. ⊠*Ohotu* ⓓ*B.P. 140, Avatoru 98775* ☎*96–02–00* ⊕*relaisjosephine.free.fr* ⟿*6 bungalows* ⌂*In-room: no a/c (some), no phone, safe, refrigerator, no TV. In-hotel: restaurant, bar, beachfront, diving, water sports, bicycles, no elevator, airport shuttle, parking (no fee)* ⊟*MC, V* ⓘⓄⓘ*MAP.*

WHERE TO EAT

"Where are we going to dinner?" is not a question you'll hear much on Rangiroa or the Tuamotus for that matter. The two hotels—Kia Ora and the Novotel—have sizeable restaurants with water views and plenty of menu choices. If you're staying at a pension you'll be dining on home-cooked meals; dishes often include bouillabaisse, tuna carpaccio (raw tuna), *poisson cru* (raw tuna marinated in lime and coconut milk), barbecued fish, and mahimahi with vanilla sauce. In many cases the meals will be tastier than resort fare, which can be bland and is always pricey.

As there are only five restaurants on the island, it's best to book ahead especially in the high season of June to August.

HOTEL RESTAURANTS

$$$$ ✕**Le Dauphin Gourmand.** When you dine at this outdoor restaurant
FRENCH you'll feel like you're dining in a home, not a restaurant. Located on a terrace overlooking Tiputa Pass, there are just five tables for diners and a large table where the hostess, Josephine, often entertains her guests. The three-course set menu may include tuna tartare, fish soup, grilled scampi, or mahimahi with ginger and Chinese spices, while a coconut or chocolate and rum tart are often on the menu for dessert. ⊠*Les Relais de Joséphine, Ohutu* ☎*96–02–00* ⊟*MC, V* ⊘*No lunch.*

$$–$$$ ✕**Te Rairoa Restaurant.** This lagoon-side restaurant is Rangi's "big-night-
PACIFIC RIM out" restaurant. There's plenty of choice on the á la carte menu ranging from escargot with garlic parsley butter, and pan-friend scallops to start, and several different varieties of fish (deep sea bass, salmon, sturgeon, and Emperor) for main course. A treat is the dessert buffet (1,000 CFP) where you can graze on several delicacies. Be aware that some dishes may be quite bland, an unfortunate trend in international resorts. ⊠*Hotel Kia Ora, Main road, Avatoru 5 km from airport* ☎*93–11–11* ⌔*Reservations essential* ⊟*AE, DC, MC, V.*

INDEPENDENT RESTAURANTS

$-$$
FRENCH

✕**Restaurant Le Kai Kai.** This is a very pleasant spot for lunch if you're cycling along the main road; you can also check your e-mail here but the Internet connection is rather slow. As there are free transfers from the hotels, you can enjoy a few drinks over dinner. There's a three-course set menu (3,300 CFP)

with two to three choices per course, and an á la carte menu featuring mussels in white wine; grilled tuna steak with soy sauce, garlic and ginger; and coffee ice cream with Kahlua for dessert. ⊠*Main roadroad, Avatoru 5 km from the airport* ☎96–03–39 ⚓*Reservations essential* ▤*MC, V* ☺*Closed Wed. night.*

$-$$
PIZZA

✕**Le Vaimario.** This restaurant attracts quite a crowd of locals on weekends and a few guests from the nearby Novotel Hotel. As one of only two independent restaurants on the island it gets busy during the high season. Dine indoors or out under a thatched roof on a mainly French menu with a long list of pizzas (all 1,250 CFP) as well. You might start with homemade foie gras, followed by shrimp sautéed with orange and ginger, and then end with a classic French treat such as profiteroles. *Main road, Avatoru, Near Novotel Hotel, 6 km (4 mi) from village* ☎96–95–96 ▤*MC, V* ☺*11:30–2, 6:30–9; Closed Sun. night and Mon.*

OUTDOOR ACTIVITIES

This divers' paradise has five scuba dive operators and others running drift snorkeling and dolphin-watch/glass-bottom boat trips in Tiputa Pass. There are day excursions to paradisiacal locations within the lagoon and tours to French Polynesia's only vineyard.

BIKING

On the main road near the airport, **JJLoc** (☎96–03–13) is a one-stop shop for bikes and scooters. It also has a small pearl shop. You can also hire bikes and scooters at **Arenahio Location** (☎96–82–45), which is about a mile east of Avatoru village on the main road.

BOATING & SAILING

If you don't won't to get wet but still want to see coral and fish, **Matahi Excursions** (☎96–84–48), near the Ohotu wharf, offers glass-bottom boat tours to Tiputa Pass's calmer waters.

DIVING & SNORKELING

Located at the Hotel Kia Ora, **Blue Dolphins Diving Center** (☎96–03–01 ⊕*www.bluedolphinsdiving.com*) offers four dives a day—two within the lagoon and two to the passes. Sites include Hammerhead Valley in Tiputa Pass, named after a shark species you might encounter.

Raie Manta Club (☎96–84–80 ⊕*www.raiemantaclub.com*) has Rangiroa covered with a kiosk at both Avatoru and Tiputa passes. Dives start from 6,200 CFP and there are kids' dives, too.

Rangiroa Activites (☎96–73–59 ⊕*www.rangiroa-snorkeling.com*) offers a two-in-one excursion that includes drift snorkeling in the Tiputa Pass and a dolphin-watch cruise. The tour costs 4,570 CFP per person with free pension/hotel pickup.

FISHING
Rangiroa Nautical and Aquatical Activities Center (☎96–04–96). Owner Serge Giroux does it all: he runs two-hour fishing trips, half-day snorkel and dolphin cruises, and full-day excursions to the Blue Lagoon, Sables Roses, and Iles aux Recifs.

LAGOON EXCURSIONS
Tane Excursions (☎96–84–68) offers a Blue Lagoon tour, as well as a combined Blue Lagoon/Ils aux Recifs tour, for 7,500 and 10,500 CFP, respectively. The second tour requires a lot of time in the boat.

Te Reva Tane e Vahine (☎96–82–51). Owner Jean-Pierre Tavita puts on a great Blue Lagoon tour and motu picnic (from 7,500 CFP). He and his daughter even weave little baskets out of palm fronds right before your eyes.

JET SKIING
Water Games (☎96–04–49) offers guided Jet Ski tours of the lagoon for an hour to half a day. Prices start at 12,000 CFP for an hour per ski.

SHOPPING

You'll save money in Rangi as there isn't much to buy; that is, unless you're lured into purchasing pearls.

GIFTS–SOUVENIRS
Ocean Passion (✉*Main roadroad, near airport* ☎96–02–72). You can't miss the brightly colored pareos and T-shirts hanging in front of this little white shop; that is, if it's open on that particular day. Hand-painted pareos range from 1,000 CFP.

GROCERIES
Magasin Henriette (✉*Coastal road, Ohotu* ☎77–56–12 ☉*Mon.–Sat. 6–6, Sun. 6:30–8:30* AM). Apart from buying food items, you can pick up sunglasses, pareos, and Tahitian shirts and board shorts. It's across the road from Les Relais de Joséphine.

Magasin Sarl (✉*Main street, Avatoru* ☎96–83–92 ☉*Mon.–Sat. 5:30–noon and 2:30–6:30, Sun. 5:30–8:30* AM). Pick up a pastry, a croissant, mineral water, and other groceries at this store next to the Catholic church.

PEARLS

Boutique Ikimasho (✉ *Main road, near Shell gas station, Avatoru* ☏ *96–84–46* ⊕ *www.ikimasho-black-pearls.com* ⊙ *Daily 9–6*). This boutique in the heart of Avatoru sells single pearls, bracelets, necklaces, pendants, and earrings, as well as a selection of artwork.

Gauguin's Pearls (✉ *Main road, near airport,* ☏ *93–11–30*). There's an on-site boutique selling single pearls and pearl jewelry. Free tours of the pearl farm are easily arranged.

SPAS

SPAS IN HOTELS & RESORTS

Hotel Kia Ora (✉ *Main road* ☏ *93–11–11* ⊕ *www.hotelkiaora.com*) provides the closest thing to spas services in Rangiroa. Its long list of massages includes a Thai massage with a Polynesian flavor. Massages cost 6,000 CFP an hour.

Novotel Rangiroa Lagoon Resort (✉ *Main road, 1 mi from airport* ☏ *93–13–50* ⊕ *www.accorhotels.pf* ⊙ *On request*) doesn't have a spa, but it does have a Thai massage therapist who can be booked for in-room treatments, which range from 6,000 to 12,000 CFP.

AFTER DARK

You'll catch up on your beauty sleep in Rangiroa—and all the Tuamotus—as there's no nightlife beyond having a few drinks at your hotel and taking in the twice-weekly cultural dance shows at Hotel Kia Ora. Some pensions invite local dancers to perform at their establishments, but these are impromptu occasions rather than organized events.

COCKTAIL TIME

Lagon Bleu (☏ *93–13–50* ⊕ *www.accorhotels.pf* ⊙ *Daily noon–10 PM*), at Novotel Rangiroa Lagoon Resort, is a casual spot and the perfect place to grab a drink as the sun goes down.

Miki Miki Bar (☏ *93–11–11* ⊙ *Daily noon–11 PM*), at Hotel Kia Ora, is a lovely bar with an old world charm, a bit like a gentlemen's club with plush sofas. From the bar's terrace you can watch—and feed—the fish.

PERFORMANCES

Hotel Kia Ora (✉ *Main road, Avatoru* ☏ *93–11–11* ⊕ *www.hotelkiaora. com* ⊙ *6 PM–8:30 PM*) has a cultural dance performance and Polynesian buffet every Wednesday and Sunday night, priced at 5,500 CFP. Nonguests pay 500 CFP for the show only; they can come for dinner, too.

FAKARAVA

Fakarava is oblong shaped and has an almost continuous string of reef and motu stretching for 40 km (25 mi) on its eastern edge. It's the second largest of the Tuamotu atolls, located 450 km (280 mi)

A BRIEF HISTORY OF THE TUAMOTUS

Historians believe most of the islands were inhabited in the 11th century. European explorers visited over a 300-year period; the first being Ferdinand Magellan in 1521. The last of the 78 islands were discovered in 1835, but it wasn't until the 1950s that the French navy drew a precise map of the region.

Pearl shell trading began as early as 1813 and French Catholic missionaries arrived in the 1820s, converted the islanders, and established the copra industry. France annexed the islands in 1853. The islands became a major economic center following the establishment of black-pearl farms in the 1960s. At same time the archipelago was forced into the world spotlight when France chose Muroroa and Fangataufa atolls—800 km (497 mi) south of Rangiroa—as its nuclear testing sites. Tests were carried out for 30 years until 1996. These atolls remain off-limits to visitors today.

5

northeast of Tahiti, and 120 km (75 mi) southeast of Rangiroa. It's renowned for the drift diving in its two passes—Garuae (also spelled Ngarue) in the north near the main town of Rotoava (and the airport) and Tamakohua Pass, 48 km (30 mi) across the lagoon in the south. The tiny village of Tetamanu, situated by the southern pass, was once the capital of the Tuamotus and houses the first church built in the archipelago in 1874.

In 2006 the entire atoll was deemed an UNESCO biosphere reserve; to preserve the lagoon no overwater bungalows have been built in it. Fakarava was "discovered" by Russian explorer Fabian Gottlieb Von Bellingshausen in 1820; some 20 years later missionaries arrived, in the guise of fanatical Catholic priest Honore Laval, and began building churches.

ESSENTIALS

Emergencies **Police (gendarmerie)** (☎ 93–40–40). **Cabinet Medical** (☎ 98–42–24).

Visitor Info **Fakarava Tourisme Committee** (☎ 98–41–51 ✉ hinanohellberg@mail.pf).

WHAT TO SEE

TOWNS

Rotoava. Situated on the northeast corner of Fakarava, this village of 750 people is where the action happens on the atoll. There's a pretty Catholic church, a primary school, a few telephone booths that take phone cards, a pharmacy with a doctor and nurse, and a post office with Internet connection. There is no bank or ATMs but the two general stores now accept credit cards. It does have a 15-km (9-mi) road and a cycling lane, so biking is a fun way to explore the area.

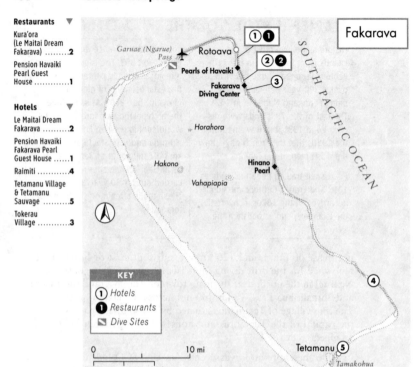

Tetamanu. It's hard to believe that this village of a dozen people was once the capital of the Tuamotus. The coral church, built in 1874, is still there, along with the Tetamanu Village pension right next to the Tamakohua Pass. The pension operates its own dive center. The owners of the Raimiti pension (about 9.6 km [6 mi] north of the pass) consider themselves Tetamanu citizens and are included in the dozen. The village and pensions are about 48 km (30 mi) from the airport and a 90-minute boat ride away.

BEACHES
Beaches are easy to visit—just climb aboard your bike and cycle along the one road until you spot a good one.

WHERE TO STAY

There's one stylish resort on the island and a dozen family-run hotels and guesthouses. Most are found in the northeast corner along the only paved road on the island, which stretches about 15 km (9 mi) from the airport south via the main town of Rotoava. No accommodation offers air-conditioning and almost all pensions have cold-water bathrooms; the Le Maitai Dream resort has hot water. There are three pensions in around Tetamanu, which is about 48 km (30 mi [or 90 minutes by boat]) from the airport.

RESORTS

$$–$$$ ☷ **Le Maitai Dream Fakarava.** Opened in 2002, this little sister to the Bora Bora property is the most luxurious accommodation on the atoll. Each of the 30 stylish bungalows, some with beach and some with garden settings, have all the creature comforts you could want, except for air-conditioning. The indoor-outdoor restaurant has magnificent lagoon views, while the Kiri Kiri Bar provides an eclectic range of entertainment, from pareo tying to cooking lessons and live music. There's an onsite diving center, and coral just off the beach for snorkelers. **Pros:** Most creature comforts; bar and entertainment. **Cons:** No a/c. ⊠*Rotoava* ☏*B.P. 19, Rotoava 98763* ☎*93–41–50* ⬖*28 bungalows* ⌂*In-room: no a/c, refrigerator. In-hotel: restaurant, bar, beachfront, diving, water sports, bicycles, no elevator, laundry service, concierge, airport shuttle, parking (no fee)* ▤*AE, MC, V* ⵏⵔ*EP.*

SMALL HOTELS/GUESTHOUSES

$$ ☷ **Pension Havaiki Fakarava Pearl Guest House.** This all-in-one pension and pearl farm is a great place to stay. Owner Joachim Dariel conducts free visits of the farm and there are free bikes to explore the town of Rotoava. There are six beach bungalows and two two-bedroom garden bungalows with fans, bathrooms with cold water, and lovely Polynesian touches like shell wind chimes and oval bathroom mirrors set in shell frames. **Pros:** There's a pearl farm on the premises; a variety of meals are offered. **Cons:** No a/c; no hot water. ⊠*Rotoava* ☏*B.P. 121, Rotoava* ☎*93–40–15* ⊕*www.havaiki.com* ⬖*8 bungalows* ⌂*In-room: no phone, no TV. In-hotel: restaurant, bar, beachfront, diving, water sports, bicycles, no elevator, laundry service, concierge, public Internet, airport shuttle* ▤*AE, MC, V* ⵏⵔ*MAP.*

$$$ ☷ **Raimiti.** This is a Robinson Crusoe experience in name and nature. Five "Robinson" bungalows line the lagoon, sleep two people, and have cold-water showers; the Crusoe bungalow—on the ocean side—sleeps four and has hot water. This is the sister property to Residence Linavera in Moorea. If you love isolation, with a touch of style, this is the place for you. It's 90 minutes by boat from the airport, and about 16 km (10 mi) from Tetamanu village. Minimum stay is two nights. **Pros:** Beautiful isolated location; all your meals and touring are included. **Cons:** some hot water; isolated may not be your thing. ⊠*Tetamanu* ☏*B.P. 1, Papetoai, Moorea 98729* ☎*55–05–65* ⊕*www.raimiti.com* ⬖*6 bungalows* ⌂*In-room: no a/c, no phone, no TV. In hotel: restaurant, bar, beachfront, diving, water sports, no elevator, laundry service, concierge, airport shuttle* ▤*AE, MC, V* ⵏⵔ*AP.*

$$$$ ☷ **Tetamanu Village & Tetamanu Sauvage.** This is the place to come if you want to dive. The two locations are right by the pass; Tetamanu Sauvage is on a motu a short distance from the main property. The "village" has six bungalows and the "sauvage" has five. There's a two-night minimum stay and dives start at 5,500 CFP. **Pros:** Great diving; great location; private bathrooms. **Cons:** Private bathrooms have no hot water. ⊠*Tetamanu* ☏*B.P. 6534, Faa'a, Tahiti 98703*

☎42–77–70 ⊕*www.tetamanuvillage.pf* ⇆*11 bungalows* ⌂*In-room: no a/c, no phone, no TV (some). In-hotel: restaurant, bar, beachfront, diving, water sports, no elevator, concierge, airport shuttle* ▭*AE, MC, V* ⎰◯⎱*MAP.*

$$ 🖵**Tokerau Village.** Located about half a mile or so from Le Maitai Dream, this pension has four bungalows set in a beautiful, well-maintained garden. Each bungalow has a double and single bed, fan, and mosquito net, as well as a private bathroom with cold-water shower. **Pros:** Beachfront; close to town. **Cons:** No a/c; no hot water. ⊠*Rotoava* ⌂*B.P. 53, Rotoava 98763* ☎*98–41–09* ✎*tokerauvillage@mail.pf* ⇆*4 bungalows* ⌂*In-room: no phone, no TV. In-hotel: restaurant, bar, beachfront, diving, water sports, bicycles, no elevator, concierge, airport shuttle* ▭*AE, MC, V* ⎰◯⎱*MAP.*

WHERE TO EAT

Dining options run from the fancy—Le Maitai Dream's Kura'ora—to the communal—family-run guesthouses—on Fakarava. Rotoava has three small snack bars where you can get cold drinks and a quick meal, as well as a pizzeria and a bakery.

HOTEL RESTAURANTS

$$$–$$$$ ✕**Kura'ora.** Guests dine under white canvas umbrellas on a terrace on
PACIFIC RIM   the edge of the lagoon by day, or at tables set with white linen and sparkling glassware by night. This restaurant is casual chic and is the most elegant on the island. Start with foie gras or mussels and move on to grilled salmon or whatever fresh lagoon fish has come in with the catch. Desserts include coconut and papaya tarts served with vanilla ice cream. Stop by the Kiri Kiri bar for a pre-dinner cocktail. ⊠*Le Maitai Dream Fakarava, Rotoava* ☎*93–41–50* ⌣*Reservations essential* ▭*AE, MC, V* ⊙*Lunch and dinner.*

$–$$ ✕**Pension Havaiki Pearl Guest House.** Nonguests dining at this little pen-
PACIFIC RIM   sion and pearl farm will be offered a two-course set menu. Dishes will vary depending on what the hostess Clotilde has made that evening, but may include mahimahi with honey sauce, oysters with coconut sauce, tuna sashimi, or even barbecued steak imported from New Zealand. Phone first to ask about transfers. ⊠*Rotoava* ☎*93–40–15* ⌣*Reservations essential* ▭*AE, MC, V* ⊙*Lunch only in June; Dinner rest of year.*

OUTDOOR ACTIVITIES

Divers in the know come from far and wide to drift dive in Ngarue Pass, a 1-km-wide expanse with a swift flowing current, or the smaller Tetamanu Pass. Snorklers also have plenty to explore in the lagoon where the water is a tepid 80°F. There are bikes to ride on the one 9-mi road and excursions to pearl farms, pink-sand beaches, and motu with nesting birds and scurrying crabs. Note that excursions may not operate every day.

BOATING & SAILING
Moorea Loca Boat Fakarava (✉ *Pension Paparara, Rotoava* ☎ *98–42–66* ⊕ *www.haere-mai.pf*) does not require a license to rent a 12-foot boat, which you can rent for one-, two-, four-, and eight-hour increments. Transfers are provided.

DIVING & SNORKELING
Top Dive Fakarava (☎ *98–43–76* ⊕ *www.topdive.com*) is based at the Le Maitai Dream resort. On offer: drop-off dives in the ocean, beginners' dives in the lagoon, and drift dives in the two passes that literally teem with sharks, turtles, rays, and other amazing marine life.

Tetamanu Diving Center (☎ *77–10–06 mobile* ⊕ *www.tetamanuvillage. pf*) is the only dive center at Tamakohua Pass—the 200-meter pass in the south of the atoll. The coral is amazing and schools of gray sharks love it here.

LAGOON EXCURSIONS
Tamatoa 2 (✉ *Rotoava* ☎ *98–41–13*), a 24-foot boat based at Pension Vaiama Village, takes 12 passengers on excursions to bird islands, motu picnic spots, and Tetamanu village. The other pensions also run lagoon excursions, which are around 7,500 CFP per person.

PEARL FARMS
Established in 1989, **Pearls of Havaiki** (☎ *93–40–15* ⊕ *www.havaiki. com*) is the oldest farm in Fakarava. Guests staying at the attached pension—and visitors alike—can dive to inspect the oyster shells with owner Joachim Dariel and play a kind of "pearl" lottery to see what's inside.

SHOPPING

Alas, shopoholics will be disappointed with the lack of options, apart from pearls. However, if you do like pearls, you'll be able to buy individual pearls and pearl jewelry at **Pearls of Havaiki** (☎ *93–40–15* ⊕ *www. havaiki.com*). They also have an array of mother-of-pearl pieces. If you want to visit a pearl farm, check out **Hinano Pearls** (☎ *98–41–51* ✍ *hianohellberg@amail.pf*), about 19 km (12 mi) south of Rotoava. To arrange a visit, call or e-mail the owners.

AFTER DARK

Fakarava is not a party town, but if you want entertainment head to the Le Maitai Dream. The resort is named after the famous rum-based Polynesia concoction, which its bar, **Kiri Kiri Bar** (☉ *10 AM–11 PM*), serves along with other tropical drinks. There's also live music and demonstrations, such as pareo tying. The resort also offers weekly **Polynesian dance performances** (✉ *6,000 CFP*) during the high season. It's best to call ahead, as performances are scheduled based upon the number of guests at the time.

TIKEHAU

Tikehau is one of the most beautiful of the Tuamotu atolls; it's an almost perfect oval of coral reef that encloses a brilliant blue lagoon measuring 26 km (16 mi) in diameter. There are pink-sand beaches perfect for picnics, a town with four churches, an island of thousands of nesting birds, and some of the best diving and snorkeling around. With a population of just over 400, things haven't changed much in almost half a century. People still work in copra production, agriculture, and fishing, though more are employed on pearl farms these days.

Although the island was not "discovered" by the West until the early 19th century, archeological remains suggest the island may have been inhabited more than 2,000 years ago. Russian naval officer Otto von Kotzebve is credited with first sighting Tikehau in 1815. The French eventually set up a mission in the 1860s. In 1987, a Jacques Cousteau–led research team claimed that the lagoon had the greatest concentration of fish species of anywhere in French Polynesia—a claim that continues to lure avid divers.

ESSENTIALS

Emergencies **Police (gendarmerie)** (☎ *96–22–99*). **Cabinet Medical** (☎ *96–23–49*).

Taxis **Mr. Ignace Tupahiroa** (☎ *77–28–02*).

Visitor Info **Tikehau Tourisme Committee** (☎ *96–22–42*).

WHAT TO SEE

TOWNS

Tuherahera. The name of the main town and the motu on which the airport is built, this busy little center has four churches (three on the same corner and the other near the quay), a town hall, medical center, a general store, and a snack bar, but no bank. Most of the pensions are located near the town and folks are transferred by car; the Tikehau Pearl Resort is 10 minutes away and requires a boat transfer.

BEACHES

Tikehau beaches are easier to explore than Manihi's as there's a 10-km (6-mi) road that runs along the atoll from the airport, through the town, and to the handful of pensions just east of the airport. If you have a bicycle, you'll be able to discover calm lagoon side beaches and the rougher ocean side beaches, but you'll need to take an excursion to **Sables Roses,** a tiny motu adrift in Tikehau's gorgeous lagoon, with towering coconut trees and pink-sand beaches. The day trips (☎ *7,000 CFP* ☉ *10* AM–*3* PM) here are leisurely affairs—swimming, snorkeling, and beachcombing. When the tide's out it's possible to walk across the shallow channels to other motus and even out to the ocean side.

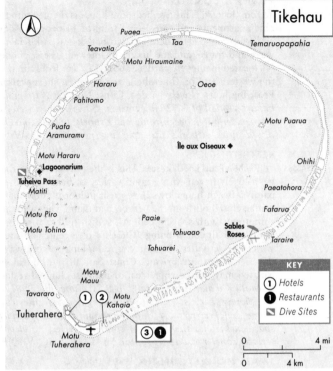

SIGHTS

Ile Aux Oiseaux. This island in the middle of the lagoon is a haven for thousands of boobies (birds, people!), sooties, noddies, and terns. It's a noisy day out, to say the least, but the birds are amazing and there's usually a picnic included in the trip. Day trips take off from Tikehau Pearl Resort. ⌑ *7,000 CFP.* ☉ *10* AM–*3* PM.

WHERE TO STAY

Tikehau is a *new* frontier when it comes to accommodations, and that's half the appeal. So don't expect the luxuries of home, and you won't be disappointed. Only three of the island's 10 hotels and pensions have hot water and only one has air-conditioning, but what you'll get is clean, comfortable family-run lodgings with three meals a day and a little thatched hut by the lagoon. The Tikehau Pearl Resort has most of the creature comforts including air-conditioned overwater bungalows. Only half the pensions accept credit cards, and as there is no bank in town, you'll need to bring a wad of cash. The Pearl resort and most of the small hotels can organize excursions.

VILLAS & CONDOMINIUMS

¢ ⊞ **Fare Hanariki.** This five-bedroom house is divided into two comfortable apartments and can sleep a total of 14 people in double, single, and foldaway beds. There are two bathrooms, a kitchen with microwave and fridge, and the luxury of Internet access, phone, and a TV. It's located in a lovely garden, about 150 feet from the water's edge at the western end of Tuherahera motu, only a short walk from shops. **Pros:** Big house; lovely garden. **Cons:** No a/c. ⊠ *Tuherahera* ✎ *fare-hanariki@mail.pf* ☎ *2 apartments* ♿ *In-room: no a/c, refrigerator, kitchen. In-hotel: beachfront, water sports, bicycles, no elevator, laundry facilities, airport shuttle, parking (no fee)* ▤ *MC, V* ⧠ *EP.*

RESORTS

$$$–$$$$ ⊞ **Tikehau Pearl Beach Resort.** This is the only resort on the island, and it's a lovely haven with a good variety of beach and overwater bungalows. Beach bungalows have great indoor-outdoor bathrooms that can be closed off from the bedroom at night. The overwater suites are sumptuous with soaring ceilings, stylish timber furniture, deep oval baths, and air-conditioning. There's a dive center on-site and a good variety of activities. **Pros:** If you're looking to get away from it all, this is isolated and private. **Cons:** Not all the bungalows have a/c; isolated may not be your ideal of paradise; limited restaurant menu. ⊠ *Motu Kahaia, Tuherahera* ☎ *B.P. 20, Tuherahera 98778* ☎ *96–23–00* ⊕ *www.pearlresorts.com* ☎ *29 bungalows, 8 suites* ♿ *In-room: a/c (some), safe, refrigerator. In-hotel: restaurant, room service, bar, pool, spa, beachfront, diving, water sports, bicycles, no elevator, laundry service, concierge, airport shuttle* ▤ *AE, DC, MC, V* ⧠ *EP.*

SMALL HOTELS/GUESTHOUSES

$ ⊞ **Tikehau Village.** With nine bungalows, this is the largest of the small family-run pensions on the island. Each of the Polynesian-style thatched bungalows has a double bed and single bed, a terrace, and a bathroom with a cold-water shower. Half- and full-board plans are offered. There are free kayaks and free airport transfers. ⊠ *Tuherahera* ☎ *B.P. 9, Tuherahera 98778* ☎ *96–22–86* ✎ *tikehauvillage@mail.pf* ☎ *9 bungalows* ♿ *In-room: no a/c, refrigerator (some), no TV (some). In-hotel: restaurant, bar, beachfront, diving, water sports, bicycles, no elevator, laundry facilities, concierge, airport shuttle, parking (no fee)* ▤ *AE, MC, V* ⧠ *MAP.*

WHERE TO EAT

Just like its neighbor Manihi, Tikehau doesn't have many choices when it comes to dining. Simply put, you either eat in your hotel restaurant or avail yourself of the half- and full-board options at your pension. Home-cooked pension meals, however, have a reputation for being simple but delicious and offering large portions.

HOTEL RESTAURANTS

$$$–$$$$
PACIFIC RIM
✕**Poreho Restaurant.** You'll really know you're in the South Seas when you dining at this open-air restaurant. The gentle breezes waft in and the views—across the lagoon and out to the overwater bungalows—are fantastic. The menu has some new twists on old island favorites such as the appetizer of potted mince of mahimahi served with local potato chips and confit tomatoes, and the main course of fillet of lamb on a bed of *fafa* (taro leaves) with Marquesas Islands honey and ginger sauce. The decadent banana-and-rum cake smothered in coconut milk mousse is a great way to end the meal. ■TIP➡ It's wise to book ahead if you want to dine here, because a boat transfer, which may be an additional cost, is required. ✉*Tikehau Pearl Resort, Motu Kahaia* ☎*96–23–00* ☏*Reservations essential* ▤*AE, DC, MC, V.*

OUTDOOR ACTIVITIES

5

The Tuheiva Pass on the west coast is the place to see graceful manta rays, while visits to the nearby Lagoonarium, an aquarium within the natural lagoon, gives snorkels a chance to swim with marine life in shallow waters. The **Tikehau Pearl Beach Resort** (✉*Motu Kahaia* ☎*96–23 00* ⊕*www.pearlresorts.com*) can organize all the excursions.

BIKING

Tikehau Village (✉*Tuherahera* ☎*96–22–86*) rents out bikes and is ideally located near the island's one road.

EXCURSIONS

If you're looking to go boating, sailing, fishing, or on a lagoon excursion, contact the **Tikehau Pearl Resort** can arrange the outings for you; however, not all will be available every day. Half-day excursions with lunch are approximately 7,500 CFP.

DIVING & SNORKELING

Located at the Tikehau Pearl Resort, **Tikehau Blue Nui** (☎*96–22–40* ⊕*www.bluenui.com*) will show you all those wonderful fish that Jacques Cousteau raved about.

SPAS

Tikehau might be isolated but spa junkies can rest assured—body wraps, facials, and massages are offered at Tikehau Pearl Beach Resort's **Manea Spa** (⊗*9–5*).

AFTER DARK

You'll getting plenty of sleep on Tikehau as there's nothing to do at night beyond dinner and drinks in your own pension or at the island's only bar, **Tianoa Bar** at Tikehau Pearl Resort. Order a mai tai and let the balmy breezes and the music of the trio of Polynesian singers (June–October) lull you into a deep state of relaxation.

MANIHI

Manihi is the least developed of the four main Tuamotu islands and at 520 km (325 mi) from Tahiti, the farthest away. It was first inhabited around AD 600 and the remains of an ancient coral *marae* (ancient temple), the Kamoka, are located on the southern edge, between two of the only three pensions on the island. Dutch explorers Jacob le Maire and Willem Schouten sighted the island in 1615. Today Manihi is a major center of black pearl production with about 60 farms dotting the lagoon whose emerald waters are said to provide the perfect temperature, density, and salinity for pearl cultivation. The first farm in French Polynesia was established here in 1968. Divers come to Manihi to explore the Tairapa Pass, where they drift dive with gray sharks, turtles, and huge fish; another favorite spot is a coral garden called The Circus.

ESSENTIALS

Emergencies Police (gendarmerie) (☎ 96–42–55). **Cabinet Medical** (☎ 97–53–67).

WHAT TO SEE

TOWNS

Turipaoa. Also known as Paeua, Manihi's main town is home to most of the atoll's 1,200 people. It's located near Turipaoa Pass (also known as Tairapa Pass), a renowned diving site. With only a few streets, a grocery story, and Catholic church, it's easy to explore. There are regular free boat transfers between the town and Manihi Pearl Resort, and bikes are welcome on board. There are no banks or ATMs on Manihi.

BEACHES

All of Manihi's lodgings are located on lovely calm beaches. But, if you want to explore further than your own patch of paradise, it's best to take an organized lagoon excursions that will visit a motu edged by white- and possibly pink-sand beaches.

WHERE TO STAY

Manihi's accommodation scene can be summed up in one word—small! There are just 49 bungalows on the atoll, 40 of which belong to the Manihi Pearl Resort. The dive center is based at the resort and most excursions depart from the resort's wharf. The pensions offer a completely different experience: each has three bungalows and two of the pensions have guest kitchens. If you want to self-cater it pays to be organized and get supplies in town before heading off to the pension.

RESORTS

$$$–$$$$ 🏨 **Manihi Pearl Beach Resort.** The biggest resort on the island, it's located about half a mile from the airport, near the village of Paeua. It opened in 1985, but was rebuilt in 1996 when taken over by Pearl Resorts; its last renovation was in 2006 when air-conditioning was installed in five overwater bungalows. All the rooms are decorated with a blend of rattan, timber, and cane materials and white bedspreads and curtains.

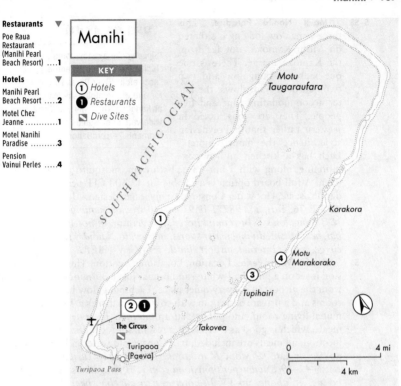

Free activities include mini-golf, beach volleyball, billiards, bicycles, and Polynesian dance classes (if there's a dozen people to make up a troupe). Shoppers will appreciate the two on-site boutiques. **Pros:** The ultimate in luxury resorts. **Cons:** No a/c. *Turipaoa ☐B.P. 1, Turipaoa 98771 ☎96–42–73 ⊕www.pearlresorts.com ⇆40 bungalows ⌂In-room: no a/c, safe, refrigerator. In-hotel: restaurant, bar, beachfront, diving, water sports, bicycles, no elevator, laundry service, concierge, airport shuttle, parking (no fee) ☰AE, DC, MC, V ❑EP.*

SMALL HOTELS/GUESTHOUSES

$ ☷**Motel Chez Jeanne.** This three-bungalow pension is on a private island 9.6 km (6 mi) north of the airport. The all-white bungalows are an A-frame western design; two are on the beach, while the other is over the water. Each has an equipped kitchen, refrigerator, and private bathroom with cold water. Owners Guy and Jeanne Herta will provide meals but need to be informed before arrival. They also provide a free visit to a pearl farm. **Pros:** If you're looking for the real Robinson Crusoe lifestyle, you'll find it here. **Cons:** Meals need to be prearranged; self-catering requires planning; in an isolated spot. *Near Motu Taugaraufara ☎96–42–90 ⇆3 bungalows ⌂In-room: kitchen, refrigerator, restaurant, bar, beachfront, water sports, no elevator, airport shuttle ☰MC, V ❑EP.*

$-$$ 🏠**Motel Nanihi Paradise.** This three-bungalow lodging is situated on Motu Kamoka, not far from the Kamoka marae. There is one one-bedroom bungalow and two two-bedroom bungalows; the latter accommodating four and five people. They are constructed in western rather than a Polynesian style, hence the name "motel." Each has a kitchen and air-con-

WORD OF MOUTH

"Since you're already doing a "high-island" (Moorea) and a "near-atoll" (Bora Bora), I'd opt for one of the atolls, say Manihi or Rangiroa. That way you'll see a wide variety of islands and environments." —LordBalfor

ditioning, along with a hot-water bathroom, mosquito netting, and linen. A full-board option is available for 13,500 CFP per person per day. **Pros:** a/c, Hot water **Cons:** Non-Polynesian design. *Motu Kamoka* ⌂*B.P. 76, Turipaoa 98771* ☎*93–30–40* ⊕*www.nanihiparadise.com* 🛏*3 bungalows* ⌂*In-room: kitchen, refrigerator. In-hotel: restaurant, bar, beachfront, diving, water sports, no elevator, laundry service, concierge, public Internet, airport shuttle* ▭*MC, V* ⑂*EP.*

$$ 🏠**Pension Vainui Perles.** Location, Location, Location. This rustic pension is set on a pink-and-white-sand beach. Just a 30-minute boat ride from the airport, it's a very quiet place. Each bungalow has two bedrooms and a private bathroom with cold water; there's a TV in a communal living room, and public dial-up Internet. The rate includes all meals, which is good as there's not a restaurant for miles. **Pros:** Good location; all meals are included; bar. **Cons:** Cold water in bathrooms; no a/c or fan. ✉*Motu Marakorako* ⌂*B.P. 51, Turipaoa 98771* ☎*96–42–89* ⊕*www.pensionvainui.com* 🛏*3 bungalows* ⌂*In-room: no a/c, no phone, no TV. In-hotel: restaurant, bar, beachfront, diving, water sports, bicycles, no elevator, public Internet, airport shuttle* ▭*MC, V* ⑂*AP.*

WHERE TO EAT

There is just one place to eat out in Manihi—the Manihi Pearl Beach Resort. There are only three other pensions on the atoll and two of the three owners provide meals as part of half- and full-board packages.

HOTEL RESTAURANTS

$$–$$$ ✗**Poe Raua Restaurant.** Situated in a lovely garden with fabulous lagoon
PACIFIC RIM   views, this restaurant is the big night out on the island. Highlights of a three-course meal may be the half-cooked tuna with ginger and mango sauce, grilled parrot fish with Marquesas butter sauce, and a warm papaya pie with coconut ice cream. If you want to splurge, there's the grilled lobster with vanilla cream at 5,000 CFP. As this is the only restaurant on the atoll, it's smart to call ahead for reservations. ✉*Manihi Pearl Beach Resort, Turipaoa* ☎*96–42–73* ▭*AE, DC, MC, V.*

BEST BETS FOR CRUISING

Shooting the pass. Divers flock to Rangiroa to drift through Tiputa Pass with dolphins, hundreds of fish, and sharks waiting to snap them up—the fish that is!

In the pink or blue! Take an excursion across Rangiroa's vast lagoon to Sables Roses (pink-sand beach) or the Blue Lagoon, for a day in paradise. The *Star Flyer* and *Haumana* call at these idyllic spots.

Wine and pearls. It sounds unbelievable but there's a vineyard in

Rangiroa—on a motu off the main town of Avatoru. If time is short, just drop into the "cave" to taste the reds, whites, or rosés. Round off the day with a visit to a pearl farm.

Time warp. Take a trip back in time across Fakarava's wide lagoon to Tetamanu to see the Catholic church built in 1874.

5

OUTDOOR ACTIVITIES

Divers will be spoiled here with three different dive environments to explore. Other activities include fishing trips and motu picnics with snorkeling.

DIVING & SNORKELING

Divers have the chance to explore three different environments here: drift diving in the Tairapa Pass; the "drop-off" on the pass's ocean side; and wonderful coral at "The Circus" inside the lagoon. Snorklers can also drift along the pass.

Located at the Manihi Pearl Beach Resort, **Blue Nui Dive Center** (☎96–42–17) is the only dive operator on Manihi. There are dive sites ideal for beginner and experienced divers inside and outside the lagoon.

OTHER WATER ACTIVITIES & EXCURSIONS

Mahini Pearl Beach Resort (☎96–42–73 ⊕*www.pearlresorts.com*) is the only real player in Manihi and it can organize all sort of water-based activities. The smaller pensions will also be able to book activities, but it is wise to check in advance whether operators pick up from the smaller pensions, which are located away from the main town.

SHOPPING

As the pearl farm capital of French Polynesia, black pearls are the big "must-buy" here. You can buy pearls at farms or at **Manihi Pearl Beach Resort** (☎96–42–73 ⊕*www.pearlresorts.com* ☉*Daily 9–5*), which has two boutiques: a pearl boutique with single pearls and jewelry and a gift shop with souvenirs such as mother-of-pearl items and clothing.

Unfortunately, a direct pearl farm purchase is no cheaper than a store-bought pearl as all pearls are sent to Pape'ete for authentication and grading and then come back to the pearl farms for sale.

SPAS

Manihi Pearl Beach Resort's **Manea Spa** (☎ *96–42–73* ⊕ *www.pearl resorts.com* ⊙ *Daily 1–7* PM) is the only spa on the island and offers enough treatments to keep guests happy for days. Therapists use the famous monoi oil (copra oil infused with tiare flowers), which is said to work miracles on the skin, in several massages involving hot volcanic stones and even black pearls. Massages start at 8,500 CFP for 30 minutes; the Manea Manea treatment of body wrap, scrub, facial, and massage is a pricey 33,000 CFP.

AFTER DARK

Your resort is your sole source of entertainment on Manihi, so gather around the bar and meet some new friends. Manihi Pearl Beach Resort offers a Polynesia dance show and buffet once a week. The show's held on various days depending on the hotel occupancy; cost is 5,650 CFP.

The Other Islands

WORD OF MOUTH

"We visited Hiva Oa and Nuku Hiva and on both stayed at the Pearl Resorts and were very pleased; both are located high on the hillsides with wonderful vistas. The islands offer more rugged beauty compared with the other Society Islands in that general region. We visited during late September and early October and experienced good weather— enjoyed hiking and some water sports."

—DJE

Written by
Bob Marriott
& Caroline
Gladstone

SCATTERED AROUND TAHITI ARE A number of island groups, mainly just specks of land in the vastness of the world's greatest ocean, but each a tiny green oasis. Some of the last places on earth to be discovered and settled by Europeans, they attracted famous explorers like Captain Cook, Bligh, and Ingraham. Later on, artists the like of Gauguin and writers such as Stevenson were to fall under the spell of their year-round hot weather, warm tropical waters, and splendid isolation. Today, the Islands act as a magnet for the discerning tourist. Raiatea, largest of the Leeward Islands and second only to Tahiti in size, is a respectable 20-minute flight northwest from the capital and with neighboring Tahaa forms a popular holiday spot.

Away to the northeast of Tahiti, the Marquesas Islands are the most isolated island group in the world—the nearest is about a three-hour flight from Pape'ete. The Gambiers, part of the Tuamotu Archipelago, are to the southeast, with the Australs the last group to be discovered lying to the south. These are tiny patches of paradise, places where it is still possible to find that touch of romance and create the feeling of being in your own little world. They're not so easily accessible, but even if only for a few days try to make time for a visit and enjoy relaxing on an exquisite island paradise.

RAIATEA AND TAHAA

Raiatea and Tahaa are basically one island connected by a fairly narrow channel and are undoubtedly among the more culturally romantic spots in the South Pacific. Raiatea, the largest island in French Polynesia after Tahiti, is known as the "sacred isle" and holds a special religious and cultural significance as the cradle of Polynesian culture. The island was a favorite destination of English explorer Captain Cook and has some of the region's most significant archeological sites. Local oral history explains that as the home of Tapuapuatea, the first Royal Marae, this island was the place where important ceremonies and gatherings took place. Ethnic groups from as far away as New Zealand and Easter Island can trace their heritage back to the island. Most of the population of around 11,000 live in the north around Uturoa, the main town and second only to Pape'ete in size. Raiatea has a rugged interior with its highest point, Mount Tefatua (Toomaru), reaching 3,335 feet (1,016 meters); it's often known as the mountain of 1,000 waterfalls.

Neighboring Tahaa has a population of less than 5,000 and is less than a quarter of the size of Raiatea. The island has a quiet charm, which takes visitors back to earlier days. Tahaa is often known as the "vanilla island" because the aromatic and exotic beans are the island's main export along with pearls, copra, and noni juice. There are no beaches but the lagoon is dotted with numerous *motu*—tiny, sandy islets—where you can while away the hours, sunbathing or swimming, which in most parts is like observing a giant deep-sea aquarium.

GETTING HERE AND AROUND

Air Tahiti has six—sometimes more—daily flights from the Faa'a International Airport in Tahiti to Raiatea Airport; it's a 40 minute flight that costs US$320 (round-trip). There are also flights from Moorea, Bora Bora, and Huahine, so island-hopping is a possibility. Tahaa has no airport but there are regular shuttle boats and ferries to the island from Raiatea. The boat trip takes around 20 minutes.

In Raiatea transport from the airport to hotels and lodgings is generally provided by minibuses and *L'Truck,* a colorful open-sided bus that transports passengers for a small fee. Taxis are available at the airport for flight arrivals, and a taxi stand is located near the market in Uturoa's center.

Cars, scooters, and bicycles can be hired on both islands and though only about half the roads are paved they are safe for driving and with traffic being at a minimum it should present no problem.

WHEN TO GO

The wet season in French Polynesia is November to April—three quarters of the annual rainfall (70 inches [1.8meters] at Pape'ete) falls during this period. This is considered the off-season and vacationers can expect temperatures of 27–30°C (80–86°F) with possible cloud cover and heavy humidity, in the smaller islands; however, there is always the possibility of a cooling breeze.

6

RAIATEA

Known as the "Sacred Island," Raiatea is a fascinating haunt for archaeologists and historians as it's one of the islands in the Pacific where Polynesian culture can trace its roots. Visitors will find many of the older Polynesian structures still in place and are fascinating places to explore. In the 16th century, Raiatea developed a powerful cult dedicated to Oro the God of War and built a large meeting ground, the Taputaputea Marae, which is still intact. Human sacrifice was practiced until around the middle of the 18th century and visitors should look for the sacrificial stone. Several tour operators run visits to the *marae* (ancient temples) along with some degree of informed commentary—although in fairness Polynesian storytelling can embellish things a little.

The Faaroa River is the only navigable waterway in French Polynesia and it can be traveled by powerboat or

NEED A REASON TO CELEBRATE?

The Hawaiki Nui Canoe Race, held for three days every October, starts on Huahine, goes on to Raiatea and Tahaa, and ends with an open-sea crossing to Bora Bora. More than a hundred canoes take part in the race, which is followed by feasting, dancing, and music.

Held in Raiatea around the last week in October, the Stone-fishing Festival has participants beating the water's surface with stones to drive fish into a trap. There's also craft and produce displays, canoe racing, and fire-walking.

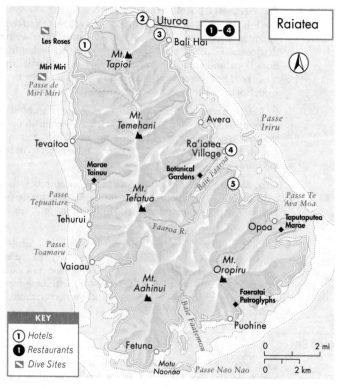

outrigger canoe. Running through the Faaroa Gorge it passes some spectacular scenery with steep-walled jungle foliage holding dozens of bird species and wild hibiscus. Trekking up Mount Temehani, a well-known landmark that's said to be Oro's birthplace, is relatively demanding. Keep a lookout for the rare, five-petal *tiare apetahi*. Said to be impossible to grow anywhere else, this white, indigenous flower can only be found above 1,300 feet (396 meters). ■TIP→ **Look, but don't touch. It's against the law to pick them.**

GETTING HERE & AROUND

Apart from being the most popular yachting center in French Polynesia, Raiatea is a favorite stopover for cruise ships, which dock right in town. The wharf area is only one block from the main street and most of the shopping and nearby attractions are within easy walking distance. The ferryboats, which run a regular service between the wharf and Tahaa, are close by and there are always eager tour operators ready to take visitors off to a number of activities.

The island is about 100 km (62 mi) around with comparatively safe driving on uncrowded, paved roads. Uturoa, the island's main town, has a population of about 5,000 and only a handful of streets, so it's fairly hard to get lost here.

ESSENTIALS

Visitor Info **Tahiti Tourisme Raiatea** (✉ *Marina Station of Uturoa* ☎ *B.P. 1628, Uturoa 98735* ☎ *60-07-77* ✉ *raiatea-info@Tahiti-tourisme.pf* ⊘ *Mon.–Fri. 8-4. Closed weekends unless a cruise ship is in port).* **Te Tepuna Association** (☎ *B.P. 884,Uturoa 98735* ☎ *66-16-65* ⊕ *www.raiatea-vacances.com).*

WHERE TO STAY

There are only two hotels on the island but a number of pensions or lodging places. *See the price chart in Chapter 1, Tahiti, for information on pricing.*

HOTELS

$$ $$$ 🏨 **Raiatea Hawaiki Nui Hotel.** The most luxurious and largest hotel on the island, the units have all modern conveniences and the overwater units even have a fish-viewing panel. Regular feeding sessions from the pier bring in shoals of tropical fish and there is an outdoor terrace overlooking the ocean and the pool. The restaurant has a very good name with seafood a popular choice and a friendly staff and music in the bar can bring in the locals on a Friday and Saturday night. **Pros:** Rooms have both a/c and a ceiling fan; there are disabled facilities available in the hotel and rooms; there are cultural activities available such as dance shows and Tahitian feasts. **Cons:** No Internet service available to guests. *about 2 km (1.2 mi) south of Uturoa* ☎*B.P. 43, Uturoa 98735* ☎*60-05-00* ⊕*www.pearlresorts.com* ⇌*20 bungalows, 8 rooms* ⚐*In-room: refrigerator, safe. In-hotel: restaurant, room service, bar, pool, waterfront, diving, water sports, bicycles, no elevator, laundry service, concierge, airport shuttle* ▤*AE, MC, V* ⦿*BP.*

$ 🏨 **Raiatea Lodge Hotel.** This is a charming colonial-style building with teak furnishings that stands in more than 2 acres of grounds. A large swimming pool is surrounded by gardens with an abundance of rare plants. All rooms have air-conditioning, television, safe, and private terrace. The hotel also has a fine restaurant (noted not just for its food but also for beautiful sunsets), with French and Tahitian cuisine served nightly and a good selection of wine. **Pros:** Free use of bicycles, kayaks, and snorkeling equipment. **Cons:** No overwater bungalows. *4 km southwest of the airport on Miri Miri pass* ☎*B.P. 680, Uturoa 98735* ☎*60-01-00* ⊕*www.raiateahotel.com* ⇌*15 rooms, 1 suite* ⚐*In-room: no a/c (some), safe, kitchen (some), refrigerator (some), no TV (some), Internet. In-hotel: restaurant, room service, bar, pool, waterfront, diving, water sports, bicycles, laundry service, concierge, public Internet, airport shuttle* ▤*AE, DC, MC, V* ⦿*EP.*

FAMILY HOTELS

¢ 🏨 **Pension Te Maeva.** These two bungalows are situated in a beautiful garden set on a hillside with a stunning, panoramic view over the lagoon. A small swimming pool is on the property. **Pros:** Common-area kitchen facilities; private bathrooms have hot water; household linen and mosquito nets provided. **Cons:** It's about 16 mi outside of Uteroa. ✉*PK 23, Opoa* ☎*B.P. 701, Uturoa 98735* ☎*66-37-28* ⊕*www. temaeva.com* ⇌*2 bungalows* ⚐*In-room: no a/c, no phone, kitchen, refrigerator. In-hotel: phone, restaurant, bicycles, laundry facilities, public Internet, airport shuttle* ▤*No credit cards* ⦿*EP, MAP, AI.*

$ 🏨 **Sunset Beach Motel.** This motel is situated on the west coast around a mi from the airport and about 2½ from Uturoa. The bungalows stand on a very large, flat area, landscaped and surrounded by coconut palms, and there is an excellent camping area. Just don't let the name fool you as there is no beach, but you can swim in the lagoon from the jetty. **Pros:** Bungalows have hot water; household linen and mosquito nets provided. **Cons:** No Internet access. ⊠ *PK 5 Apooiti, Uturoa* 🖂 *B. P. 397, Uturoa 98735* ☎ *66–33–47* ⊕ *www.sunset.raiatea.com* ➪ *22 bungalows* 🔥 *In-room: no a/c, no phone, kitchen, refrigerator. In-hotel: waterfront, diving, water sports, bicycles, no elevator, common phone, airport shuttle* ⊟ *MC, V* ◑ *BP.*

$ 🏨 **Vini Beach Lodge.** This Polynesian-owned and -operated beach lodge is located right by Vini Beach with panoramic views of Faaroa Bay. All bungalows have a terrace, ceiling fans, and a fully equipped kitchenette. **Pros:** Private rooms with hot water; mosquito nets provided; English is spoken. **Cons:** There's a rental fee for bikes and kayaks. ✛ *South of Uturoa on Faaroa Bay* 🖂 *B.P. 1384, Uturoa 98735* ☎ *60–22–45* ⊕ *www.raiatea.com/vinibeach* ➪ *7 bungalows* 🔥 *In-room: no a/c, no phone, kitchen (some), refrigerator (some), no TV (some). In-hotel: restaurant, bar, pool, waterfront, water sports, bicycles, laundry facilities, public Internet, airport shuttle* ⊟ *V* ◑ *EP, MAP, AI.*

WHERE TO EAT

Raiatea has a good selection of restaurants with an across-the-board selection of food ranging from French to Polynesian, Chinese, and Italian. This is a "boatie" or "yachtie" type environment with a number of the better-known dining places clustered around Uturoa's harbor; things can get quite busy on Friday and Saturday nights. Seafood is always outstanding on the menu but the selection should satisfy most diners, though they may find the wine list more constricting. It should perhaps be pointed out that many of the restaurants are as much noted for their outstanding views or sunsets as for the food.

Another way of dining are *les roulottes* which are found here and on other islands in Polynesia. The name means basically "rolling food trucks" and they supply simple island food, usually on the cheap side. They are a favorite of many locals who either eat at the truck or take the food home. *See the price chart in Chapter 1, Tahiti, for information on pricing.*

¢–$ ✗ **Chez Michéle.** In the town center close by the Hinano Hotel, this
FRENCH indoor-outdoor restaurant is popular with locals. It serves inexpensive French, Chinese, and Tahitian food and opens very early in the morning for breakfast. ⊠ *B.P. 315, Uturoa* ☎ *66–14–66* ⊟ *No credit cards* ◷ *Closed Sat. evenings and Sun.*

¢–$ ✗ **Club House.** Perhaps the largest restaurant in Raiatea, the Club House
FRENCH faces the yacht harbor and is shaded by a thatch-roofed canopy. It's a reasonably priced place that serves a decent breakfast, lunch, and dinner. Regular entertainment on the weekends, and amazing sunset views, are a big draw for guests. ⊠ *Apooti marina, Uturoa* ☎ *66–11–66* ⊟ *No credit cards.*

RAIATEA ESSENTIALS

The currency is the Pacific franc (CFP). The exchange rate at this writing is approximately 76 CFP to US$1. Business hours are typically weekdays from 7:30 to 11:30 and 1:30 to 5:30. Most businesses are open for a half day Saturday and are closed Sunday.	To date, the Internet has largely passed Raiatea by, and cyber cafés have yet to make an impact. Many shops offer what they call "cyber points"—basically a computer in the back of the shop and little else. **Techni-Iles** (☎66–34–06) at the Europcar office in Uturoa has two computers, but you can also bring your own laptop.

$–$$
FRENCH
✕**Quai des Pêcheurs.** This moderately priced restaurant is on the fishermen's wharf right on the harbor front; reservations recommended for dinner. Naturally enough fish is a house specialty, but French food is also served. The bar is popular on Saturday nights. ⊠ *Gare Maritime on the Uturoa waterfront, Uturoa* ☎66–43–19 ⊟*AE, MC, V* ۞*Daily noon–2* PM, *7–9* PM.

¢–$
CHINESE
✕**Sea Horse.** This Chinese restaurant is a favorite among boaties as it's in the Maritime Complex by the wharf; reservations recommended on the weekends. All the usual Chinese food fare is served up, as well as local dishes, at a reasonable price. ⊠ *Gare Maritime on the Uturoa waterfront, Uturoa* ☎66–16–34 ⊟*MC, V* ۞*Closed Sun.*

SPORTS & ACTIVITIES

Both Raiatea and Tahaa have a network of trails that include hidden pools and waterfalls, and several groups run horseback trail rides, walking tours, and 4WD safaris.

BEACHES

Raiatea and Tahaa don't have beaches, so locals and tourists head out to the many motu, or islets for their sand and surf; quite a business has been built around transporting picnicking tourists to them. Some are not quite deserted islands, but they can give a feeling of being on one. Several companies specialize in half-day trips, including one that takes an outrigger-canoe-type craft across the vivid blue and green lagoon. A glass-bottom boat tour of the lagoon offers an easy way to take in the terrific diversity of marine life in what is basically an enormous outdoor aquarium.

SNORKELING

Snorkeling is easily the most popular activity for visitors and can be done almost anywhere in the lagoon's clean and colorful waters. While the coral itself is not nearly as vivid as in other places (there is a good deal of scientific and political argument over why), the marine life here is rich. Neither sharks nor anything threatening can be found in the reef, so it is safe. One caveat, though, is that well out into the lagoon—and in proximity to the outer reef or channels—currents can be strong.

6

OTHER WATER SPORTS

French Polynesia is on the world professional surfing tour, and the outer reefs of Raiatea and Tahaa are regarded, at times, as simply stunning. The numerous passes from the lagoon to the ocean are the best spots, but locations vary with weather and swells.

Windsurfing is expensive in Raiatea, mainly because of the high insurance rates and potential lawsuits. The lagoon between Raiatea and Tahaa is regarded as an excellent location, but you must bring your own gear. Somewhat paradoxically, the sport of kite boarding (or fly surfing, as the French call it) is popular in Raiatea—and to the casual observer it may seem a great deal riskier than windsurfing. Riders, atop a small surfboard, are hauled along by a large kite, often at great speeds. Experts can perform jumps, leaps, and even somersaults, making for spectacular viewing. More sedate sailing is readily available, and the world's largest sailboat charter company, The Moorings, has long had a base at Raiatea.

Bill fishing (or sportfishing) is popular in the waters outside the reef; most professional fishing charters are based out of Uturoa.

HIKING, HORSES & 4WD TOURS

The interior of both islands is rugged, and a variety of options are available for touring. These treks range from gentle eco-walks to 4WD safari trips in Range Rovers and jeeps. Operators of the latter take visitors through lush tropical jungle, up onto high ridges, and through vanilla and pineapple farms. Horseback trail rides on the slopes of Raiatea's Mt. Tamahani are also popular.

SHOPPING

As is typical across the Pacific, the locals in Raiatea shop for fresh food, including fish, at the local market. Located near the harbor on the main street, the market also sells arts and crafts. It opens at sunrise, and Wednesday and Friday are the busiest days. The freshest produce is sold on Sunday, but before dawn—the market closes at 7 AM on Sunday.

Both islands have an active community of artisans, but one of the more unusual is **Jean Luc Liaut** (☏ *66–32–14* ⊕ *www.raiatea.com/temanuata*), a native Raiatean whose fishing boat Te Manu Ata is based in Uturoa and is available for charter. He has turned handmade fishing lures into an art form, and his products are sought globally.

The usual art and handicraft shops sell a wide variety of woodcarvings and shell and pearl items, with most guaranteed to have been locally made. Local artists often sell at the **Hawaiki Nui Federation** (☏ *66–12–37*) at Uturoa airport and the Maritime Harbor.

TAHAA

Located just north of Raiatea, and only a few minutes by shuttle boat, the fragrant scent of vanilla envelops Tahaa, giving it its nickname, "the vanilla island." The island produces more than 80% of French Polynesia's vanilla, and visiting a vanilla plantation here will be a

Pearls of Wisdom

BUYING PEARLS

The Tahitian Pearl is legendary among jewelry lovers, and most people traveling to this island destination hope to bring home a black pearl of their own. Luckily, these calcareous concretions are sold throughout Raiatea and Tahaa—they come from the lagoon between them. While a good deal of hype and mystique is attached to the pearl, simple common sense and an appreciation of their beauty will help most buyers make the right choice.

So, where should you shop? On Raiatea you can stop by **Arri Boutique** (☎ 66–35–54), **La Palme D'Or** (☎ 66–23–79), or **Tico Pearls** (☎ 66–14–00), all of which are in Uturoa. See Pearl Farms, below for places to shop in Tahaa.

PEARL FARMS

But what if you want to know more about the pearl? Maybe you'd like to know how a pearl is made. If so, a trip to a pearl farm is in order. Visitors learn how pearls are prepared for grafting, as well as the varieties and their characteristics. Visitors can also buy pearls or jewelry direct from the farms.

The following farms, which are all located in Haamene, Tahaa, are open daily, 4:30 AM–6 PM and offer free admission.

Loose pearls and 18-carat-gold-set jewelry can be purchased at **Motu Pearl Farm** (☎ 65–69–18 ✉ araia@mail.pf).

Near Vaipoe Farm, **Poerani Farm** (☎ 65–60–25 ✉ rani-poe@mail.pf) has lovely grounds and will arrange for visitors pickups, for a fee.

Vaipoe Pearl Farms (☎ 65–60–83 ✉ vaipoe.excursions@mail.pf) has a gift shop that sells its own cultivated black pearls, jewelry, and handicrafts. They accept MasterCard and Visa, which is rare.

blissful experience as the plantations are located in luxuriant valleys among pineapples and coconuts.

The island, which is less than a quarter of the size of Raiatea, hosts a population of less than 5,000. Its quiet nature has allowed it to retain the charms of old-time Polynesia. There are four black pearl farms on Tahaa and all are open for tours by the public. Though the island does not have beaches, it does have a number of motu, which dot its outer reef. Mount Ohiri (1,811 feet [552 meters]) towers over this tortuous coastline and wild interior.

ESSENTIALS

Visitor Info **Tahaa Tourism Committee** (✉ B.P. 250, Haamene 98734 ☎ 60–81–66).

WHAT TO SEE

Hibiscus Foundation for Protected Turtle Species. Based at the Hibiscus Hotel, this sanctuary rescues sea turtles that have been caught in commercial fishnets—most get sold on the lucrative black market. More than 1,300 turtles have been nursed back to heath at the sanctuary which tags the healthy turtles before releasing them into open waters.

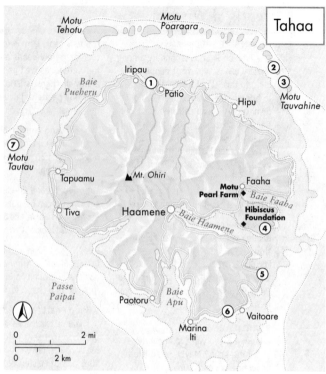

For US$100 you can sponsor and name a turtle and receive updates on its progress in the wild. ⊠ *Haamene Bay* ☎ *65–61–06* ⊕ *www.hibiscus tahaa.com* ☼ *Turtle feedings, daily 9* AM ⊠ *Free.*

WHERE TO STAY & EAT

Eating establishments on Tahaa are few and far between, but food is most often provided at all lodging places. *See the price chart in Chapter 1, Tahiti, for information on pricing.*

HOTELS

$$$ 🏨 **Hôtel La Pirogue.** Though it's on a private island north of Tahaa, the hotel is still only about an hour from the Raiatea Airport. The bungalows are situated either on the beach or set among beautiful green gardens and the restaurant overlooks the crystal clear lagoon. Various tours and excursions are on offer from the hotel. **Pros:** A beautiful setting right by the water. **Cons:** It's a boat ride to get anywhere else. ⊠ *On Motu Porou, north of Tahaa* ⌂ *B.P. 668, Uturoa, Raiatea 98735* ☎ *60–81–45* ⊕ *www.hotellapirogue.com* ⇗ *9 bungalows* ⚹ *In-room: no a/c, refrigerator, DVD, Internet. In-hotel: restaurant, room service, bar, beachfront, diving, water sports, no elevator, laundry service, concierge, airport shuttle* ▤ *AE, MC, V* ⊚ *BP.*

$$$$ 🏨**Le Taha'a Island Resort & Spa.** This Relais & Châteaux property is built in the traditional Polynesian style and is only 35 minutes from the Raiatea airport by boat. The public areas are built into trees, giving you a Swiss Family Robinson feel as well as unobstructed views of the sparkling blue water all around you and Bora Bora in the distance. Beach villas have private swimming pools and overwater bungalows have direct access to the lagoon. The resort's Manea Spa offers waterside massages among other amazing services. **Pros:** Onsite spa; only hotel on the motu; has shop that offers everyday items. **Cons:** Expensive. ⊠ *Motu Tautau, west of Tahaa* ☎ *B.P. 67, Patio, Tahaa 98733* 📞 *60–84–00* ⊕ *www.letahaa.com* 🛏 *12 villas, 11 bungalows, 37 suites* ⌂ *In-room: refrigerator, DVD (some), Internet. In-hotel: 3 restaurants, room service, 2 bars, tennis court, pool, spa, beachfront, diving, water sports, bicycles, laundry service, concierge, public Internet, airport shuttle* ⊟ *AE, DC, MC, V.*

> ### THE GOLDEN CROP
>
> After saffron, vanilla is the world's most lucrative crop and about three-quarters of the French Polynesian output comes from here. It's easy to see why vanilla is so expensive. The flowers are fertilized by hand, because the insects that would normally do the fertilization are not present in this region. The pod takes nine months before it's ready for picking. A drying period of 15 to 20 weeks will then elapse before the pods are ready for use and they will normally be taken to Tahiti for processing and export.

$$$$ 🏨**Vahine Island Private Island Resort.** Only 20 minutes by boat from Tahaa and 30 minutes by boat from the Raiatea airport, this exclusive hideaway paradise is on a 10-acre private island north of Tahaa. Spectacular far-reaching views take in the main island and extend to Raiatea, Bora Bora, and Huahine. Three units are over water, three on the beach, and three hidden among a riot of tropical flowers. The restaurant features local seafood and exotic flavors with a French touch. There's also horseback riding available. **Pros:** It's an exclusive hideaway paradise. **Cons:** No Internet service. *On Motu Tuvahine, 1½ mi north of Tahaa* ☎ *B.P. 510, Uturoa, Raiatea 98735* 📞 *65–67–38* ⊕ *www.vahine-island.com* 🛏 *6 bungalows, 3 suites* ⌂ *In-room: no a/c, safe, kitchen (some), refrigerator, DVD. In-hotel: restaurant, room service, bar, beachfront, diving, water sports, bicycles, laundry service, concierge, airport shuttle* ⊟ *AE, MC, V* ⊙ *MAP.*

FAMILY HOTELS

$$$ 🏨**Fare Pea Iti.** This small property on the northern tip of the island features Tahitian-style bungalows on a private beach. The bungalows are backed by a tropical garden and have stunning views across the lagoon from the terraces. All meals can be provided on request. **Pros:** Private bathrooms with hot water. **Cons:** It's way off the beaten track if you happen to like shopping and nightlife. *On the sea in Iripau* ☎ *B.P. 128, Patio 98733* 📞 *60–81–11* ⊕ *www.farepeaiti.pf* 🛏 *3 bungalows* ⌂ *In-room: no a/c, no phone, kitchen, refrigerator. In-hotel: restaurant, bar, pool, waterfront, water sports, bicycles, laundry facilities, Internet, airport shuttle* ⊟ *AE, MC, V* ⊙ *EP.*

$ **⊞Hibiscus Hotel.** Leo and Lolita Morou, who also run the property's sea turtle protection center, are the proprietors at this beautifully located hotel. Each of the seven bungalows overlook the water. The restaurant serves Tahitian and French fare daily and is open to the public. Grab a drink at the bar and listen to the yachties who come ashore here. **Pros:** Bathrooms have hot water. **Cons:** There are no private bathrooms. ⊠*Haamene Bay* ⌂*B. P. 184, Haamene 98734* ☎*65–61–06* ⊕*www.hibiscustahaa.com* ⟲*7 bungalows* ⌂*In-room: no a/c, no phone, no TV. In-hotel: bar, beachfront, water sports, laundry facilities, public Internet, airport shuttle* ⊟*AE, MC, V* ⦿*MAP.*

> ### WORD OF MOUTH
>
> "I suggest going to Tahaa. There is a string of little motus off the northeast coast that are so beautiful, with great views and snorkeling." —ALF

¢ **⊞Pension Api.** Situated near the southern tip of the island, this lodging has three bungalows offering clean no-frills accommodation. The owners also run a small lunch and take-away service. **Pros:** Common kitchen area for guests to use. **Cons:** There's no Internet access; TV is shared. ⊠*Vaitoare* ☎*65–99–88* ✉ *jjwatlp@mail.pf* ⟲*3 bungalows* ⌂*In-room: no a/c, no phone, no TV. In-hotel: beachfront, water sports, bicycles, laundry facilities, airport shuttle* ⊟*No credit cards* ⦿*EP or MAP.*

$$$ **⊞Tiare's Breeze.** Located in the island's hilly section, two private bungalows with handcrafted thatched roofs have incredible panoramic views of the sparkling Haamene Bay below. You'll fall asleep beneath the stars and wake up to fresh island fruit and French pastries that have been delivered to your doorstep. **Pros:** A great place for reflection and quiet time; linens and mosquito nets provided; private bathrooms with hot water. **Cons:** The bungalows overlook the water, but are not on the water. ⊠*Haamene Bay* ⌂*B.P. 178, Haamene 98734* ☎*65–62–26* ⊕*www.tiarebreeze.com* ⟲*2 bungalows* ⌂*In-room: no a/c, no phone, kitchen, refrigerator. In-hotel: beachfront, water sports, bicycles* ⊟*AE, MC, V.*

SPORTS & ACTIVITIES
See Sports & Activities, in Raiatea, above, for information about Tahaa.

THE MARQUESAS ISLANDS

The Marquesas, known locally as "the land of men," lies 4,000 km (2,485 mi) south of Hawaii; the archipelago is the farthest island group from a continent. Geographically the islands fall into two groups: those that are centered around Nuku Hiva (Ua Huka, Ua Pou, Hatu Iti, Eiao, Hatutaa, and Motu One) in the north, and those centered around Hiva Oa (Futu Huku, Tahuata, Motane, and Fatu Hiva) in the south.

When Mother Nature thrust the islands from the sea, little allowance was made for the needs of humans. There are no coral-walled lagoons or protective reefs, and safe anchorages are limited. These wild and

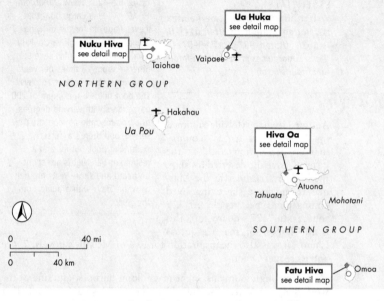

SOUTH PACIFIC OCEAN

Ua Huka
see detail map

Nuku Hiva
see detail map

Taiohae

Vaipaee

NORTHERN GROUP

Hakahau

Ua Pou

Hiva Oa
see detail map

Atuona

Tahuata

Mohotani

SOUTHERN GROUP

Motu One

Eiao

Hatutu

0   40 mi

0   40 km

Fatu Hiva
see detail map

Omoa

mountainous islands are the remains of extinct volcanoes—some peaks reach more than 3,000 feet (914 meters) high—with steep cliffs, lush vegetation and a rugged natural beauty that can be breathtaking.

Six of the 12 islands are inhabited with a total population of 8,000 people—the horse and goat population far outnumbers the people. Believed to be some of the oldest settled islands in Polynesia, there are ancient fortifications and stone palisades with some of the largest carved stone figures to be seen outside of Easter Island. The archipelago also claims to be the original home of tattooing.

■ TIP→ **Time in the Marquesas is 30 minutes ahead of Tahiti.**

WHEN TO GO

There is no real dry season in the Marquesas and temperatures vary but are generally higher than in Tahiti, though you don't have to worry about cyclones here. Rainfall is often short-lived but heavy, and is evenly spread throughout the year with the main precipitation in June and August. People coming from the northern hemisphere often visit in July and August, while in the southern they take the long break at Christmas. Book early if you plan on traveling during these times.

GETTING HERE & AROUND
Four of the islands have airfields, the rest are accessible by boat; helicopter services are available but expensive.

ESSENTIALS
Visitor Info Tahiti Tourisme Raiatea (⊠ *Marina Station of Uturoa* ⌂ *B. P. 1628, Uturoa 98735* ☎ *60–07–77* ⊕ *www.marquises.pf* ✎ *raiatea-info@ tahiti-tourisme.pf).*

NUKU HIVA

Author Herman Melville summed up Nuku Hiva as a "country that no description could fit the beauty." Melville deserted his ship, the whaler *Acushnet* in the Marquesas and for a short time lived among the Typee people. At 329 square km (127 square mi), this is the largest of the Marquesas Islands; it was also the inspiration for two of Melville's novels, *Typee* and its sequel *Omoo*.

> ### DOING IT ALL
>
> If you'd like to see a number of the Marquesas islands, jump aboard the *Aranui 3* (⊠ *Pape'ete* ☎ *42–62–42* ⊕ *www.aranui.com* ▭ *AE, MC, V*), a cargo boat that leaves Pape'ete for the outlying islands—Nuku Hiva, Hiva Oa, Fatu Hiva, and Ua Huka, plus several others—about 16 times per year; the journey takes about 15 days. The boat holds a maximum of 200 passengers with varying degrees of accommodation, meals are served, and there's a nursery, swimming pool, library, and a restaurant-bar. Nights are spent on board and shore visits are half or whole days with a guide from the ship.

With towering mountains, eight magnificent harbors, and one of the world's highest waterfalls, Nuku Hiva is richly blessed. Few doubt that its 2,400 inhabitants live in paradise.

GETTING HERE AND AROUND
Air Tahiti flies direct to Nuku Hiva from Pape'ete every day of the week; the flight time averages around 2½ hours. There is no public transport, but cars and bikes can be rented and there are plenty of taxis. Horse riding is also a popular way of getting around but plan to do a fair bit of walking.

ESSENTIALS
Car Rental Europcar (☎ *92–04–89* ⊕ *www.europcar.pf).* **Nuku Rent-a-Car** (☎ *92–08–87).*

Taxis Andre Teikiteetini (☎ *92–02–07).* **Jean-Claude Dupont** (☎ *92–08–22).* **Elisabeth Kautai** (☎ *92–08–87).* **Martine Haiti** (☎ *92–01–19).*

Visitor Info Nuku Hiva Tourism Committee (⊠ *Taiohae* ☎ *92–03–73* ⊕ *www. marquises.pf* ⊙ *Mon.–Fri. 7:30–4).*

WHAT TO SEE
Taiohae. In the shadow of towering, 2,834-foot (864 meters) Mt. Muake, this is the island's main town. Located in the center of the southern coast at the foot of deep Taiohae Bay, the town is in the center of an ancient volcanic crater, half of which has collapsed into the

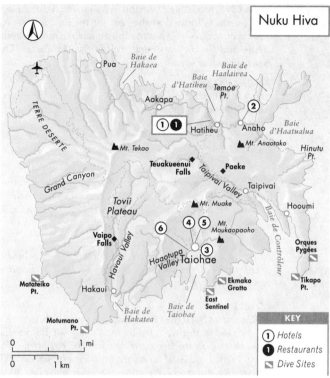

ocean, creating a bay. A modern administrative center complete with gendarmerie (police), it has a particularly French feel to it. Taiohae sculptors work in shops behind the village. Most of the island's banks, schools, stores, and shops are in Taiohae. **The Cathedral of Notre-Dame of Marquesas** is built with various rock from the six islands of the Marquesas. The wood carvings inside combine Marquesan art with religion, including a dramatic wooden pulpit.

Tovii Plateau. The plateau provides the island with its only flat agricultural area, while a mountain range, dominated by 4,015-foot (1,223 meters) Mt. Tekao, looms above.

Taipivai. Melville based his celebrated novel *Typee* on his experiences in Nuku Hiva and the time he spent in the valley of Taipivai. The large and fertile valley is around 16 km (10 mi) from Taiohae and can be reached by boat. Taipivai features the best archaeological sites in the Marquesas.

Hatiheu Bay. Scottish author Robert Louis Stevenson favored Hatiheu Bay, which is on the northern coast. Nearly a thousand feet above the bay, a statue of the Virgin looks down; in the valley is the *Naniuhi tohua* meeting place used by pre-Christian Marquesans, which includes a dance platform, ceremonial stones, and petroglyphs carved in boulders.

Anaho Bay. The village of Anaho, with it's small thatched-roofed Catholic church, is located at the head of the bay. It's backed by jagged green mountains—this has to rank among the most beautiful places on earth—and has the only coral shelf in the Marquesas. There's also an expansive white sand beach.

WHERE TO EAT

As restaurants are a rarity, most lodging establishments will supply meals. Look out for the les roulottes, or rolling food trucks that set up by the harbor and at other points usually in the evenings. This is fast food with a twist, as you can get meals such as grilled steak and fish, chicken, plenty of chips and even pizza and omelettes. *See the price chart in Chapter 1, Tahiti, for information on pricing.*

$-$$ ✕**Restaurant Hinako Nui.** Set in the village of Hatiheu on the north coast, a thatched roof and sea views add a certain charm to this eating-house that specializes in local seafood. *B.P. 199, Taiohae 98742* ☎*92–02–97* ▤*No credit cards.*

WHERE TO STAY

Nuku Hiva has only one hotel, but numerous family hotels or pensions to choose from. *See the price chart in Chapter 1, Tahiti, for information on pricing.*

HOTELS

$$-$$$ ▦**Keikahanui Nuku Hiva Pearl Lodge.** Set in a lush tropical garden, this superior lodge overlooks the bay and village of Taiohae; jagged mountains covered in thick vegetation form the backdrop. The restaurant serves French and local food with the accent on seafood. The bar opens onto the swimming pool and a terrace, which is just 50 steps above a deserted, black sand beach. **Pros:** Tahitian feasts, dance shows, and local music and other cultural activities are offered; a/c and Internet access in the rooms. **Cons:** No spa; no wedding facilities. ✉*B.P. 53, Taiohae 98742* ☎*92–07–10* ⊕*www.pearlresorts.com* ⇆*20 bungalows* ⚄*In-room: safe, refrigerator, DVD, Internet. In-hotel: restaurant, bar, pool, waterfront, diving, water sports, bicycles, laundry service, concierge, airport shuttle* ▤*AE, MC, V* ❮❶❯*MAP.*

FAMILY HOTELS

$$ ▦**Hinako Nui.** On the north coast, two hours by car from Taiohae, Chez Yvonne, as it's also known, stands on a hillside in a well-maintained garden only 164 feet (50 meters) from the sea. There's one family bungalow and four standard bungalows all equipped with private bathroom. Hinako Nui Restaurant is a two-minute walk away and all guests take their meals there. **Pros:** Linens provided; private bathrooms with hot water; common kitchen available for guests. **Cons:** This is really in an out-of-the-way location *B.P. 199, Taiohae 98742* ☎*92–02–97* ✉*hinakonui@mail.pf* ⇆*5 bungalows* ⚄*In-room: no a/c, no phone, refrigerator (some), no TV. In-hotel: restaurant, bar, laundry facilities, airport shuttle* ▤*No credit cards* ❮❶❯*AI.*

¢   ▦**Kao Tia'e.** Raymond & Maya Vaianui run these five seaside bungalows nicely situated in Anaho Bay. One of the island's very few restaurants—the Hinako Nui at Chez Yvonne (*see review, below*)—is not far away. **Pros:** If you love peace and quiet this is the place. **Cons:** In an emergency you could have problems. *⌂B.P. 290, Taiohae 98742* *☎92–00–08 ⟳5 bungalows ⌂In-room: no a/c, no phone, no TV. In-hotel: restaurant, bar, laundry facilities, airport shuttle ▤No credit cards ℐⓄⅠMAP.*

¢ **Mave Mai Pension.** Jean-Claude and Regina Tata have a house in the Taiohae Village with eight rooms, three of which have a balcony. There is a library/reading lounge where guests can relax and watch TV, excursions are available and there's an on-site car rental. **Pros:** Linens and mosquito nets provided; private bathrooms with hot water. **Cons:** It is on the mountainside. *✉Taiohae Center ⌂B.P. 378, Taiohae 98742* *☎92–08–10 ⊕www.haere-mai.pf ⟳8 rooms ⌂In-room: no phone, kitchen (some), refrigerator (some), no TV. In-hotel: restaurant, diving, water sports, laundry facilities, airport shuttle ▤MC, V ℐⓄⅠMAP.*

¢ **Paahatea Nui.** Justin and Julienne Mahiatapu run this pension situated right in the village of Taiohae. Each bungalow has a ceiling fan and a private hot water bathroom, plus there's one room with a private (hot water) bathroom. A fully equipped kitchen is at the client's disposal. **Pros:** Beach access; bay views. **Cons:** You might score one of the three rooms with a shared bath. *⌂B.P. 201, Taiohoe 98742 ☎92–00–97* *✍paahateanui@mail.pf ⟳6 bungalows, 4 rooms ⌂In-room: no a/c, no phone. In-hotel: restaurant, waterfront, water sports, bicycles, laundry facilities, airport shuttle ▤No credit cards ℐⓄⅠCP.*

¢ **Pension Moana Nui.** Located in the village of Taiohae, this pension has a bungalow and seven rooms. The house and five of the rooms have a/c and all have a private bathroom with hot water. **Pros:** Linens provided; private bathrooms with hot water; common kitchen available for guests. **Cons:** There could be outside traffic to the restaurant. *⌂B.P. 33, Taiohae 98742 ☎92–03–30 ✍pensionmoananui@mail.pf* *⟳1 bungalow, 7 rooms ⌂In-room: no a/c (some), no phone. In-hotel: restaurant, bar, waterfront, diving, laundry facilities, public Internet, airport shuttle ▤AE, DC, MC, V ℐⓄⅠEP, MAP.*

SPORTS & ACTIVITIES

Operators offer 4WD safaris around the island, including trips to the Hakauii Valley and Mt. Muake. Guided horseback rides are also offered. One of the better ways to soak up the beauty of the island is by speedboat; you can avoid many of the more rugged roads ashore. With rich fishing nearby, sportfishing charters are readily available.

Dancing is regularly performed—both formally for visitors and also informally. One need only listen for the sound of wooden drums beating to find a group of boys and girls practicing their dances. Audiences are usually welcome and made to dance as well.

Private individuals offer their boats for rental. For information on this, contact the tourism committee or the family pensions.

The Fabric of Marquesas

Also called *hiapo,* tapa used to be the main form of cloth in the pre-European Pacific. The fabric's popularity has faded because of the introduction of new, synthetic fabrics and is now practiced only on Fatu Hiva, though only a handful of women make it. The cloth is made from banyan or paper mulberry bark that has been cut into 10-inch-wide strips and soaked in water for several days. The soaked bark is then pounded for hours with a special wooden beater on a stone anvil. The wooden beat-ers, which are incised with grooves, are themselves considered pieces of art and are usually passed down the family line. Once the tapa is beaten out, it is scraped with seashells—a process that removes most of the outer bark—before being sun-dried. Strips are often glued together using liquids obtained from tree-roots. The artists then paint it in dark brown colors and patterns that are distinctive to the island—tapa patterns are often reflected in tattoos.

OUTFITTERS

4WD Tours Mave Mai Tours (✉ *Taiohae* ☎ *92–08–10* ✎ *pension-mavemai@ mail.pf*). **Nuku Hiva Transports** (✉ *Taiohae* ☎ *92–06–80* ✎ *pension-mavemai@ mail.pf*).

Hiking Marquises Rando (✉ *Taiohae* ☎ *92–07–13* ⊕ *www.marquisesrando.com*).

Horse Riding Sabine Teikiteetini (✉ *Taiohae* ☎ *92–08–25*).

Scuba Diving Centre de Plongee des Marquises (✉ *Taiohae* ☎ *92–00–88*).

HIVA OA

Isolated and wildly beautiful, Hiva Oa—known as the garden of the Marquesas—was the wild paradise that French artist Paul Gauguin escaped to in 1901 and where he lived out the rest of his days. In Gauguin's day, the island was quite isolated, being some 1,609 km (1,000 mi) from Tahiti, and it was far beyond the influence of the busy world of the early 20th century. Happily, it's still pretty much the same. The 316-square-km (122-square-mi) island, with a population of around 2,000, is dominated by Mt. Temetiu, which is the highest peak in the Marquesas chain at 4,186 feet (1,275 meters). No coral reef shelters Hiva Oa's rugged shoreline, so it's continually pounded by the surf and most of it remains inaccessible. The interior is just as rugged, but lushly forested and covered by a wide variety of trees and flowers.

GETTING HERE AND AROUND

There's a daily round-trip flight between Pape'ete and Atuona that takes approximately 3½ hours. There's also a daily flight from Atuona to Nuku Hiva (about 35 minutes) and there are four weekly flights to Ua Huka, taking around an hour each, so air traffic between the islands is reasonable. Between-island flights sometimes involve a short stopover at another island to pick up or put down passengers. It's all pretty relaxed. There are also boats between the islands but these are

Hiva Oa

PACIFIC OCEAN

Cap Matefenua

Pointe Teohotepapa

Baie de Natue

Oipona me'ae

Mt. Vaipoo

Pointe Matapuava

Baie de Puamau

Pointe Matapuava

①

Puamau

Hanaupe

Cap Teohoahivehi

Motuua

Hekeani

Baie de Hanapaoa

Hanaiapa

Hanapaoa

Tiki Moe One ◆

Mt. Ootua ▲

Pointe Pakahokaha

Pointe Matatepai

Baie de Hanaiapa

Mt. Feani ▲

✈

Tehueto ◆

Jacques Brel ◆ Memorial

Tahuata

Baie de Tahauku

Atuona ② – ⑤ see inset

Mt. Temetiu ▲

Baie de Taaoa

Pointe Teaehoa

Taaoa

Baie de Hanamenu

Pointe Kiukiu

Pointe Tepaapaa

Tahuata

0 ⊢ 4 km

0 ⊢ 4 mi

Atuona

Calvaire Cemetery ◆

Paul Gauguin Cultural Centre & Jacques Brel Cultural Centre ◆

⑤

③

Post Office ◆

④

Lighthouse ◆

Tohua Pepeu ◆

Musée Gauguin ◆

Atuona

Tahauku

②

0 ⊢ 1/8 km

0 ⊢ 1/8 mi

6

normally chartered by negotiation with local owners. The islands don't have public transport but there are always bicycles for hire and horses. Some type of taxi service and vehicle rentals either with or without a driver are always an option.

ESSENTIALS

Car Rentals **Atuona Rent-a-Car** (☎ *92–76–07*).

Taxis **Ida Clark Taxis** (☎ *92–71–33*).

Visitor Info **Hiva Oa Tourism Committee** (✉ *Tahu'Uku Wharf, Atuona* ☎ *92–78–93* ⊕ *www.marquises-hivaoa.org.pf*).

WHAT TO SEE

Those who fancy themselves botanists will have a field day with Hiva Oa's wide variety of flora including pandanus, banyan trees, sugarcane, coconut palms, and ti plants as well as such flowers as heliconia, bougainvillea, plumeria, and ylang-ylang. Grapefruit, mango, papaya, vanilla, banana, and guava are common crops.

Hiva Oa's main settlement is **Atuona,** which lies at the head of the Bay of Traitors. The legacy of Gauguin's time spent on the island is its main attraction.

The Paul Gauguin Cultural Centre has no original works by the artist but does display reproductions of some of the paintings from his time in Polynesia. A replica of his thatched Maison du Jouir (House of Pleasure) has been rebuilt nearby. ✉ *Atuona* ☎ *92–73–32* ✐ *commune@commune-hivoa.pf* ☉ *Mon.–Thurs. 8–11 and 2–5, Fri. 7:30–2:30, Sat. 8–11* 🎫 *$6.*

The **Jacques Brel Cultural Centre** is adjacent to the Paul Gauguin Centre and they share a ticket office. The center honors the life of Brel (1929–1978), a Belgian singer and actor that lived in Atuona for several years at the end of his life. Brel's Beachcraft Bonanza plane—which he named *Jojo,* after one of his most famous songs—is on permanent display. A souvenir market now stands next to the museum. ✉ *Atuona* ☎ *92–73–32* ✐ *commune@commune-hivoa.pf* ☉ *Mon.–Thurs. 8–11 and 2–5, Fri. 7:30–2:30, Sat. 8–11* 🎫 *$5.*

If you'd like to see Gauguin's final resting place, pay a visit to the **Calvaire Cemetery,** which is behind Atuona's gendarmerie (police station); there should be a signpost. A stone engraved PAUL GAUGUIN, 1903 marks the spot. On the tombstone is a replica of a statue of an *oviri* (savage) that is said to symbolize the values for which the artist searched in the Marquesas. Brel is also buried here.

The island has some of the most interesting archaeological sites in French Polynesia and these can all be seen on a 4WD excursion. The village of **Taaoa** is west of Atuona and can be reached by a zigzag track that reaches an elevation of 1,300 feet (400 meters). The village has a great view over the bay, and there's a large archaeological site consisting of several hundred *paepae* (stone platforms).

In the opposite direction the village of **Puamau** is situated east of Atuona; the journey takes 2½ hours by 4WD over a mountain trail that crosses the island, passing through the island's airport, the north shore, and the villages of Hanapaaoa and Nahoe. Puamau is overshadowed by a circle of high cliffs and is home to the Pekekea historical site which consists of the tomb of Queen Vahinetitoiani that's protected by two gigantic "tiki"—Mani and Pauto. Higher up the trail sits one of the most important archaeological sites in the Marquesas: Iipona, a temple site with the largest stone carving found outside of Easter Island. The site is guarded by a 7-foot-tall (2 meter) tiki that's known as Takai', the valley's namesake. Takai' is accompanied by two smaller tiki: Tauatepepe on the right and Pepetamuimui to the left. There are also many tiki heads displayed about the paepae, and on one of the platforms there is also the striking statue of Makali Taua Pepe, representing a woman giving birth to a creature that is half man, half goat.

OFF THE BEATEN PATH Although it has no airport, the neighboring island of **Tahuata**—the only landing place of Spaniard Alvaro De Mendana, the first European to see the islands—can be reached by boat or helicopter and is popular with visiting yachties. Approximately 600 people live in either the village of Vaitahu, which is backed by a massive green cliff-face, or in several smaller villages around the island. Hapatoni is a delightful village by the sea, the seafront road being constructed with very old carved slabs. It can be reached by boat from Vaitahu village in about 15 minutes. There are no normal roads on the island and getting around can be difficult; horseback is the favored mode of transport. There are several lovely beaches that look tantalizing, but take precautions before taking the plunge as the dreaded nono will be there in large numbers. Petroglyphs can be seen in an inland valley and there are also relics of the fighting between the local people and the French in earlier days. Today, villagers sell carvings, paintings, and monoi (a fragrant mix of coconut and tiare flower extracts that's used as a body moisturizer).

WHERE TO STAY & EAT

Just like Nuku Hiva, there's only one hotel on Hiva Oa, but numerous family hotels to choose from. If you're looking for independent dining options you won't find them. Don't worry though, you won't go wrong dining where you're staying, but if you'd like to self cater, there are grocery stores in Atuona and Puamau. *See the price chart in Chapter 1, Tahiti, for information on pricing.*

HOTELS

¢–$ **Hiva Oa Hanakee Pearl Lodge.** The lodge's 14 bungalows sit on a hillside facing majestic Mount Temetui among luxuriant vegetation. Each has amazing views over Traitors Bay and the distant island of Tahuata and feature works of local artists. **Pros:** Wedding facilities on the property; Tahitian feasts are offered; local music is performed. **Cons:** No spa. *B.P. 80, Atuona 98741* 🕾*92–75–87* ⊕*www.pearl resorts.com* 🛏*14 bungalows* ⚄*In-room: safe, refrigerator, DVD (some), Internet. In-hotel: restaurant, bar, pool, waterfront, diving, bicycles, laundry facilities, concierge, public Internet, airport shuttle* 🖃*AE, D, MC, V* ❡*MAP.*

6

FAMILY HOTELS

¢ ⊞**Chez Marie-Antoinette.** Mrs. Marie-Antoinette runs this homey pension located towards the end of the island. **Pros:** If you want the basics, this is your place; linen is provided. **Cons:** No sea access; no kitchen facilities; no a/c; no hot water. ✑*B.P. 163, Atuona 98741* ☎*92–72–27* ✉*heitah.etienne@mail.pf* ✍*3 rooms* ⌂*In-room: no a/c, no phone, no TV. In-hotel: restaurant, water sports, laundry facilities, airport shuttle* ▬*No credit cards* ¶◎*MAP.*

$ ⊞**Pension Kanahau.** Kanahau Pension features wooden bungalows built on stilts that provide guests with magnificent views of Atuona. Each bungalow has its own private bathroom with hot water. **Pros:** Linen and mosquito nets provided; common kitchen area; cultural activities are available for a charge. **Cons:** No sea access; no a/c; no Internet or phone. ⊠*On Tahauku Bay* ✑*B.P. 101, Atuona 98741* ☎*91–71–31* ⊕*pensionkanahau.com* ✍*4 bungalows* ⌂*In-room: no a/c, no phone. In-hotel: diving, laundry facilities, concierge, airport shuttle* ▬*No credit cards* ¶◎*EP.*

$$ ⊞**Relais Moehau.** Georges and Tahu Gramont have eight spacious rooms in their lovely house situated in Atuona village with terraces overlooking the Bay of Traitors and Mount Temetui. **Pros:** Sea access; linen provided; private bathrooms with hot water. **Cons:** No kitchen facilities; no a/c. ✑*B.P. 50, Atuona 98741* ☎*92–72–69* ⊕*www.relaismoehau. pf* ✍*8 rooms* ⌂*In-room: no a/c (some), no phone (some), refrigerator (some). In-hotel: restaurant, bar, diving, laundry facilities, public Internet, airport shuttle* ▬*MC, V* ¶◎*MAP.*

¢ ⊞**Temetiu Village.** Mr. Gabriel Heitaa runs Temetiu Village, which is located in Atuona. The bungalows are set on a hillside with panoramic views of Traitors Bay, Hanakee Islet, and Mt. Temetiu. **Pros:** Linen and mosquito nets provided; private bathrooms with hot water. **Cons:** No kitchen facilities; no a/c. ✑*B.P. 52, Atuona 98741* ☎*91–70–60* ⊕*temetiu.blogspot.com* ✍*6 bungalows* ⌂*In-room: no a/c, no phone. In-hotel: restaurant, bar, pool, diving, laundry facilities, public Internet, airport shuttle* ▬*AE, MC, V* ¶◎*EP, MAP.*

SHOPPING

The villages on both Hiva Oa and Tahuata offer a range of locally made handicrafts including wood, stone, and coral carvings. Distinctive, hand-painted tapa cloth is also available all over the island. Many of the islanders wear their own handicrafts, most notably the vivid tattoos that are enjoying a resurgence in French Polynesia; you can get one of these more permanent reminders of your trip, though the tattoo will be created with a modern needle rather than the more traditional (and painful) methods.

SPORTS & ACTIVITIES

Local operators offer guided tours to traditional archeological sites, either on foot, horseback, or 4WD vehicle. Helicopter rides over the island's lush and rugged interior are also fairly popular, giving visitors a bird's-eye view of stunning valleys and waterfalls. Mountain bikes can be rented, although the trails are rugged. The sea is dangerous around Hiva Oa, but the best beach for swimming is near the town of Taaoa—it has black sand. Nahoe and Hanamenu are pretty bays

MARQUESAS ISLANDS ESSENTIALS

These islands are a far cry from the more traveled islands in Polynesia. Island time—the concept that nothing happens in a hurry—is the norm, and accommodations can be less than luxurious. Visitors need to have a degree of patience and adventure. Here are a few more tips to surviving the "Land of Men."

■ Accommodations are often quite basic, a/c is virtually nonexistent, and many bathrooms lack hot water.

■ Check with your accommodations to see if they provide a mosquito net. If not, make sure you bring one and have your bug repellent handy—you'll definitely need it.

■ Don't drink the water.

■ Credit cards are not widely accepted, so bring cash.

■ Leave the driving to the locals, as many roads are accessible only by 4WD and have serpentine bends with horrendous drops in mountainous areas.

■ Islands generally have an information office but banks are rare and Internet access can be sketchy at best.

■ The currency in the islands is the Pacific franc (CFP). At this writing, the exchange rates were CFP76 to US$1, but rates are subject to change.

■ Most stores and offices are open Monday to Friday, from 7:30 to 11:30 and 1:30 to 5:30, as well as a half-day on Saturday. Very few places are open on Sunday.

worth a quiet visit. Several outfitters offer deep-sea fishing trips from the harbor at Atuona.

If you're a hiker, **Moena O Te Manu Excursions** (☎92–74–44) offers half- or full-day treks to see petroglyphs, waterfalls, valleys, and the Temetiu Peak, as well as 4WD excursions. **Entreprise Deligny** (☎92–71–59) offers 4WD excursions throughout Hiva Oa. You can see the island from atop a horse from **Hamau Ranch** (☎92–70–57). They offer horseback riding with a professional guide for half- or full-day excursions. Divers should head to **Subatuona Temetiu Village** (☎92–70–88 ✍eric.lelyonnais@wanadoo.fr). Eric Le Lyonnais will put excursions together for you.

UA HUKA

Arid and small, at approximately 78 square km (30 square mi), Ua Huka (which means "great house" in the Polynesian language) is home to around 570 people, but they are greatly outnumbered by many more horses and goats; the island is also home to the stately—and endangered—Marquesan imperial pigeon. A vast plateau dotted with wild cotton and fragrant herbs spreads out from the base of Mount Hitikau. The island, the smallest of the northern Marquesas, is celebrated for its wood carvings made from the local scrub. It's also home to the Marquesas' most ancient archeological sites.

GETTING HERE AND AROUND

Air Tahiti makes four flights a week from Pape'ete to Ua Huka. The flight usually take in another island, making the trip about 4½. There are also flights to and from other islands. There is no public transport or car rental firms but several of the pensions hire out vehicles, usually with a driver.

ESSENTIALS

Visitor Info **Ua Huka Tourism Committee** (⊠ *Vaipaee* ☎ *92–60–19* ✐ *scalla-mera.Florentine@mail.pf).*

WHAT TO SEE

Vaipae'e. The island's main village, Vaipae'e, is a short walk from the dock at Baie de Vaipae, a narrow bay between high cliffs. The village's main attraction is the **Musée Communal** (☎ *92–60–13* ☉ *Open by request only* ✉ *Free, donations welcome*), the oldest museum in the Marquesas. Its collections include mortuary canoes and various decorations such as bracelets, earrings, sperm whale teeth, and adzes. Local wood-carvers work and sell their wares here.

Vaikivi. At the center of the island—three hours by foot but quicker on horseback—are the archeological remains of Vaikivi, where you can admire a series of petroglyphs on the rocks of this ancient volcanic crater. Around 50 carved petroglyphs have been discovered here, including a depiction of an outrigger sailing canoe, others show a human face and an octopus.

Papuakeikaha Arboretum. East of Vaipae'e, on the road to the airport, is this remarkable botanical garden spread out over 42 acres. It showcases more than 300 plant species (most of which are unlabeled, so take an illustrated guide if possible) from all over the world. Most of the major local flora, including the majestic local palm and papaya, are represented among the offerings. The citrus fruit collection, from which emanate distinctively tangy aromas, is reputed to be the best in the world. An aviary displays local birds, including the ultramarine lorikeet. ⊠ *Vaipaee* ☎ *92–61–51* ☉ *Mon.–Fri. 6:30 AM–4:30 PM, Sat.–Sun. by request* ✉ *Free.*

The Museum of Wood "Jardin" is also situated in the Arboretum. ⊠ *Vaipaee* ☎ *92–60–13* ☉ *By request* ✉ *Free.*

Hane. The village of Hane, protected on the east by Motu Hane, also has a little museum dedicated to the sea, with a display of canoes through the ages, paddles, and many other objects. The oldest archeological site so far discovered in the Marquesas, Haíatuatua, is also here. It has been dated to between AD 250 and 300.

Sea Museum of Hane ✉*Mr. Joseph Vaatete–98744 Vaipaee–Ua Huka.* ☎*92–60–13* ⊘*By request* ⊞*Free.*

Meiaute. At the foot of Mount Hitikau, you can see a great series of monumental tiki carved from red rock. Many organized tours call here.

In the tiny village of Hokatu about 2 mi east of Hane look for the **Geology and Petroglyphe Museum,** which is tiny but interesting. ☎*92–60–55* ⊘*By request* ⊞*Free.*

WHERE TO STAY
You'll only find family hotels, or pensions, on Ua Huka. *See the price chart in Chapter 1, Tahiti, for information on pricing.*

FAMILY HOTELS
¢ **Chez Maurice & Delphine.** This pension is located on the mountainside with splendid views of the bay. Excursions such as horse riding, a visit to the archaeological sites and a tour around the island by speedboat can be arranged. They will also rent out a car with driver. Guests can be initiated into wood carving free of charge. **Pros:** Linens and mosquito nets provided; private bathrooms with hot water; common kitchen available for guests. **Cons:** No water sports available. ✉*Vaipaee* ☎*92–60–55* ⊕*www.haere-mai.pf* ⟿*5 bungalows* ⌂*In-room: no a/c, no phone, refrigerator, no TV. In-hotel: restaurant, waterfront, laundry facilities, airport shuttle* ⊟*No credit cards* ⦿*MAP.*

$ **Pension Auberge Hitikau.** Celine Fournier has three rooms in a house located in the valley just below the peak of the volcano. She is happy to offer lessons in drag fishing—a local method that involves throwing a net—or to organize picnics. **Pros:** You can rent a car with or without a driver; excursions organized; linens and mosquito nets provided; common kitchen available for guests. **Cons:** Shared bathrooms. ✉*Hane* ☎*92–61–74* ⟿*3 rooms* ⌂*In-room: no a/c, no phone, refrigerator (some), no TV. In-hotel: restaurant, bar, water sports, laundry service, airport shuttle* ⊟*No credit cards.* ⦿*EP, MAP, AI.*

$$ **Le Reve Marquisien.** Marie-France Aunoa keeps this pension situated on the mountainside overlooking the valley. **Pros:** Linens provided; private bathrooms with hot water; common kitchen available for guests. **Cons:** No credit cards. ✉*Vaipaee* ☎*92–61–84* ⌀*revemarquisien@mail.pf* ⟿*4 bungalows* ⌂*In-room: no a/c, no phone. In-hotel: restaurant, laundry facilities, airport shuttle* ⊟*No credit cards* ⦿*AI.*

SPORTS & ACTIVITIES
Local tour operators provide a variety of options for exploring the island's archaeological sites on hiking, horseback, and ATV tours. You can also take boat tours to two small islands off Ua Huka's southwest point. One island is red, the other white, and both are covered in thousands of terns. The islanders themselves take the tern eggs for food, a matter of some controversy.

CLOSE UP

The Impressionist's Inspiration

Born in Paris in 1848, Paul Gauguin is one of the finest post-Impressionist painters. The son of a journalist originally from Peru, Gauguin moved from Paris to Lima with his family in 1849. His father died en route and the family remained in Lima for four years before moving back to France, where Gauguin received his formal education. Later he became a member of the merchant marines, traveling for six years before finally settling down in France in 1870 as a stockbroker.

When Gauguin's mother died in 1867, his guardian, a wealthy art collector by the name of Gustave Arosa, introduced him to the world of painting. Gauguin began collecting art and painting, but it wasn't until he met Camille Pisarro, who introduced him to Paul Cézanne and other French Impressionists, that he became an accomplished, full-time painter.

Gauguin moved to Panama in 1887 to work on the Panama Canal, but stayed only a few weeks before moving to Martinique, where ill health and poverty forced him back to France. In Brittany he developed the painting style for which he has become best known and became friendly with Vincent Van Gogh. In 1891, Gauguin moved to Tahiti, but after two years he returned to France. It was an embarrassing return, but Gauguin had brought back some excellent work and managed to mount an exhibition in Paris and set up a studio in Montparnasse. Unfortunately, his heart was in the tropics and he returned to Tahiti in 1895. During this period he created many of his famous works, but his poor health and lack of money, combined with scathing articles he wrote for a local newspaper, made him many enemies. In 1901 Gauguin left Tahiti for the Marquesas and settled in the village of Atuona on the island of Hiva Oa. Here he built his "House of Pleasure" and, with money coming in from Paris, probably enjoyed his happiest period. Unfortunately he died two years later and his remains are buried in the Calvaire Cemetery in Atuona.

If you visit the island's interior, be on the lookout for the giant Marquesan imperial pigeon (Ducula galeata), which has recently been reintroduced by the Ornithological Society of Polynesia (MANU). It is a beautiful gray bird with a green and red sheen on its plumage and a spectacular white and gray-black cere protruding almost to the tip of the bill, making it preeminent amongst Polynesian avifauna. At one time the bird could only be found in a few valleys on Nuku Hiva, in severely depleted numbers. Since the species faced imminent extinction—made worse by the fact that it survived on only one island—MANU set up a reintroduction program on Ua Huka, in order to create a second population and to increase its probability for survival. This program is in the valley of Vaiviki.

FATU HIVA

The southernmost island in the Marquesas archipelago, Fatu Hiva is also the most isolated. The island has high sheer cliffs, craggy slopes, and a mass of untamed vegetation. The lush jungles are divided by narrow ravines and marvelous valleys, much of the island's allure lies in its wild beauty, including the Bay of Virgins (known locally as Hana Vave or, in French, Baie des Vierges). Many people believe that the bay is the loveliest in all of Polynesia.

Activities include deep-sea fishing, sailing, and horseback riding. Trekking is also popular though it can be tough-going in the heat and unruly vegetation. Though there are no great beaches, swimming is possible, but you'll need to watch out for sharks.

Accommodations are fairly basic and credit cards are not widely accepted. Although there are one or two food stores and a Post Office, shops are a rarity, but the women will display their wares on the harbor front when a ship comes in. The islands were once famous for skilled tattoo artists. Today, the art form is experiencing a resurgence.

GETTING HERE & AROUND

Fatu Hiva does not have an airport, but there's a boat from Hiva Oa. As it's not a regular service, the trip has to be organized through the Pensions; the trip takes about 3½ hours.

The island has no form of public transport or taxis, but there are two 4WD services that are also contracted through the pensions. Most people walk, but biking and horseback riding are also popular modes of transport.

WHAT TO SEE

Rain is a frequent visitor to Fatu Hiva, explaining the island's lushness. The east coast of the island is largely mountainous and inaccessible. The center of the island is a large plateau, where the majority of the vegetation is either grass or pandanus trees, whose leaves are an important ingredient in many dishes. Mount Tauauoho (3,150 feet [960 meters]), to the south of the plateau, is the highest point on the island.

About 500 people live on the island in two villages: **Omoa**, which has a simple but beautiful Catholic church, and the even smaller **Hanavave.** Many of the inhabitants carry dramatic tattoos in the local tradition and proudly display them to visitors. The islanders are legendary for their generosity and friendship, and if necessary it's perhaps best to repay this generosity with gifts rather than cash.

Only 4.8 km (3 mi) of sea separate the villages but land access is by a 16-km (10-mi) narrow path that winds over the mountains. Walking this can take around four to five hours—getting around is not an easy option.

Vaiee-Nui Falls are in the valley behind Hanavave. The journey is described by some as an easy walk of around an hour but it must be remembered that rain is frequent on Fatu Hiva, and a muddy path can turn the easy walk into a tough hike. If you make the trip, be sure to take swimming gear; the pool at the base of the falls simply calls out for a swim.

WHERE TO STAY

There are no real restaurants on the island, and no place to stay in Hanavave. Omoa does have family-owned and -run pensions that offer meals, but keep in mind that these rooms are in people's homes and

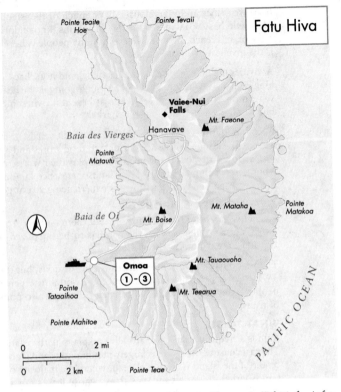

may be pretty basic. *See the price chart in Chapter 1, Tahiti, for information on pricing.*

¢ **Chez Lionel.** Lionel Cantois's place is about a mile from Omoa's harbor. It's surrounded by lush vegetation and is close to a river where swimming is possible. **Pros:** Seaside access; mountain views; linen and mosquito nets are provided. **Cons:** Only some of the private bathrooms have hot water. *⊕1.5 km (1 mi) from the wharf ⌂B.P. 1, Omoa 98740 ☎92–81–84 ✎chezlionel@mail.pf ⛵1 bungalow, 2 rooms ☖In-room: no a/c, no phone, kitchen (some), refrigerator (some), no TV (some). In-hotel: restaurant, laundry facilities, public Internet, airport shuttle ⊟No credit cards ⵔMAP.*

$ **Chez Norma.** Mrs. Norma Ropati's pension has six rooms available. Her private home is in the village of Omoa, close by the dock. She also runs a small restaurant from the same address offering the chance to taste a *kaikai enana*, a traditional Marquesas meal that includes *poe* (pudding-like), *fri* (plantains), goat meat, coconut milk, and fish. **Pros:** Private bathrooms with hot water; linens provided. **Cons:** No water views; no a/c or ceiling fans; no Internet service. *656 feet (200 meters) from the Omoa Quay, Omoa ☎92–80–13 ⛵4 rooms ☖In-room: no a/c, no phone, no TV. In-hotel: laundry facilities, airport shuttle ⊟No credit cards ⵔAI.*

$$ 🏠**Pension Heimata.** This pension is located in the village of Omoa. You'll stay in one of two rooms in the home of Mrs. Albertine Tetuanui. **Pros:** Common bathrooms have hot water; three meals a day can be provided. **Cons:** There are no private bathrooms; this is as basic as it gets, there are not a lot of extras or amenities here. *Downtown, 1,640 feet (500 meters) from the Omoa Quay, Omoa* ☎*92–80–58* 🛏*2 rooms* 🔌*In-room: no a/c, no phone, no TV. In-hotel: airport shuttle* 💳*No credit cards* 🍴*EP, MAP.*

SHOPPING

Watch out for *umu hei monoi.* This local specialty, made from dried bananas, is said to include dried coconut oil, sandalwood, spearmint, jasmine, ginger, pineapple, basil, and gardenia.

> ### BEWARE THE NONO
>
> This tiny bug—found near bodies of water in humid, low-lying areas—is definitely the local curse; it's silent but (not seriously) deadly. They attack exposed skin—ankles, legs, and the backs of knees are particularly susceptible—and cause a slight swelling, which is followed by the most acute itching. Don't scratch! Apply lemon or lime juice to offset the itch, though you may fare better by adding the juice to a decent cocktail and drowning your sorrows. The only effective way to deal with this pest is to wear long sleeves and pants, use a good insect repellent, and apply *manoi oil* to bites.

Local scented oils are often offered for sale. You'll also find *umuhei* (aromatic bouquets), mainly made from sandalwood.

Local carvers work in miro, rosewood, and sandalwood, as well as local rock. You'll find mainly bowls, platters, and the ubiquitous tiki. Local women make traditional tapa cloth from the hand-beaten bark of the mulberry tree.

THE GAMBIER ISLANDS

Located more than 1,000 mi east of Tahiti, the 10 islands and 18 islets of the Gambier Archipelago are more than a little off the regular tourist track. However, the archipelago's atmosphere and history draw the traveler dedicated to seeing somewhere out of the ordinary with many of its resources as yet untouched and bays and creeks abounding with fish. The volcanic soils have produced a lush landscape and there are mini-orchards (usually in the residents' backyards) groaning under the weight of papayas, mangoes, and breadfruit. The lagoon is azure blue and the quiet bays of the main island of Mangareva are often dotted with yachts.

The island's earliest known inhabitants date back to the 10th century, and for a period of some 500 years, the islanders—who numbered in the thousands—lived and traded timber with other island groups, including the Marquesas. Excessive logging, however, denuded the islands and with the loss of trade they fell into a bleak period marked by civil war and even cannibalism. The first European to "discover" the

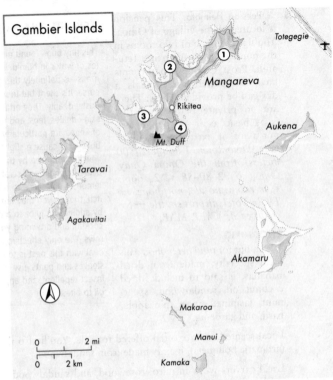

Gambier Islands

islands was Captain John Wilson, an Englishman who arrived aboard the HMS *Duff* in 1797. He named the island group after British Admiral Gambier who had help fund his sea voyage. Wilson was a member of the London Missionary Society, which had had great success converting members of the Society Islands to Protestantism. However, it was Catholicism that took hold in the Gambier Island, arriving in the form of French priest Father Honore Laval and a small entourage of priests in 1834. History doesn't paint a glowing picture of Father Laval, who is said to have systematically destroyed the islands' culture in an obsessive drive to convert the inhabitants to Catholicism; several marae were destroyed in his quest although a few remain on the other islands. He set about building the enormous St. Michael's Cathedral, which was completed in 1848 and can hold an amazing 2,000 people, almost twice the number of the island's population. Other Catholic missionaries built chapels, a convent, a school, mills, weaving workshops, watchtowers, and baker's ovens.

GETTING HERE AND AROUND

Trips need to be carefully planned, as flights are limited and vary in frequency depending on the season and holiday periods. The Tahiti-Gambier return fights can operate as frequently as weekly (and sometimes twice-weekly); but will drop back to fortnightly (every two weeks) and three times a month in the low season. Flying time is around four and a half hours, though bad weather can greatly affect this. Flights depart from Pape'ete around 5:40 AM, arriving in Mangareva around 11:05 AM. The airport is located on Motu Totegegie, about 5 km (3 mi) north of the port at Rikitea. Boats meet each flight and transport passengers to the town of Rikitea.

A hassle-free way to organize a trip to Gambier is with an Air Tahiti package that includes accommodation and transfers. It can be combined with an island-hopping itinerary to other archipelagos. Charter flights can be arranged to the island with Air Archipels.

You can travel by ship but it's a long, uncomfortable journey. The Nuku Hau cargo/passenger ship makes a voyage every 25 days. Meals are served on board but there are no berths. Leaving Pape'ete, it heads for the Tuamotu group first, calling at about five islands before reaching Mangareva.

ESSENTIALS

Airlines Air Archipels (☎81–30–30). **Air Tahiti** (☎86–40–23 ⊕www.airtahiti.com).

Passenger Ship Nuku Hau (✉Pape'ete, Tahiti ☎45–23–23 or 54–99–54).

Visitor Info Gambier Tourism Committee (✉Chez Bianca & Benoit, Rikitea, Mangareva ☎97–83–76 ✎scallamera.Florentine@mail.pf).

MANGAREVA

Mangareva, with a population around 1,000, is the farthest island from Tahiti (1,033 mi away) and virtually the only inhabited one. It's certainly the only one with tourist accommodations. Pearl farming is the primary industry and there's a farm in the lagoon.

About 5 mi long and less than 3 mi wide, the island's steep-sided and strikingly terraced with two main peaks, Mt. Duff (1,444 feet [440 meters]) and Mt. Mokoto 129 feet (423 meters). It shares a lagoon with five small islands, the largest of which are Aukena, Akamaru, and Taravai. A string of motu and a coral reef—measuring some 64 km (40 mi) in circumference—surrounds the lagoon.

A cradle of Catholicism in the Pacific, Mangareva has several remains of religious buildings dating from the mid-1800s. The altar at Saint Michel Cathedral, in the village of Rikitea, is inlaid with mother-of-pearl and studded with black pearls.

Things have changed little in the past 100 years or so; today the small town of Rikitea has just a few small grocery stores, one café (which is really a grocery store selling sandwiches), a post office, medical center and the cathedral. There's no bank, though there is an ATM. As only one of the four pensions on the island accepts credit cards, it is wise to bring adequate cash.

WHERE TO STAY

There are just four lodgings—each run by a local family—on Mangareva. Three are situated in the town of Rikitea or a few minutes away, while the fourth (Pension Jojo) is 15-minute car trip away. You'll get an intimate experience, sharing meals with other guests and sometimes the owner's family in a communal dining room. Some accommodations have shared kitchens and you'll always be able to do your laundry.

The pension owners are the experts on the island and operate all tours—around the island itself and to the three main islands in the lagoon. The owners of pension Bianca & Benoit also head the Gambier Tourism Committee. *See the price chart in Chapter 1, Tahiti, for information on pricing.*

¢–$ 📷 **Chez Bianca & Benoit.** Located on the mountainside at the base of Mt. Duff, this pension has panoramic views of Aukena Bay and is about a half mile from the dock. The three rooms are located in a two-story house and share a communal bathroom with hot water and have access to a lounge room with TV and telephone. All meals are available and are taken around a communal table. Tours of Mangareva, as well as the three other main islands can be arranged together with fishing and motu picnics. If your stay is less than three nights, full board is compulsory. **Pros:** Linens and mosquito nets provided; private bathrooms with hot water; common kitchen available for guests. **Cons:** Rooms share a bathroom; no a/c. ✉ *B.P. 19, Rikitea 98755* ☎ *97–83–76* ✎ *biancabenoit@mail.pf* 🛏 *5 bungalows, 3 rooms* ⚒ *In-room: no a/c, no phone, refrigerator (some), no TV. In-hotel: bar, water sports, bicycles, laundry facilities, airport shuttle* ▭ *No credit cards* ⦿ *CP.*

$ 📷 **Chez Jojo.** Jocelyne Mamatui has two bungalows and one room located right on the lagoon with wonderful views of Aukena and Akamaru islands. The pension is a 15-minute drive from Rikitea. Bungalows have private bathrooms; the room has a shared bathroom. There is daily housekeeping and meals are taken in the dining room of the host's house and will often include vegetables from her garden. There's also a bar selling wine and beer only. Island tours (from 25,000 CFP) and fishing trips can be arranged. **Pros:** Linens and mosquito nets provided; private bathrooms with hot water. **Cons:** Not centrally located and requires transport into town; shared bathroom; no a/c. ✉ *B.P. 1, Rikitea 98755* ☎ *97–82–61* 🛏 *2 bungalows, 1 room* ⚒ *In-room: no a/c, no phone. In-hotel: restaurant, bar, waterfront, diving, water sports, bicycles, laundry facilities, airport shuttle* ▭ *No credit cards* ⦿ *CP.*

$ 📷 **Pension Maro'i.** Marie Teakarotu keeps this pension, which is located on the edge of the lagoon a few minutes from the village. The four bungalows each have a double bed, a single bed, a terrace, and a bathroom with hot water. There's also a shared kitchen and a communal dining room. **Pros:** Linens and mosquito nets provided; private bathrooms with hot water. **Cons:** No a/c. ✉ *Gatavake* ⌂ *B.P. 04, Rikitea 98755* ☎ *97–84–62* ✎ *btghinarau@mail.pf* 🛏 *4 bungalows* ⚒ *In-room: no a/c, no phone, no TV (some). In-hotel: restaurant, bar, waterfront, water sports, bicycles, laundry facilities, public Internet, airport shuttle* ▭ *AE, MC, V* ⦿ *EP, MAP, AI.*

$ ⊡**Tara Etu Kura Pension.** There's just one bungalow and one room at this pension right in the village of Rikitea. The bungalow has a private bathroom with hot water, but the room has a shared bathroom. Guests also have a communal kitchen at their disposal. An excursion to the three other islands in the lagoon can be arranged. **Pros:** Central location; linens and mosquito nets provided; bathrooms have hot water. **Cons:** Room has a shared bathroom; no a/c. ⊠*B.P. 75, Rikitea 98755* 🖀*97–83–25* ➴*1 bungalow, 1 room* ⌂*In-room: no a/c, no phone. In-hotel: restaurant, waterfront, laundry facilities, airport shuttle* ▭*No credit cards* ❙◯❙*CP.*

SPORTS & ACTIVITIES

Most pensions organize hikes and picnics while bikes, kayaks, and snorkeling gear can normally be rented if they are not supplied free or charge. The pensions will also organize fishing trips or tours of Mangareva and the nearby islands of Aukena, Akamaru, and Taravai. You can also hike to the top of Mt. Duff on your own, but be sure to ask directions from your pension owner first as the trailhead is hard to find.

Mangareva is a popular stopover for "yachties" on sailing adventures around the South Pacific islands; it's conveniently positioned between Pitcairn (which can only be reached by boat) and the Tuamotu Islands to the north.

There is not much to buy; however, there are artisans making mother-of-pearl ornaments that would make very nice souvenirs. A visit can be arranged as part of an island tour.

THE AUSTRAL ISLANDS

Lying well to the south of Tahiti, the six islands of the Austral group have scenery that is often spectacular but rarely seen as it's well off the usual tourist path.

No particular events apart from Christmas and New Year seem to stir the peace of this place. As on many of the islands it's worth a visit to a church on the Sabbath to hear the singing. The Polynesians voices are particularly harmonious and on Tubuai they have a style all their own.

GETTING HERE & AROUND

Tubuai, Raivavae, Rurutu, and Rimatara can be reached by air from Tahiti but Ile Maria is uninhabited and Rapa is isolated and difficult to reach. Tubuai is the administrative center and is on a regular flight schedule from Tahiti. Flights at present are four times a week and less between the other islands.

WHEN TO GO

The climate is more temperate with less rain than Tahiti, and the cooler season is from May to September; November through March are the popular months to visit. The islands have suffered severe damage from cyclones, which is an ongoing problem in this part of the Pacific.

TUBUAI

Life is quiet for the 2,000-some inhabitants of Tubuai, which is 644 km (400 mi) south of Tahiti. It's a mellow, subtropical island of approximately 70 square km (27 square mi) and the capital of the Austral Islands chain. Mts. Taitaa (1,280 feet [390 meters]) and Tonorutu (1,023 feet [312 meters]) dominate the horizon, and the island is fringed by a barrier reef scattered with motu (small coral islets), while its lagoon side offers brilliant, white-sand beaches. Polynesians have lived on the island for more than 2,000 years. English explorer James Cook first mapped it in 1777; the island was annexed in 1881 by France.

Today, much of the economic life of the island is devoted to fishing and growing fruit and vegetables destined for Pape'ete. Tubuai has a temperate climate, tropical yet cooler than Tahiti and well-watered and fertile, producing coconuts, taro, arrowroot, and bananas. Tubuai has one of the least-studied ecosystems in the Pacific; it is rich in flowers and plant life along with birds. Species like the Kuhl's lorikeet, the Rimatara reed-warbler, and the Rapa fruit-dove are unique to the island.

GETTING HERE AND AROUND

Flying time from Tahiti to Tubuai nonstop is about three hours; most flights stop at one of the other islands extending the flight by another hour.

Getting around the island is easy as one road encircles the island and another cuts across the middle. Roads are not usually paved but mainly packed sand or gravel. There is no public transport, but cars and bicycles can be rented and family pensions usually organize picnics and rent out boats and other beach-type equipment. Hitching a lift is pretty common, too.

ESSENTIALS

Car Rental Europcar Tubuai (⊠ *Taahueia* ☎ *95-04-12*).

Visitor Info Harii Taata Association (✆ *B.P. 27, Mataura 98754* ☎ *95-07-12* ✉ *maletdoom@mail.pf*).   ●

WHAT TO SEE

More than half the people live in the town of **Mataura** on the northern coast, about 1.5 km (1 mi) east of the wharf. You'll find shops and a small market in the village, though in truth there is little for the tourist to buy.

Tubuai had a role in the best-known naval mutiny, that aboard HMS *Bounty* in 1789. After master's mate Fletcher Christian seized the ship, setting Captain William Bligh adrift, the mutineers sailed the South Pacific looking for a place to hide, eventually ending up on Pitcairn Island. In the course of their travels they spent time in Tubuai, building Fort George, southeast of **Taahueia** and around 3 km (2 mi) east of the wharf. Nothing remains of the original fort, but a replica has recently been built.

Near **Mahu** on the south coast is the home and grave of parliamentary speaker Noel Ilari, who was jailed by the French government in the

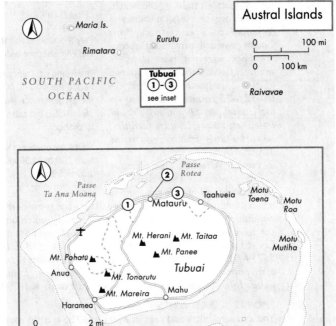

1950s on false charges. Details of the saga are on his gravestone. His home is now a modest guesthouse.

Tubuai has a number of marae, or Polynesian meeting grounds, along with *ahu* (platforms for the dead). They are generally poorly maintained in the Christian environment.

WHERE TO STAY

You'll find small family run hotels in and around Mataura, Tubai's main town. *See the price chart in Chapter 1, Tahiti, for information on pricing.*

¢ 🏨 **Chez Karine & Tale.** Karine—an American—and her husband Charles Tahuhuterani have two bungalows set on the hillside with beach access and a terrace with an ocean view. Each has a private bathroom with hot water. Meals can be served if you order in advance. **Pros:** Linens and mosquito nets provided; private bathrooms with hot water; airport transfers are free. **Cons:** Facilities are sparse. ⌖*B.P. 34, Mataura 98754* ☎*93–23–40* ✉*charles@mail.pf* ➷*1 bungalow* ⌂*In-room: no a/c, no phone, kitchen, refrigerator. In-hotel: diving, water sports, bicycles, airport shuttle* ▭*No credit cards* ⏧*CP.*

¢ 🏨 **Chez Yolande.** Sam and Yolande Tahuhuterani offer a real family experience for their guests as they can share their days with a Polynesian family. Located right by the beach, Sam will organize lagoon tours and Yolande cooks great food. **Pros:** Linens provided; private bathrooms with hot water; airport transfers are free. **Cons:** Facilities are sparse. ⌂*B.P. 23, Mataura 98754* ☎*95–05–52* ⮐*5 rooms* ⌂*In-room: no a/c (some), no phone, no TV. In-hotel: restaurant, laundry facilities, airport shuttle* ▭*No credit cards* ⦿*EP, MAP.*

¢ ⌧**Pension Vaiteanui.** This pleasant family pension is located on the hillside overlooking the road and is

just ten minutes from the Mataura village. The rooms are in a modern building with a private bathroom. Meals can be taken on-site, though you have to order in advance. **Pros:** Linens and mosquito nets provided. **Cons:** The bathroom is shared with other guests. ⌂*B.P. 141, Mataura 98754* ☎*93–22–40* ✉*bodinm@mail.pf* ⮐*6 rooms* ⌂*In-room: no a/c, no phone, no TV. In-hotel: restaurant, bar, diving, laundry facilities, public Internet, airport shuttle* ▭*No credit cards* ⦿*EP, MAP, AI.*

SPORTS & ACTIVITIES

You can rent bikes and cars in Mataura. The coastal road around the island is beautiful, peaceful, and easy to negotiate on foot or bike. Mt. Taita, also known as "the sleeping man," is the best destination for a gentle mountain hike.

The lagoon beaches are clean and safe. Picnic trips are offered across the lagoon to a number of islets on the reef. Largely untouched by the outside world, the islets give a taste of incredible isolation. Wilson Doom rents out his 24-foot boat for full- or half-day island tours or picnics on a motu.

For the adventurous, Tubuai is on the extreme international surfing route, but this is an activity for the skilled rather than the beginner since the best waves are to be found on the ocean side of the barrier reef.

CONTACTS

Boat Rentals **Wilson Doom** (☎*95–07–12* ✉*maletdoom@mail.pf*).

Scuba Diving **La Bonne Bonteille** (☎*95–08–41* ⊕ *www.labonnebouteille plongee.com*).

SHOPPING

When ships or tour groups are in port, islanders offer a variety of local weavings created from the pandanus leaves. Their hats, in a particularly old-fashioned style, are popular, as are fans. Some woodcarvings are also offered, especially at Mahu.

Cruising in French Polynesia

WORD OF MOUTH

"On the ship, your costs are more fixed. Food is very expensive when on land, and when you sail on the Paul Gauguin, other than excursions and souvenirs, your trip is paid for up front. Age wise, there's a real mix on the ship, and definitely more to do at night than on land."

—beckaboo

"A cruise is a good way to see the various islands of Tahiti without breaking the bank."

—judilie

Linda Coffman
Updated
By Caroline
Gladstone

CRUISING FRENCH POLYNESIA IS A "dream come true" experience that's perfect for the first-time passenger. The average cruise length is seven days, in which time you'll visit four islands. It may sound like a Caribbean cruise, but that's where the similarity ends. When ships call at French Polynesian ports passengers enter a time warp encountering sleepy havens where life goes on as it has for decades.

The real magic of a sea voyage is gliding across the blue ocean and watching the islands—be they volcanic hulks swathed in clouds or sparkling white atolls forested with coconut palms—loom into view. Moorea's shark-toothed mountains, Bora Bora's brooding Mt. Otemanu, and Huahine's jungle-covered twin peaks will take your breath away. Watch the water change from azure blue to soft turquoise as your ship navigates the pass between the reef, and enters the lagoon.

You can enjoy this ticket to paradise on board a variety of vessels from six-star motor yachts with every imaginable luxury, to cargo ships that let you follow in the wake of Herman Melville and Paul Gauguin.

CHOOSING YOUR CRUISE

Deciding whom you'd like to share your cruise with is the first step to picking the perfect water-bound trip. Do you want to share your ship with 687 other passengers or just seven like-minded souls on a catamaran? Next you'll need to decide what kind of ship you'd like. Would a floating resort with pools, a casino, two restaurants, bars, and entertainment be best? Do you yearn to hoist the sails and feel the wind in your face, or does securing a passage on a working ship visiting remote islands fulfill all those "run away to sea" fantasies?

French Polynesian is blessed with an amazing diversity of vessels. You won't see a carbon copy of your ship in port; you may not even see another ship during your week at sea. There's a style for every type of passenger and all the options deliver that South Seas experience that has captivated writers for centuries.

Sometimes the choice of ship comes down to price; other times it's about adventure, or maybe all you want is complete relaxation without having to lift a manicured finger. One thing's for sure—you won't find floating leviathans in these waters; even the bigger ships are a quarter the size of the mighty Caribbean vessels. Fares range from $250 a day on the 670-passenger *Pacific Princess* to $1,500 a day on Bora Bora Cruises' two motor yachts.

It's a good idea to choose the itinerary first and then see what ships, in your price bracket, appeal to you. Your fellow passengers are likely to be aged 40 and over; usually seasoned travelers. The less expensive, more adventurous itineraries attract a younger crowd, and vice versa. All vessels (except the really small ships) depart from Pape'ete.

ITINERARIES

SOCIETY ISLANDS

This is the classic itinerary and all vessels, bar the *Aranui 3* cargo ship, visit at least three of French Polynesia's islands. Seven- and six-night cruises are the norm with calls at three to four islands apart from Tahiti itself. There are no days at seas as distances between islands are short; even the Archipels sailing catamarans take only a few hours to get to each island.

The small motor yachts and sailing boats depart from either Bora Bora or Huahine and visit Bora Bora, Huahine, Tahaa, and Raiatea; the bigger ships departing from Pape'ete also call at Moorea and anchor in its bays: Cook's and Opunohu. Small ships allow passengers plenty of time to snorkel and kayak, and usually have free excursions. All ships anchor in the lagoon and transport passengers to shore by tenders (small boats used to shuttle people back and forth between the ship and land).

SOCIETY ISLANDS & TUAMOTU

This is a wonderful itinerary to follow, if you have the time, as it combines the most popular ports of both island groups in 10- and 11-night cruises starting from Pape'ete. Itineraries—aboard either the *Star Flyer, Paul Gauguin,* or the *Pacific Princess* (in late 2009)—include two full days at sea, except in the case of Paul Gauguin, which is in port every day. Ports of call include Bora Bora, Tahaa, Raiatea, Huahine, and Moorea in the Societies, and Rangiroa in Tuamotu. *Star Flyer* is small enough to enter Rangiroa's vast lagoon where it spends a day cruising and overnights at anchor there; you can also add the port of Fakarava to the 11-night itinerary.

TUAMOTU ISLANDS AND RANGIROA LAGOON

This is the domain of small catamarans (motor and sail) operated by Huamana Cruises and Archipels Cruises. You can explore the vast Rangiroa Lagoon (measuring 72 km by 26 km [45 mi by 16 mi]) on two-, three-, four-, six-, and seven-night itineraries. This will involve lazy days cruising through the pristine waters, anchoring by pink sandy beaches, picnics on small *motu* (islets), and village visits. A two- or three-night cruise will call at the Blue Lagoon; a four-nighter will visit the pink-sand beaches and the "above-sea" coral outcrops of Iles aux Recifs; a six- or seven-night cruise will combine the two. The Archipels catamarans also sail across the ocean to Fakarava and the rarely visited atoll of Toau, both part of the Tuamotu group. All cruises depart from Rangiroa.

MARQUESAS ISLANDS AND TUAMOTU

The most exotic and port-intensive cruises are the 14-night voyages to the Marquesas on the cargo/passenger ship, *Aranui 3*. Leaving Pape'ete, it makes its first call at Takapoto in the Tuamotu group and then visits the six inhabited Marquesas islands: Ua Pou, Nuku Hiva, Tahuata, Fatu Hiva, Hiva Oa, and Ua Huka. Picking up and delivering goods as it goes, it makes two stops each at Ua Pou and Nuku Hiva—on the way out and on the way home. It operates 16 cruises a year, departing

Pape'ete on Saturdays. In a new move the *Paul Gauguin* will also visit the islands during two 2009 itineraries—14-night (departing April 14) and 11-night (departing May 26) one-off cruises calling at Hiva Oa and Nuka Hiva and visiting Futa Hiva during the May cruise only. The itinerary also takes in the Tuamotu and Society groups.

WHEN TO GO

As the average temperature in French Polynesia is a balmy 26°C (78.8°F) year-round, any time is really a good time to cruise. Decisions are limited only by the cruise lines' schedules. Most lines operate year-round, although not every itinerary is offered on a regular basis. For example, while both *Star Flyer* and *Paul Gauguin* have separate Society Islands and Tuamotu/Society itineraries, there are many more Society cruises on offer due to the popularity of this better known group of islands. *Aranui 3*'s Marquesas voyages operate year-round, but the *Pacific Princess*'s Society/Tuamotu itineraries are seasonal; they start in early October and run through December.

CRUISE COSTS

Cruise fares vary considerably by itinerary, type of ship and the category of accommodations. Seasonality doesn't affect French Polynesia too much and you'll find only marginal differences in prices (i.e., *Star Flyer*'s economy season is only $150 to $200 cheaper than its value season). Published rates are highest for exclusive small ships (carrying 8, 24, or 60 passengers); daily rates can range from $900 to $1,500 a day, which is three to four times the cost of a cruise on a Princess Cruises or Star Clippers ship. However, these small ships usually include wines with meals, other alcoholic drinks, excursions, port and fuel charges, and tips. The less expensive ships do not include drinks, excursions, or taxes, and daily fares will start at $250 to $350 per person depending on the ship. The five-star ship *Paul Gauguin,* sits somewhere between the premium cruises and the ultra-luxury, as its daily fares start at $530 a day and include wines, spirits, soft drinks, beer, and tips, but not taxes. Budget around $210 to $300 for taxes on most ships. Single travelers will pay a supplement for sole use of a double cabin, and this price obviously varies.

EXTRAS

You've paid your cruise fare and you've probably told yourself that you won't need to spend another cent. However, if you haven't booked an ultra-luxury small ship where butlers pour your drinks and there's no tab to sign, you'll be in store for quite a few extra costs. First, there are the taxes (*see Taxes, below*), which average about $210 to $280 for a seven-day cruise. Find out whether your ship includes them in the fare or will add them to your account at the end of the cruise.

Shore excursions can max out your credit card if you book one at every port, but if you have the chance, you really shouldn't pass up the opportunity to experience at least one snorkel and ray feeding

Saving Money on Your Cruise Fare

You can save on your cruise fare in several ways. Obviously, you should shop around. Some travel agents will discount cruise prices, though this is becoming a thing of the past. One thing never changes—do not ever, under any circumstances, pay brochure rate. You can do better, often as much as half off published fares. These are a few simple strategies you can follow:

■ **Book early:** Cruise lines discount their cruises if you book early, particularly during the annual "Wave" season between January and March.

■ **Cruise during the off-season:** French Polynesia doesn't have the same seasonal differences as cruises in the Caribbean. The off-season is from around November to May (excluding the Christmas period) and it may be possible to pick up a deal.

■ **Book late:** Sometimes you can book a last-minute cruise at substantial savings if the ship hasn't filled all its cabins.

■ **Choose accommodations with care:** Cabins are usually standardized and location determines the fare. Selecting a lower category can result in savings while giving up nothing in terms of cabin size and features.

■ **Book a "guarantee":** You won't be able to select your own cabin because the cruise line will assign you one in the category you book, but a "guarantee" fare can be substantially lower than a regular fare.

■ **Cruise with friends and family:** Book a minimum number of cabins, and your group can generally receive a special discounted fare.

■ **Reveal your age and affiliations:** Fare savings may be available for seniors and members of certain organizations, as well as cruise line stockholders.

■ **Cruise often:** Frequent cruisers usually get discounts from their preferred cruise lines.

7

excursion and one 4WD excursion through Society Islands' rugged hills. The *Star Flyer,* one of the less-expensive cruise operators, charges the following per person: a three-hour ray and shark feed on Bora Bora, $93; a 4WD tour to Bora Bora's WWII cannons, $103; a four-hour jungle hike in Raiatea, $77; a three-hour snorkel tour in Tahaa, $105; and a 3½-hour quad bike tour on Moorea, $134.

Drinks are another expense on most ships. A rule of thumb is you'll pay about the same for a drink as you would in a four- or five-star hotel bar. Some ships have wine-package deals (buy seven bottles in advance for the cruise and save money), while sometimes there are free cocktail parties. Phone calls are also very costly, so try to avoid them and use your cell phone or use the public phones when you get into port. Onboard shopping and casinos (there's a casino on two of the ships) eat up your money, too. As can tipping, though it's not expected in French Polynesia (*see Tipping, below*).

CRUISE LINES

One size definitely does not fit all in cruising. What's appealing to one passenger may be unacceptable to another. Ultimately, most cruise complaints arise from passengers whose expectations were not met. Make no mistake about it: cruise lines have distinct personalities, but not all luxury or mainstream cruise lines are alike, although they will share many basic similarities. The cruise industry is a fluid one—that means that when new features are introduced, they may not be found on all ships, even those within the same cruise line.

So which cruise line is best? Only you can determine which is best for you. You won't find ratings by Fodor's—either quality stars or value scores. Why? Because ratings are personal and heavily weighted to the reviewer's opinion. Your responsibility is to select the right cruise for you—no one knows your expectations better than you do yourself.

THE FRENCH POLYNESIAN CRUISE FLEET

French Polynesia is a small-fry destination on the world cruising map. You won't find numerous ships, from any one cruise line, based in the region. What you will find, though, is one ship from a trio of well-known cruise lines and a handful of little ships (some are actually sailboats), which cruise these waters and nowhere else.

The proximity of the Society Islands to each other has spawned a new breed of boutique ships, while the sheer necessity of transporting cargo to distant outposts has also popularized the almost extinct mode of transport called freighter or cargo travel.

PREMIUM CRUISE LINES—MID-SIZE SHIP

Premium cruise lines' ships exude a refined atmosphere, have stylish, well-maintained surroundings, and deliver a polished and attentive brand of service. They offer all sorts of activities most people associate with traditional cruise ships (passenger contests and pool games), but in keeping with the ship's elegant surroundings they'll be fun but subdued. In addition to traditional cruise activities, onboard lectures are common and production shows are quite sophisticated.

Premium line cruise ships tend to be newer mid-size to large vessels that carry 600 to 1,000 passengers. Decor is glamorous and subtle, with toned-down colors and extensive original art. Staterooms range from inside cabins for three or four people to outside cabins with or without balconies to suites.

Princess Cruises' mid-size ship, *Tahitian Princess,* perfectly fits this bill and has cruised the Society and Tuamotu islands seasonally since 2002. The ship's last cruise is scheduled for early December 2008; it will be replaced by its sister ship, the *Pacific Princess,* which will begin cruising in October 2009.

PRINCESS CRUISES Rising from modest beginnings in 1965, when it began offering cruises to Mexico with a single ship, Princess has become one of the world's most well-known cruise lines. Its fleet sails to more destinations each year than any other major line. Princess was catapulted to stardom in 1977, when its flagship became the setting for *The Love Boat* television series, which introduced millions of viewers to the still-new concept of a seagoing vacation. The name and famous "sea witch" logo have remained synonymous with cruising ever since. While the recent addition of three medium-size vessels to the fleet—including *Pacific Princess* and *Tahitian Princess*—offers a welcome smaller-ship choice, Princess more often follows the "bigger is better" trend when designing new ships.

Alternative restaurants—dining options other than the main dining room that usually have better quality food, but sometimes charge a surcharge to eat there—are a staple throughout the fleet, but vary by ship class. Enrichment programs featuring guest lecturers and opportunities to learn new skills or crafts are welcome additions to a roster of adult activities, which still includes staples such as bingo and art auctions.

The average age on a Princess boat is 45, though you do see a mix of younger and older couples on board. Princess suggests tipping $10 to $11 per person, per day. Gratuities are automatically added to onboard accounts; 15% is added to bar bills. ⏛*Princess Cruises, 24305 Town Center Dr., Santa Clarita, CA 91355-4999* ☎*661/753–0000 or 800/774–6237* ⊕*www.princess.com.*

Pacific Princess & Tahitian Princess. These identical ships, each weighing 30,277 tons, are the lightweights of the Princess fleet. Launched in 1999, they belonged to the now-defunct Renaissance Cruises fleet (they had the rather pedestrian names of *R Three* and *R Four*, respectively) and were acquired by Princess after Renaissance collapsed, and thus, have quite a different look. The interiors have a plush European elegance that echoes passenger ships of the 1920s; the central staircase, for example, would not have been out of place on the *Titanic,* albeit a much smaller version of that ill-fated ship. Public rooms have cherry wood–paneled walls and rich Oriental carpets, and one of the bars has a trompe l'oeil ceiling (painted with a fresco depicting a rural scene). There are four restaurants: the 338-seat Club Restaurant with large ocean-view windows; the Sabatini's Trattoria that serves a three-hour set degustation menu (and costs an extra $20 per person); an American-style steak house; and the Lido café which is open for casual dinners and pizzas. There's a spa operated by Steiner, high-tech weight machines and treadmills, and steam rooms. Entertainment—cabaret acts and local Polynesian troupes—takes place in the 345-seat Cabaret Lounge. More than 60% of the cabins have private balconies, suites have bathtubs, and the owner's suites (the best accommodations) have Jacuzzis.

A 10-night cruise starts at $2,178 per person, twin share. ⇦*344 cabins* ♿*In-room: safe, refrigerator. In-boat: 9 passenger decks, 2 specialty restaurants, dining room, buffet, ice-cream parlor, pizzeria, pool, gym, hair salon, hot tubs, showroom, dry cleaning, laundry service, computer room* ⊟*AE, DC, MC, V.*

7

LUXURY CRUISE LINES—SMALL SHIPS

Comprising only 5% of the market, the exclusive luxury cruise lines, which includes Regent Seven Seas Cruises (RSSC), offers high staff-to-guest ratios for personal service, superior cuisine in a single seating, and a highly inclusive product with few onboard charges. These ships offer much more space per passenger than you will find on premium cruise lines. Lines differ in what they emphasize, with some touting luxurious accommodations and entertainment and others focusing on exotic destinations and onboard enrichment.

The *Paul Gauguin* is a classic, small luxury ship purposely built for French Polynesian waters. Built by a French company and owned by Grand Circle Travel, it's operated by the U.S.-based Regent Seven Sea Cruises.

REGENT SEVEN
SEAS CRUISES

Regent Seven Seas Cruises (RSSC) was part of Carlson Hospitality Worldwide, one of the world's major hotel-and-travel companies until December 2007, when it was bought by Apollo Management, a New York investment company. By all accounts nothing is set to change with the new ownership (the same company also owns Oceania Cruises). RSSC line was formed in December 1994 with the merger of the one-ship Diamond Cruises and Seven Seas Cruises lines. From these modest beginnings, RSSC has grown into a major luxury player in the cruise industry, adopting the "Regent" label in early 2006. Subtle improvements throughout the fleet are ongoing, such as computer service with Wi-Fi capability for your own laptop and cell phone access, even when you are at sea. New bedding with down comforters and Egyptian cotton linens, Regent-branded bath amenities, flat-screen televisions, DVD players, and new clocks will be added to all accommodations.

The line's spacious ocean-view staterooms have the industry's highest percentage of private balconies; you'll always find open seating at dinner; tips are included in the fare and no additional tipping is expected. Specialty dining varies by ship within the fleet: the French menus on *Paul Gauguin* are devised by two-star Michelin chef Pierre Vigato from his own Apicius restaurant in Paris.

Regent has introduced an all-inclusive beverage policy that offers not only soft drinks and bottled water but also cocktails and select wines at all bars and restaurants throughout the ships. Activities are oriented toward onboard enrichment programs, socializing, and exploring the destinations on the itinerary. Spa and salon services are provided by the high-end Carita of Paris. While RSSC's vessels are adult-oriented and do not have dedicated children's facilities, a "Club Mariner" youth program for children is offered on selected sailings. Although passengers tend to be older and affluent, they are quite active. ☏ *Regent Seven Seas Cruises, 1000 Corporate Dr., Suite 500, Fort Lauderdale, FL 33334* ☎*954/776–6123 or 877/505–5370* ⊕*www.rssc.com.*

The **Paul Gauguin** operates slightly differently from other RSSC ships in that it follows French regulations that restrict the number of passengers it's allowed to carry: it currently carries 348 even though there is room for more. Local regulations also stipulate a minimum amount to be spent in the casino and boutique (around $15 to $20). The ship underwent a $6 million refurbishment in 2006, which added new soft furnishings in public areas and generally spruced up an already very stylish ship. Designed especially for travel in these waters, it has a room called Fare Tahiti (a traditional thatched hut) with books, videos, and other materials on the unique art, history, and culture of the islands. Three original Gauguin sketches are displayed under glass. Expert lecturers on Tahiti and Gauguin are on each cruise and provide a wealth of information.

Half of the cabins have balconies and the top-grade suites have butler service. Both the main dining room and the specialty restaurant (with alternative French and Italian menus) are open-seating, and complimentary table wines are provided at dinner. There's a Connoisseur Club for those who want to smoke cigars and sip cognac and premium wines at extra cost.

A seven-night *Paul Gauguin* cruise starts at $3,695 per person, twin share. ⬇174 cabins ♿In-room: safe, refrigerator, DVD (some). In-boat: 7 passenger decks, specialty restaurant, dining room, buffet, pool, gym, fitness classes, hair salon, showroom, dry cleaning, laundry service, computer room 🖷AE, DC, MC, V.

LUXURY CRUISE LINES—BOUTIQUE SHIPS

Not all boutique ships are luxury. Some are simply small and provide an intimate experience. However, when luxury meets boutique, the result is an amazing experience akin to being aboard a private yacht. The service will be impeccable; passengers will be feted with champagne breakfasts on the beach, sitting at tables set with white linen cloths as their feet are caressed by the limpid lagoon waters. Exclusive excursions and Jet Skiing will often be complimentary, and all drinks, with the exception of premium wines and champagnes, will be included. Getting the idea? Bora Bora Cruises' two motor yachts—the 60-passenger *Tu Moana* and the *Ti'a Moana*—offer just this type of luxury; as does the eight-person *Roa* operated by Roa Yachting. The 24-passenger Haumana Cruises' catamaran, the *Haumana*, is just a trifle less posh (not quite as much caviar on the menu perhaps) but luxurious just the same.

BORA BORA CRUISES **Bora Bora Cruises** is a French Polynesian operation, whose two ships ply the waters of the Society Islands on a six-night round-trip cruise itinerary from Bora Bora. It is owned by Mehiti Degage, a French Polynesian business woman who has been around boats all her life—her father, Eugene Degage, is the owner of the Tahiti—Moorea interisland ferry operations, Aremiti Ferries. Bora Bora Cruises was launched in 2003. Its two ultra-sleek motor cruisers were built in Australia and are identical apart from variations in interior decor and design.

Degage prides herself on outfitting the ships with the very best: from the Philippe Starck washbasins in the bathrooms to a glass staircase in the lounge and Italian leather sofas. The experience and service would be similar to that delivered by the very top-end luxury cruise lines of Seabourn and SeaDream Yacht Club; in fact SeaDream Yacht Club CEO, Larry Pimintel, advised Degage on certain aspects of delivering a luxury cruise product.

Bora Bora Cruises is all about intimate encounters: a six-day cruise includes several private beach picnics where not only tables and chairs but beds are set up on the sand for guests to recline upon. The staff of the onboard Nomade Spa set up a massage tent on the beach. There are champagne breakfasts and private picnics, while one of the extra-special treats is the motu cinema—the screen is a sail sheet strung between two coconut trees and the movie is *Tabu,* which was filmed in Bora Bora in 1928.

While mainly an adult vacation, children are welcome and one cabin has been set aside with games and there's a staff member to supervise them. The cruise fare includes drinks, some tours, transfers, and tips. A six-night Bora Bora cruises costs approximately $8,990 per person, twin share. ⌂*Bora Bora Cruises, BP 401876, Fare Tony, Pape'ete 98713* ☎*54–45–05* ⊕*www.boraboracruises.com.*

Tu Moana and ***T'ia Moana*** are two identical ships that have an all-white sleek profile, but different interior decor and color schemes. Both have beautiful timbers (floors, wall panels, and furniture) with *Tu Moana* featuring darker wood, and *T'ia Moana* a lighter look. Cabins are spacious at around 1,600 square feet (1,486 square meters) and have LCD TVs mounted on the wall and DVD and CD players. All decks have mini galleries displaying pieces of Polynesian artwork (tikis, drums, framed tapas, and paintings). The dining room is exquisite with teak floors, floor-to-ceiling windows, and banquettes and individual chairs, with tables for two, four, or six. The cuisine is French with Polynesian accents, and Michelin-starred chefs advise on menus. Breakfasts and lunches are usually served on deck. There is a lovely deck bar with rattan chairs and sofas with very soft cushions. Those who want an even more luxurious (and exclusive) experience can book a cabin—or all six cabins—on the top Vavau deck. You'll have your own dining area, butler, and dedicated staff. The ship has a small gymnasium, Jacuzzi, and a spa offering massages, body wraps, and facials. ⌂*30 cabins* ⌂*In-room: safe, refrigerator, DVD. In-boat: 5 passenger decks, 2 dining rooms, buffet, pool, gym, fitness classes, hot tubs, showroom, laundry service, children's programs (5–14)* ▭*AE, DC, MC, V.*

ROA YACHTING   Roa Yachting was established in French Polynesia in 2007. It's a French motor yacht charter company with 13 years' experience operating in the Mediterranean. It currently has one motor yacht based in the region—the *Roa*—which can be booked for three or six nights of cruising, complete with all meals, services, and activities. It can also be chartered, with a captain and crew, but without meals or extra services.

This is a high-end intimate cruising experience best suited for a family or a group of friends. The motor yacht can accommodate eight people in four cabins and is priced (per person) depending on the number of people aboard—the per-person rate is less expensive when the whole yacht is booked. The fare includes all meals, soft drinks, taxes and tips, and one activity or excursion each day: these may include water-skiing, a canoe trip, a scuba diving, a quad bike ride; Jet Skiing is only available on the six-night itinerary. The three-night cruise visits Tahaa and Raiatea; the six-night cruise adds Huahine and spends more time in each port. Guests, however, can instruct the captain to stay longer in a certain port or not to visit a port if they are enjoying their little piece of paradise anchored at one island. ☏ *Roa Yachting, BP 511, Vaitape, Bora Bora 98730* ☎ *71–83–86* ⊕ *www.roayachting.com.*

The **Roa** is a 77-foot-long Falcon motor yacht with four cabins (two with king beds; two with twin beds), a communal living area known as "The Square," and a small dining room. Each cabin has a private bathroom with shower, toilet, sink, and bidet. The front-facing double cabin has two bathroom areas: one for toilet, bidet, and sink; the other for shower. The rear double cabin has a private staircase leading to the deck.

The Square is 323 square feet in area, large enough for sofas and chairs; it also has a large plasma TV screen where DVDs are shown.

The *Roa* carries a glass-bottom kayak, a rubber dinghy, and fishing gear. The aft deck area has a large teak table and eight chairs for breakfast and lunch meals. The lower deck has a ladder for easy access to the lagoon. The vessel has the latest navigational equipment, including radar, GPS, and depth sounders, and cruises at 25 knots. A three-night cruise costs approximately $5,115 per person with eight passengers. Prices increase when fewer people are on board. ⛵ *4 cabins* ♿ *In-boat: passenger deck, dining rooms* ▤ *AE, DC, MC, V.*

HAUMANA CRUISES   Eugene Degage, who owns the Tahiti–Moorea ferry company, Aremiti, owns this luxury cruise line. He is the father of Mehiti Degage, who runs Bora Bora Cruises. The 12-cabin catamaran, *Haumana,* which means "Spirit of Peace" in Tahitian, previously operated around the Society Islands. It repositioned to the Tuamotu islands when the two Bora Bora Cruises' yachts came on line.

Huamana offers an intimate, casual experience on a elegant vessel. It cruises solely within the huge Rangiroa Lagoon on three- and four-night itineraries which can be taken back-to-back. The three-night Blue Lagoon Cruises runs from Wednesday night until Saturday morning; the four-night Pink Sands Cruise runs from Saturday night until Wednesday morning; the combined seven-night itinerary is known as the Rainbow Cruise. The ship, which tows two tender boats behind, cruises at night and drops anchor by day at gorgeous beaches and deserted motu. Passengers while away the day swimming, snorkeling, and shark feeding. The programs include visits to villages and during each cruise there is one lunch or meal served on the beach complete with a "floating" bar—a buoyant arrangement of bottles bobbing in the lagoon. This is another all-inclusive operation, with the fare including wines at lunch and dinner, all nonalcoholic drinks, excursions, and activities such as kayaking and fishing, diving, and Jet Skiing are extra. ⬧ *Haumana Cruises BP 9254, Motu Uta, Pape'ete 98713* ☎*50–06–74* ⊕*www.tahiti-haumana-cruises.com.*

Haumana, an all-white 12-cabin twin-hulled catamaran, was built in Australia and is 110 feet long and 45 feet wide. Since moving to the Tuamotu from the Society Islands it has been renovated and now has 12 rather than 19 cabins, each with around 160 square feet of space. The all-white cabins have large windows, air-conditioning, queen-size beds, TV, DVD, and CD player; bathrooms are equipped with hair dryers. Four have an extra sofa bed to accommodate a child under 12.

The restaurant is located on the top deck, with panoramic windows and glass doors leading out onto the deck, where meals are also taken. Breakfast is buffet style; dinner á la carte with French and Polynesian dishes. Lucky anglers can hand their catch of the day to the chef who will whip up a special fish dinner for them. The Sky Lounge, furnished with long turquoise sofas beautifully built into the contours of the ship, is the place to socialize over a few drinks. A sundeck, Jacuzzi, and marine platform, from where kayaks and the Jet Skis are launched, completes the neat little ship. A three-night Blue Lagoon cruise costs approximately $2,774 per person, twin share; four nights costs approximately $3,295; seven nights is approximately $5,469. ⬧*12 cabins* ⬧ *In-room: safe, refrigerator, DVD. In-boat: 3 passenger decks, dining room, buffet, hot tubs* ▤*AE, DC, MC, V.*

PASSENGER/CARGO SHIPS

Once upon a time it was possible to buy a cheap passage on a freighter ship and go where the cargo and captain took you. Much loved by fans of Errol Flynn movies, this was an alternative mode of travel for the adventurous with time on their hands. The vessel provided somewhere to sleep, somewhere to eat, and no doubt somewhere to drink. While it's still possible to take a freighter journey these days, between the U.S. and Australia for instance, it's a rare treat to encounter a trader that operates a regular cruise to such an exotic destination. The *Aranui 3* is rightly tagged "Freighter to Paradise." It's been plying the route between Tahiti and the Marquesas islands since 2000 (as its two predecessors did before it from the 1950s). But today's vessel offers comforts that the stowaways and adventurers of yesterday could have only dreamed of…air-conditioning, a pool, a gym (unheard of!), *and* great meals. But, it's the adventure to such an amazing part of the world, where the folk come down to the port to welcome the ship, and the amazing islands with towering mountains, thunderous surf, and quiet lagoons, that will linger in memory.

ARANUI CRUISES **Compagnie Polynesienne de Transport Maritime,** or CPTM, operates the *Aranui 3*. Few outsiders have heard of it, but everyone in French Polynesia knows the *Aranui*. The company is owned by the Wong family, originally from Hong Kong, who settled in Tahiti after WWII. They began operating cargo ships to the Marquesas in 1950s and in 1959 acquired the first Aranui from a New Zealand company. Aranui means "great highway" in the Maori language and the owners decided to keep the name as the ship symbolized a highway between Tahiti and the remote islands. When the cargo business hit a downturn in the 1980s, the owner, Jules Wong, decided to take on passengers. The family acquired another ship, a former Baltic trader (the *Aranui II*), but eventually the demand outgrew the ship and they decided to build their own vessel with a range of cabins and more modern facilities. The current *Aranui 3* began service in 2000, delivering the cargo and the same romantic experience in considerably more comfort. ⌂*Aranui Cruises BP 220, Pape'ete 98713* ☎*42–62–42* ⊕*www.aranui.com.*

The **Aranui 3** is a cross between a freighter and a cruise ship, with cargo containers up the front and passenger quarters at the back (or aft). It has 85 cabins and a dormitory that sleeps about 30 passengers. Eight of the 10 suites have balconies, and along with the 12 deluxe cabins they also have refrigerator and bathroom and bathtub. There are 63 standard cabins with two lower berths, porthole, and private bathroom with shower. While the ship has most of the facilities of a typical mainstream cruise ship (restaurant, pool, gym, lounge, and library), it's the experience of being part of the lifeblood of these distant islands that makes the journey unique. The *Aranui 3* calls at ports with names few have ever heard and would be hard pressed to find on a map—Hakahau, Taiohae, and Atuona, the tiny settlements on the islands of Ua Pou, Nuku Hiva, and Hiva Oa. And there are half a dozen more little known ports on the itinerary. As the cargo is being unloaded at each port—and the Marquesan crew is loading on the copra, pearl shells, and other island produce—passengers are free to wander around the town or take excursions to villages where the likes of Robert Louis Stevenson and Herman Melville lived more than a century before. There are visits to ornate churches, artisans' workshops, and the former house and grave of artist Paul Gauguin who spent his last years on the island of Hiva Oa.

Entertainment is provided by the ship's Polynesian musicians, while an expert on Marquesan history, anthology, art, or some other specialty subject accompanies each cruise. ⇥*85 cabins, 1 dormitory* ⌂*In-room: safe, refrigerator (some), TV (some). In-boat: 7 passenger decks, dining room, pool, gym, laundry facilities, laundry service* ▭*AE, DC, MC, V.*

SAILING SHIPS—FOUR-MASTED

Some people love sailing and others hate the idea of hoisting and winching sails. On a large, four-mast barkentine-rigged sailing ship (a fully-rigged ship with three or more masts) you can do absolutely nothing—just as you would do on a normal cruise ship—or lend a hand with the ropes and sails or climb the rigging to the crow's nest. There are few such vessels operating as cruise ships today, and so few opportunities to sit on the bowsprit as the ship comes into port or lie in the giant widow's nets strung out high above the waves. French Polynesia is lucky to have *Star Flyer,* a replica 19th-century clipper ship—a cruise aboard it is not to be missed.

STAR CLIPPERS   In 1991, Star Clippers presented a new tall-ship alternative for sophisticated travelers who want nonconventional adventures at sea. The vessels are the world's largest barkentine and full-rigged sailing ships— four- and five-masted beauties filled with modern, high-tech equipment as well as amenities more often found on private yachts. The ships rely on sail power while at sea unless conditions require the assistance of the engines. The day officially begins when the captain holds an informative daily briefing on deck with a bit of sailing lore tossed in. Star Clippers are not cruise ships in the ordinary sense with strict agendas. You can lounge on deck and simply soak in the nautical ambience or join crewmembers steering the ship, as well as learn about navigational techniques from the captain. Star Clipper ships are more upscale than Windjammer Cruises (another sailing cruise line popular in the U.S.), and have larger public rooms, swimming pools, and extras such as hair dryers, TVs, and phones. They are not as luxurious as the Windstar ships that used to cruise French Polynesia, but they are true sailing vessels, albeit with motors. Prices, however, are a bit more affordable on Star Clippers ships and often less than you would pay on a high-end cruise ship.

This is not a cruise line for the physically challenged; there are no elevators and ramps or staterooms or bathrooms with wheelchair accessibility. While children are welcome and may participate in shipboard activities suited to their ability, there are no dedicated youth facilities.

Star Clippers recommends the following gratuities: room steward, 3 euros per day; dining-room staff, 5 euros per day. A 15% gratuity is added to all bar bills. Gratuities may be charged to your shipboard account; onboard charges are billed in euros. *Star Clippers, 4101 Salzedo Ave., Coral Gables, FL 33146* ☎*305/442–0550 or 800/442– 0551* ⊕*www.starclippers.com.*

Star Flyer is one of a pair of identical ships in the fleet (the other is the *Star Clipper*). Built in Belgium in 1990 at a cost of $25 million and launched the following year, it was the first clipper sailing ship to be built for 140 years and became the first commercial sailing vessel to cross the North Atlantic in 90 years. It has since plied that route many times, crossing from the Caribbean to the Mediterranean to take up seasonal duties in both regions. In December 2007 it was deployed to French Polynesia to operate regular seven-day cruises around the Society Islands and 10- and 11-day cruises to the Tuamotus. Current schedules are in place until 2010.

Life on board *Star Flyer* is casual and friendly and there's absolutely no need for jackets, ties, cocktail dresses, or high heels. Some sailing fans have said a cruise on *Star Flyer* is like "dying and going to yachtsman's heaven"—the deck creaks under foot, the ship sways in the breeze, and it's a glorious sight under full sail. The four masts are 206 feet (63 meters) tall, and there's a crow's nest at the top for those agile enough to climb up. Two of the boat's wonderful features are its bowsprit—a long pole at the front on which you can sit—and widows' nets—two very sturdy nets that are strung out on both sides of the ship from the bowsprit in which you can lie high above the ocean below.

The ship carries 170 passengers in 85 cabins and has an elegant dining room where both buffet and set menus (with several choices per course) are served. There's a small lounge, bar, and library, but most passengers prefer to sit on the deck after dinner. The ship sails at night and drops anchor each morning in a quiet bay: one of the favorite rituals is "captain's story time," when passengers gather around the captain at the helm to listen to seafaring tales. Entertainment is low-key and fun. A local band will perform here and there, there will be a few deck games, and the crew will stage a concert or two. If you want to cool off, there are two very small "dip" pools.

A seven-day cruise on *Star Flyer* starts at $2,457. ⇨*85 cabins* ⚫*In-room: safe. In-boat: 4 passenger decks, dining room, 2 pools, fitness classes* ▤*AE, DC, MC, V.*

SAILING SHIPS—CATAMARANS

Sailing is a magical way to experience French Polynesia's beautiful lagoons and open waters. Although these vessels are obviously sailing boats and not cruise ships, they operate regular cruise itineraries and are sold by travel agents around the world. Two six-night itineraries operate year-round: one in the Society Islands and the other around the Tuamotus. Each boat has a captain and a chef/hostess, who is occasionally assisted by a local guide.

Guests are pampered in a style similar to the luxury boutique ships, but without the extensive facilities. The cruises include some shore excursions such as 4WD tours and village visits. Food is French with Polynesian accents.

ARCHIPELS POLYNESIAN CRUISES François Profit, a 15-year veteran maxi-yacht—a yacht large enough to have competed in the America's Cup—and former first-class captain in the French merchant navy, founded the company in 1992. His fleet of six deluxe sailing catamarans cruise the waters of the Society Islands and the Tuamotu.

Society Islands cruises depart weekly on Saturdays and travel between Huahine, Raiatea, Tahaa, and Bora Bora. Unlike other cruises, these are not round-trip cruises. The trip begins in either Huahine or Bora Bora and ends at the other port (it does not turn around and return to the port of embarkation). There are two different Tuamotu itineraries: three- and four-day cruises within the Rangiroa lagoon, visiting the Blue Lagoon and Pink Sand beaches, and a seven-day cruise operated once a month during the full moon. This latter itinerary travels from Fakarava to the rarely visited island of Toau and to Rangiroa. ⌂*Archipels Polynesian Cruises, BP 1160, Opunohu-Papetoai, Moorea 98729* ☎*56-36-39* ⊕*www.archipels.com.*

Each of the six 56-foot-long **catamarans** has 1,600 square feet of useable space, four air-conditioned cabins with private bathrooms, a large salon with panoramic windows, a small library with board games, and a spacious deck. Each catamaran is equipped with dinghies, windsurfers, snorkeling and fishing gear, and ocean kayaks. Cabins and bathrooms are cleaned daily, and sheets changed every three days. The cruise fare includes all meals as well as table wines and cold natural lemonade. Other drinks, including cocktails and premium wines, are at extra cost. Also included are excursions to beaches and villages, and guided snorkeling, fishing, and kayaking tours, as well as airport transfers.

A six-night Society Islands cruise or a six-night Tuamotu Atoll cruise is $2,525 per person, twin share. A three-night Rangiroa lagoon cruise is $1,460 and two-night cruises are $1,095 per person, twin share. *4 cabins In-boat: 2 passenger decks, dining room, bar AE, DC, MV, V.*

BEFORE YOU GO

To expedite your pre-boarding paperwork, some cruise lines have convenient forms on their Internet Web sites. As long as you have your reservation number, you can provide the required immigration information, pre-reserve shore excursions, and even indicate any special requests from the comfort of your home. Less-"wired" cruise lines might mail pre-boarding paperwork to you or your travel agent for completion after you make your final payment and request that you return the forms by mail or fax.

TRAVEL DOCUMENTS

After you make the final payment to your travel agent, the cruise line will issue your cruise tickets and vouchers for airport-to-ship transfers. Depending on the airline, and whether you have purchased an air-sea package, you may receive your plane tickets or e-ticket vouchers at the same time; you may also receive vouchers for shore excursion, although most cruise lines issue these aboard ship.

PASSPORTS & VISAS
See Passports & Visas, in Essentials in Travel Smart French Polynesia for passport and visa information.

⚠ **Children under the age of 18—when not traveling with** *both* **parents— almost always require a letter of permission from the absent parent(s).** Airlines, cruise lines, and immigration agents can deny children initial boarding or entry to foreign countries without proper proof of identification and citizenship *and* a notarized permission letter from absent or non-custodial parents. Your travel agent or cruise line can help with the wording of such a letter.

WHAT TO PACK

The traditional cruise wardrobe falls into three categories: casual, informal, and formal. However, things are a little different in French Polynesia as it's a very casual place where people rarely dress up, even in the best resorts. Informal, a vague term by all accounts, is about as dressy as it gets and usually means slacks and a shirt for men and a dressy casual outfit for women. One thing is for sure though…you'll never need to pack a glittering gown or tuxedo. In fact some ships (such as the *Star Flyer*) ban ties for men. You won't be shot if you wear one, you'll just feel a bit silly and end up taking it off.

The majority of the ships stress that casual—and a smattering of smart casual clothing—is all that's required. Evening casual means khakis and nice polo or sport shirts for men. Ladies' outfits are dresses, skirts and tops, or pants outfits. By sticking to two or three complementary colors and a few accessories, you can mix up tops and bottoms for a different look every night. Cruise documents should include information on dress code (if the ship has one) and may indicate if there are any "formal" evenings during the cruise. If in doubt call your travel agent or e-mail the cruise line directly.

If you do wish to make a sartorial statement, then the very elegant *Paul Gauguin* and the two Bora Bora Cruise Line yachts are most likely the best places. Otherwise it will be casual wear on deck by day, i.e., swimwear, a cover-up, and sandals for the pool, and shorts and sundress around the rest of the ship.

Time spent ashore touring and shopping calls for comfortable clothing and good walking shoes. Days are hot and can be sticky, so comfortable clothing is the way to go. Lagoon and ocean beaches can be strewn with coral, so pack a pair of reef shoes, or plastic shoes. And don't forget a hat, sunglasses, and sunblock.

An absolute essential for women is a shawl, or light sweater, to ward off the chill of aggressive air-conditioning in public rooms. Put things you can't do without—such as prescription medication, spare eyeglasses, toiletries, a swimsuit, and change of clothes for the first day—in your carry-on. Most cruise ships provide soap, shampoo, and conditioner.

ACCESSIBILITY ISSUES

As recently as the early 1990s, "accessibility" on a cruise ship meant little more than a few inside staterooms set aside for passengers with mobility issues. Most public restrooms and nearly all en suite bathrooms had a "step-over" threshold. Newer ships are more sensitive to the needs of passengers with disabilities, but many older ships still have physical barriers in both cabins and public rooms. And once you get off the ship—particularly in ports with unpaved and sometimes lumpy coral pathways—your problems will be compounded.

French Polynesia, with its variety of ships—many of which are very small—presents many challenges to physically disabled passengers. Only two, the *Paul Gauguin* and the *Pacific Princess* (which begins operating in October 2009) have wheelchair accessible cabins, with one and three cabins, respectively. These ships also have elevators and wide hallways. The other ships in the region would not be suitable, particularly the *Star Flyer* and the *Aranui 3* as the island visits from these require landings by tender boat and seas can be rough at times; this exercise is sometimes problematic even for the able-bodied to negotiate under adverse conditions. Some people with limited mobility may also find it difficult to embark or disembark the ship when docked due to the steep angle of gangways during high or low tide at certain times of day.

Passengers who have service animals should check with the cruise line to ascertain if there are any quarantine restrictions in French Polynesia that would prevent them taking the animal ashore.

INSURANCE

Comprehensive trip insurance is especially valuable if you're booking a very expensive or complicated trip (particularly to an isolated region) or if you're booking far in advance. Who knows what could happen six months down the road? A comprehensive policy tends to cover almost anything that can go wrong (although these days terrorism is unlikely to be covered), from illness, evacuation, cancellation, and lost documents and luggage. If you don't mind taking the risk and don't want to spend too much money, then consider buying medical-only coverage at the very least.

See Trip Insurance, in Essentials in Travel Smart French Polynesia for travel and medical insurance contacts.

ARRIVING & EMBARKING

Most cruise ship passengers fly to the port of embarkation. If you book your cruise far enough in advance, you'll be given the opportunity to purchase an air-and-sea package, which may—or may not—save you money on your flight. You might get a lower fare by booking your air independently, so it's a good idea to check for the best fare available. Independent air arrangements might save you enough to cover the cost of a hotel room in your embarkation port so you can arrive early.

In almost all cases in French Polynesia you will have to spend at least one, or perhaps two nights in Pape'ete, as airline schedules do not necessarily coincide with cruise departures. If your cruise ship or yacht is leaving from the Society Islands or the Tuamotus, you'll have to take a domestic flight to Bora Bora, Huahine, or Rangiroa. On arrival at their tiny airports, you'll be met by a representative of the cruise line.

Your agent will be aware of flight and cruise schedules and will likely suggest a package of pre- and post-cruise accommodation together with transfers. French Polynesian transfer companies are very efficient, and if you have the appropriate voucher you won't be left standing alone at the airport.

BOARDING

Once the planning, packing, and anticipation are behind them, veteran cruise passengers sometimes view embarkation day as anticlimactic. For the uninitiated, however, embarkation can be a bit overwhelming, but in French Polynesia, your experience should be efficient and laid-back.

CHECK-IN

There is only one cruise dock in Pape'ete and it's in Place Vaiete right in the heart of town. Your cruise ship will be waiting for you, so there's no chance you'll get lost. As cruise ships and passenger numbers are small (except in the case of the *Pacific Princess,* which can carry 688 passengers), you shouldn't encounter long lines. Actual boarding time is often scheduled for noon, but some cruise lines will begin processing early arrivals and then direct them to a "holding" area.

During check-in, you will be asked to produce your documents and any forms you were sent to complete ahead of time, plus proof of citizenship and a credit card (to cover onboard charges). You'll be issued a boarding card that often also doubles as your stateroom "key" and shipboard charge card. At some point—either before you enter the check-in area or before proceeding to the ship—you and your hand luggage will pass through a security procedure similar to those at airports.

BOARDING THE SHIP

Once boarding begins, you will inevitably have your first experience with the ship's photographer—usually on the larger ships. Smile and relax. This is the first day of your vacation and you're under no obligation to purchase any photos.

Procedures vary from ship to ship, but you'll no doubt be greeted by at least one crewmember and asked to produce your boarding card and, possibly, a picture ID for the security officer. At some point you may be photographed for security purposes—your image will display when your boarding card is "swiped" into a computer as you leave and reboard the ship in ports of call. Depending on the cruise line, you will be directed to your cabin, or a steward will relieve you of your carry-on luggage and accompany you. Stewards on high-end cruise lines not only show you the way, but also hand you a glass of champagne as a welcome-aboard gesture. However, if you board early, don't be surprised if you are told cabins are not "ready" for occupancy—passageways to accommodations may even be roped off. In that case you can explore the ship, sample the luncheon buffet, or simply relax until an announcement is made that you can go to your cabin.

ON BOARD

Check out your cabin to make sure that everything is in order. Try the plumbing and set the air-conditioning to the temperature you prefer. Your cabin may feel warm while docked but will cool off when the ship is underway. You should find a copy of the ship's daily schedule in the cabin. Take a few moments to look it over—you'll want to know what time the muster drill—a compulsory safety exercise—takes place (a placard on the back of your cabin door will indicate directions to your emergency station), as well as meal hours and the schedule for various activities and entertainments.

It will also be a while before your checked luggage arrives, so your initial order of business is usually the buffet, if you haven't already had lunch. Bring along the daily schedule to check over while you eat.

While making your way to the lunch buffet, you may encounter bar waiters offering trays of colorful and exotic drinks, often in souvenir glasses that you can keep. Beware—they are not complimentary! If you choose one, you will be asked to sign for it.

If want to book shore excursions and spa treatments, it's a good idea to do this early to avoid disappointment, along with reservations at the specialty restaurants.

PAYING FOR THINGS ON BOARD

Let's step back a moment and take a look at what happened when you checked in at the pier. Because a cashless society prevails on cruise ships, an imprint was made of your credit card, or you had to place a cash deposit for use against your onboard charges. Then you were issued a charge card that usually doubles as your stateroom "key." Most onboard expenditures are charged to your shipboard account with your signature as verification, with the possible exception of casino gaming—even so, you can often get "cash advances" against your account from the casino cashier.

An itemized bill is provided at the end of the voyage listing your purchases. In order to avoid surprises, it's a good idea to set aside your charge slips and request an interim printout of your bill from the Purser to insure accuracy. Should you change your mind about charging onboard purchases, you can always inform the Purser and pay in cash or traveler's checks instead. If your cash deposit was more than you spent, you will receive a refund.

TIPPING

The ships that travel in French Polynesian waters either have a no-tipping policy—these include the *Paul Gauguin,* Bora Bora Cruises, and Haumana Cruises—or will automatically add the gratuity to your cruise account. Tipping is not customary in French Polynesia—that is, in restaurants and other service industries—so it may be simply up to you if wish to tip a porter at the dock. If you do, then 200 CFP is adequate.

The *Pacific Princess* adds $10 to $11 a day for every passenger including children; the *Star Flyer* allows you to pay your gratuities in advance, which are 10 euros per person per day. There's a 10% to 15% charge added to all bar bills, so don't tip the bartender.

DINING

All food, all the time? Not quite, but it's possible to literally eat away the day and most of the night on a cruise. A popular cruise directors' joke is, "You came on as passengers, but you'll be leaving as cargo." Although it's meant in fun, it does contain a ring of truth. Food—tasty and plentiful—is available 24 hours a day on many cruise ships, and the dining experience at sea has reached almost mythical proportions. Perhaps it has something to do with legendary midnight buffets, the absence of menu prices, or maybe it's the vast selection and availability.

RESTAURANTS Every sizeable ship has at least one main restaurant and a *Lido,* or casual, buffet alternative. Increasingly important are specialty restaurants. Meals in the primary and buffet restaurants are included in the cruise fare, as are afternoon tea and snacks, and late-night buffets. Most mainstream cruise lines levy a surcharge for dining in alternative restaurants that may, or may not, also include a gratuity, although there generally is no additional charge on luxury cruise lines.

You may also find a pizzeria or a specialty coffee bar on your ship. Although pizza is complimentary, expect an additional charge for specialty coffees at the coffee bar and, quite likely, in the dining room as well. You'll also likely be charged for sodas and drinks during meals other than iced tea, regular coffee, tap water, and fruit juice.

There's often a direct relationship between the cost of a cruise and the quality of its cuisine. The food is very sophisticated on some (mostly expensive) lines, including Regent Seven Seas Cruises, Bora Bora Cruises, and Haumana Cruises.

The *Paul Gauguin* has three restaurants, including the elite La Verandah whose menus have been devised by Le Condon Bleu chefs and showcase dishes from various regions in France. Passengers must reserve this fine-dining restaurant, but no extra charge is levied. Bora Bora Cruises' two motor yachts serve some of the best food in French Polynesia; French Michelin-starred chefs are often invited on board to prepare meals and advise on menus.

It's fair to say that a few concessions should be made when cruising in French Polynesia. Apart from the larger Princess and RSSC

Drinking & Gambling Ages

Many underage passengers have learned to their chagrin that the rules that apply on land are also adhered to at sea. On most mainstream cruise ships you must be 21 in order to drink alcohol. There are exceptions—for instance, on cruises departing from countries where the legal drinking age is lower than 21. By and large, if you haven't achieved the magic age of 21, your shipboard charge card will be coded as booze-free, and bartenders won't risk their jobs to sell you alcohol.

Gambling is a bit looser, and 18-year olds can try their luck in the few casinos that operate on the ships in French Polynesian waters; both *Paul Gauguin* and *Pacific Princess* have casinos and slot machines. Casinos are trickier to patrol than bars, though, and minors who look "old enough" may get away with dropping a few coins in an out-of-the-way slot machine before being spotted on a hidden security camera. If you hit a big jackpot, you may have a lot of explaining to do to your parents.

ships and the luxury Bora Bora Cruises that either have large food storage and preparation areas—or charge a hefty cruise fare—the smaller ships are hampered by lack of galley space and the price of delivery food to far-flung islands, which is the case for those ships not departing from Pape'ete.

DINNER SEATINGS
There's no need to worry about the traditional seating arrangements that apply on many large cruise ships. There are no such seating arrangements on ships in French Polynesia. They all have an open-seating policy.

SPECIAL DIETS
Cruise lines make every possible attempt to insure dining satisfaction. If you have special dietary considerations—such as low salt, kosher, or food allergies—be sure to indicate them well ahead of time and check to be certain your needs are known by your waiter once on board. In addition to the usual menu items, "spa," low-calorie, low-carbohydrate, or low-fat selections, as well as children's menus, are usually available. Requests for dishes not featured on the menu can often be granted if you ask in advance.

DRINKING ON BOARD
It's hard to avoid the ship's bars since they are social centers, but alcoholic drinks are not usually included in your cruise fare, and bar bills can add up quickly. Drinks at the captain's welcome-aboard cocktail party and at cocktail parties held specifically for past-cruisers are usually free. But if you pick up that boldly colored welcome-aboard cocktail as your ship pulls away from the dock, you may very well be asked to sign for it, and the cost will then be added to your shipboard account.

You should expect to pay about the same price for a drink on board a ship as you would in a medium- to slightly high-priced bar at home: $4 to $5 for a domestic beer, $7 to $10 for a cocktail, $5 to $9 for a glass of wine, $1.25 to $2 for a soft drink. On virtually all ships, an automatic 15% gratuity will be added to your tab. What most people don't consider is that specialty coffees are also added to your bar tab, so if you order a cappuccino—and on some ships that applies even if it's in the dining room after dinner—you'll see a charge of $2 to $4 on your bar bill.

Wine by the bottle is a more economical choice at dinner than ordering it by the glass. Any wine you don't finish will be kept for you and served the next night. Gifts of wine or champagne ordered from the cruise line (either by you, a friend, or your travel agent) can be taken to the dining room. Wine from any other source will incur a "corkage" charge.

THE CAPTAIN'S TABLE
Legend has it that a nouveau riche passenger's response to an invitation to dine with the captain during a round-the-world cruise was, "I didn't shell out all those bucks to eat with the help!" Although there are some cruise passengers who decline invitations to dine at the captain's table, there are far more who covet such an experience. You'll know you've been included in that exclusive coterie when an embossed invitation arrives in your stateroom on the day of a formal dinner. RSVP as soon as possible—if you're unable to attend, someone else will be invited in your place.

Who's invited? If you're a frequent repeat cruiser, the occupants of an owner's suite, or if you hail from the captain's hometown or speak his native language, you may be considered. Honeymoon couples are sometimes selected at random, as are couples celebrating a golden wedding anniversary. Attractive, unattached female passengers often round out an uneven number of guests. Requests made by travel agents on behalf of their clients sometimes do the trick, too.

ENTERTAINMENT

Although mainstream cruise lines in the Caribbean, Alaskan, and the Mediterranean turn on slick entertainment in grand showrooms and cabaret acts featuring magicians, comedians, and jugglers, you won't find big production shows or much sleight of hand onstage in the calm lagoon waters in French Polynesia. What you'll get though are balmy nights under starry skies, Polynesian singers and ukulele players, and cultural dance shows.

Bora Bora Cruises kicks off its first night with a luxurious beach barbecue followed by the screening of the 1931 movie *Tabu*—a love story between a young Tahitian man and his forbidden love interest—on a sail cloth strung between two palms trees; if there's rain or thunder, it adds to the drama. *Star Flyer* may stage a couple of deck games, a trivia quiz night, or a crew concert throughout the cruise. The *Aranui 3* travels with a Polynesian trio; the Marquesan crew has been known to join in or put on a few concerts of their own.

The *Pacific Princess* and *Paul Gauguin* are the only ships large enough to have showrooms, casinos, and numerous bar areas. Although there are no big shows, the *Paul Gauguin* has Polynesian entertainment most nights including dancing and singing. The *Pacific Princess* travels with a band, another trio of musicians and a solo pianist/singer. These are the ships if you like cheek-to-cheek dancing.

The real treats are the folkloric shows or other entertainments arranged to take place while cruise ships are in port. Local performers come aboard, usually right before the ship sails, to present their country's songs and dances. It's an excellent way to get a glimpse of the cultural history of their performing arts.

Several of the upscale ships have in-cabin DVD players; the larger ships (and even the small *Roa* yacht) will screen movies in the public room for everyone to enjoy. Enrichment programs are the new popular pastime at sea. While these are not on the same large scale as the big cruise liens, French Polynesian ships invite expert speakers (historians, anthropologists, and maybe an author or two) to share their knowledge with passengers; lighter diversions such as pareo tying and Tahitian dance classes are on offer at times. Computers and the Internet are entertainment for many people; both *Pacific Princess* and *Paul Gauguin* have computer rooms and charge a fee for Internet connection.

CASINOS

Both the *Pacific Princess* and *Paul Gauguin* have casinos with gaming tables and slot machines. These can be quite lively areas, considering there aren't too many other entertainment options on board. Casino hours vary based on the itinerary or location of the ship; most are required to close while in port, while others may be able to offer 24-hour slot machines and simply close table games. Every casino has a cashier, and you may be able to charge a cash advance to your onboard account, for a fee.

SPORTS & FITNESS

Onboard sports facilities depend on the size of the ship. The boutique ships find no need to have swimming pools, but some have Jacuzzis and all carry kayaks, and fishing and snorkeling gear, which are complimentary. One or two have their own Jet Skis, but passengers pay extra to use them.

The three largest ships (*Paul Gauguin, Pacific Princess,* and *Aranui 3*) have swimming pools and fitness centers, while all, with the exception of *Aranui 3,* have hot tubs. Even the smallish *Star Flyer* has room for two pools, but these are simply dip pools for cooling off. The *Princess* and the RSSC ship also have jogging tracks and steam rooms; *Pacific Princess* has a golf driving net and the old staple of cruise life, the shuffleboard court.

SPAS

With all the usual pampering and service in luxurious surroundings, simply being on a cruise can be a stress-reducing experience. Add to that the menu of spa and salon services at your fingertips and you have a recipe for total sensory pleasure. Spas have also become among

CLOSE UP

Health & Safety at Sea

Safety begins with you, the passenger. Once settled into your cabin, locate life vests and review posted emergency instructions. Make sure vests are in good condition and learn to secure them properly. Make certain the ship's purser knows if you have a physical infirmity that may hamper a speedy exit from your cabin, so that in an emergency he or she can quickly dispatch a crewmember to assist you. If you're traveling with children, be sure that child-size life jackets are placed in your cabin.

Within 24 hours of embarkation, you'll be asked to attend a mandatory lifeboat drill. Do so and listen carefully. If you're unsure about how to use your vest, now is the time to ask. Only in the most extreme circumstances will you need to abandon ship—but it has happened. The time you spend learning the procedure may serve you well in a mishap.

In actuality, the greatest danger facing cruise-ship passengers is fire. All cruise lines must meet international standards for fire safety, which require sprinkler systems, smoke detectors, and other safety features. Fires on cruise ships are not common, but they do happen, and these rules have made ships much safer. You can do you part by *not* using an iron in your cabin and taking care to properly extinguish smoking materials. Never throw a lit cigarette overboard—it could be blown back into an opening in the ship and start a fire.

All large ships have an infirmary to deal with minor medical emergencies, but these infirmaries are not suitable for dealing with major procedures. The ship's doctor should be able to treat you as well as any general practitioner or clinic ashore for minor problems. For really complicated medical conditions, such as a heart attack or appendicitis, the ship's medical team evacuates passengers to the nearest hospital ashore. While at sea, evacuation expenses can rise as fast as the helicopter that whisks the patient away. You'll need supplementary insurance to cover evacuation costs.

Two of the most prevalent diseases that spread through cruise-ship populations are influenza and noroviruses that cause intestinal and stomach upsets. Annual influenza vaccination is the primary method for preventing influenza and its complications. But to prevent all kinds of infections—including noroviruses—frequent hand washing is also essential; take advantage of the dispensers of hand-sanitizer, and use it when entering any dining room. Or slip into the restroom to wash your hands with soap and hot water.

the most popular of shipboard areas, particularly if there are sea days involved in a cruise.

Spa offerings have come a long way, and today's large cruise lines hand the operation over to a well-known land-based beauty house: Princess ships have Steiner Leisure spas (which operate on 100 ships worldwide), while RSSC's vessels use the expertise of French house, Carita Spa. Treatments will involve massages, body scrubs, and wraps that incorporate the most exotic ingredients—cinnamon, coconut, honey and even coffee—along with skin and hair treatments. The larger ships also have hair salons and manicurists.

CLOSE UP

Crime on Ships

Crime aboard cruise ships has occasionally become headline news, thanks in large part to a few well-publicized cases. Most people never have any type of problem, but you should exercise the same precautions aboard ship that you would at home. Keep your valuables out of sight—on big ships virtually every cabin has a small safe. Don't carry too much cash ashore, use your credit card whenever possible, and keep your money in a secure place, such as a front pocket that's harder to pick. Single women traveling with friends should stick together, especially when returning to their cabins late at night.

Your cruise is a wonderful opportunity to leave everyday responsibilities behind, but don't neglect to pack your common sense. After a few drinks it might seem like a good idea to sit on a railing or lean over the rail to get a better view of the ship's wake. Passengers have been known to fall. "Man overboard" is more likely to be the result of carelessness than criminal intent.

The most innovative spa is aboard the two yachts of Bora Bora Cruises—the spa is brought to you as you play on the beach and therapists set up lovely tents made of soft billowing materials and massage tables.

All spa treatments incur extra charges and can be quite a bit more than similar treatments you'll have at home.

SHIPBOARD SERVICES

COMMUNICATIONS

Just because you're out to sea doesn't mean you have to be out of touch. However, ship-to-shore telephone calls can cost $5 to $15 a minute, so it makes more economic sense to use e-mail to remain in contact with your home or office. Princess and RSSC ships have wireless connections in cabins and also Internet cafés on board. Connections can be slow (they are generally slow in French Polynesia) and this will add up, especially if the price is $1 a minute or more.

Cell phone coverage is quite good in most of the islands of French Polynesia, so take your mobile phone and make sure you've activated "roaming" on your account. Picking up a signal on a ship is more difficult than it is on land, but as you'll be pulling into an island every day (with the exception of cruises that travel out to the Tuamotus), so you should have ample opportunity to make calls.

LAUNDRY & DRY CLEANING

Pacific Princess and *Aranui 3* have coin-operated self-service laundries, although both the *Pacific Princess* and *Paul Gauguin* provide a valet laundry service. The small ships don't have these facilities, so take enough clothes to last or do some hand washing.

SHORE EXCURSION DESK

Manned by a knowledgeable staff, the Shore Excursion Desk can offer not only the sale of ship-sponsored tours, but may also be the place to learn more about ports of call and garner information to tour independently. The boutique ships tend to run their own tours and they are included the fare; *Aranui 3* also has complimentary touring. Costs are incurred when outside operators are involved or the ship's own motorized equipment is used (such as Jet Skis).

DISEMBARKATION

All cruises come to an end eventually, and the disembarkation process on large ships begins the day before you arrive at your ship's final port. During that day your cabin steward delivers special luggage tags to your stateroom, along with customs forms and instructions. The luggage tags go onto your larger bags, which are placed outside your stateroom door for pickup during the hours indicated.

A statement itemizing your onboard charges is delivered before you arise on disembarkation morning. Any discrepancies in your onboard account should be taken care of before leaving the ship, at the purser's desk. Breakfast is served in the restaurant on the last morning. If you're on a big ship, you'll be asked to wait in a lounge or on deck for your tag color or number to be called. On small ships the procedure will likely involve just walking off the ship while a crewmember carries your luggage.

As the ships finish their cruises in Pape'ete or one of the smaller islands, there are usually no customs regulations to adhere to. You'll proceed through customs immigration when you get to the airport.

CUSTOMS & DUTIES

TAXES

Make no mistake about it; French Polynesia has lots of taxes, over and above the ones you've already paid as part of the cruise fare. First, there are the ones that appear on your bill. The **VAT** (value-added tax) is an additional 6% tax on all accommodation including cruise ships. The **Tourist Development Tax** is a 200 CFP (approx: $2.60) per person per day charge on hotels/cruise ships; children under 12 traveling with their parents are exempt. There's also the **Visitor Tax** (aka sojourn tax), which is another 150 CFP (approximately $1.94) per person per day. This tax is included in the bill if you visit Bora Bora, Moorea, Huahine, Rangiroa, Raiatea, Tahaa, Matavia, Tikehau, Nuka Hiva, and Tahiti—as cruise ships frequent all these islands, the tax will be charged.

You will also be charged a 10% VAT on tourist services, which is a little vague but in reality means travel agency services and rental cars. There's also a VAT on purchases. You can reclaim the VAT on purchases; it's advisable to ask when you purchase an item, as some goods take off the tax and save you the hassle of applying for a VAT refund.

If you have to apply for a refund, you fill in a form and deposit it at a special "post box" at Faa'a Airport in Tahiti.

U.S. CUSTOMS

See Customs & Duties, in Essentials in Travel Smart French Polynesia for information on customs requirements to and from French Polynesia.

ALLOWANCES You're always allowed to bring goods of a certain value back home without having to pay any duty or import tax. But there's a limit on the amount of tobacco and liquor you can bring back duty-free. The values of so-called "duty-free" goods are included in these amounts. When you shop abroad, save all your receipts, as customs inspectors may ask to see them as well as the items you purchased. If the total value of your goods is more than the duty-free limit, you'll have to pay a tax (most often a flat percentage) on the value of everything beyond that limit. For U.S. citizens who have been in French Polynesia for at least 48 hours, the duty-free exemption is $800. But the duty-free exemption includes only 200 cigarettes, 100 cigars, and 1 liter of alcohol (this includes wine); above these limits, you have to pay duties, even if you didn't spend more than the $800 limit.

SENDING PACKAGES HOME Although you probably won't want to spend your time looking for a post office, you can send packages home duty-free, with a limit of one parcel per addressee per day (except alcohol or tobacco products or perfume worth more than $5). You can mail up to $200 worth of goods to yourself, or $100 worth of goods to a friend or relative; label the package "personal use" or "unsolicited gift" (depending on which is the case) and attach a list of the contents and their retail value. If the package contains your used personal belongings, mark it "personal goods returned" to avoid paying duty on your laundry. You do not need to declare items that were sent home on your declaration forms for U.S. Customs.

UNDERSTANDING TAHITI & FRENCH POLYNESIA

Vocabulary

TAHITIAN VOCABULARY

The Tahitian alphabet has only thirteen letters, five of which are vowels: "a" as in *bar,* "e" as in *they,* "i" as in *machine,* "o" as in *mold,* and "u" as in *flute.* The eight remaining letters—f, h, m, n, p, r, t, v—are pronounced like their English consonant counterparts, with the following exceptions: "h" is pronounced "sh" when preceded by "i" or followed by "o," and "r" is sometimes rolled.

ENGLISH	FRENCH	TAHITIAN
USEFUL WORDS & PHRASES		
afternoon	après-midi	avatea
airplane	avion	manureva
ask	demander	ani
asleep	endormi	ta'oto
bad	mauvais	ino
baggage	bagages	ota'a
bank	banque	fare moni
beach	plage	tahatai
bed	lit	roi
beer	bière	pia
breakfast	petit-déjeuner	tafe poipoi
butter	beurre	pata
car	voiture	pereoo
cash	espèces	moni
church	église	fare pure
coffee	café	taofe
dance	danse	aô
depart	partir	reva
dinner	dîner	amura'a-avatea
doctor	médecin	taote
drink	boisson	inu
eat	manger	amu
everybody	tout le monde	te taatoa raa
farewell	adieu	parahi
girl	fille	poti'i

ENGLISH	FRENCH	TAHITIAN
hospital	hôpital	fare ma'i
lunch	déjeuner	tama'a
man	monsieur	tane
medicine	médicament	raau
midnight	minuit	tuiraa-pô
money	argent	moni
name	nom	i'oa
noon	midi	avatea
passport	passeport	buka ratere
post office	bureau de poste	fare rata
room	chambre	piha
store	boutique	fare toa
understand	comprendre	ta a papu
water	eau	pape
welcome	bienvenue	ia ora na
wife	épouse	ava
woman	femme	vahine
yes	oui	e, oia
goodbye	au revoir	parahi oe
good evening	bonsoir	ia ora na oe i teie po
good morning	bonjour	ia ora na oe
I'd like to eat	je voudrais manger	ina aro vau e tamaa
how are you?	comment allez vous?	eaha te huru?
thank you	merci	mauruuru
what time is it?	quelle heure est-il?	hora ahai teie?
where is the bank?	Où est la banque?	tehia te fare moni?

Travel Smart
French Polynesia

WORD OF MOUTH

"You might want to consider booking an Air Pass
through Air Tahiti, which gives you the opportunity
to visit several islands at a cheaper cost than individual flights. If you do purchase that, you'd want
to fly to Moorea from Pape'ete, and then to Bora
Bora from Moorea, then back to Pape'ete."
— BarbiJKM

GETTING HERE & AROUND

French Polynesia is a group of 118 islands totaling 8,220 square km (3,174 square mi), stretching out over 2,000 km (1,243 mi) of vast ocean. Some of the islands are atolls, ring-shaped coral reefs that encircle an interior lagoon, and some, like Tahiti, seem to be mountains surrounded by reefs. The only thing the islands have in common is that they are the very definition of paradise: flush with blue and green colors, warm winds, vibrant reefs, and lush plant life, including *uru* (breadfruit) trees, ferns, and flowers such as frangipani and *tiare,* the symbol of French Polynesia.

There are five archipelagos (chains of islands) that make up the different cultural divides of French Polynesia: the Society, Gambier, Austral, Tuamotu, and Marquesas. Some of the islands have infrastructure, like paved roads, car-rental companies, and public transportation; however, the more remote you go, the more likely "infrastructure" means dirt tracks and lots of scenery. Tahiti, part of the Society islands, is the largest and most developed island in French Polynesia. It is made up of two nearly circular islands, one large (Tahiti Nui) and one small (Tahiti Iti), joined by an isthmus. There is one main looping road encircling the mountainous interior, and the outskirts are fringed by black-sand beaches, surf breaks (like the famous Teahupoo), and lagoons. Pape'ete is the colorful capital of Tahiti.

▌ BY AIR

TO FRENCH POLYNESIA

French Polynesia is located roughly halfway between California and Australia, which makes it a popular stop-off point for people traveling to and from Australia and New Zealand. Many airlines offer great package deals for island-hopping, not just within French Polynesia, but including Fiji and Hawaii as well. Ask your travel agent or the airline to see if there are any deals.

A variety of airlines fly into Tahiti's Faa'a International Airport. If you are flying from the U.S., you can fly direct from Los Angeles and San Francisco, or you travel via Hawaii for roughly the same price. There are no direct flights from Canada.

WITHIN FRENCH POLYNESIA

Given the vast expanse of French Polynesia, most of the travel to and from the islands is by plane. You can either charter a flight (be prepared to pay), or hop on the interisland flights offered by Air Tahiti and Air Moorea, which fly to 38 islands in the five archipelagos. Flight frequencies tend to change like the tides, so make certain you check before purchasing a ticket: some areas, like the Gambier archipelago, only have flights going in and out once a week. There is no main air travel service in French Polynesia, but Air Tahiti is the kingpin. If you have any questions about interisland travel, ask them or your travel agent.

Based at Faa'a, Air Tahiti and Air Archipels—a private air charter service that's been operating since 1996—can arrange charter flights to many of the islands.

Airline Contacts Air France (☎ 47-47-47 ⊕ www.airfrance.com). **Air Moorea** (☎ 86-41-41 ⊕ www.airmoorea.com). **Air New Zealand** (☎ 800/262-1234 in U.S. ⊕ www.airnz.com). **Air Tahiti** (☎ 45-55-55 ⊕ www.airtahiti.com). **Hawaiian Airlines** (☎ 800/367-5320 in U.S. ⊕ www.hawaiianair.com). **Qantas** (☎ 800/227-4500 in U.S. ⊕ www.qantas.com.au). **United Airlines** (☎ 800/538-2929 in U.S. ⊕ www.united.com).

Airlines & Airports Airline and Airport Links.com (⊕ www.airlineandairportlinks.com).

Airline Security Issues Transportation Security Administration (⊕ www.tsa.gov).

Charter Companies **Air Tahiti** (☎ 86–40–23 ⊕ www.airtahiti.com). **Air Archipels** (☎ 81–30–30 ⊕ www.airarchipels.com).

AIR PASSES

There are several air passes available for hopping between islands: the Discovery Pass (Moorea, Huahine, Raiatea; $330), the Bora Bora Pass (Moorea, Bora Bora, Huahine, Raiatea, Maupiti; $475), the Lagoon Pass (Moorea, Rangiroa, Fakarava, Manihi, Tikehu, Ahe; $530), and the Bora Bora–Tuamotu Pass (Moorea, Bora Bora, Huahine, Raiatea, Maupiti, Rangiroa, Fakarava, Manihi, Tikehu, Ahe; $940). These passes allow for a cost-effective and convenient way to travel, but they come laden with terms and conditions, some of which include having to start in Tahiti, but not being able to return to it; all islands of the same archipelago must be visited at one time; only one stopover is allowed per island; the pass is only valid for 28 days after the first departure. Check out the Air Tahiti Web site for a more thorough discussion of terms and conditions, as they often change.

Air Passes **Air Tahiti** (☎ 86–42–42 ⊕ *www.airtahiti.com*). **ETahiti Travel** (☎ 83–51–60 ⊕ *www.etahititravel.com*).

AIRPORTS

Tahiti's Faa'a International Airport is the only international airport in French Polynesia. The airport is located about 5 km (3 mi) from the capital city of Pape'ete on the northwest side of Tahiti Nui, Tahiti's large island. The airport offers basic amenities, such as snack bars, souvenir shops, public phones, public restrooms, a post office, bank counters, ATM machines, and a restaurant. The main terminal is for Air Tahiti. The Air Moorea counter is in another building 656 feet (200 meters) away. There are bus and taxi services to take you to and from the airport—buses are the cheaper option, but they don't always run on time.

Most of the runways on the 38 other islands that receive air traffic are paved and of good quality. Some of the more remote islands, however, have unpaved landing strips. The term "airport" can vary from island to island, but the majority of them feature shelter, public restrooms, public phones, souvenirs, and a snack bar.

Airport Information **Faa'a International Airport** *(PPT)* (☎ 86–60–61 ⊕ www.tahiti-aeroport.pf).

▌ BY BOAT

There is a network of ferries in French Polynesia that allows for the transport of locals and merchandise between islands. Interisland boat travel varies widely, from the speedy daily transfers between Tahiti and Moorea, to the twice-weekly transfers from Tahiti to Huahine, to the small cargo vessels know as *goelettes,* which take passengers along with their main freight transport. If you go even farther out to the Gambier archipelago, there are boats that, every three weeks or so, travel a 15-day circuit around the more remote atolls. Make sure you know what you're getting: boat transport can be anything from luxury travel to unrolling a sleeping bag on the deck and providing your own meals, especially on freight transport. Ask questions, and be prepared. If you're short on time, flying is the better option.

The two main ferries traveling from Tahiti to outlying islands are the *Moorea Express* and the *Aremiti*. For information on boat travel between other French Polynesian islands, the best option is to ask your accommodation or visit the port in person for prices and timetables.

The cargo passenger ships *Hawaiki Nui* and the *Vaeanu* run inter-island "cruises" as part of their delivery run, and call at Huahine, Raiatea, Tahaa, and Bora Bora. The *Hawaiki Nui* takes 12 passengers accommodated in cabins and on deck (two voyages a week); the *Vaeanu* takes

90 passengers with 58 on deck and 32 in cabins (three voyages a week). These cargo/passenger boats are for those who don't mind roughing it. There are restaurants on board.

Boat Contacts Aremiti (☎ 42-88-88 ⊕ www.aremiti.pf). **Hawaiki Nui** (☎ 54-99-42). **Moorea Express** (☎ 82-47-47 ⊕ www.mooreaferry.pf). **Vaeanu** (☎ 41-25-35).

▌BY BUS

Several of the major islands in French Polynesia have the infrastructure for public transportation. Buses are called *L'Trucks,* and even though most have evolved beyond the flat-bed trucks with benches, they can still be a bit rustic. Stops are marked with a blue sign, and most fares are set per route, rather than distance traveled (note that you pay your fare at the end of your trip). Although schedules are set, don't expect the buses to run on time.

▌BY CAR

Car rentals are available on nearly every major island in French Polynesia. If you are going to the outlying islands, cars are scarce, and often can only be rented with a driver. Given the astronomical price of renting a car, not to mention petrol, consider other transportation options outside of the major islands: scooters are often available for rental (outside of Tahiti), boat transfers are a great way to get around, and biking is popular and safe—the roads are primarily flat and, outside of Tahiti's main cities, there isn't much traffic. Hotels often provide transportation, or rent bikes, scooters, and even cars, so it's best to check with your accommodation first before looking into rentals from airports or major city centers.

You only need to bring your national driver's license to drive in French Polynesia.

Most islands have one main paved road encircling their perimeters. Some of the larger islands (like Tahiti) have paved roads that wind into the interior, but most roads (aside from the primary perimeter one) are generally dirt tracks suitable only for 4WD.

Driving is on the right-hand side of the road and is relatively straightforward. That being said, keep your wits about you, as local drivers can often leave you with your heart in your throat.

GASOLINE

In French Polynesia, petrol stations (as they're called) are easy to find and are competitively priced in the main city centers. However, once you start driving in the more remote areas, petrol stations are few and far between. Plan ahead and make sure you have a full tank before heading out to explore. Petrol is sold by liters, and the cost can range widely—just plan on it being expensive. The good news is that, given the size of French Polynesian islands, it's nearly impossible to go through a lot of gas. Cash is usually the only payment accepted, and most stations are self-service.

RENTAL CARS

Rental cars are available in French Polynesia's major islands from international agencies, such as Hertz, Budget, and Avis. However, renting a car is extremely expensive, and the price of petrol makes it even more so. Given compact size of the islands, the lack of paved roads, and the variety of ways to get around, it's recommended that you arrive at the island first and see what your travel needs are before committing to renting a car. Often your accommodation can provide boat or vehicle transfers, or rent bikes, scooters and even cars, so check with them before you make any arrangements.

ROADSIDE EMERGENCIES

Discuss with the rental agency what to do in the case of an emergency, as this sometimes differs between companies. Make sure you understand what your insurance covers and what it doesn't, and it's a good rule of thumb to let someone at your accommodation know where you are heading and when you plan to return. If you find yourself stranded, hail a bus or speak to the locals, who may have some helpful advice about finding your way to a phone or a bus-stop. Keep emergency numbers (car rental agency and your accommodation) with you, just in case.

BY CRUISE SHIP

Charter cruises are a unique and luxurious way to see Tahiti and French Polynesia. Most companies offer a variety of cruises, from one-day excursions to seven-day odysseys. Traveling by yacht isn't cheap, but if you want to see a variety of remote islands, and engage in water sports like diving and snorkeling, then cruising can be the best value for your money. There are a large number of French Polynesia–based charter companies to choose from, including Tahiti Yacht Charter, which offers a variety of cruise options, from a seven-day cruise for two with your own skipper/cook, to creating your own itinerary. Archipels Croisieres spend three to seven days cruising French Polynesia on an eight-passenger catamaran. Moorings Signature Vacations seven-day cruises on crewed yachts explore Tahiti and the surrounding islands. Princess Cruises offers a 10-day cruise throughout French Polynesia.

Cruise Line Contacts **Tahiti Yacht Charter** (☎ *45–04–00, 800/404–1010 in U.S.* ⊕ *www. tahitiyachtcharter.com).* **Archipels Croisieres** (☎ *56–36–39* ⊕ *www.archipels.com).* **Moorings Signature Vacations** (☎ *888/952–8420 in U.S.* ⊕ *www.mooringssignature.com).* **Princess Cruises** (☎ *800/774–6237 in U.S.* ⊕ *www.princess.com).*

BY HELICOPTER

You can also take a helicopter with the French Polynesia's only company, Polynesia Helicopters, which operates from Tahiti-Faa'a International Airport.

Contacts **Polynesia Helicopters** (☎ *54–87– 20* ⊕ *www.polynesia-helicopter.com).*

BY TAXI

Taxis are available on well-developed islands like Tahiti and Moorea, but, like everything, they are extremely expensive. A longer cab ride can be as expensive as renting a car for the day. That being said, most taxis are clean and responsible. Most charge flat fares from the airport to hotels, but other trips are metered. Ask whether there is a special surcharge for baggage—this can often be waived with a little fast-talking. On the more remote islands, taxi service is more sporadic. Taxis may be available only from 6 AM to 6 PM, or the town "taxi" may actually be a well-known local with a car who shuttles tourists where they want to go. Your accommodation will often arrange airport transfers for you, so if traveling to the outlying areas, make certain you inquire with them, or at the airport.

ESSENTIALS

▌ACCOMMODATIONS

There is a wide range of accommodation options in French Polynesia, but they all have one thing in common: they're expensive. You're paying for paradise, so expect to pay twice or even triple what you think the room might be worth. French Polynesia doesn't have a thriving backpacker culture, but hostels (called "guesthouses") can be found. The bulk of the accommodation options are pensions and hotels, and then there are the luxury resorts with over-the-water bungalows of which dreams are made. Most hotels quote their rates in the local currency and they don't include the hefty taxes that will be added to your bill: the 6% *taxe sur la valeur ajoutée* (TVA, or value-added tax), the 5% government tax, and the *tax de sejour* (accommodation tax), which is charged per person per night. *See Taxes, below, for more tax information, and see the individual price charts in each chapter for accommodation price information.*

▌TIP→ Assume that hotels operate on the European Plan (**EP**, no meals) unless we specify that they use the Breakfast Plan (**BP**, with full breakfast), Continental Plan (**CP**, Continental breakfast), Full American Plan (**FAP**, all meals), Modified American Plan (**MAP**, breakfast and dinner) or are all-inclusive (**AI**, all meals and most activities).

BED & BREAKFASTS

There are a few bed-and-breakfasts scattered around French Polynesia, although it's difficult to find a traditional B&B by Western standards. The term "bed-and-breakfast" is often used to describe everything from home-stays to hotels, so check with your host about what's on offer before confirming your reservation, just to make certain it's what you're after.

Reservations Services **BNB Choices** (⊕ www.bnbchoices.com). **Rentalo.com** (⊕ rentalo.com/vacation-rentals/tahiti).

Pamela Lanier's Bed & Breakfasts (⊕ www. lanierbb.com/french_polynesia). **Bed and Breakfast.Net** (⊕ www.bedandbreakfast.net).

GUESTHOUSES

Guesthouses in French Polynesia can mean anything from family-run pensions to hostel-style accommodations. Roughly translated, it means cheaper rates, the chance to mix with other travelers and locals, a kitchen, and rustic facilities, such as lukewarm water and outdoor bathroom compounds. Guesthouses are a good option for people traveling on a budget, but note that they usually don't accept credit cards.

Reservation Contacts **Haere Mai** (⊕ www. haere-mai.pf).

HOME EXCHANGES

Home exchanges are growing more and more popular in French Polynesia. Although you're primarily looking at exchanges on the main islands of Tahiti and Moorea, it's still a unique way to experience the islands. The best resource for home exchanges is to explore the Internet.

Reservation Contacts **Home Exchange** (⊕ www.homeexchange.com). **Home Welcome** (⊕ www.homewelcome.com/oceania/french-polynesia). **Vacation Rentals** (⊕ www.vrwd. com/vacation-home-excahnges/oceania).

HOTELS

"Hotel" is another word in French Polynesia that has multiple meanings, from a dreary overpriced room to five-star accommodation. Prices vary greatly, as does the value for money. Although hotels are more comfortable and offer more amenities than pensions and guesthouses, mid-range hotels may leave you feeling jilted—a three-star accommodation in Sydney or San Francisco offers a lot more than a three-star property in French Polynesia. Deals and travel pack-

LOCAL DO'S & TABOOS

CUSTOMS OF THE COUNTRY

French Polynesia is a very relaxed and friendly place, and it is easy to feel welcome. The greatest currency you'll have is a smile. Here, it's considered rude not to greet someone you pass on the street—a simple smile or hello will suffice—and politeness goes a long way. Remember that French Polynesia is on island time, and it's acceptable that things move more slowly. Religion's also a large part of daily life and, even though it's not pressed upon travelers, it's important to respect and not ridicule or debate their choices. Food, also, is the heart and soul of Polynesia, and appreciative lingering over meals, large appetites, and smiles are the reward for those who have prepared a meal for you.

GREETINGS

First and foremost, smile, and acknowledge everyone you meet. Men tend to be greeted with handshakes, women with kisses on each cheek, although they can be interchanged.

SIGHTSEEING

Polynesian etiquette is quite simple: be friendly and polite. Skimpy bathing suits are okay at the resorts and while you're swimming, but don't parade around in them. Most landowners don't mind you trespassing, but ask first if possible, and don't pick fruit from the trees or leave gates open. It's not necessary to go to church, but dress conservatively and be respectful if you do. If you want to take someone's photo, ask first. If you want to give money to a beggar, do so, but favor him/her with a smile and an acknowledgement, as well. Show respect to the elderly. Keep public displays of affection to a very bare minimum.

OUT ON THE TOWN

The two things most people find trying in French Polynesia are the lax antismoking laws (smoking is allowed in most restaurants), and island time—shops are closed during the lunch hour, restaurant service may be considered slow by Western standards, and you'll find that no one is in a hurry to serve you. Don't take this personally, it's just the custom. Three stumbling blocks that take a little getting used to are being allowed to eat with your hands in restaurants, asking for the check (it will not be brought to your table until you do so, under the assumption that you are still enjoying your meal), and removing your shoes when entering someone's house. Even if they insist that it's not necessary, it is a sign of respect to make yourself comfortable.

LANGUAGE

The main languages spoken in Tahiti are Tahitian and French. Although English is widely spoken, especially in the tourist areas, learning and using a few French and/or Tahitian phrases is both useful and appreciated. Thankfully, high-school French is enough to get you by, and Tahitian is easy to pronounce. Here are a few phrases to try: *la ora na* (Hello), *nana* (an informal hello), *Parahi* (Good-bye, *nana* can also be used), *E* (Yes), *Aita* (No), *Mauruuru* (Thank you), *E'e* (Excuse me), *To'u i'oa 'o* (My name is...), *Tei hea?* (Where is...?). For a few pronunciation tips, a little practice with vowels is usually enough to get you by: "a" as in father, "e" as in hey, "i" as in magazine, "o" as in floor, "u" as in the "oo" in moo.

Another trick of the trade is the glottal stop, the apostrophe'd gap that separates words, and separates native speakers from tourists. A glottal stop indicates a pause. For example, Pape'ete would be pronounced with a slight pause between "Papa" and "ete". Keep an ear open, and you'll start to get the hang of the language quickly.

ages abound, however, and are worth looking into.

Reservation Contacts Hotel Advisor (⊕ *frenchpolynesia.hoteladvisor.com*). **Pacific Island Travel** (⊕ *www.pacificislandtravel.com*). **South Travels** (⊕ *www.southtravels.com*).

LUXURY RESORTS

French Polynesia is the stereotype for paradise, and the islands know how to do luxury. From private islands, to helicopter transfers, to iconic over-the-lagoon bungalows, if you've dreamed it, it's here. Most luxury hotels offer spa services, sumptuous food, four-poster beds draped with netting, and a wealth of activities—just expect to pay for it all. Paradise doesn't come cheap, and most luxury resorts are not all-inclusive. Still, if there was ever a holiday to splurge on, French Polynesia fits the bill.

Reservation Contacts Luxury Link (⊕ *www.luxurylink.com*). **Perfect Escapes** (⊕ *www.perfectescapes.com*). **Tahiti Escapes** (⊕ *www.visit-tahiti.com/luxury.html*).

PENSIONS

Pensions are the step between the hostel and the hotel. They are usually simple family-run establishments with eclectic furnishings. Some pensions are gems, with tidy thatched bungalows and warm showers. Others are little more than threadbare rooms with calendar pages for artwork. Still, pensions are a great way to mix and mingle with the locals, who take pride in being your host. Pensions are also good value for money, and you're guaranteed to bring home a story or two. Room prices usually include half board (breakfast and dinner), full board (all meals), or the use of a kitchen. Credit cards are often not accepted.

Reservation Contacts Diving World (⊕ *www.diving-world.com/tahiti-pensions. html*). **Hideaway Holidays** (⊕ *www.hideawayholidays.com.au/ppt_pensions.htm*). **Tahiti Travel Connection** (⊕ *www.tahititravel.com.au/pensions/index.asp*).

▌COMMUNICATIONS

INTERNET

The Internet is still a relatively new phenomenon in French Polynesia, although Internet cafés are growing more and more popular on developed islands like Tahiti and Moorea. Few hotels offer room access, so check first before you lug your laptop overseas; however, most hotels do have communal computers with Internet access so you can check your e-mail. The cost is usually around 900 CFP per minute.

Contact Cybercafes (⊕ *www.cybercafes.com*) lists over 4,000 Internet cafés worldwide.

PHONES

The good news is that you can now make a direct-dial telephone call from virtually any point on earth. The bad news? You can't always do so cheaply. Calling from a hotel is almost always the most expensive option; hotels usually add huge surcharges to all calls, particularly international ones. In some countries you can phone from call centers or even the post office. Calling cards usually keep costs to a minimum, but only if you purchase them locally. And then there are mobile phones *(⇨ below)*, which are sometimes more prevalent—particularly in the developing world—than landlines; as expensive as mobile phone calls can be, they are still usually a much cheaper option than calling from your hotel.

Compared to other remote areas, the phone system in French Polynesia is modern and easy to use, but it's also costly—if you use hotel phones you will be charged about US$10 a minute, with a connecting charge as well. Public phones can be found in each village, and you'll also find them around the islands on the side of the road. A Telecarte (phone card) is required to use these phones and can be bought at the Pape'ete Airport snack bar and in many supermarkets, shops, and news agencies. Phone cards come in denominations of 1,000, 2,000, and 5,000 CFP.

The country code for French Polynesia is 689.

CALLING WITHIN FRENCH POLYNESIA

There are no area codes within French Polynesia, so numbers should be dialed directly. Phone cards are a good option for calling between islands. Local calls usually cost around 35 CFP for four minutes, with island-to-island calls being more expensive.

CALLING OUTSIDE FRENCH POLYNESIA

To call the United States from French Polynesia dial 00 + 1 + area code + number. To call French Polynesia from the United States dial 011 + 689 + number. If you get stuck, ring information at 3612.

MOBILE PHONES

If you have a multiband phone (some countries use different frequencies than what's used in the U.S.) and your service provider uses the world-standard GSM network (as do T-Mobile, Cingular, and Verizon), you can probably use your phone abroad. Roaming fees can be steep, however: 99¢ a minute is considered reasonable. And overseas you normally pay the toll charges for incoming calls. It's almost always cheaper to send a text message than to make a call, since text messages have a very low set fee (often less than 5¢).

If you just want to make local calls, consider buying a new SIM card (note that your provider may have to unlock your phone for you to use a different SIM card) and a prepaid service plan in the destination. You'll then have a local number and can make local calls at local rates. If your trip is extensive, you could also simply buy a new cell phone in your destination, as the initial cost will be offset over time.

■TIP➔ If you travel internationally frequently, save one of your old mobile phones or buy a cheap one on the Internet; ask your cell phone company to unlock it for you, and take it with you as a travel phone, buying a new SIM card with pay-as-you-go service in each destination.

You will need to check with your provider to see if your mobile phone will work in French Polynesia. If it doesn't, you can either rent a phone from one of the companies below, or you can tap into the local network—Tikiphone Vini Network. However, your network needs to be a roaming partner of Tikiphone Vini Network, otherwise there's the option of picking up a prepaid calling card from them to make and receive calls on your phone while traveling. Phone rentals are also available.

Contacts **Tikiphone Vini Network** (⊕ www.vini.pf). **Cellular Abroad** (☎ 800/287-5072 ⊕ www.cellularabroad.com) rents and sells GMS phones and sells SIM cards that work in many countries. **Mobal** (☎ 888/888-9162 ⊕ www.mobalrental.com) rents mobiles and sells GSM phones (starting at $49) that will operate in 140 countries. Per-call rates vary throughout the world. **Planet Fone** (☎ 888/988-4777 ⊕ www.planetfone.com) rents cell phones, but the per-minute rates are expensive.

▌CUSTOMS & DUTIES

Customs requirements can change at any time, so it's best to check with a travel agent before departing for Tahiti. Some general rules of thumb, however, are to limit the amount of perfume, alcohol, and cigarettes you bring into the country. Don't bring any live animals or pets, or cultured pearls of a non–French Polynesian origin. Also, take note that you are limited to the number of rolls of unexposed film (10) you can take into French Polynesia, and that any telecommunications or radio equipment must have an import license. For departing the country, you can leave with $800 worth of goods per traveler, including one quart of liquor and 200 cigarettes. Any items of worth (medicine, pearls, art, antiques, etc.) need an accompanying purchase documentation. Generally, customs in French Polynesia are fair and simple: make certain you have proper paperwork to document anything of worth entering or exiting the country, and follow all the basic rules—don't travel with the usual hazards and don't stash shells or animal products in your bag before leaving.

U.S. Information **U.S. Customs and Border Protection** (⊕ *www.cbp.gov*).

▌ EATING OUT

French Polynesian islands have a wide variety of eateries on offer, mostly Polynesian, French, or Chinese in influence. If you can sample a *hima'a*—a traditional Polynesian meal of fish, pork, taro roots, and coconut milk wrapped in banana leaves and cooked for hours in a pit over hot stones—take the opportunity, as it's a real treat. Vegetarians are out of luck as far as vegetarian-specific cuisine, but they will be in paradise with a wide variety of breads and tropical fruit (vegetables themselves, though, are a rarity). The islands are also very child-friendly; although most restaurants still allow smoking, the atmosphere is welcoming for children and there are plenty of options for them to choose from. Baby food and formula are also readily available throughout the islands.

MEALS & MEALTIMES

Polynesians love their food, and mealtimes are traditionally large gatherings of family and friends. Most restaurants are open from 10:30 AM to 11 PM, although most places are closed on Sundays. Markets can also be found, opening around 6 AM, and can be a great place to find snacks, as well as a unique and cost-effective ways of feeding yourself, especially if you have cooking facilities at your accommodation. Breakfast is usually the lightest meal, and heavily French-influenced: bread with butter, jam, and fruit, and either coffee or tea. Lunch tends to be the largest meal, and often consisting of *poisson cru*, raw fish in coconut milk. Dinner can be large or light, depending on the individual's preference, and is usually a mixture of tropical fruit, taro root, raw or cooked fish, pork, or lamb or beef imported from New Zealand or Australia. In some of the more remote islands, you will find goat or even dog on the menu. If you stumble across turtle, remember that it's an endangered species, refuse to eat it, and make certain you tell the establishment why—it's the only way to permanently take turtle off the menu. Remember that it's okay to eat with your hands in Polynesian custom, and that, in French custom, the bill is not brought to you until you request it.

Unless otherwise noted, the restaurants listed in this guide are open daily for lunch and dinner. *See the individual price charts in each chapter for restaurant price information.*

PAYING

Credit cards are accepted in most tourist areas, although smaller and more remote establishments are usually cash-only affairs.

For guidelines on tipping see Tipping below.

RESERVATIONS & DRESS

Regardless of where you are, it's a good idea to make a reservation if you can. In some places (Hong Kong, for example), it's expected. We only mention them specifically when reservations are essential (there's no other way you'll ever get a table) or when they are not accepted. For popular restaurants, book as far ahead as you can (often 30 days), and reconfirm as soon as you arrive. (Large parties should always call ahead to check the reservations policy.) We mention dress only when men are required to wear a jacket or a jacket and tie.

When dining out, dress in French Polynesia tends to be casual, tidy, and fit for the weather: loose and colorful clothing. Although you will see the occasional flowered Hawaiian shirt or flip-flops at nice restaurants, do everyone a favor and avoid the temptation: dress respectfully for your hosts, rather than donning the cabana gear. For men, a golf shirt and khakis are perfect. For women, this is the perfect excuse to wear a colorful sundress.

WINE, BEER & SPIRITS

What is paradise without a cold cocktail? Thankfully Polynesians are fairly lax about alcohol, and it's readily available at bars, restaurants, and supermarkets. The local beer is a brand called Hinano, which is light and refreshing, especially after a day spent in the sun. It is sold in bottles, cans, and on tap. You can find imported beers for imported prices, as well. Red and white wines, mostly imported from France, are also available. It's best to order these from restaurants and hotels that know how to treat wine, as the heat and elements can do a number on the vintage if it hasn't been properly looked after.

▌ ELECTRICITY

Electricity in French Polynesia is 220V, 60Hz, although some of the larger hotels offer 110V for shavers and the like. It is recommended that you bring your own converter (French-style plugs with two round pins), although some resorts offer converters upon request at the front desk. French Polynesia is a group of islands so power problems aren't uncommon, especially on some of the more remote islands or during tropical storms.

Consider making a small investment in a universal adapter, which has several types of plugs in one lightweight, compact unit. Most laptops and mobile phone chargers are dual voltage (i.e., they operate equally well on 110 and 220 volts), so require only an adapter. These days the same is true of small appliances such as hair dryers. Always check labels and manufacturer instructions to be sure. Don't use 110-volt outlets marked FOR SHAVERS ONLY for high-wattage appliances such as hair dryers.

▌ EMERGENCIES

The emergency number for police in French Polynesia is 17, although the police system isn't exactly robust—the more remote islands can have one or two policemen in total. In Pape'ete, there's a police station, and more officers, but don't count on immediate help. If you would like to report a crime, visit the police station or your local consulate.

For a medical emergency, dial 15, or call the SOS Medecins, an emergency unit of doctors and medical personnel. You can also ring Mamo General Hospital in Pape'ete, which is the largest hospital in French Polynesia. If you find yourself in a medical emergency in a remote area, your accommodation/hosts are usually in the best position to help you.

Contacts SOS Medecins (☎ 42–34–56). **Mamo General Hospital** (☎ 42–01–01 *for emergencies, 46–62–62 for general information*).

▌ HEALTH

SPECIFIC ISSUES IN FRENCH POLYNESIA

Health hazards in French Polynesia are generally environmental: dehydration, prickly heat, heatstroke, fungal infections, sunburn, diarrhea, food poisoning, coral cuts, and occasionally dengue fever.

Tap water is generally safe to drink on developed islands like Tahiti, but drink the readily available bottled water in outlying islands, especially if the only water available is well water. If you don't have access to bottled water and aren't certain, however, the usual tricks of boiling or water-purifying tablets work well. Fruits and vegetables should be peeled, and be careful of uncooked meat.

Wash your hands frequently, and treat cuts with extra caution: a small skin puncture can quickly turn septic in the tropics. Wash the injury well, and treat with an antiseptic ointment or iodine. Keep the wound as dry as possible (so no bandages or Band-Aids). If the wound is starting to spread, or if it isn't healing, see a doctor.

With mosquitoes, the simplest solution is to keep as much skin covered as possible with long-sleeved shirts and trousers. Avoid perfumes or scented lotions, use mosquito repellant containing DEET, and use a mosquito net or coil when sleeping, if possible.

Health care in French Polynesia is generally of a good standard, but the remote islands can pose a problem, just because of their locality. Make certain that your insurance covers emergency transports, keep your receipts, and expect to pay cash for most treatments.

OVER-THE-COUNTER REMEDIES

Pharmacies in French Polynesia carry most of the over-the-counter medications that you will need for headaches, upset stomachs, minor aches and pains, and cuts and bruises. They also provide a selection of basic cosmetic and health care products (like shampoo and toothpaste), sunscreen, and mosquito repellant and coils. Make certain you stock up on anything you need before traveling to the outer islands, as supplies are more difficult to come by.

SHOTS & MEDICATIONS

There are no required vaccinations to enter French Polynesia, but typhoid fever, hepatitis A, and hepatitis B are recommended, and an International Certificate of Vaccination is required for travelers over one year old who are entering from a yellow fever–infected area of the world. Generally, dengue fever, a viral disease spread by mosquitoes, can pose an occasional threat, especially to pregnant women or children. The disease tends to run in outbreaks, so check the CDC's Health Information for International Travel, or the World Health Organization's Web site for up-to-date information.

Health Warnings National Centers for Disease Control & Prevention (*CDC* ☎ 877/394–8747 *international travelers' health line* ⊕ *www.cdc.gov/travel*). **World Health Organization** (*WHO* ⊕ *www.who.int*).

▪ HOURS OF OPERATION

Business hours can be a bit scattered in French Polynesia. In general, shops and offices tend to keep hours from 7:30 AM to 5 PM, with a two-hour lunch break around 11:30, Monday through Friday. On the weekends, those hours change to 7:30–11:30 AM on Saturdays, and most establishments are closed on Sundays.

HOLIDAYS

French Polynesians love a good celebration, and draw on both Polynesian and French holidays, as well as religious ones, to make up a diverse and colorful calendar. Public holidays, when all businesses and government offices are closed, include New Year's Day, the Arrival of the First Missionaries (March 5), Easter, May Day (May 1), VE Day (May 8), Ascension (late May), Pentecost and Pentecost Monday (early June), International Autonomy Day (June 29), Bastille Day (July 14), Assumption (August 15), All Saints' Day (November 1), Armistice Day (November 11), and Christmas Day.

▪ MAIL

There are post offices on all of the main islands. City branches tend to be open Monday through Friday, 7:30–3; the Faa'a Airport branch is also open on Saturdays and Sundays from 6:30 to 10 AM. The postal service is friendly and efficient: it usually takes a week to 10 days to mail something to Europe, Australia, or the U.S., with postcards costing about 120 CFP. If you would like to have something sent to you in French Polynesia, you can have it mailed care of your place of accommodation or arrange to have it sent to a local post office branch.

SHIPPING PACKAGES

Although the postal service is generally reliable, don't expect the same services in Tahiti that are available in Europe or the U.S., such as shipping parcels from stores or courier services. Some hotels and shops will mail purchases for you, but you will need to ask, rather than counting on this as the norm. FedEx does access French Polynesia.

Contact Fed Ex (⊕ www.fedex.com/pf).

▪ MONEY

French Polynesian paradise is worth the price. If it wasn't, you wouldn't find travelers shelling out the enormous amount of cash required to visit this spectacular destination year after year. It is expensive: French Polynesia is far away from anything, most goods need to be imported, and what infrastructure there is makes a living from tourism. Once you understand that, it makes planning your trip much easier to stomach. A mix of credit card purchases and cash transactions is the best way to plan for your trip, especially since banks and ATMs aren't as readily available as they are in other destinations.

Prices throughout this guide are given for adults. Substantially reduced fees are almost always available for children, students, and senior citizens.

Currency Conversion Google (⊕ www. google.com). **Oanda.com** (⊕ www.oanda.com). **XE.com** (⊕ www.xe.com).

ATMS & BANKS

Your own bank will probably charge a fee for using ATMs abroad; the foreign bank you use may also charge a fee. Nevertheless, you'll usually get a better rate of exchange at an ATM than you will at a currency-exchange office or even when changing money in a bank. And extracting funds as you need them is a safer option than carrying around a large amount of cash.

▪TIP➔ PIN numbers with more than four digits are not recognized at ATMs in many countries. If yours has five or more, remember to change it before you leave.

ATMs (or DABs, as they're known in French) are hit-or-miss in French Polynesia. They can usually be found on the major islands (Bora Bora, Huahine, Tahiti, Moorea, Raiatea, and Rangiroa) and offer some of the best exchange rates, but finding an ATM in the outlying areas—especially one that works—can be tricky. Don't count on having access to one. There are three primary banks on the islands: Banque de Polynesie (a branch of which can be found at Faa'a Airport), Banque de Tahiti, and Banque Socredo—note that international bank cards tend to only work at ATMs associated with this particular bank.

CREDIT CARDS

Throughout this guide, the following abbreviations are used: **AE**, American Express; **DC**, Diners Club; **MC**, Master-Card; and **V**, Visa.

It's a good idea to inform your credit-card company before you travel, especially if you're going abroad and don't travel internationally very often. Otherwise, the credit-card company might put a hold on your card owing to unusual activity—not a good thing halfway through your trip. Record all your credit-card numbers—as well as the phone numbers to call if your cards are lost or stolen—in a safe place, so you're prepared should something go wrong. Both MasterCard and Visa have general numbers you can call (collect if you're abroad) if your card is lost, but you're better off calling the number of your issuing bank, since MasterCard and Visa usually just transfer you to your bank; your bank's number is usually printed on your card.

If you plan to use your credit card for cash advances, you'll need to apply for a PIN at least two weeks before your trip. Although it's usually cheaper (and safer) to use a credit card abroad for large purchases (so you can cancel payments or be reimbursed if there's a problem), note that some credit-card companies *and* the banks that issue them add substantial percentages to all foreign transactions, whether they're in a foreign currency or

not. Check on these fees before leaving home, so there won't be any surprises when you get the bill.

■ TIP→ Before you charge something, ask the merchant whether or not he or she plans to do a dynamic currency conversion (DCC). In such a transaction the credit-card *processor* (shop, restaurant, or hotel, not Visa or Mas-terCard) converts the currency and charges you in dollars. In most cases you'll pay the merchant a 3% fee for this service in addition to any credit-card company and issuing-bank foreign-transaction surcharges.

Dynamic currency conversion programs are becoming increasingly widespread. Merchants who participate in them are supposed to ask whether you want to be charged in dollars or the local currency, but they don't always do so. And even if they do offer you a choice, they may well avoid mentioning the additional sur-charges. The good news is that you *do* have a choice. And if this practice really gets your goat, you can avoid it entirely thanks to American Express; with its cards, DCC simply isn't an option.

Credit cards are readily accepted in all major cities and tourist areas, but the out-lying islands prefer cash, so plan to carry both. Given the high rates tacked to bank exchanges, credit cards are often a good way to pay for large purchases, such as transfers and accommodation, but note that some establishments and shops require a 2,000 CFP minimum purchase.

Reporting Lost Cards American Express (☎ *336/393–1111 collect from abroad* ⊕ *www.americanexpress.com*). **Diners Club** (☎ *303/799–1504 collect from abroad* ⊕ *www.dinersclub.com*). **MasterCard** (☎ *800/627–8372 in the U.S. or 636/722– 7111 collect from abroad* ⊕ *www.mastercard. com*). **Visa** (☎ *410/581–9994 collect from abroad* ⊕ *www.visa.com*).

CURRENCY & EXCHANGE

The local currency, *franc cours pacifique* or CFP, is currently exchanging at a rate of 1 CFP to US13¢. Known locally as "francs," you will see the letters CFP on all menus and on prices in most local shops. (Pearl shops will also have euro and U.S. dollar pricing). The world money markets refers to the currency as XPF and this is what you will see in a bank and what will appear on your credit card statement).

Coins come in 1, 2, 5, 10, 20, 50, and 100, while notes are in 500, 1,000, 5,000, and 10,000 values. Most travelers exchange money at airports or hotels, but there are banks in touristy areas, as well. Hefty surcharges are attached to any transaction, so the best option is to make fewer of them, even if it means carrying more cash. Since Tahiti is still a relatively safe place to travel, certain precautions (such as using the hotel's safe, when possible, or not being overly demonstrative with money) goes a long way to discouraging petty thieves.

■**TIP→**Even if a currency-exchange booth has a sign promising no commission, rest assured that there's some kind of huge, hidden fee. (Oh . . . that's right. The sign didn't say no *fee*.) And as for rates, you're almost always better off getting foreign currency at an ATM or exchanging money at a bank.

TRAVELER'S CHECKS

Traveler's Checks are still accepted in major cities or large resorts, but outside of well-traveled areas they are an endangered species. Given the large bank fees tacked to changing Traveler's Checks, cash or credit cards are the better option.

Contact **American Express** (☎*888/412–6945 in the U.S., 801/945–9450 collect outside of the U.S. to add value or speak to customer service ⊕www.american express.com*).

▌PACKING

The French Polynesian islands are a casual destination where most time is spent out-of-doors, so function trumps fashion—there's no need to dress to impress, but looking tidy is always appreciated by your island hosts. Comfortable and loose-fitting clothes, sundresses, and bright colors fit in anywhere. Bring what you need to stay covered from the intense tropical sun (brimmed hats, sunscreen, sarongs, and loose, long-sleeved shirts are essential), as well as items you'll need to play in the ocean (your own snorkel and fins, sturdy reef shoes, and a few swimsuits). Mosquito repellent, a raincoat, and a first-aid kit are essential.

■**TIP→**Although most essentials are readily available at the larger resorts or city centers, you pay a premium for anything that isn't grown on the island, so it's best pack a plentiful supply.

▌PASSPORTS & VISAS

The entry requirements for French Polynesia are quite similar to France, but they can and do change, so check with a travel agent before you depart. Every traveler needs a round-trip ticket and a passport valid for six months beyond their stay in the country. U.S. and Canadian citizens can stay up to one month without a visa. As French Polynesia is a French overseas territory, extensions can be obtained by applying to the French High Commissioner or by applying locally to the Police aux Frontieres, located in the Faa'a airport or next to the Visitors Bureau in Pape'ete, but this needs to be done one week before the expiration date on the visa. There is a 3,000 CFP fee, and the extension is good for up to three months.

Contacts **Embassy of France** (✉*4101 Reservoir Rd. NW, Washington, D.C., 20007* ☎*202/944–6200* ⊕*www.info-france-usa.org*).**Police aux Frontieres** (☎*42–40–74*).

▌ RESTROOMS

Facilities in French Polynesia are usually simple and clean, but they can be anything from exotic structures made of tile, ceramic and glittering glass, to rustic outhouses on some of the more remote islands. Having your own stash of toilet paper or tissues can come in handy, and it is polite to only use the facilities at a petrol station or restaurant if you purchase something in return.

Find a Loo **The Bathroom Diaries** (⊕ *www.thebathroomdiaries.com*) is flush with unsanitized info on restrooms the world over—each one located, reviewed, and rated.

▌ SAFETY

French Polynesia is still a very safe place to travel, provided you don't take it for granted. As with every destination, pickpockets and petty thieves take whatever opportunities you give them, so leaving your camera on your towel while you have a swim is not recommended. Also, locals still indulge in illegal drunk-driving, so keep aware and steer well clear of any erratic drivers. The chance of crime increases in the larger cities like Pape'ete, where a rise in drug abuse is causing a parallel increase in violent crime. Take care walking late at night. However, the greatest risks while traveling in French Polynesia are posed by the environment itself: heatstroke, sunburn, reef cuts, and riptides, for example, are notorious culprits, so minimize sun exposure, ask questions, and tread carefully.

Contact **Transportation Security Administration** (*TSA;* ⊕ *www.tsa.gov*).

General Info & Warnings **Australian Department of Foreign Affairs & Trade** (⊕ *www.smartraveller.gov.au*). **Consular Affairs Bureau of Canada** (⊕ *www.voyage.gc.ca*). **U.K. Foreign & Commonwealth Office** (⊕ *www.fco.gov.uk/travel*). **U.S. Department of State** (⊕ *www.travel.state.gov*).

▌ TAXES

Although there is no departure tax in French Polynesia, it's made up in other creative and exorbitant taxes. The TVA (or *taxe sur la valeur ajoutee,* value-added tax) is a hefty 16% added to purchases in shops, 10% added in bars/excursions/restaurants, and 6% added to your accommodation bill, which tends to accumulate taxes. You will also be charged the 5% government tax and the *tax de sejour* (accommodation tax), which is charged per person per night.

A sojourn or "visitor" tax of 150 CFP per person/per day is tacked on to international cruises and international classified hotel rooms. A sojourn tax of 50 CFP per person per day is added to bills in the smaller family-run hotels and pension. Children under 12 staying with their parents are exempt from the sojourn tax, for a visit of up to three days in each hotel. Sojourn taxes apply in the most frequently visited islands (Tahiti, Moorea, Bora Bora, Huahine, Raiatea, Tahaa, Rangiroa, Mataiva, Tikehau, Nuku Hiva, and Tuamotu).

Altogether your hotel bill in a resort will have 11% added to it, plus 150 CFP per person per day. Pensions and guesthouses have usually included the VAT and the sojourn tax in the cost of the room or bungalow. Shops, restaurants, activities and tourist services include the VAT (which ranges from 6% to 10% depending on the product) in their prices.

When making a purchase, ask for a V.A.T. refund form and find out whether the merchant gives refunds—not all stores do, nor are they required to. Have the form stamped like any customs form by customs officials when you leave the country or, if you're visiting several European Union countries, when you leave the EU. After you're through passport control, take the form to a refund-service counter for an on-the-spot refund (which is usually the quickest and easiest option), or mail it to the address on the form (or the envelope with it) after you arrive home. You receive the total refund stated on the form, but the processing time can be long, especially if you request a credit-card adjustment.

TIME

French Polynesia is two hours behind Pacific standard time (so, 10 hours behind London and three hours behind Los Angeles). During daylight saving time (April to late October), that extends to three hours. For added confusion, the Marquesas are a half hour ahead of the rest of French Polynesia, so check flight times carefully if you're island-hopping.

TIPPING

Tipping is not expected in Polynesian culture. If the service is extraordinary, tipping as a compliment is always appreciated, but isn't customary.

TOURS

Given its remote location, the option for island-hopping around French Polynesia, and the variety of things to do, you'll find a number of options that are suited to your travel style, whether based around scuba-diving or your dream wedding. If you prefer the freedom to pick and choose for yourself, however, it's easy to plan your day-to-day activities once you've arrived on an island, giving yourself the freedom of no commitments.

Contacts American Society of Travel Agents (*ASTA* ☎ *703/739–2782 or 800/965–2782* ⊕ *www.astanet.com*). **United States Tour Operators Association** (*USTOA* ☎ *212/599–6599* ⊕ *www.ustoa.com*).

TRIP INSURANCE

Comprehensive travel policies typically cover trip-cancellation and interruption, letting you cancel or cut your trip short because of a personal emergency, illness, or, in some cases, acts of terrorism in your destination. Such policies also cover evacuation and medical care. Some also cover you for trip delays because of bad weather or mechanical problems as well as for lost or delayed baggage. Another type of coverage to look for is financial default—that is, when your trip is disrupted because a tour operator, airline, or cruise line goes out of business. Generally you must buy this when you book your trip or shortly thereafter, and it's only available to you if your operator isn't on a list of excluded companies.

If you're going abroad, consider buying medical-only coverage at the very least. Neither Medicare nor some private insurers cover medical expenses anywhere outside of the United States (including time aboard a cruise ship, even if it leaves from a U.S. port). Medical-only policies typically reimburse you for medical care (excluding that related to preexisting conditions) and hospitalization abroad, and provide for evacuation. You still have to pay the bills and await reimbursement from the insurer, though.

Expect comprehensive travel insurance policies to cost about 4% to 7% or 8% of the total price of your trip (it's more like 8%–12% if you're over age 70). A medical-only policy may or may not be cheaper than a comprehensive policy. Always read the fine print of your policy to make sure that you are covered for the risks that are of most concern to you. Compare several policies to make sure you're getting the best price and range of coverage available.

■TIP➔OK. You know you can save a bundle on trips to warm-weather destinations by traveling in rainy season. But there's also a chance that a severe storm will disrupt your plans. The solution? Look for hotels and resorts that offer storm/hurricane guarantees. Although they rarely allow refunds, most guarantees do let you rebook later if a storm strikes.

It's important to make certain that your health insurance has provisions for emergency evacuation. Medical treatment in French Polynesia is generally good, but severe cases may need to be airlifted elsewhere, which can be extremely expensive. Also, although credit cards and U.S. insurance are starting to be more widely accepted, cash is still usually expected for most treatments. Speak with your insurance company as how best to handle this situation.

Comprehensive Travel Insurers Access America (☎ 800/729–6021 ⊕ www.access america.com). **AIG Travel Guard** (☎ 800/826–4919 ⊕ www.travelguard.com). **CSA Travel Protection** (☎ 800/873–9855 ⊕ www. csatravelprotection.com). **HTH Worldwide** (☎ 610/254–8700 ⊕ www.hthworldwide. com). **Travelex Insurance** (☎ 800/228–9792 ⊕ www.travelex-insurance.com). **Travel Insured International** (☎ 800/243–3174 ⊕ www.travelinsured.com).

Insurance Comparison Sites Insure My Trip. com (☎ 800/487–4722 ⊕ www.insuremytrip. com). **Square Mouth.com** (☎ 800/240–0369 or 727/490–5803 ⊕ www.squaremouth.com).

Medical Assistance Companies AirMed International Medical Group (⊕ www. airmed.com). **International SOS** (⊕ www. internationalsos.com).

Medical-Only Insurers International Medical Group (☎ 800/628–4664 ⊕ www. imglobal.com). **Wallach & Company** (☎ 800/237–6615 or 540/687–3166 ⊕ www.wallach.com).

∎ VISITOR INFO

Tahiti Tourism is the main tourist hub for all of French Polynesia. You can find a local office through their Web site, which is full of comprehensive information on trip planning, weather, interisland travel, wedding planning, events, lodging, and tours. Visit the site first, but the offices are also good about responding to specific queries.

FODORS.COM CONNECTION

Before your trip, be sure to check out what other travelers are saying in Talk on www.fodors.com.

Contacts South Pacific Tourism Organization (⊕ www.spto.org). **Tahiti Tourisme** (☎ 877/468–2448 in U.S. ⊕ www.tahiti-tourisme.com).

ONLINE TRAVEL TOOLS

As far as the South Pacific goes, Tahiti is fairly plugged in, and there is considerable information to be found on the Internet. Although most Web sites seem very Tahiti-focused, they often provide information and links for other islands in French Polynesia, and they also provide the most reliable information. Just like Tahiti Tourism is the main hub for French Polynesian tourism, Tahiti Internet sites are the main hub for French Polynesian information. Tahiti.com is a hodgepodge Web site of general information on cruises, lodgings, and what to see and do. Tahiti Explorer features general tourist information, with a focus on lodging and discount packages. Tahiti Nui Travel is one of the primary tourism companies in French Polynesia; their Web site contains travel information, including package deals. Tahiti1 contains useful information on Tahitian history and culture, as well as food, festivals, and recent news. Tahitipress.pf is a comprehensive online news magazine in both French and English, with everything from surf stories to government happenings. Totally Tahiti contains a wide variety of information from culture, to air travel, to visa requirements. Polynesian Islands has some general information, but it has a unique connection of Web-links for the rest of French Polynesia. Polynesian Cultural Center offers information on Hawaiian and South Pacific cultures. The Marquesas offers information for the Marquesas islands.

All About Tahiti & French Polynesia **Tahiti-press.pf** (⊕ *www.tahitipresse.pf*). **Tahiti1** (⊕ *www.tahiti1.com*). **Tahiti.com** (⊕ *www. tahiti.com*). **Totally Tahiti** (⊕ *www.totallytahiti. com*). **Tahiti Explorer** (⊕ *www.tahitiexplorer. com*). **Tahiti Nui Travel** (⊕ *www.tahitinuitravel. com*). **Polynesian Islands** (⊕ *www.polynesian islands.com*). **Polynesian Cultural Center** (⊕ *www.polynesia.com*). **The Marquesas** (⊕ *www.marquises.pf*).

▌ WEDDINGS

To get married legally in French Polynesia the couple must reside in the country for one month before the ceremony and must allow 10 days for the marriage *banns* (notice of impending marriage) to be published.

The following documents must be translated into French and provided to the city's (or municipality) town hall where the wedding will take place: birth certificates certified within the past three months and translated into French by an official translator; a prenuptial medical certificate less than two months old; a passport providing at least one month's continuous residency; a copy of a notarized marriage contract, if one exists; birth certificates of children to be made legitimate; identification of adult witnesses, including their profession and address (parents cannot be witnesses); a certificate of singleness; and wedding (or marriage) banns publication certificate from the place of foreign residency. ■ TIP➜ **Check with your hotel or wedding planner to make sure your paperwork is in order and nothing is missing before leaving.**

U.S. and Canadian nationals are entitled to a one-month stay without a visa, so they should contact the French Embassy in their country to inquire about visa extensions so they can stay longer and quality for a legal civil wedding.

If a civil wedding is not possible, there are many traditional ceremonies that can be arranged by wedding planners at hotels. Many people get married in their home country and then have a Polynesian ceremony during their honeymoon. The traditional weddings are quite elaborate and usually take place on the beach. They can involve singers and dancers, and often the groom arrives by outrigger canoe and the couple is wrapped in a wedding quilt called a *tifaifal*.

INDEX

NOTES

NOTES

NOTES

NOTES

NOTES

NOTES

NOTES

ABOUT OUR WRITERS

Ever since she watched *Adventures in Paradise*, a popular 1960s TV series, in her childhood, Caroline Gladstone yearned to visit Tahiti. Fortunately, she found that the reality of the islands measured up to—and actually surpassed—the celluloid images. A journalist for 25 years, Caroline has been travel writing for 18 years. One of her specialties is cruise writing; she was cruise editor of Australian magazine *Traveltrade* for almost a decade. These days she works as a freelance travel and feature writer and is brushing up her French for future visits to French Polynesia. She wrote the Tahiti, Moorea, Bora Bora, Huahine, Tuamotu, and Cruising chapters for this book.

Born in Nottingham, England, Bob Marriott has lived in New Zealand with his wife Linda for many years. His travels have taken him all over the world and his writing and photographs have been published in New Zealand, Australia, the U.S., Britain, Asia, and on the Web. He's contributed to a number of Fodor's guidebooks including South-east Asia and New Zealand, and for this book he worked on the Other Islands chapter.

Carrie Miller is a travel addict who found her way from Minnesota to the National Geographic Society, where she was a writer/researcher for *National Geographic Traveler Magazine*. After an assignment to New Zealand, Carrie returned to D.C., packed up her desk, and moved to the land of the Long White Cloud. She found New Zealand to be the perfect diving board for exploring the South Pacific, and when she isn't traveling, freelancing, or watching dolphins from her front porch, you can find her in the gym, training for her first amateur boxing match...which seemed like a good story idea at the time. She worked on the book's Travel Smart French Polynesia section.